Works 2000
fast&easy™

Diane Koers

A DIVISION OF PRIMA PUBLISHING

A Division of Prima Publishing

Prima Publishing and colophon are registered trademarks of Prima Communications, Inc. PRIMA TECH and Fast & Easy are trademarks of Prima Communications, Inc., Rocklin, California 95677.

Publisher: Stacy L. Hiquet
Associate Publisher: Nancy Stevenson
Marketing Manager: Judi Taylor
Managing Editor: Sandy Doell
Senior Acquisitions Editor: Deborah F. Abshier
Associate Acquisitions Editor: Rebecca I. Fong
Project Editor: Kevin Harreld
Copy Editor: Geneil Breeze
Technical Reviewer: Anna Laura Stewart
Interior Layout: Marian Hartsough
Cover Design: Prima Design Team
Indexer: Katherine Stimson

Important: If you have problems installing or running Works 2000, go to Microsoft's Web site at **www.microsoft.com**. Prima Publishing cannot provide software support.

ISBN: 0-7615-2437-1
Library of Congress Catalog Card Number: 99-65609
Printed in the United States of America

99 00 01 02 DD 10 9 8 7 6 5 4 3 2 1

To Alex

You have the most precious smile!

Acknowledgments

I am deeply thankful to the many people at Prima Publishing who worked on this book. Thank you for all the time you gave and for your assistance.

To Debbie Abshier for the opportunity to write this book and her confidence in me. To Rebecca Fong for her speedy responses to the numerous issues that arose. I'm so glad you're onboard! To Geneil Breeze and Anna Laura Stewart for their help in making this book technically and grammatically correct. Those certainly were big jobs! And to Kevin Harreld for all of his patience and guidance. You seem to have an unending supply.

Lastly, a big thanks to my husband, Vern. You are my blessing.

About the Author

DIANE KOERS owns and operates All Business Service, a software training and consulting business formed in 1988 that services the central Indiana area. Her area of expertise has long been in the word processing, spreadsheet, and graphics area of computing as well as providing training and support for Peachtree Accounting software. Diane's authoring experience includes numerous books for Prima's *Fast & Easy* series on topics such as Microsoft Office, Microsoft Word, Lotus 1-2-3, Lotus SmartSuite, WordPerfect, and Microsoft Windows 98 as well as co-authoring Prima's *Essential Windows 98.* She has also developed and written software training manuals for her clients' use.

Active in her church and civic activities, Diane enjoys spending her free time traveling and playing with her grandsons and her three Yorkshire terriers.

Contents at a Glance

Contents

Introduction

This new *Fast & Easy* book from Prima Publishing will help you use the many and varied features of Microsoft's popular Works product. Works is designed to answer most personal and professional computing needs with a program that has a user-friendly integrated design and a feature-rich environment.

Prima's *Fast & Easy* books teach by the step-by-step approach, clear language, and illustrations of exactly what is onscreen. *Microsoft Works 2000 Fast & Easy* provides the tools to successfully learn Microsoft Works—a word processor, spreadsheet, database manager, and a personal calendar system. You'll also learn how to manage an electronic address book.

Who Should Read This Book?

The easy-to-follow, highly visual nature of this book makes it the perfect learning tool for a beginning computer user. It is also ideal for those who are new to this version of Microsoft Works, or those who feel comfortable with computers and software but have never used these types of programs before.

By using *Microsoft Works 2000 Fast & Easy*, any level of user can look up steps for a task quickly without having to plow through pages of descriptions.

Added Advice to Make You a Pro

This book uses steps and keeps explanations to a minimum to help you learn faster. Included in the book are a few elements that provide some additional comments to help you master the program, without encumbering your progress through the steps:

- **Tips** offer shortcuts when performing an action, or a hint about a feature that might make your work in Microsoft Works quicker and easier.
- **Notes** give you a bit of background or additional information about a feature, or advice about how to use the feature in your day-to-day activities.

In addition, two helpful appendixes show you how to install Microsoft Works and how to use the Microsoft Task Wizards, which are included in Works to save you time!

Read and enjoy this *Fast & Easy* book. It certainly is the fastest and easiest way to learn Microsoft Works 2000.

PART I

Discovering Microsoft Works

1

Getting Started

Congratulations! You are ready to begin working with Microsoft Works, an excellent integrated software application designed for homes, home offices, or other small businesses. In this chapter, you'll learn how to:

- Start the Works program
- Discover the Task Launcher
- Preview the various Works components
- Exit Microsoft Works

Starting Works

When Microsoft Works installs, the setup program creates several methods for you to begin using the software. If you have not yet installed Microsoft Works, see Appendix A, "Installing Works."

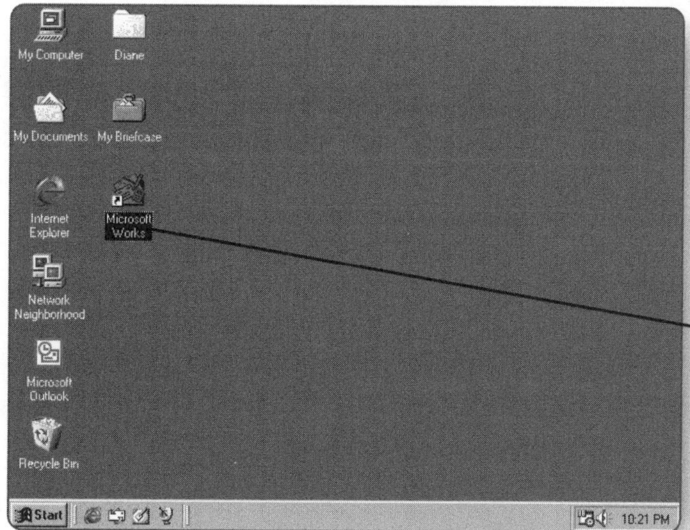

Using the Shortcut Icon

The fastest method to launch the Works program is to use the shortcut placed on your Windows desktop.

1. **Double-click** on the **Microsoft Works icon**. The Works Task Launcher program will appear.

> **NOTE**
>
> You may be prompted to register your software. Follow the onscreen instructions to register.

Using the Start Menu

If your desktop does not have a shortcut icon, you can access the Works program by using the Start button.

1. Click on **Start**. The Start menu will appear.

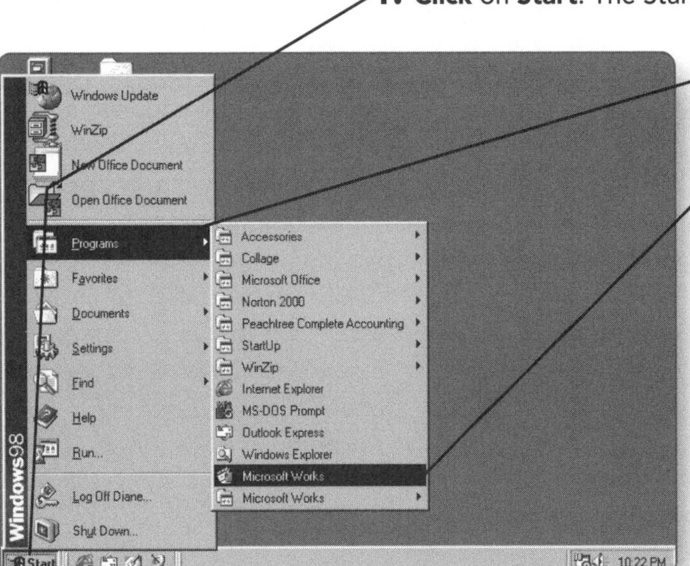

2. Click on **Programs**. The Programs menu will appear.

3. Click on **Microsoft Works**. The Works program will launch, and the Task Launcher will appear.

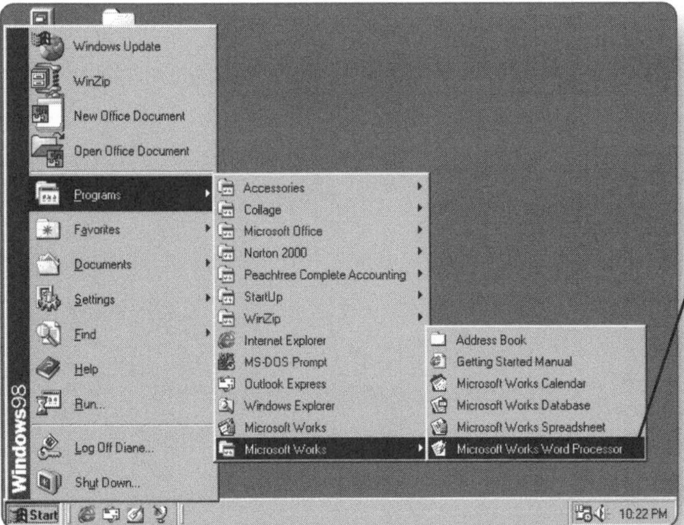

TIP

You can also click on the Microsoft Works folder and choose a Works component. This method bypasses the Task Launcher discussed in the next section.

Discovering the Task Launcher

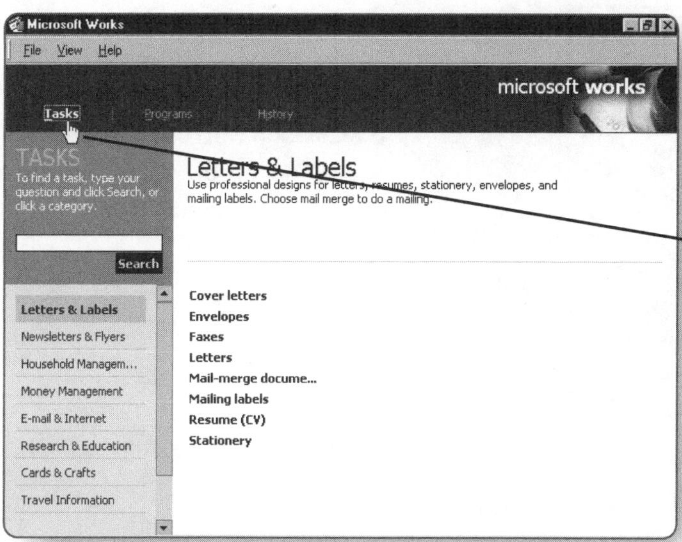

From the Task Launcher, you can access various components, create new documents, open existing documents, or use one of the Task Wizards.

1. If necessary, click on Tasks. A list of available Task Wizards, categorized by project type, will appear. Task Wizards are discussed in Appendix B, "Using Task Wizards."

2. Click on **Programs**. A listing of the Works components will appear.

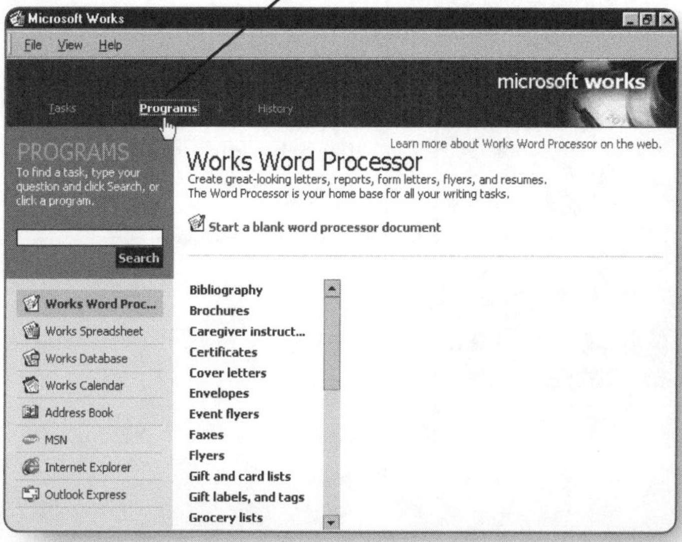

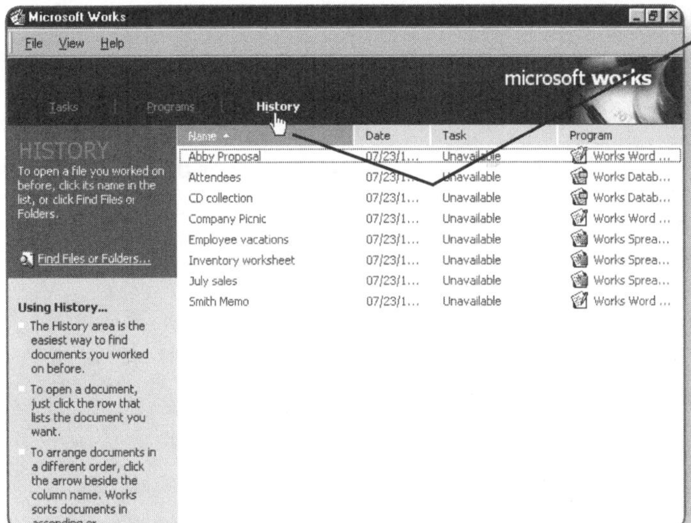

3. **Click** on **History**. After you create Works documents, a listing will appear here.

Understanding the Components of Works

Microsoft Works is considered an *integrated* application. This means that all the components work as one single program.

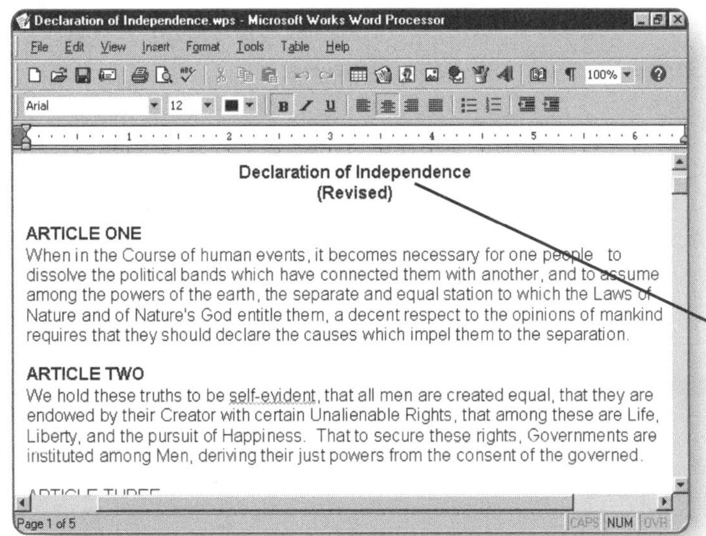

Working with Word Processing

Create memos, letters, proposals, and other text-based documents using the Works word processing module.

You'll learn how to format text in Chapter 4, "Formatting a Document."

Seeing Spreadsheets

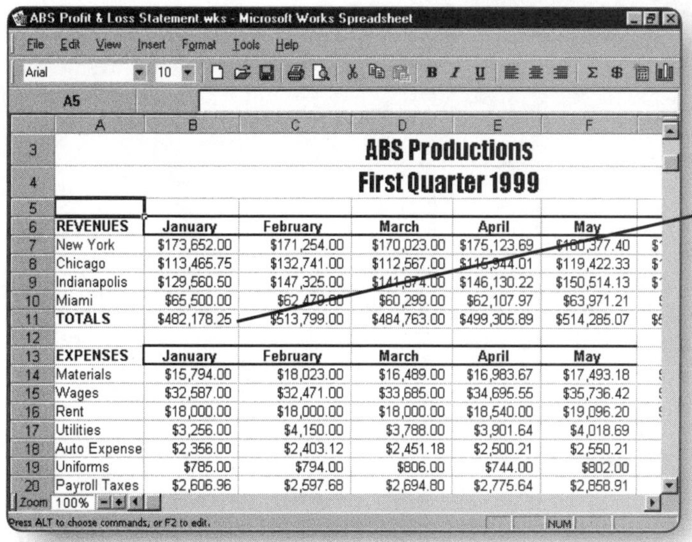

Spreadsheets are used to crunch numbers. Save time by letting the spreadsheet do the calculating for you.

You'll learn how to create formulas in Chapter 12, "Working with Formulas and Functions."

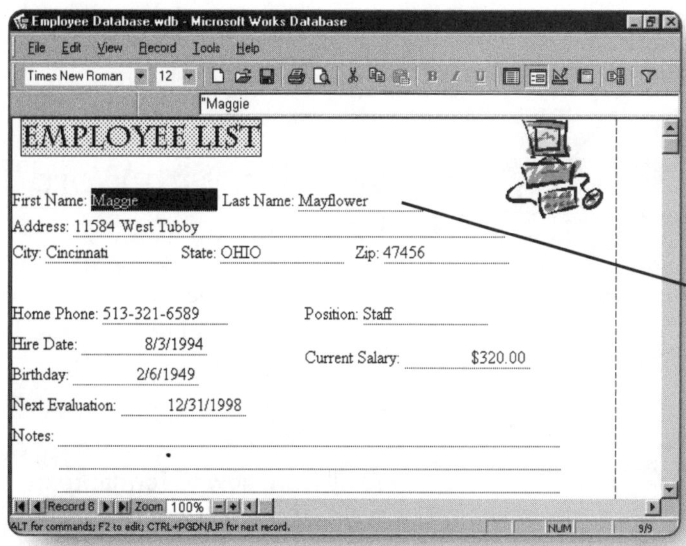

Discovering Databases

Track names, addresses, and other data by designing a Works database.

You'll learn how to add records to a database in Chapter 17 "Working with Data."

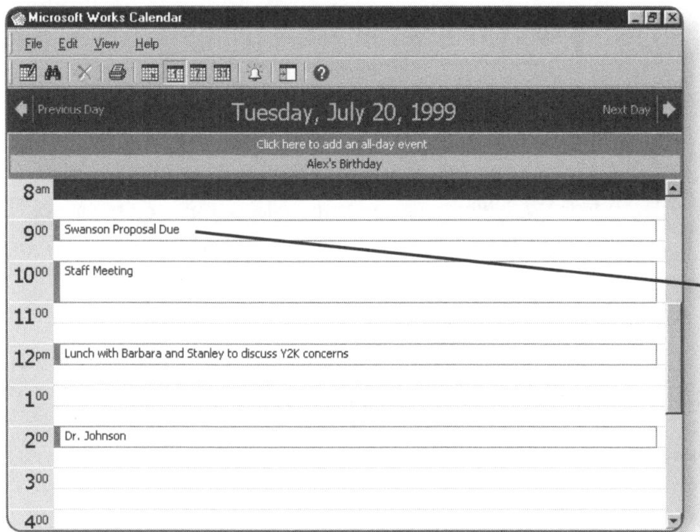

Viewing the Calendar

Schedule events and meetings with the newest feature to Microsoft Works—the Calendar.

Chapter 24, "Scheduling Using the Calendar," shows you how to keep your calendar up-to-date.

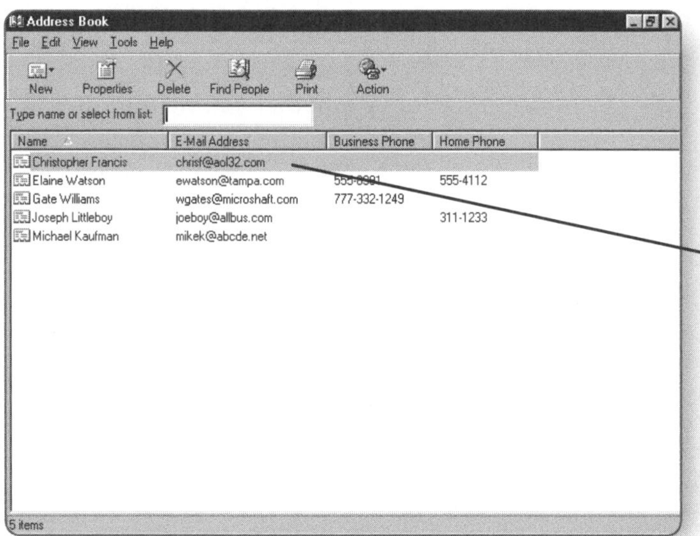

Scanning the Address Book

Use the Address Book to keep track of your family and friends.

Chapter 21, "Saving Information in the Address Book," shows you how to manage telephone numbers, e-mail addresses, birthdays, and much more.

Exiting Works

When you are finished working with Works, exit the program. This procedure protects your data and avoids possible program damage. It also frees up valuable computer memory that can be used for other programs.

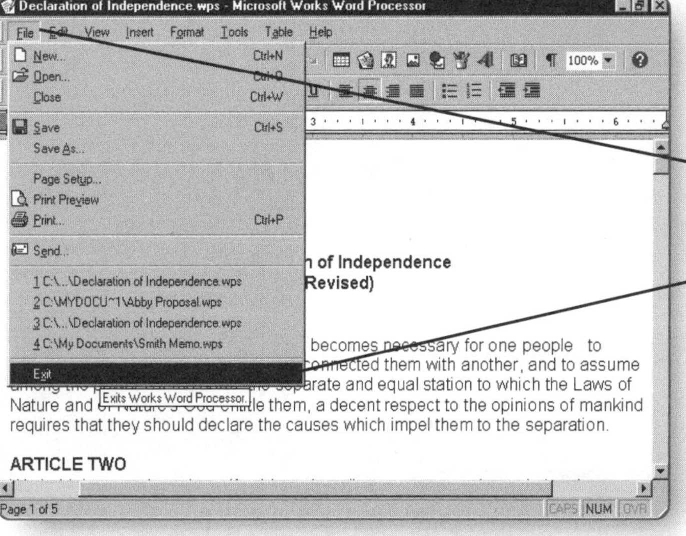

1. Click on **File**. The File menu will appear.

2. Click on **Exit**. The Works program will close.

> **NOTE**
>
> If any documents are open that haven't been saved, Works asks whether you want to save changes to those files. Click Yes if you want to save your document or click No if you want the document discarded. If you click on Yes, Works prompts you for a name for the file.

2

Seeking Help

Although you'll find many answers to your questions in this book, sometimes you need additional information. Microsoft supplies several types of assistance. In this chapter, you'll learn how to:

- Access the Help window
- Use the Help Contents and Index
- Install the Works online manual
- Get help on the Web

Accessing Help

Help with Microsoft Works is available several ways. One method, using the Help window, shows you that help is only a mouse click away.

When you begin any type of Works document, the Help window displays a menu of choices applicable to that type of document.

1. Start Microsoft **Works**. The Works Task Launcher will appear.

2. Click on **Programs**. The Works Programs screen will appear.

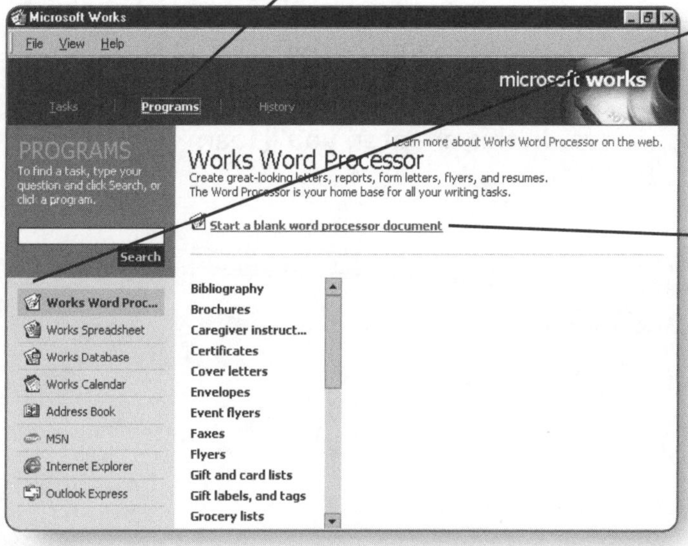

3. Click on a Works **application**. (The major applications are word processing, spreadsheets, or database). A list of possible document types will appear.

4. Click on **Start a blank word processor document** (or spreadsheet or database). A blank document will appear.

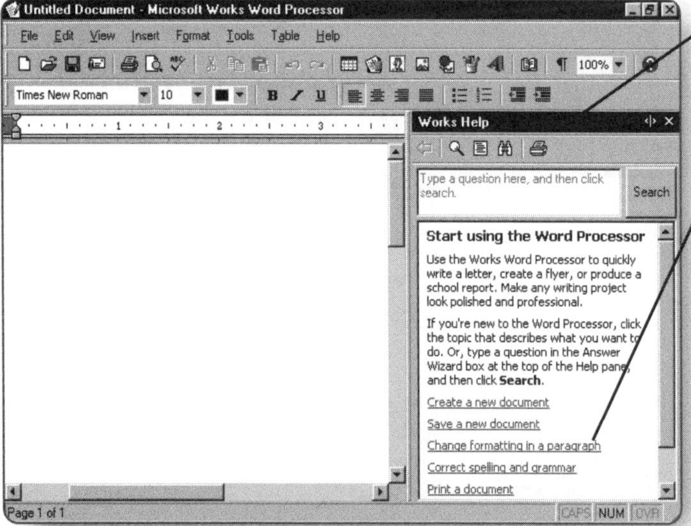

The help topics window appears to the right of the document window.

5. Click on a **topic**. The Help window will redisplay with information for the selected task.

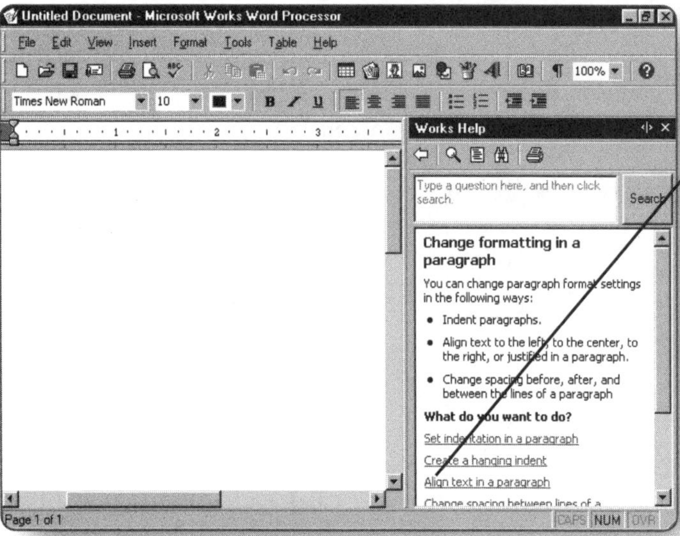

NOTE

Some features may have multiple help topic levels.

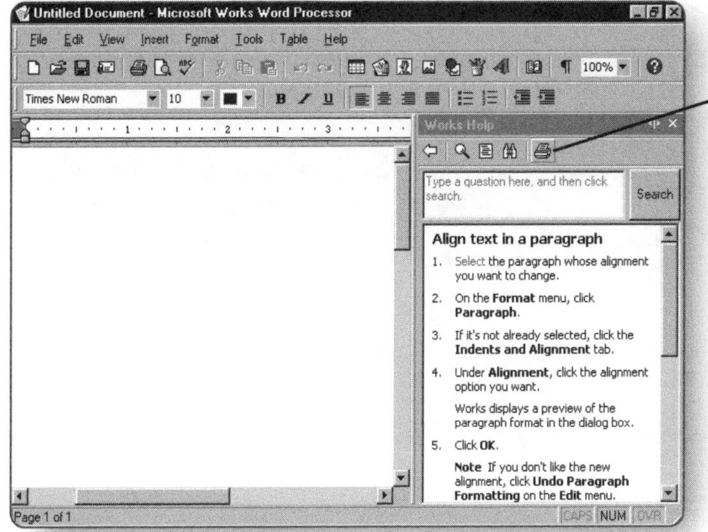

TIP

Click on Print to print a copy of the help information.

Asking the Answer Wizard

A feature new to Works 2000 is the Ask the Answer Wizard help function. This feature allows you to research a Works feature by typing a question in your own words.

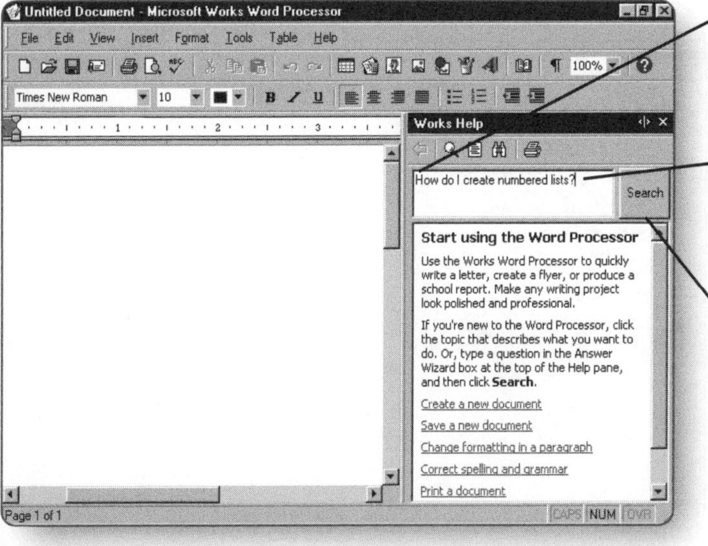

1. **Click** in the **Search text box**. The blinking insertion point will appear.

2. **Type** your **question**. The text will appear in the Search text box.

3. **Click** on **Search**. A list of possible topic matches will appear in the bottom of the Help window.

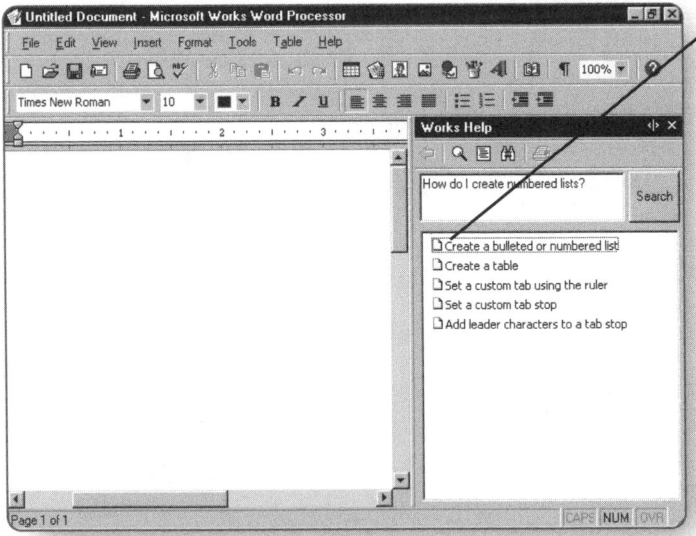

4. Click on the **topic** that most closely matches your request. Information on the feature will appear.

Looking Through the Help Contents

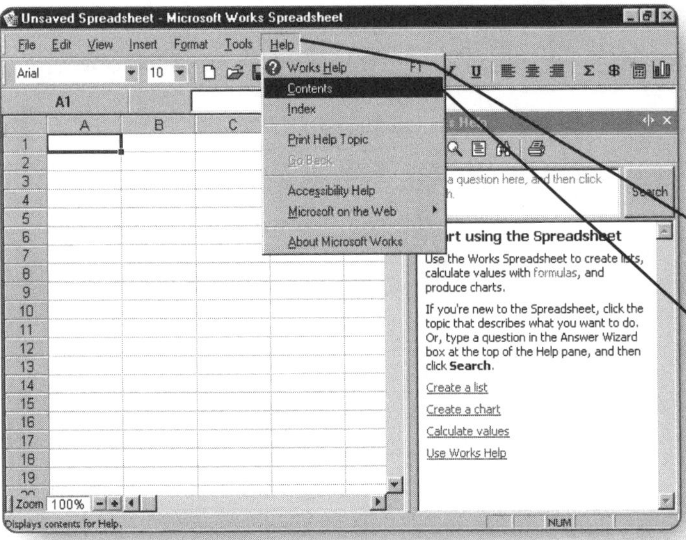

The Help Contents feature presents help information in a folderlike format, making it easy for you to browse available topics.

1. Click on **Help**. The Help menu will appear.

2. Click on **Contents.** The Help window will display a Table of Contents relevant to the Works component you are currently using. For example, if you have a spreadsheet open, the Spreadsheet Table of Contents will appear.

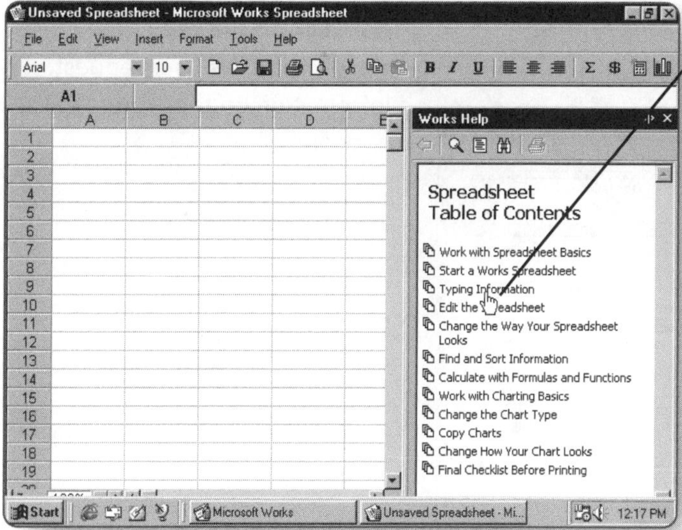

3. Click on a **general topic**. A list of subtopics will appear.

> **NOTE**
>
> A *general topic* has *specific topics* and is signified by an icon resembling multiple pieces of paper. A specific topic appears in blue text and is indicated by an icon representing a single sheet of paper. Some general topics may have other general topics listed under them.

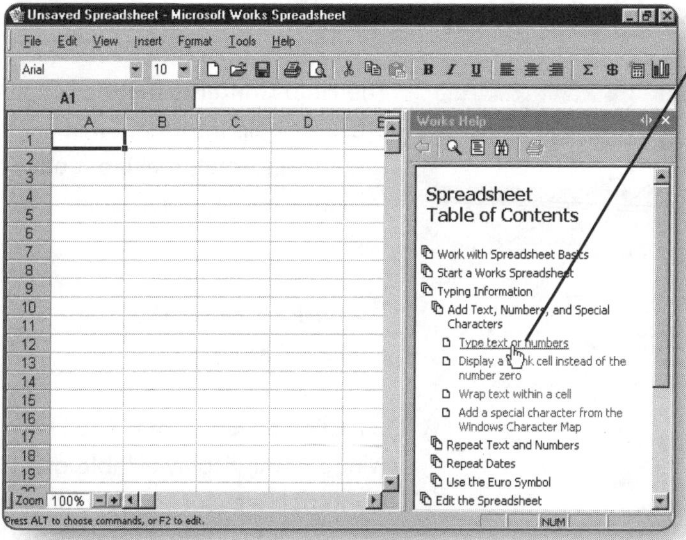

4. Click on the **specific topic** you want to view. The information on that topic will appear in the Help window.

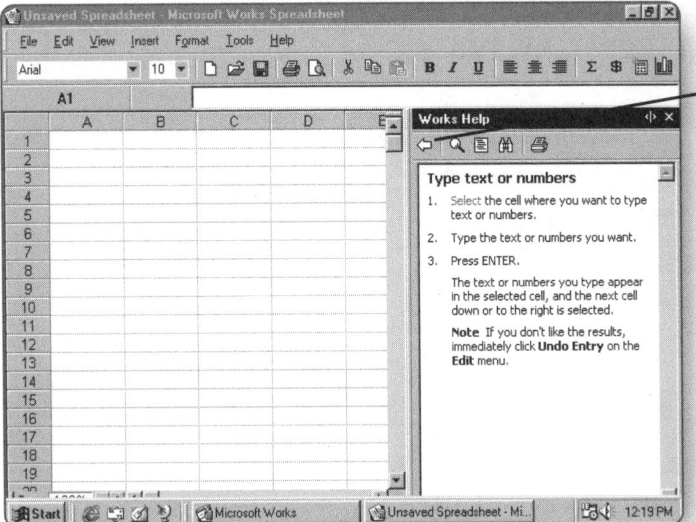

TIP

Click on the Back button to return to the previous Help screen.

Using the Help Index

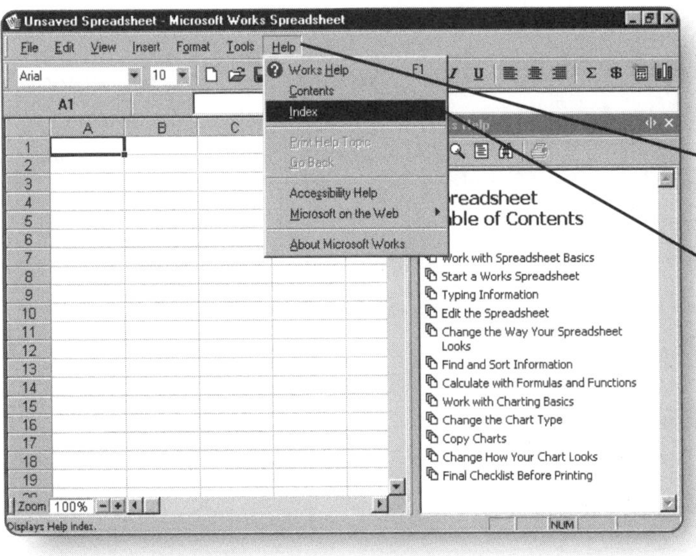

Works' help features also include an extensive index of topics.

1. Click on **Help**. The Help menu will appear.

2. Click on **Index**. A list of words relevant to the Works component you are using will appear.

The topics are listed alphabetically with some topics displaying a list of subtopics.

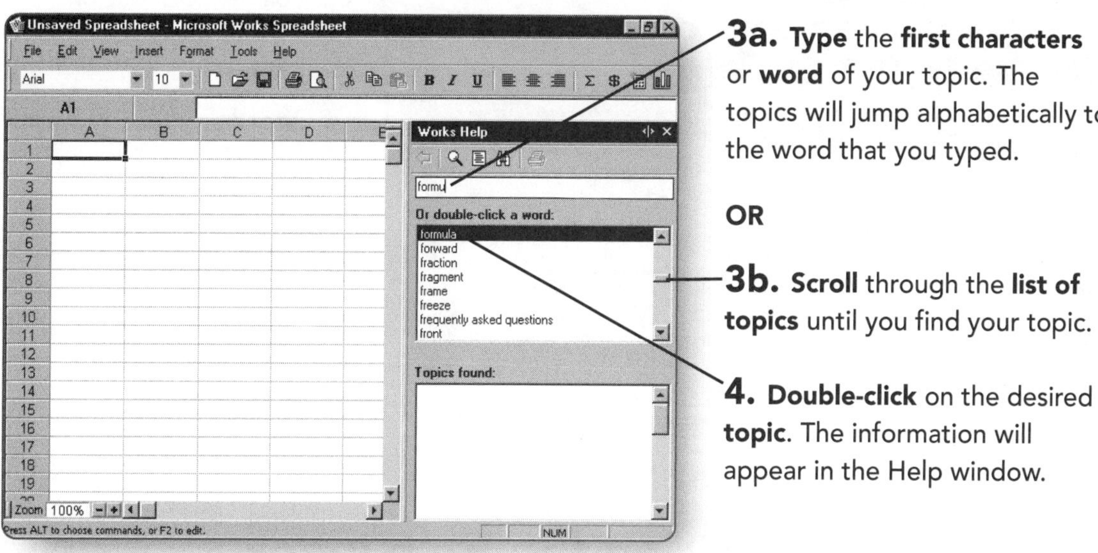

3a. Type the **first characters** or **word** of your topic. The topics will jump alphabetically to the word that you typed.

OR

3b. Scroll through the **list of topics** until you find your topic.

4. Double-click on the desired **topic**. The information will appear in the Help window.

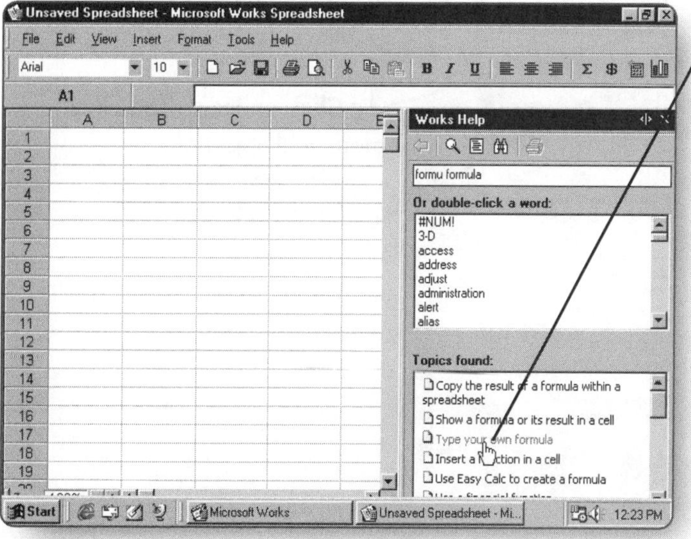

5. Click on the **topic** that most closely matches your request. Information on the feature will appear.

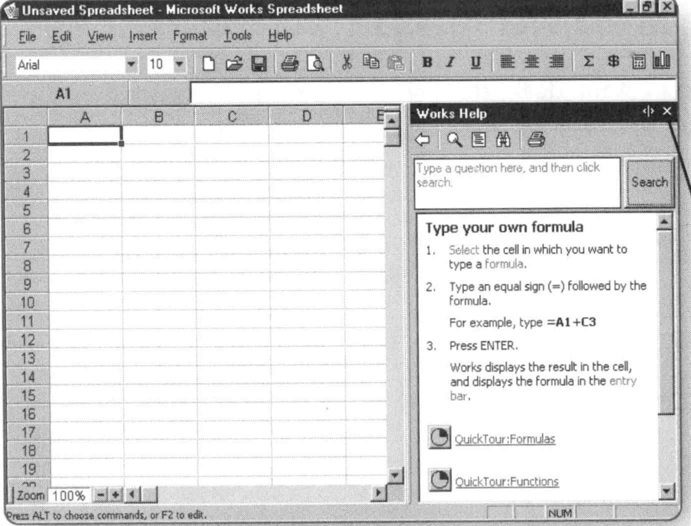

Managing the Help Window

If the Help window is in your way and you don't need it at the moment, put it away.

1. Click on the Help window **Close box**. The Help window will close.

You can reopen the Help window whenever you need it.

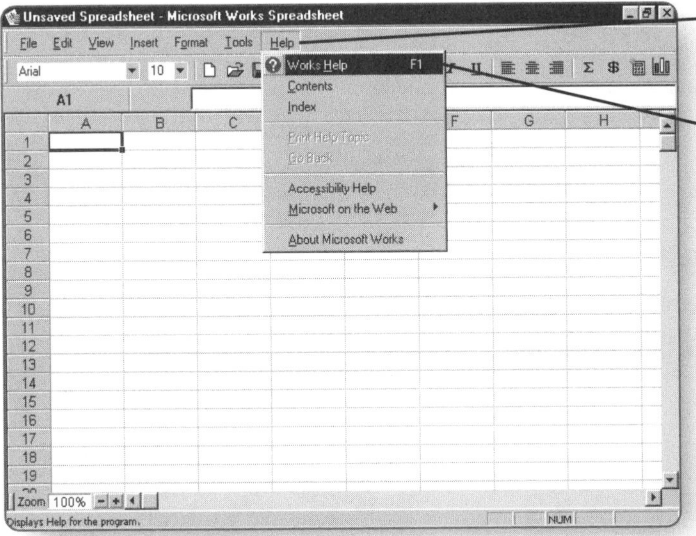

2. Click on the **Help menu**. The Help menu will appear.

3. Click on **Works Help**. The Help window will reappear.

> **TIP**
>
> Press F1 to quickly reopen the Works Help window.

> **NOTE**
>
> For the remainder of this book, the Help window will not be displayed.

First Time Help

Works automatically displays a First Time Help option the first time you select a feature. You can see a demonstration of the feature or get step-by-step instructions.

1. Click on a **feature** that you have never used before. The First-time Help dialog box will open.

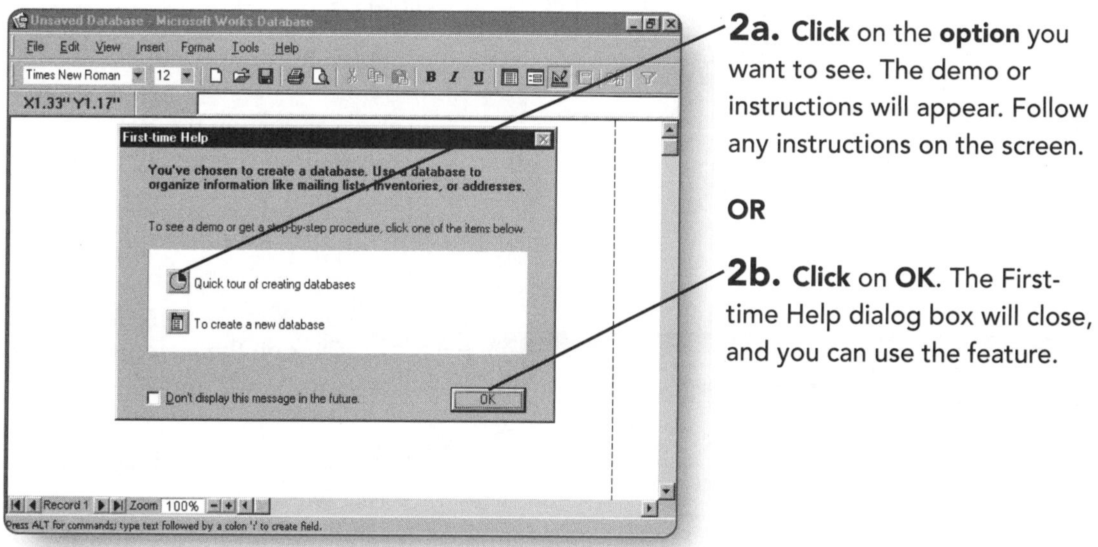

2a. Click on the **option** you want to see. The demo or instructions will appear. Follow any instructions on the screen.

OR

2b. Click on **OK**. The First-time Help dialog box will close, and you can use the feature.

Finding Help on the Web

Many sources of assistance are supplied with Microsoft Works. You've already seen several good resources. Another one is the World Wide Web. Microsoft includes technical support at its Web site.

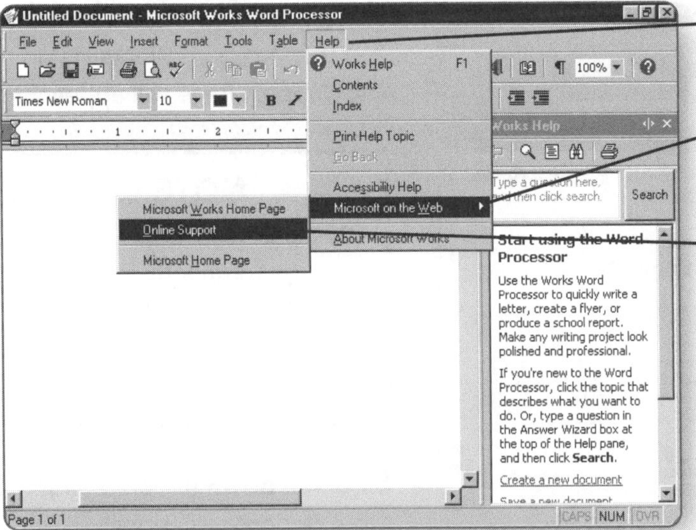

1. **Click** on **Help**. The Help menu will appear.

2. **Click** on **Microsoft on the Web**. A submenu will appear.

3. **Click** on **Online Support**. If you are not connected to the Internet, you will be prompted to do so.

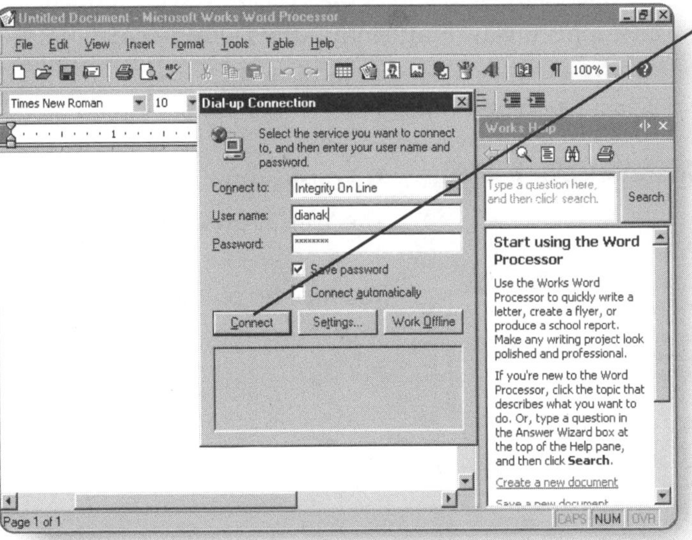

4. **Click** on **Connect**. Your Internet connection will be established.

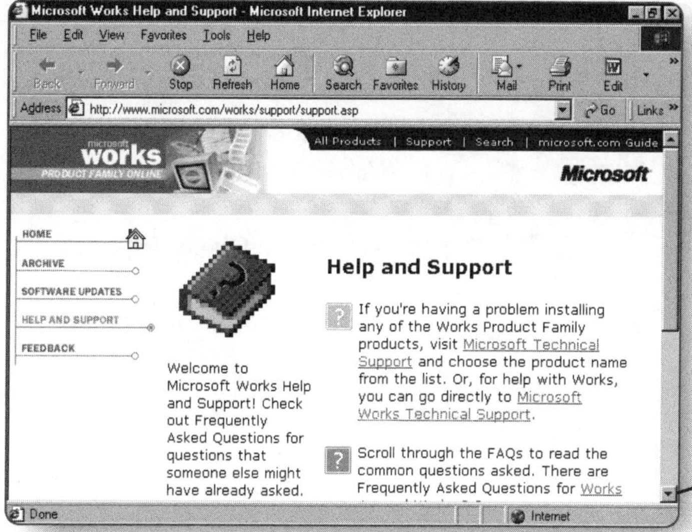

Internet Explorer 5 will launch, and the Microsoft Works Help and Support Page will appear.

> **NOTE**
>
> Because Web pages change frequently, your screen may appear slightly different from the figure.

5. Scroll down the Web page. More options will appear.

From the Microsoft Help and Support page you can obtain technical support, view Frequently Asked Questions, download free templates and Task Wizards, or even communicate with other Microsoft Works users.

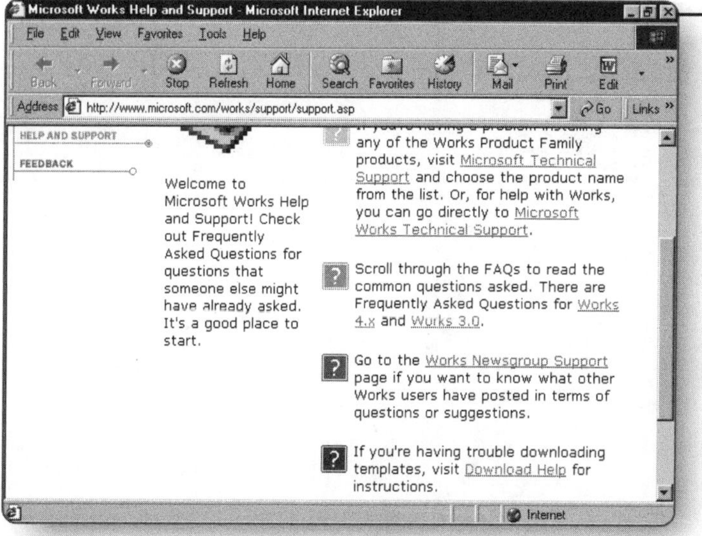

6. Click on the **Close button**. The Web browser will close.

You may be prompted to close your Internet connection.

NOTE

Depending on the version of Microsoft Windows you have on your system, your dialog box may look slightly different from the one shown.

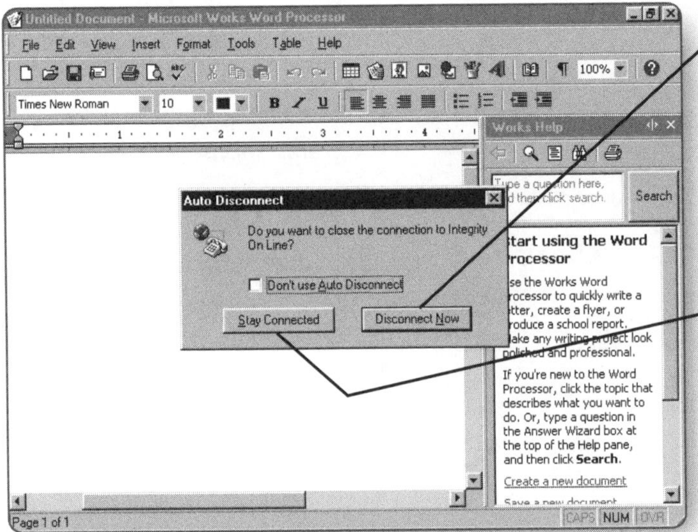

7a. Click on **Disconnect Now** if you want to disconnect. Your connection will terminate, and you will return to the Microsoft Works window.

OR

7b. Click on **Stay Connected**. Your connection will remain open, and you will return to the Microsoft Works window.

Installing the Online Users Manual

You probably did not receive any printed books with your Microsoft Works program. Most manufacturers now include documentation on the CD that comes with the software.

To use the online users manual, you need to have a program called Adobe Acrobat installed on your computer. If you don't already have it, don't worry; Works includes it on the CD as well.

Installing Adobe Acrobat Reader

You only need to install this program once. In fact, you may already have it on your computer from other software programs.

1. Place the **Microsoft Works 2000 CD** in your CD-ROM drive.

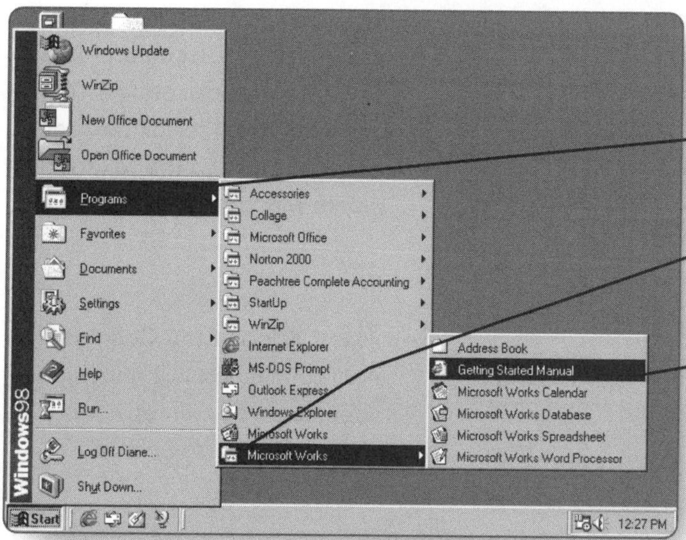

2. Click on **Start**. The Start menu will appear.

3. Click on **Programs**. The Programs submenu will appear.

4. Click on **Microsoft Works.** The Works subfolder will appear.

5. Click on **Getting Started Manual**. An Internet Explorer window will open with information on the manual.

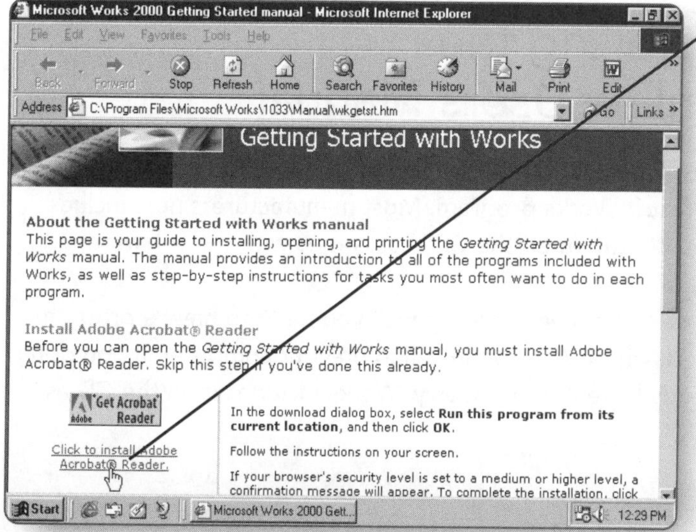

6. Click on **Click to install Adobe Acrobat Reader**. A File Download dialog box will open.

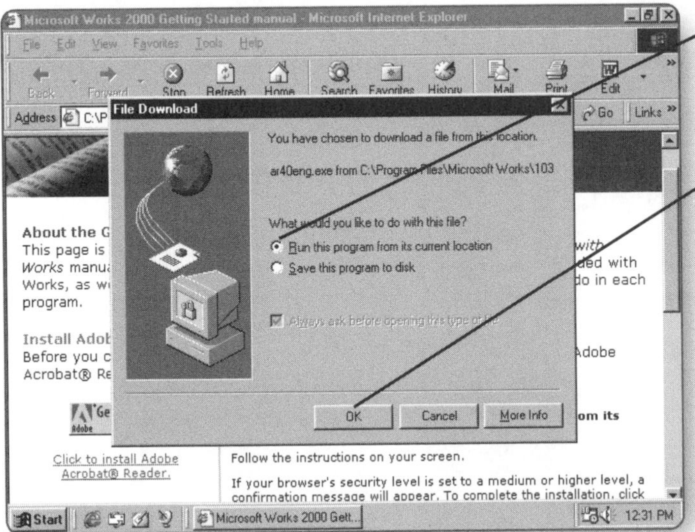

7. Click on **Run this program from its current location**. The option will be selected.

8. Click on **OK**. A security warning message will appear.

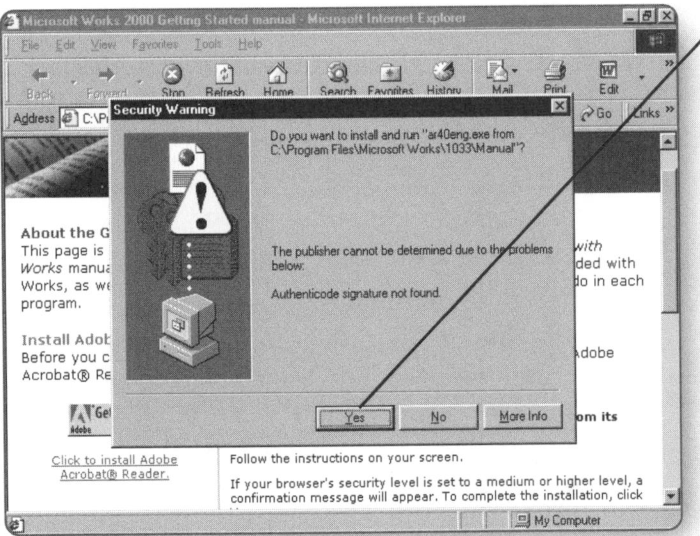

9. Click on **Yes**. The Adobe Acrobat Reader Setup program will begin.

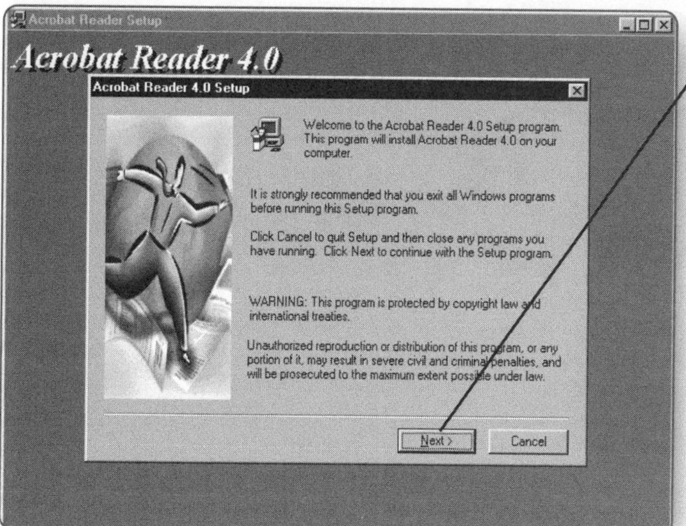

10. Click on **Next**. The Software License Agreement screen will appear.

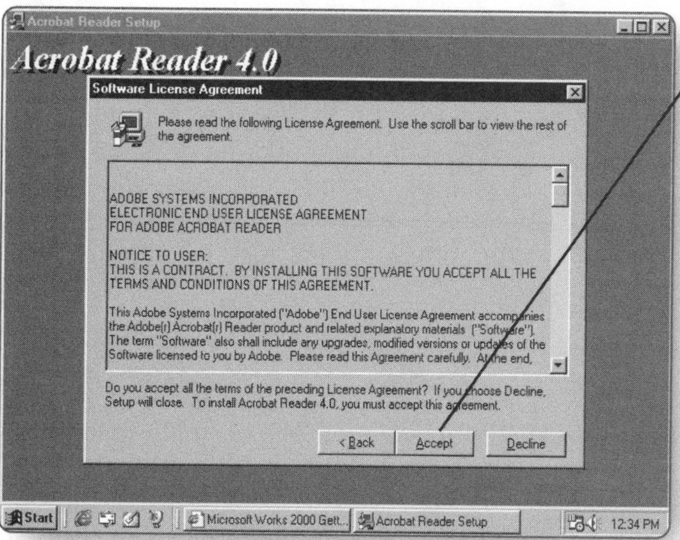

11. Click on **Accept**. The Choose Destination Location screen will appear.

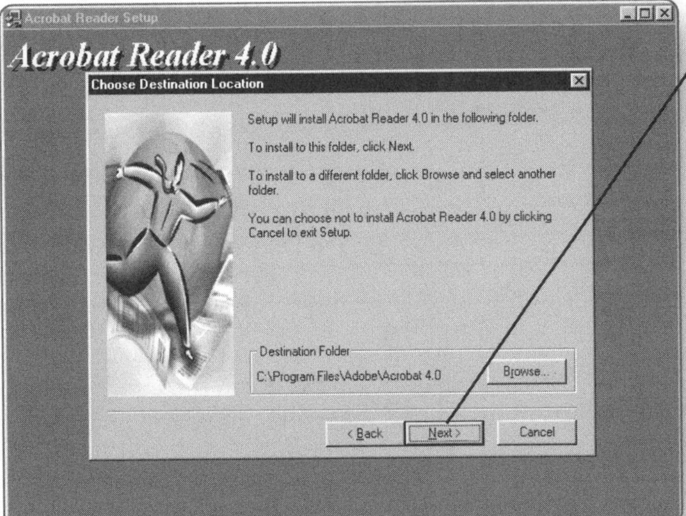

12. Click on **Next**. The Adobe Acrobat Reader program will be installed on your computer.

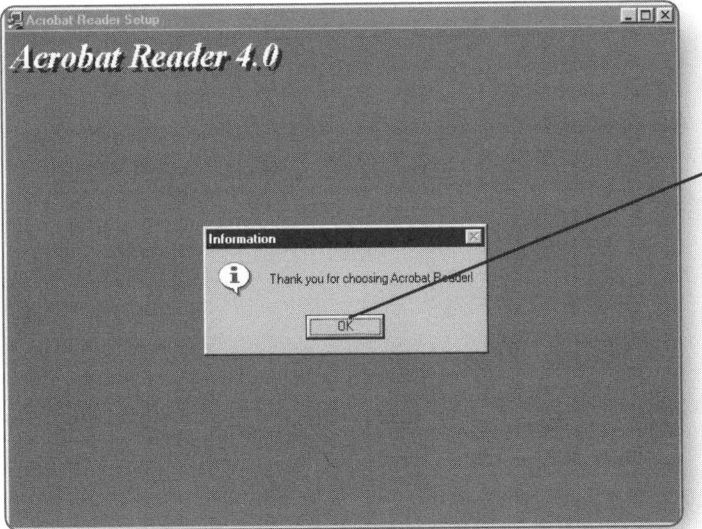

When installation has been completed, an acknowledgment box will open.

13. Click on **OK**. The dialog box will close, and your screen will return to the Internet Explorer window.

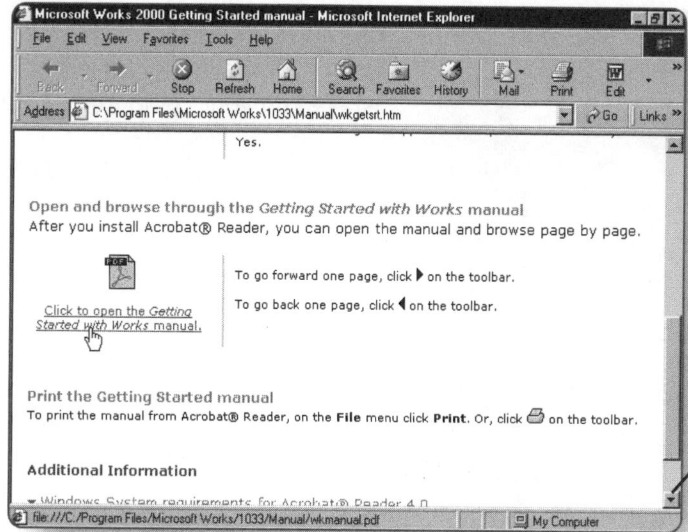

Using the Online Documentation

After the Adobe Acrobat Reader program is installed, you'll be ready to use the Works Online Documentation.

TIP

Scroll down the Internet Explorer page to find this choice.

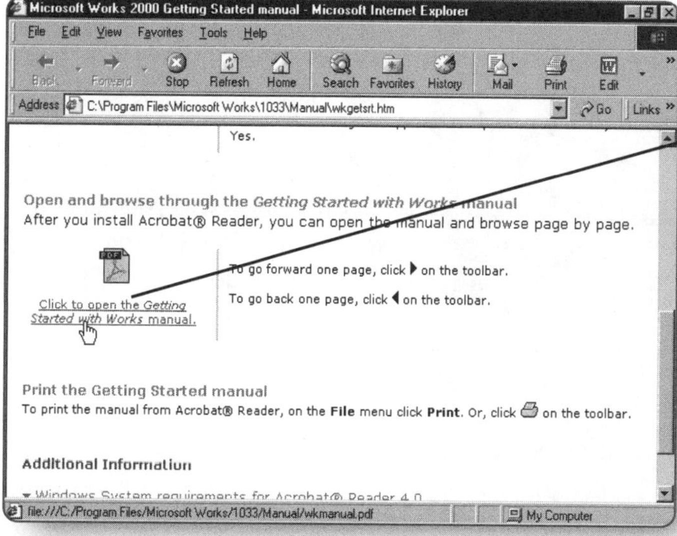

1. **Place** the **Microsoft Works 2000 CD** in your CD-ROM drive.
2. **Click** on **Click to open the Getting Started with Works manual**. The Works manual will display on the screen.

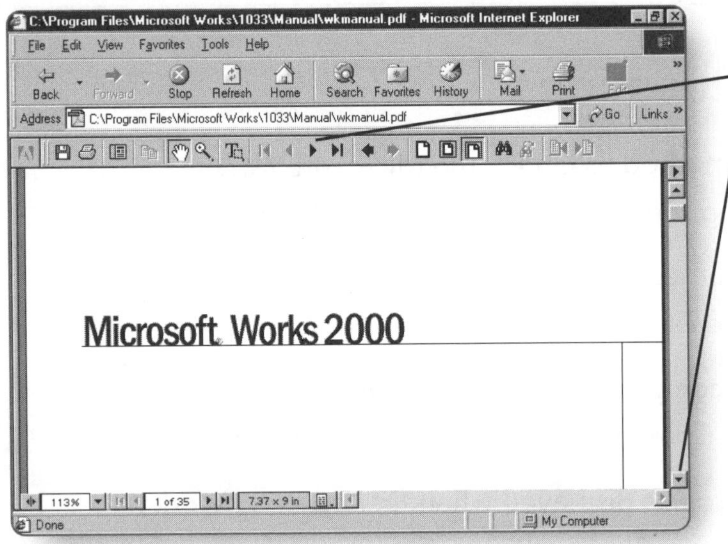

From the manual you can:

- Click on Next Page to read more of the documentation
- Scroll down to read more of the current page

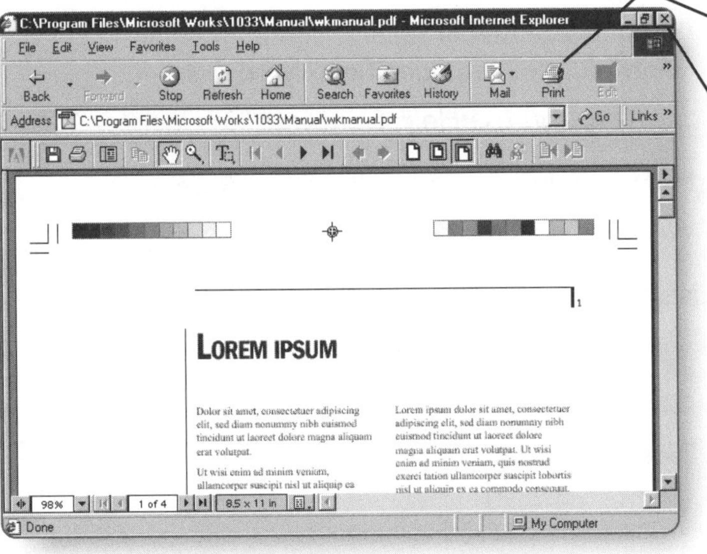

- Click on Print to print the manual
- Click on Close to close the online documentation

Part I Review Questions

1. What is the fastest method to launch the Microsoft Works program? *See "Using the Shortcut Icon" in Chapter 1*
2. What are the types of tasks you can do with the Task Launcher? *See "Discovering the Task Launcher" in Chapter 1*
3. What are the major components included with Works? *See "Understanding the Components of Works" in Chapter 1*
4. Where are the help topics displayed when first opening Works? *See "Accessing Help" in Chapter 2*
5. What is the Answer Wizard? *See "Asking the Answer Wizard" in Chapter 2*
6. In the Help Contents window, how are specific help topics indicated? *See "Looking Through the Help Contents" in Chapter 2*
7. What can you do to the Help window if it's in your way? *See "Managing the Help Window" in Chapter 2*
8. What is sometimes displayed the first time you access a feature? *See "First Time Help" in Chapter 2*
9. What are some of the ways Microsoft can assist you when you access the Microsoft Works Home Page? *See "Finding Help on the Web" in Chapter 2*
10. Instead of printed books, how do many manufacturers provide documentation? *See "Installing the Online Users Manual" in Chapter 2*

PART II

Using the Word Processor

3

Creating a Simple Document

When you need to create a letter, memo, or proposal, use the Word Processing application of Works. Word processing is great for everything text based—from the simplest letter to a professional-looking newsletter. In this chapter, you'll learn how to:

- Create a document
- Insert the current date
- Move around in a document
- Select and delete text
- Undo your mistakes
- Create and use an Easy Text entry

Opening a Blank Word Processing Document

Use the Works Task Launcher to create a new word processing document.

1. Start the Microsoft **Works program**. The Task Launcher will appear when you launch the Works program.

When the Task Launcher appears, you can select a type of project.

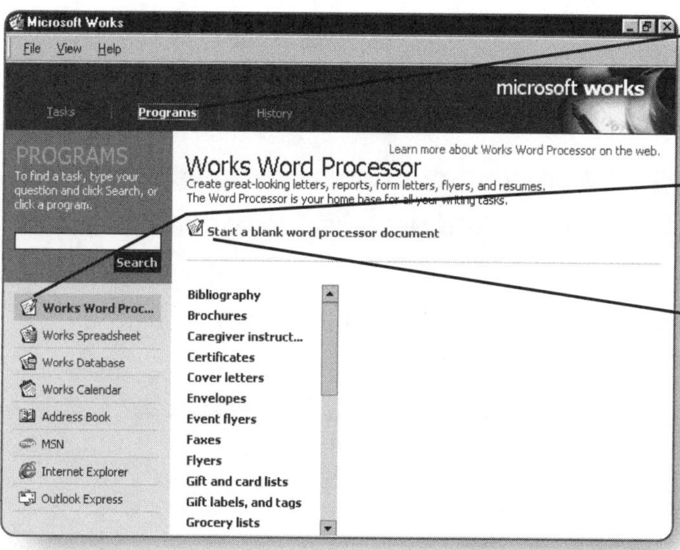

2. Click on **Programs**. A listing of the Works components will appear.

3. Click on **Works Word Processor**. A listing of Word Processing tasks will appear.

4. Click on **Start a blank word processor document**. A blank word processing document will appear.

Typing Text in a Document

When typing in a word processing document, press the Enter key only when you get to the end of a paragraph or when you want an extra blank line between paragraphs. Works takes care of the rest. If the word you are typing does not fit entirely at the end of the current line, Works puts it on the next line automatically. This is called *word wrap*.

You will find it to your benefit to follow the "Type First, Edit Later" concept. Type the text into your document and then go back and make any changes.

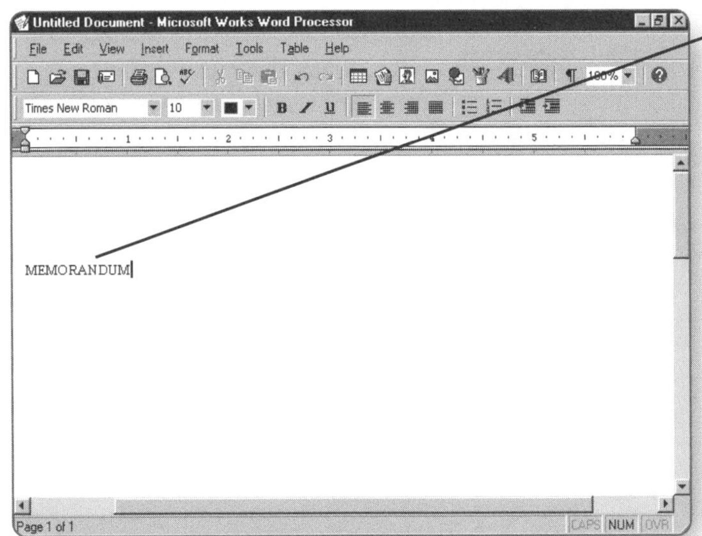

1. Type some **text**. The text you type will appear at the location of the insertion point.

If you make any mistakes while typing, you can press the Backspace key to erase any letter to the left of the blinking insertion point. You'll learn how to make other corrections later.

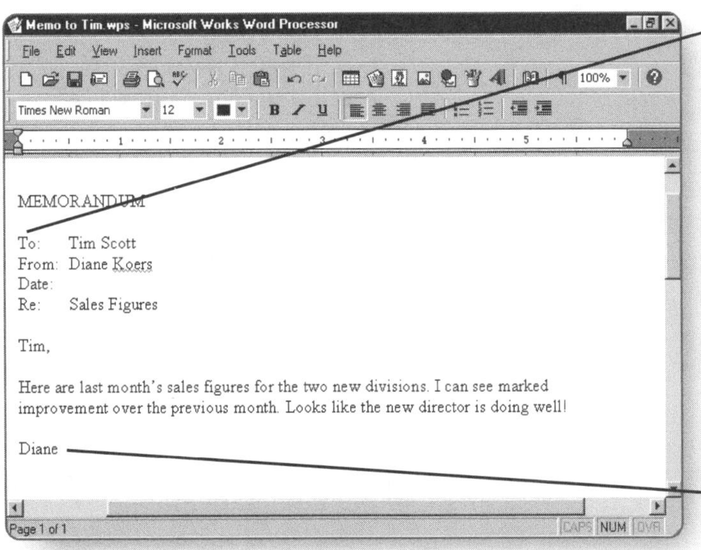

2. Press the **Enter key twice** when you have completed a paragraph. The insertion point will move down two lines.

> **NOTE**
>
> A paragraph consists of a single line of text, such as "Dear Sir," or multiple lines of text.

3. Continue typing until your document is complete.

Inserting the Date and Time

Instead of fishing around your desk looking for your calendar, let Works put today's date in your document.

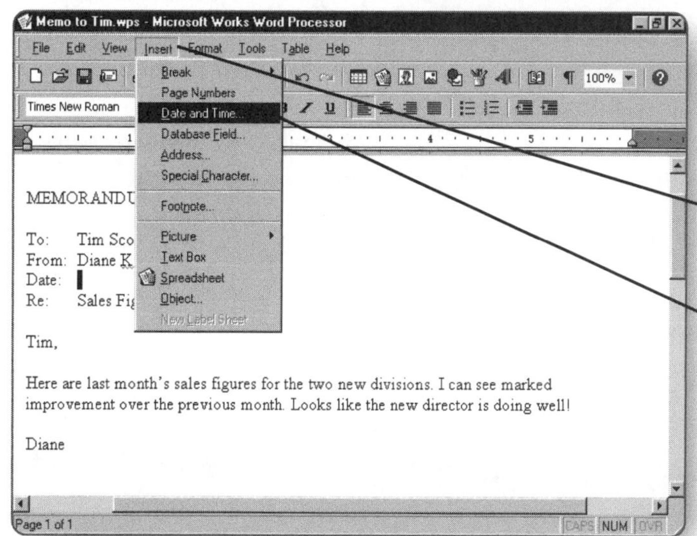

1. **Click** the **mouse pointer** where you want to insert the date. The insertion point will blink.
2. **Click** on **Insert**. The Insert menu will appear.
3. **Click** on **Date and Time**. The Insert Date and Time dialog box will open.

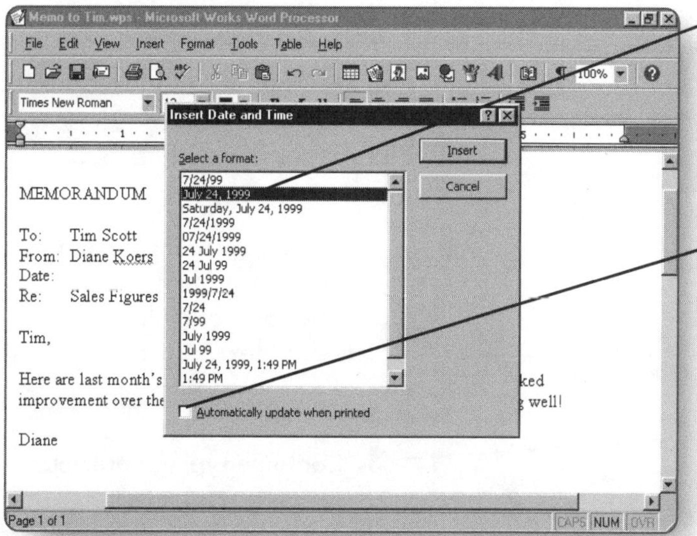

4. **Click** on a **date format**. The selected date format will be highlighted.

> **NOTE**
>
> If "Automatically update when printed" is checked, the date will change in the document every time it is opened to reflect the current date. This is called a *dynamic* date. If you do not want the date to change (a *static* date), do not check this option.

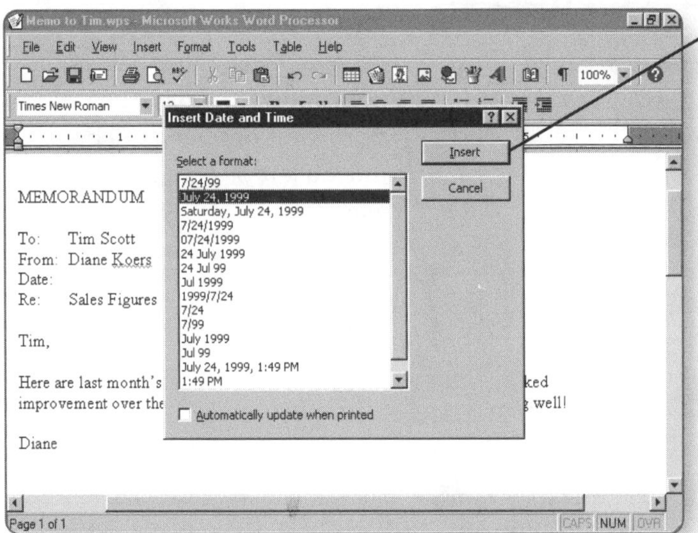

5. Click on **Insert**. The date will be inserted into your document at the location of the insertion point.

> **TIP**
>
> A shortcut to insert a dynamic date or time is Ctrl+D for the current date and Ctrl+T for the current time.

Moving Around in a Document

Works provides several quick ways to move around a word processing document.

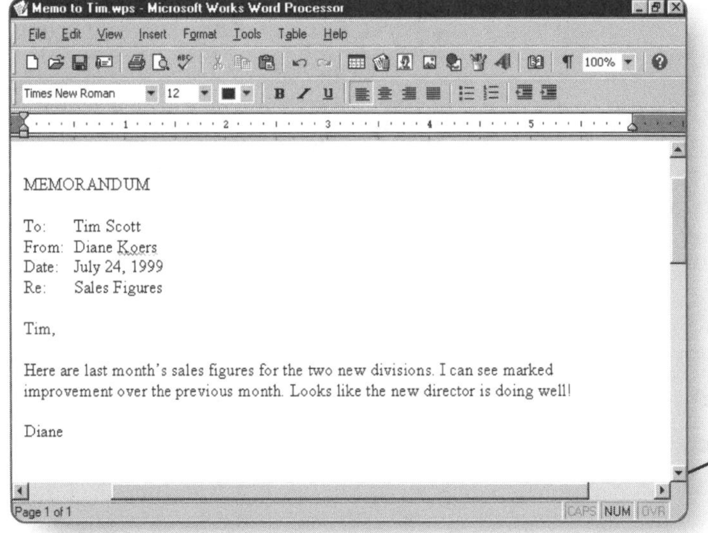

Moving Around Using the Scroll Bar

When moving through a document using the scroll bar, the insertion point does not move—only the screen display moves. You must click in the document to move the insertion point to a new location when using the scroll bar.

1. Click on the **arrow** repeatedly at either end of the vertical scroll bar. The document onscreen will be moved up or down in the window.

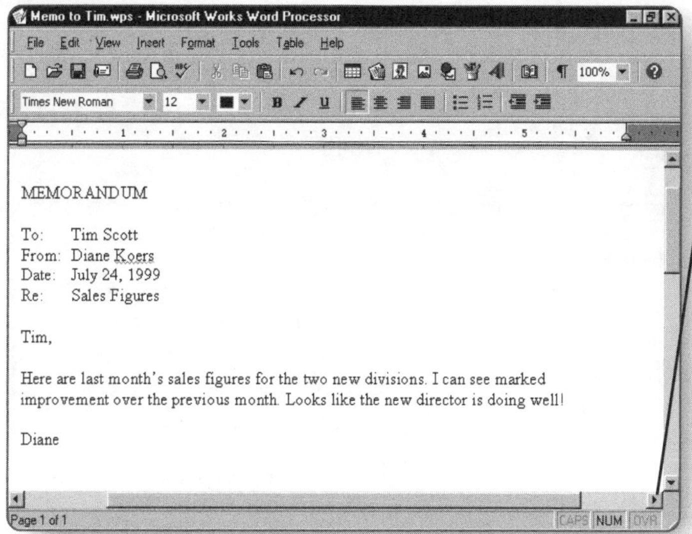

2. Click on the **arrow** repeatedly at either end of the horizontal scroll bar. The document onscreen will be moved left or right in the window.

Using the Go To Feature

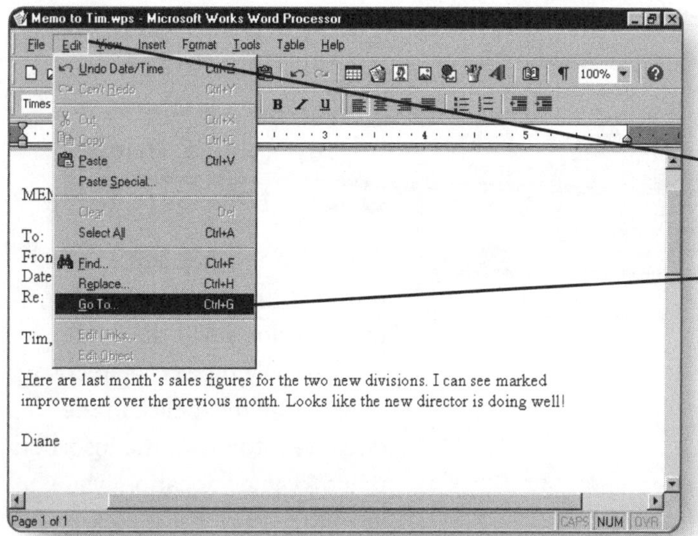

To quickly move to a specific page of a document, you can use the Works Go To Feature.

1. Click on **Edit**. The Edit menu will appear.

2. Click on **Go To**. The Find and Replace dialog box will open with the Go To tab displayed.

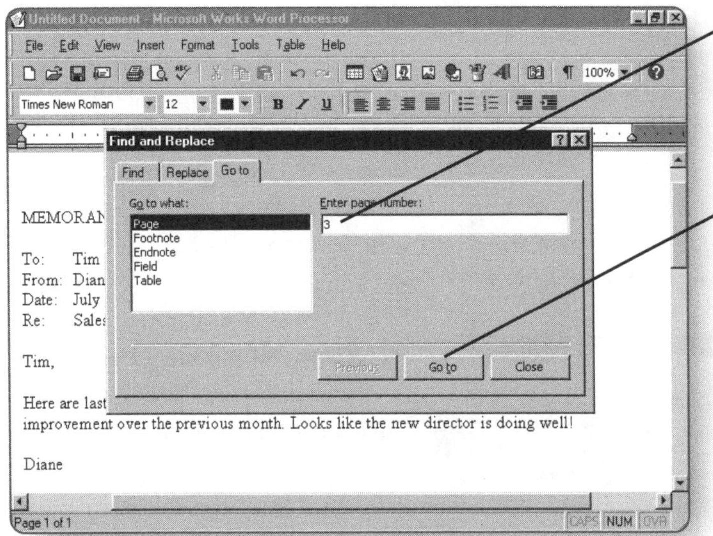

3. Type the desired **page number**. The page number will appear in the Enter page number: text box.

4. Click on **Go to**. The specified page will be displayed.

5. Click on **Close**. The Find and Replace dialog box will close.

Moving Around Using the Keyboard

You may prefer to use your keyboard to move around in your document. This minitable illustrates these shortcut keys.

To Move	Do This
Right one word	Press Ctrl+Right Arrow
Left one word	Press Ctrl+Left Arrow
To the beginning of a line	Press Home
To the end of a line	Press End
To the beginning of the paragraph	Press Ctrl+Up Arrow
To the next paragraph	Press Ctrl+Down Arrow
Down one screen	Press Page Down
Up one screen	Press Page Up
To the beginning of the document	Press Ctrl+Home
To the end of the document	Press Ctrl+End
To a specified page number	Press Ctrl+G

Inserting Text

When Works is first installed, word processing initially defaults to *insert* mode.

This means that when you want to add new text to a document, any existing text will move to the right to make room for the new text.

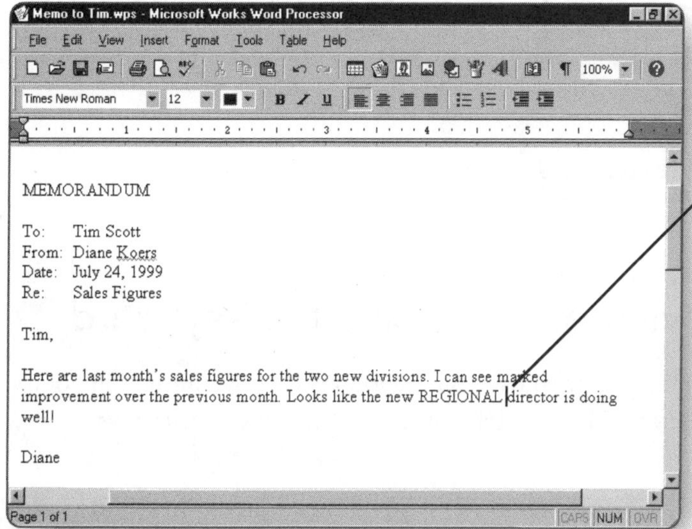

1. **Click** the **mouse** where you want to add text. The blinking insertion point will appear.
2. **Type** the **new text**. The new text will be inserted into the document.

> **NOTE**
>
> In this figure, the added word is in uppercase letters so that you can easily see the effect of inserting text.

Selecting Text

To move, copy, delete, or change the formatting of text, you first need to select it. When text is selected, it appears onscreen as light type on a dark background—just the reverse of unselected text. You can only select a sequential block of text at a time—not bits of text in different places.

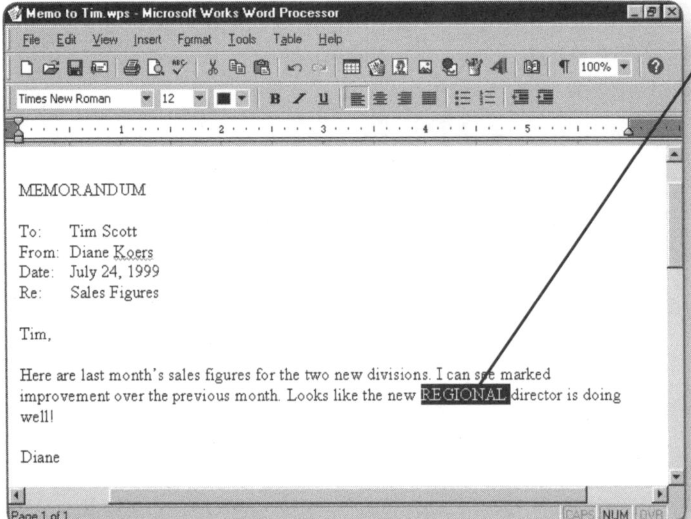

1. To select a word, **double-click** on a **word**. The word will be highlighted.

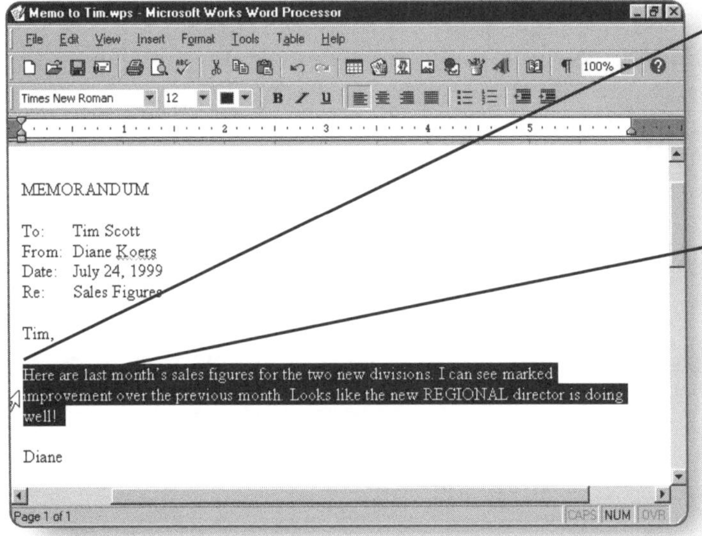

2. To select a paragraph, **position** the **mouse pointer** to the left side of a paragraph. The mouse pointer will point to the right.

3. **Double-click** the **mouse**. The entire paragraph will be highlighted.

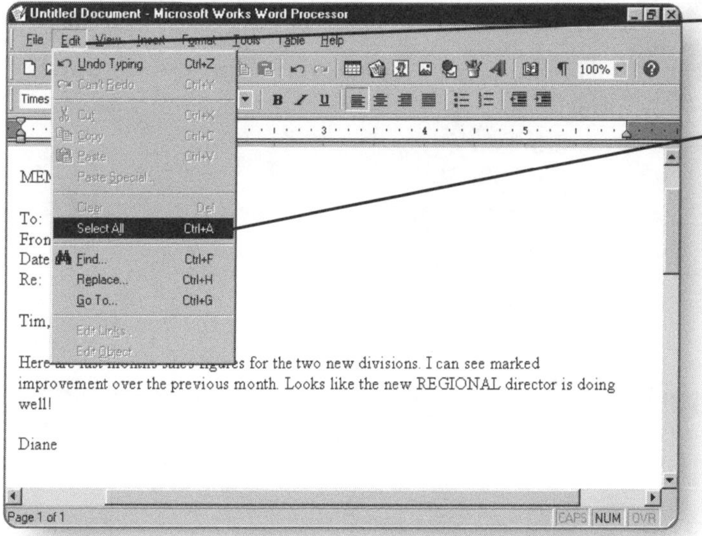

4. Click on **Edit**. The Edit menu will appear.

5. Click on **Select All**. The entire document will be highlighted.

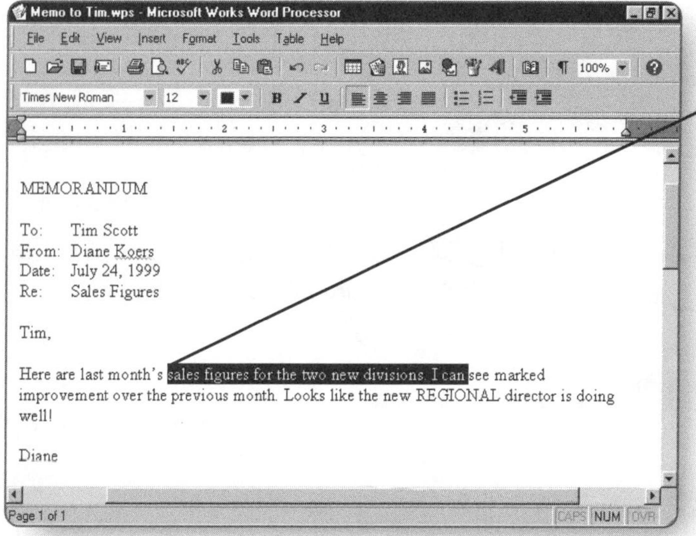

TIP

Alternatively, you can select a block of text by clicking at the beginning of the text, pressing and holding down the mouse button, and then dragging across the text. Release the mouse button. The text will be highlighted.

Text can be deselected by clicking anywhere else in the document.

Deleting Text

You can delete unwanted text one character, word, paragraph, or page at a time—or any combination.

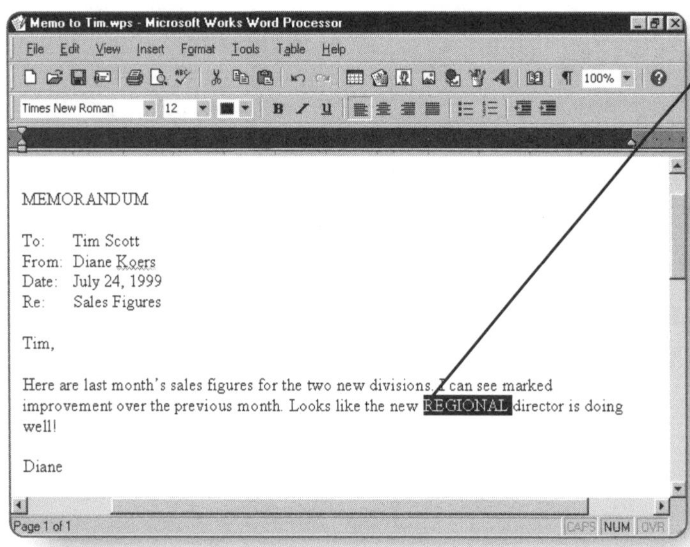

1. Select the **text** to be deleted. The text will be highlighted.

2. Press the **Delete key** on your keyboard. The text will be deleted.

As soon as the deleted text disappears, any text below or to the right of the deleted text moves up to fill in the space.

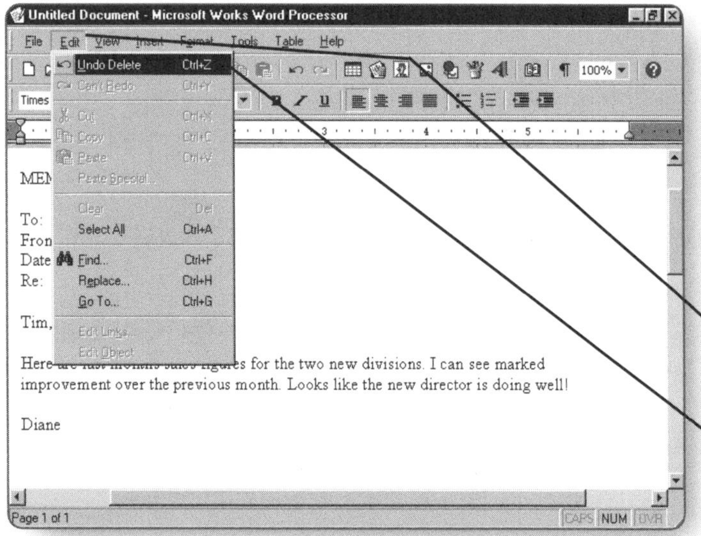

Undoing Mistakes

Microsoft Works has a wonderful feature called *Undo*. This feature reverses the last step you performed.

1. Click on **Edit**. The Edit menu will appear.

2. Click on **Undo**. The last action you took will be reversed.

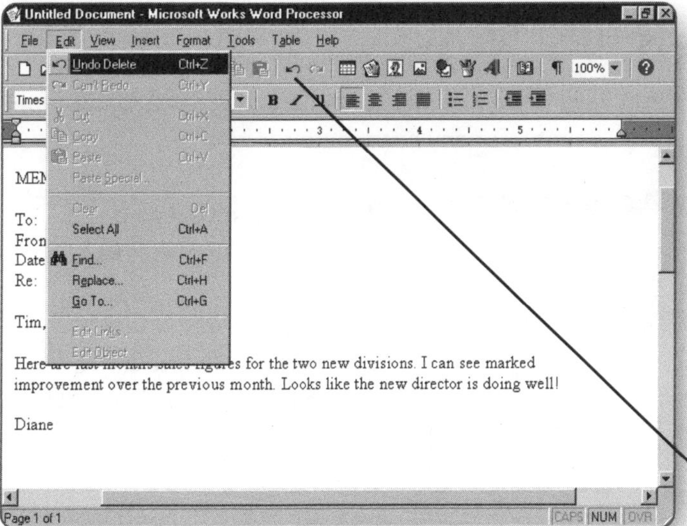

NOTE

The Edit menu lists Undo with the feature last used. For example, if you last deleted text, it will read, "Undo Delete." If the last function was to underline text, the Undo will read, "Undo Underline."

TIP

You can also click on the Undo button to reverse the last action. Each click of the Undo button reverses one previous step.

Saving a Document

Your computer could fail you at any time due to many reasons. Saving your work not only preserves changes you make in the process of creating a document but also files it electronically so that you can later find it and use it again.

Saving a Document the First Time

When you first create a document, it has no name. If you want to use that document later, you must name it so that Works can find it.

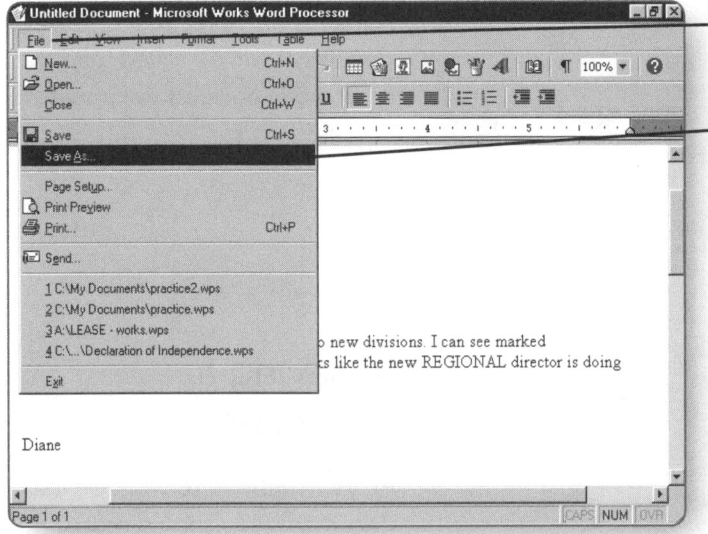

1. Click on **File**. The File menu will appear.

2. Click on **Save As**. The Save As dialog box will open.

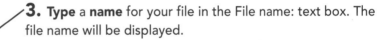

3. Type a **name** for your file in the File name: text box. The file name will be displayed.

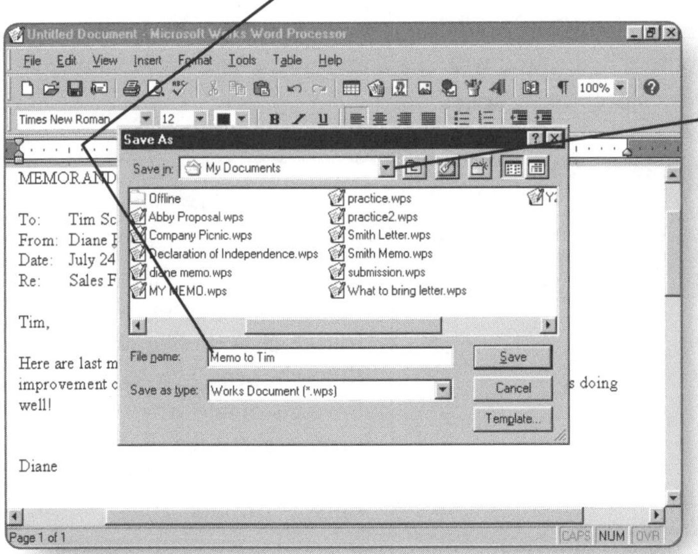

NOTE

The Save in: drop-down list shows folder options where you can save the document. The default folder that appears is My Documents. If you don't want to save it to this folder or if you want to save your document to another disk, click on the down arrow to browse and locate another folder or disk.

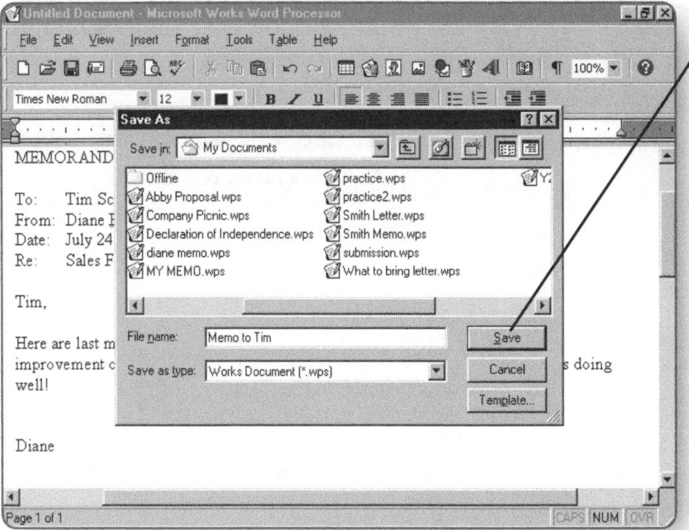

4. Click on **Save**. Your document will be saved, and the name you specified will appear in the title bar.

Resaving a Document

As you continue to work on your document, you should resave it every ten minutes or so to help ensure that you do not lose any changes.

1. Click on the **Save button**. The document will be resaved with any changes. No dialog box will open because the document is resaved with the same name and in the same folder as previously specified.

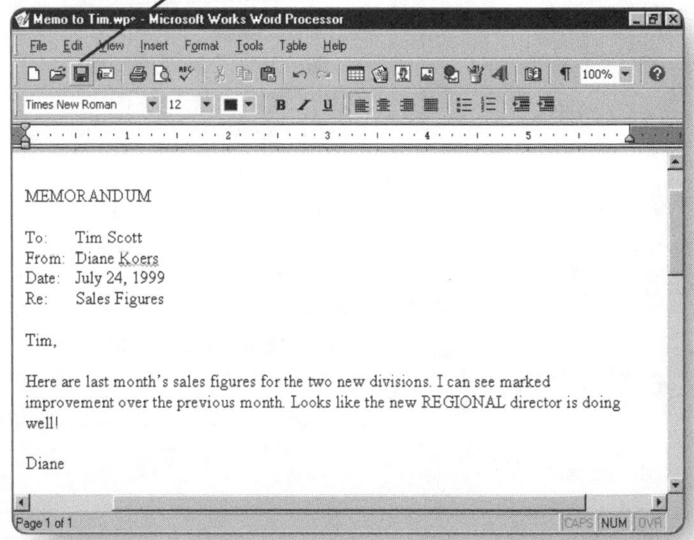

TIP

If you want to save the document with a different name or in a different folder, click on File and then choose Save As. The Save As dialog box prompts you for the new name or you can choose a different folder. The original document remains as well as the new one.

4

Formatting a Document

Appearance is everything, so Works offers several ways to improve the appearance of your document through formatting. Formatting allows you to change the look of your document by changing the look of the text. In this chapter, you'll learn how to:

- Work with text properties
- Set paragraph alignment and indentation
- Set and delete tabs
- Work with bullets and numbering

Working with Text Attributes

You can change the appearance of text in a variety of ways. For example, you can make the text bold, underlined, or italic as well as change the font typeface and size.

Making Text Bold

Applying the bold attribute to text makes the text characters thicker and darker.

1. Create a **new document** as you learned in Chapter 3. The document will be displayed on the Works screen.

2. Select the **text** to be bolded. It will be highlighted.

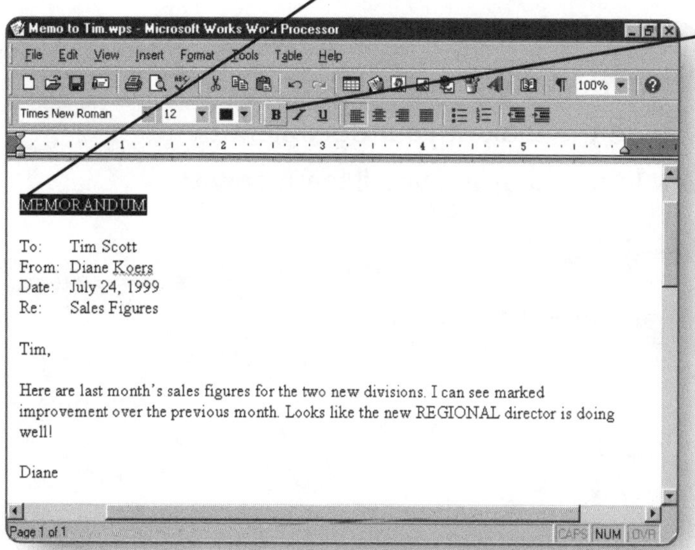

3. Click on the **Bold button**. The selected text will be in bold.

> **TIP**
>
> Repeat steps 2 and 3 to deselect the bold option.

Underlining Text

Using the underline attribute can call special attention to parts of your document.

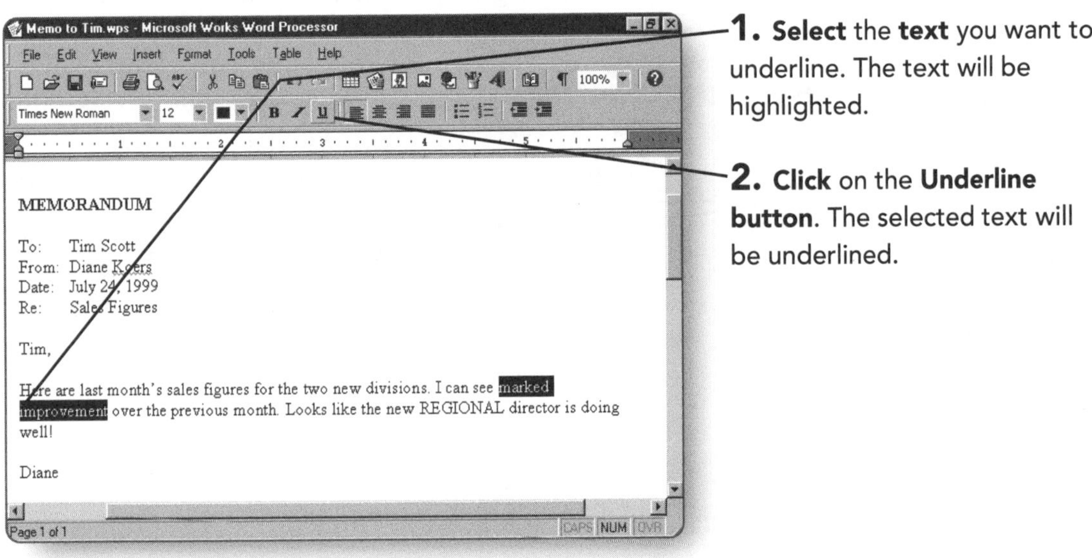

1. Select the **text** you want to underline. The text will be highlighted.

2. Click on the **Underline button**. The selected text will be underlined.

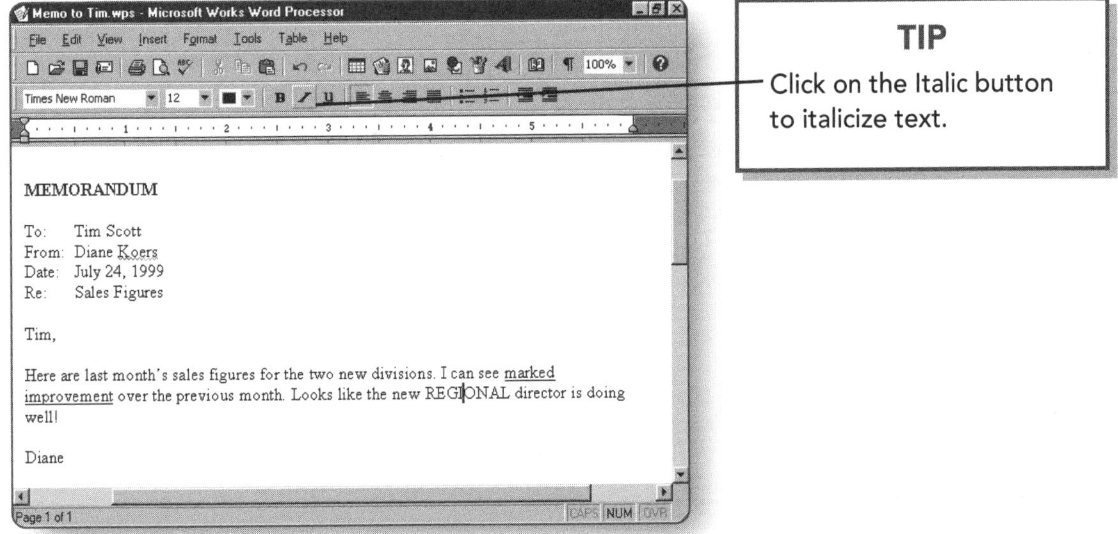

TIP

Click on the Italic button to italicize text.

Changing the Font Typeface

Changing the font typeface is another way to make text stand out from the rest of your document. The font selections you have vary depending on which fonts are installed on your computer.

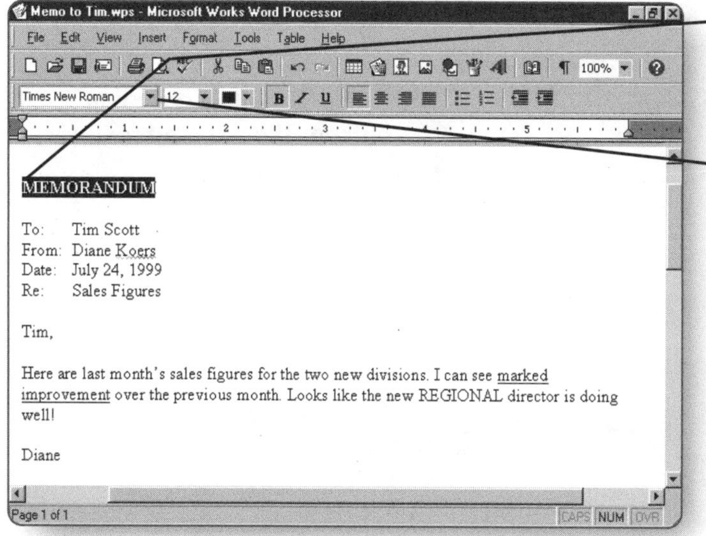

1. **Select** the **text** you want to change. The text will be highlighted.

2. **Click** on the **Font Name drop-down arrow**. A list of available fonts will appear.

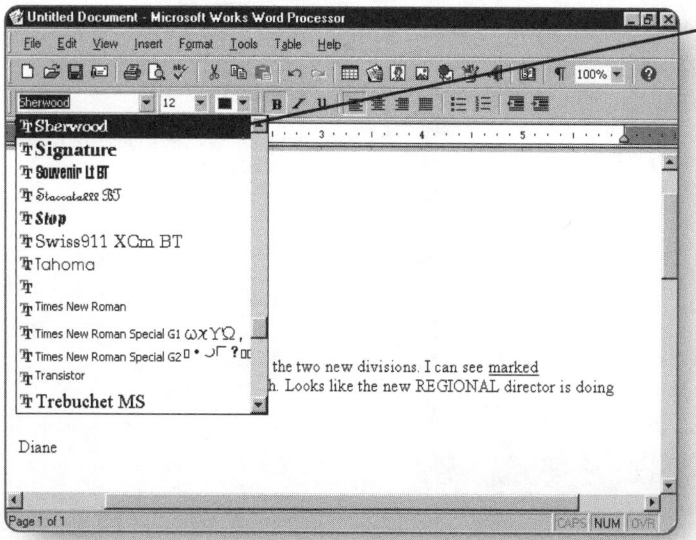

3. **Click** on a **font name** from the list. The font typeface change will be applied to the selected text.

Selecting a Font Size

You may want to make portions of your text larger or smaller than the rest of the text in your document.

1. Select the **text** you want to change. The text will be highlighted.

2. Click on the **Font Size drop-down arrow.** A list of font sizes will appear.

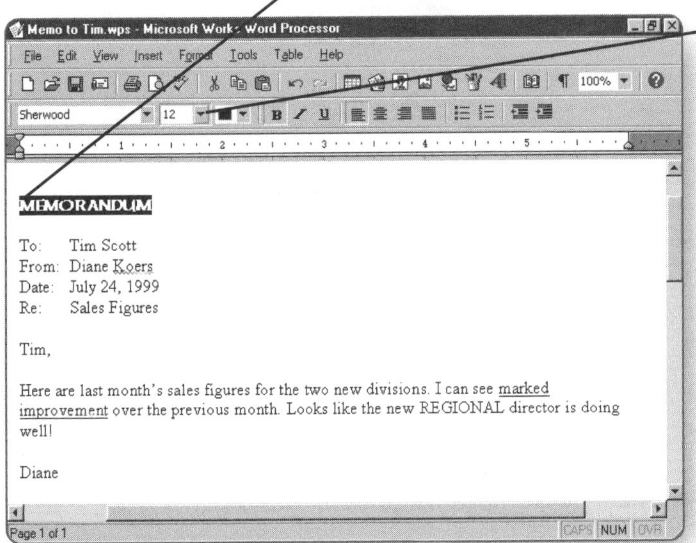

The larger the number, the larger the font size. For example, a 72-point font is approximately 1-inch tall on the printed page.

3. Click on a **new size**. The font size change will be applied to the selected text.

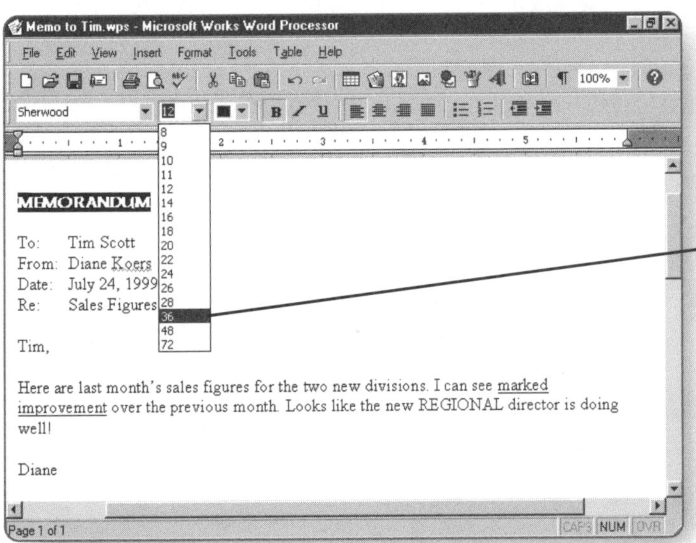

Setting Other Text Attributes

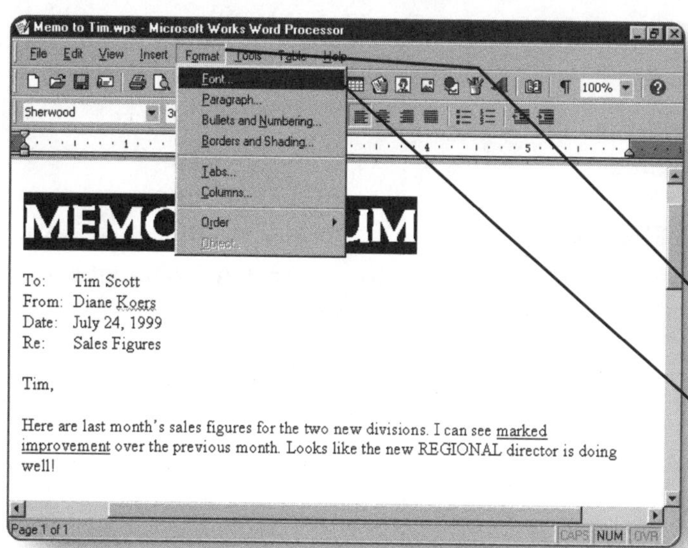

Works has a dialog box that allows you to select text attributes in a single step.

1. Select the **text** to be modified. The text will be highlighted.

2. Click on **Format**. The Format menu will appear.

3. Click on **Font**. The Font dialog box will open.

4. Click on any combination of the following **options**:

- **Font name.** Click on a name from the displayed list.
- **Font style.** Click on a style from the displayed list.

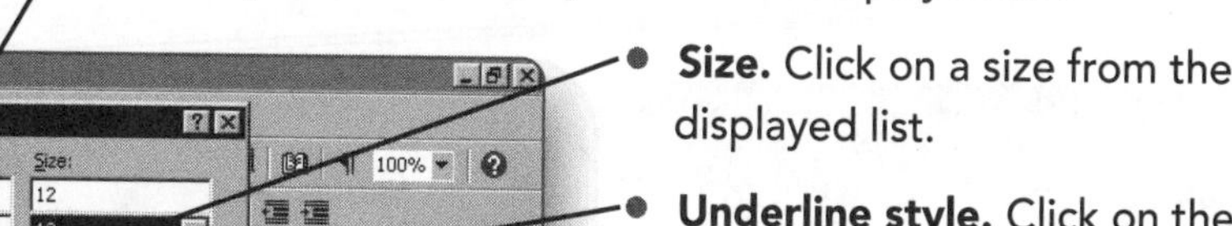

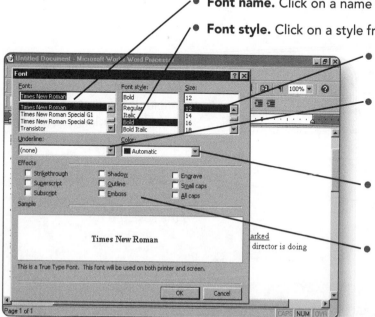

- **Size.** Click on a size from the displayed list.
- **Underline style.** Click on the drop-down arrow and choose from the available underline methods.
- **Text Color.** Click on the drop-down arrow and choose from the available colors.
- **Special Effects.** Click on any desired choices.

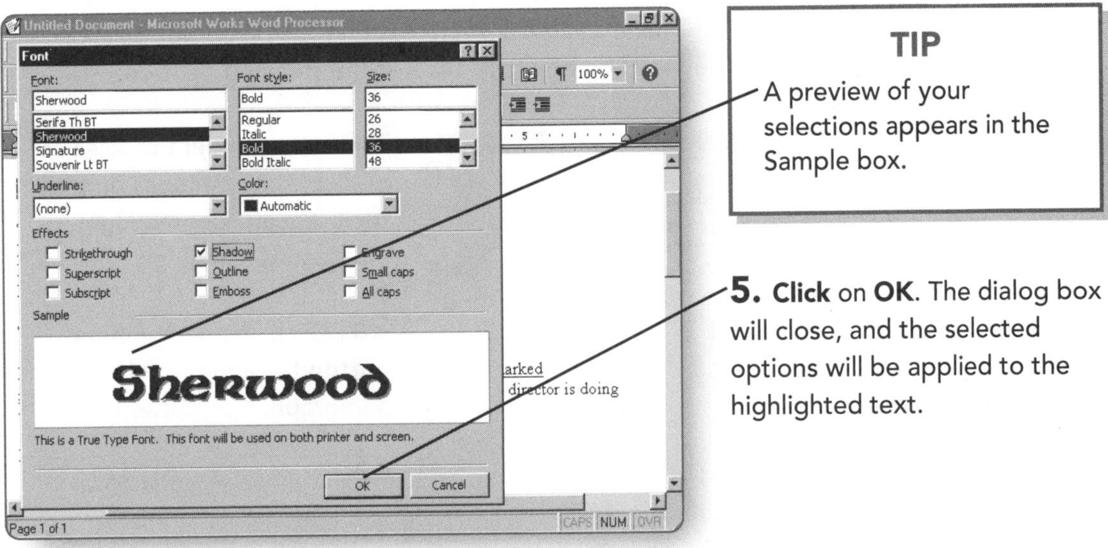

TIP

A preview of your selections appears in the Sample box.

5. Click on **OK**. The dialog box will close, and the selected options will be applied to the highlighted text.

Setting Paragraph Options

You may want to align certain paragraphs in your documents so that they are, for example, centered on a page. Headings and titles are examples of text that are usually centered. You also may need to indent paragraphs so that they stand out from other text.

Setting Paragraph Alignment

Four types of alignment are available: left, center, right, and justified.

- **Left align**. Text is even with the left margin but jagged on the right margin.
- **Center align**. Text is centered between the left and right margins.
- **Right align**. Text is even with the right margin but jagged on the left margin.
- **Justified**. Text is spaced evenly between the left and right margins.

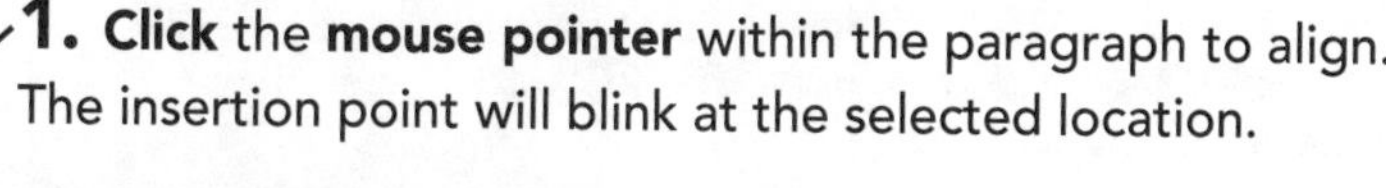

1. Click the **mouse pointer** within the paragraph to align. The insertion point will blink at the selected location.

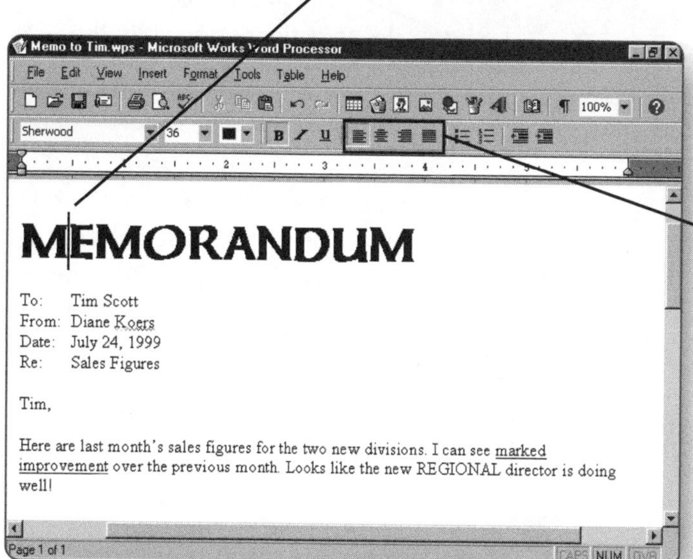

The four alignment choices are available as selections on the toolbar: Left, Center, Right, or Full Justify.

2a. Click on an **alignment button** to align the selected paragraph.

OR

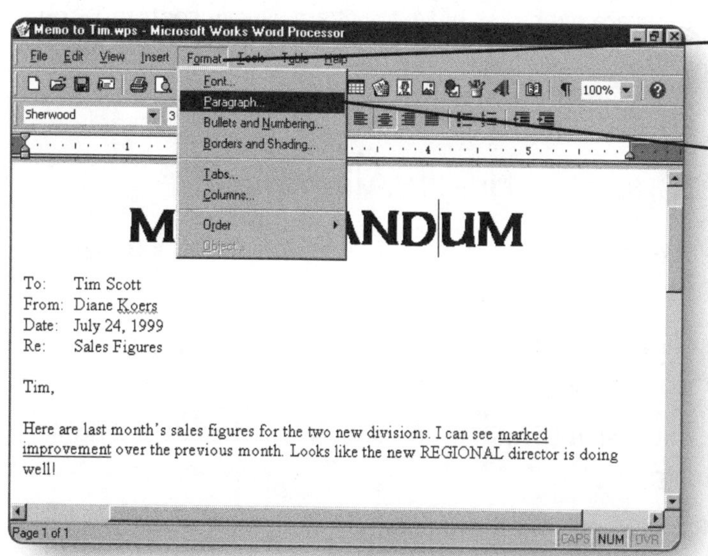

2b. Click on **Format**. The Format menu will appear.

3. Click on **Paragraph**. The Format Paragraph dialog box will open.

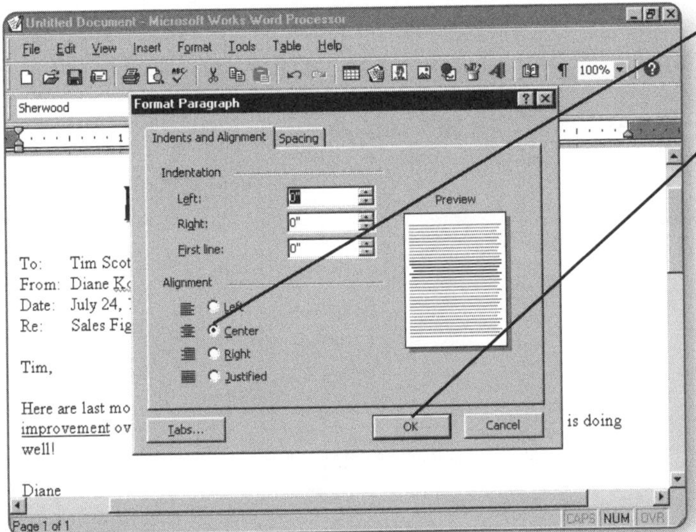

4. Click on an **alignment**. The option will be selected.

5. Click on **OK**. The Format Paragraph dialog box will close.

> **TIP**
>
> Shortcut keys to align text include: Ctrl+L to left align, Ctrl+E to center align, Ctrl + R to right align, and Ctrl+J to full justify.

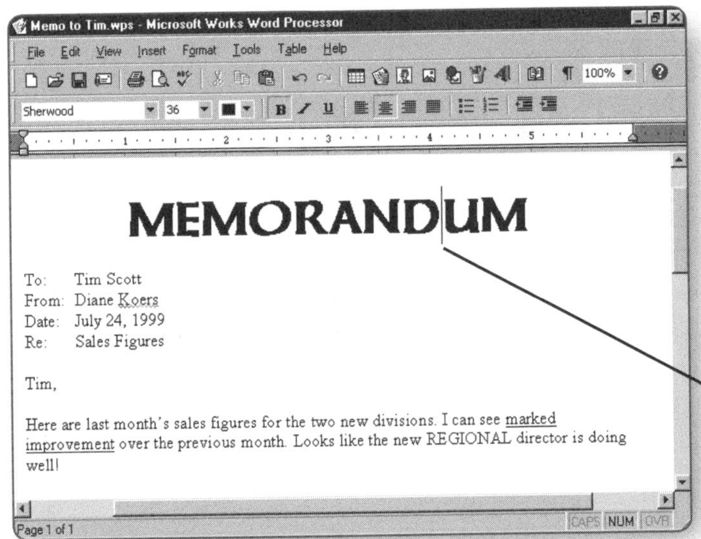

Creating Paragraph Borders

Add emphasis to a paragraph by placing a line under it or a border around it. You can have thin lines, thick lines, double lines, even dashed or dotted lines.

1. Click the **mouse** in the paragraph to be modified. The blinking insertion point will appear in the paragraph.

> **TIP**
>
> Optionally, select multiple paragraphs to put a single border around.

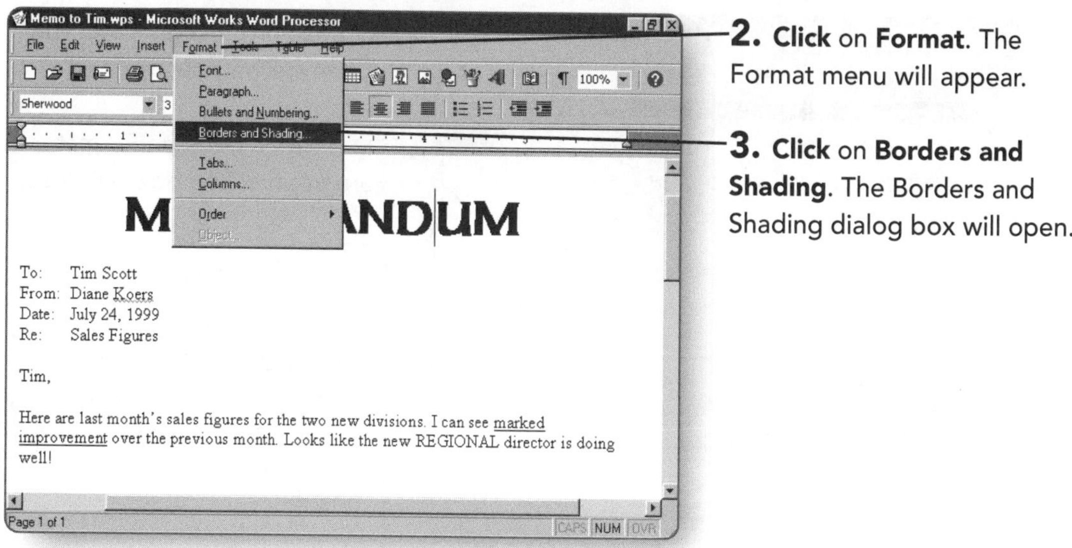

2. **Click** on **Format**. The Format menu will appear.

3. **Click** on **Borders and Shading**. The Borders and Shading dialog box will open.

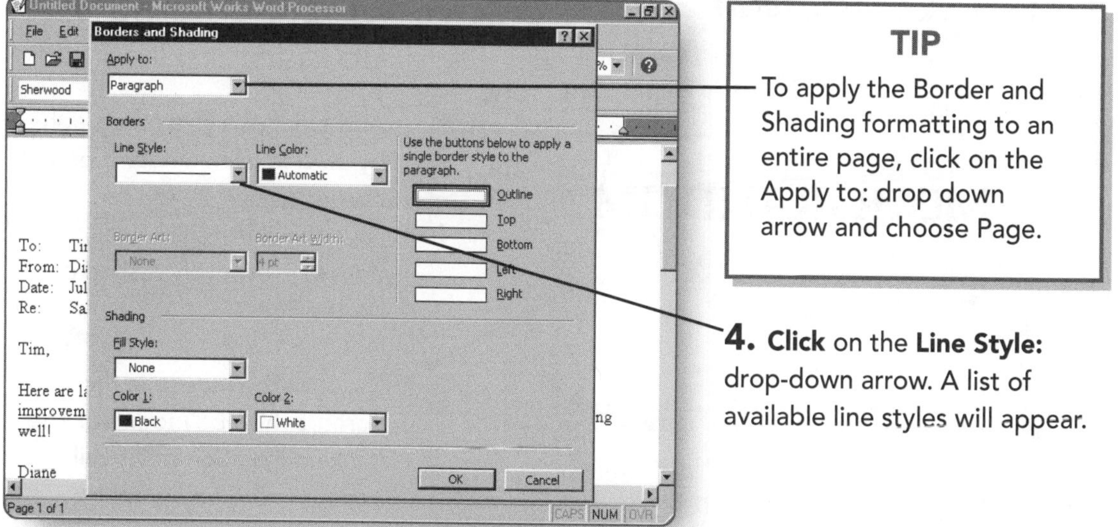

> **TIP**
>
> To apply the Border and Shading formatting to an entire page, click on the Apply to: drop down arrow and choose Page.

4. **Click** on the **Line Style:** drop-down arrow. A list of available line styles will appear.

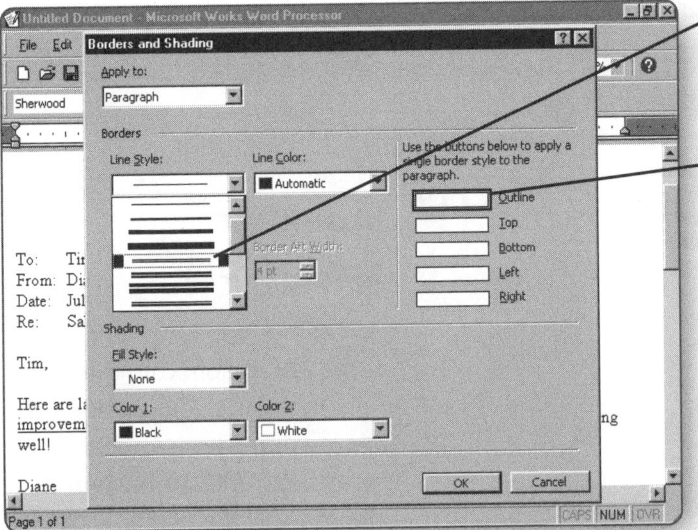

5. Click on a **style**. The selected style will display in the drop-down box.

6. Click on the desired **border placement options**. The line style will appear in selected options.

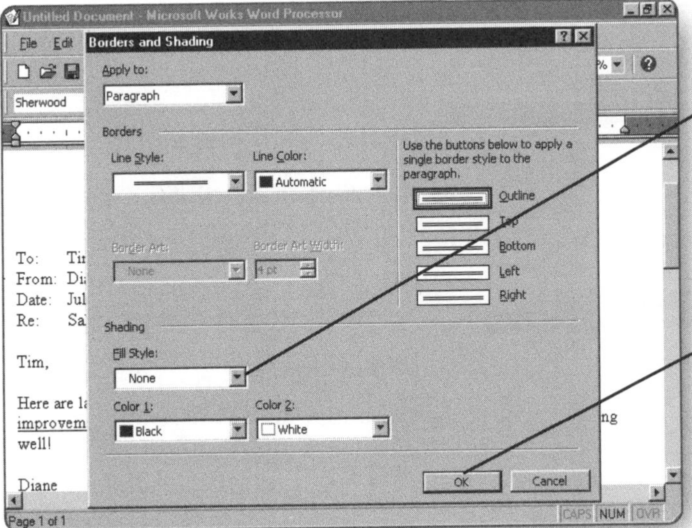

TIP

Optionally, to apply shading to a paragraph or page, click on the Fill Style: down arrow and choose a shading style.

7. Click on **OK**. The Borders and Shading dialog box will close.

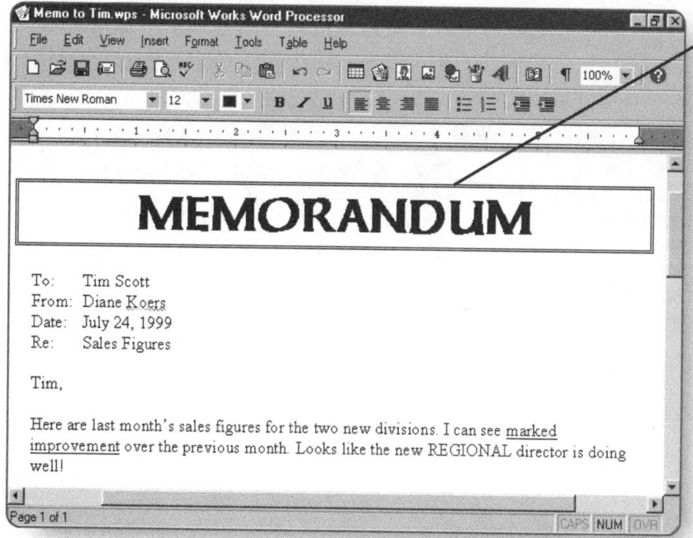

The selected options will be applied.

Indenting Paragraphs

Sometimes you want to inset an entire paragraph from the left or right margins to emphasize its information. This is known as *indenting*. Unlike a tab, which indents only the first line, all lines of the paragraph are inset when a paragraph is indented.

1. Select the **paragraphs** to be indented. The paragraphs will be highlighted.

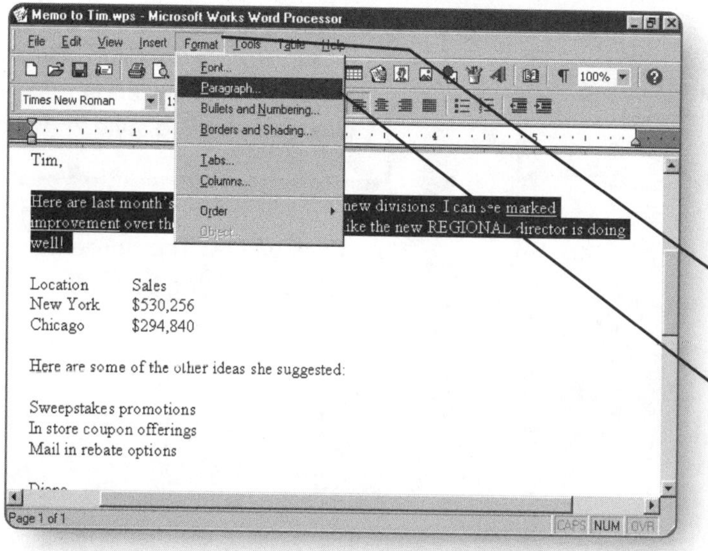

TIP

Optionally, click the mouse in a single paragraph to be modified.

2. Click on **Format**. The Format menu will appear.

3. Click on **Paragraph**. The Format Paragraph dialog box will open.

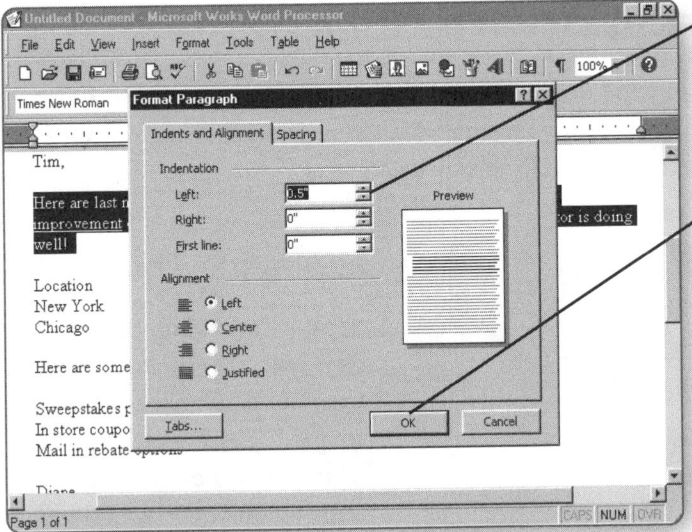

4. Click the **up/down arrows** for the Left Indentation. The indentation will increase .10 inch for each click.

5. Click on **OK**. The Format Paragraph dialog box will close.

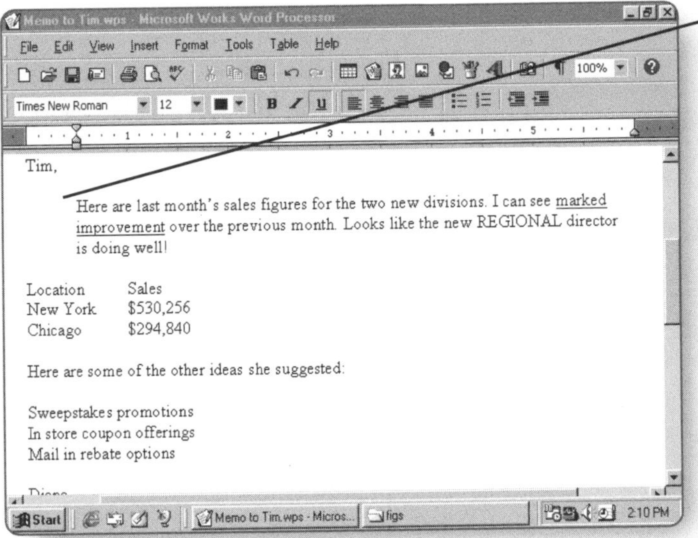

The selected paragraphs will be indented.

Creating a Tabular Table

Often you need to create columns of text in your document. Don't use your space bar to line up these columns because it is better accomplished by using tabs.

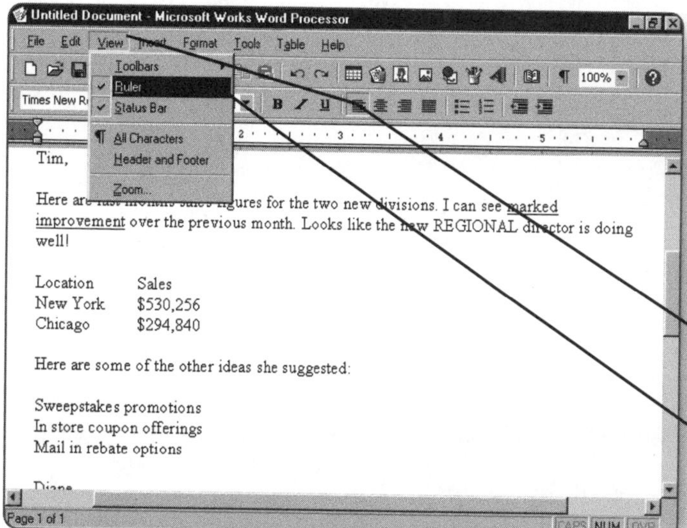

Displaying the Ruler

Setting and deleting custom tabs is easiest by using the ruler. If the ruler is not already displayed, you'll need to turn it on. The display of the ruler can be turned on or off as needed.

1. **Click** on **View**. The View menu will appear.

2. If there is no check mark already next to it, **click** on **Ruler**. The ruler bar will be displayed.

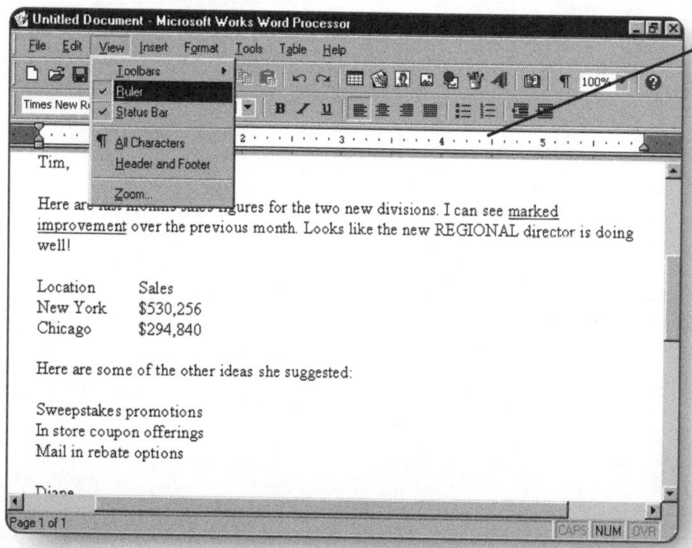

The ruler bar is displayed in inches.

> **TIP**
>
> To turn off the display of the ruler, repeat steps 1 and 2.

Using the Default Tabs

By default, tabs are set at every ½ inch.

1. Click the **mouse pointer** at the beginning of a paragraph. The blinking insertion point will appear at the beginning of the paragraph.

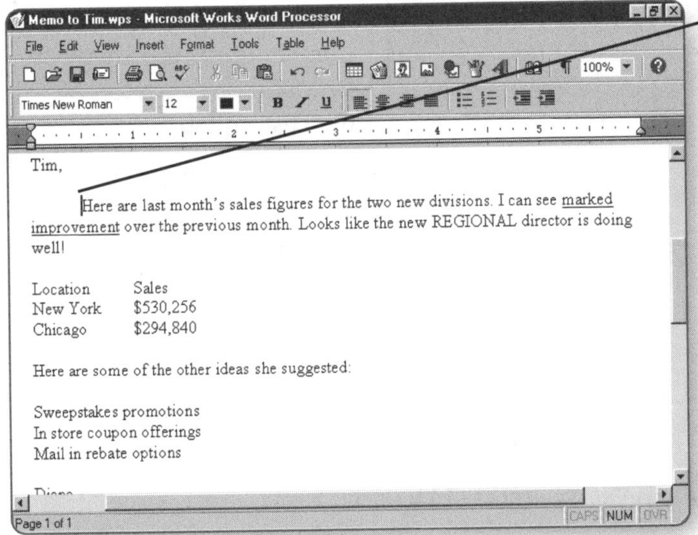

2. Press the **Tab key**. The first line of the paragraph moves to the right ½ inch.

> **TIP**
>
> Press the Tab key again to indent the first line an additional ½ inch.

Setting Tabs

Use the ruler to create your own tab settings.

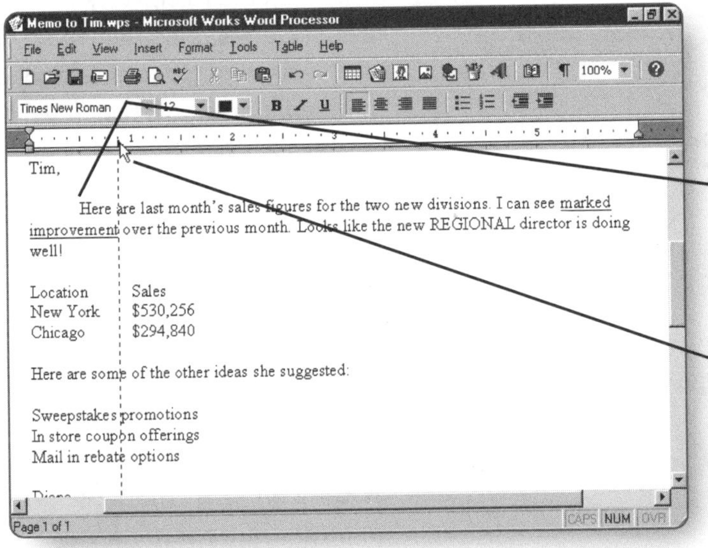

1. Click the **mouse pointer** in the paragraph to be modified. The blinking insertion point will appear in the paragraph.

2. Position the **mouse pointer** on the ruler. The mouse pointer will become a white arrow.

3. Click the **point of the arrow** on the ruler where you want to create a new tab. The tab will be set at that point.

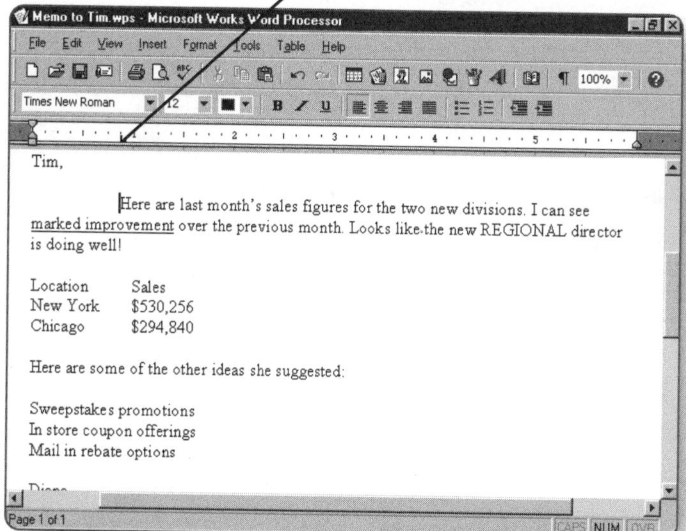

Custom tabs are indicated by a small L-shaped character on the ruler.

> **NOTE**
>
> Custom tabs override the default tabs to the left of the custom tab.

> **TIP**
>
> Move a tab by dragging the tab marker to a new location on the ruler.

Modifying Tab Styles

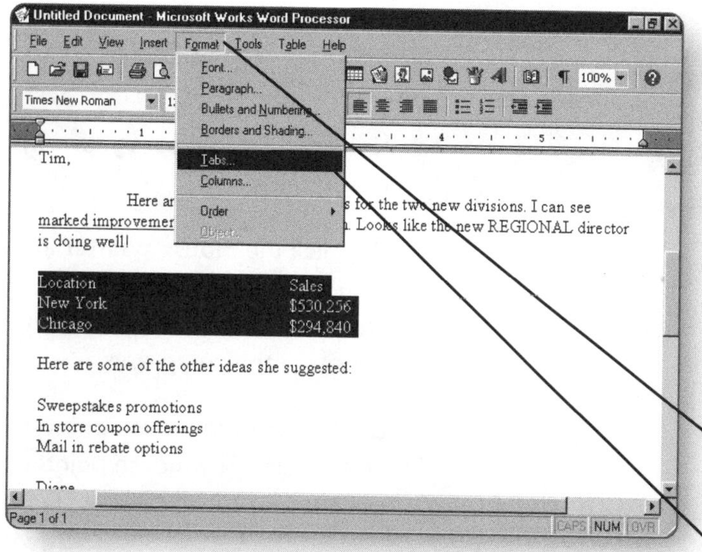

When you set a custom tab by clicking on the ruler, Works inserts a left-aligned tab. You can modify any tab to be a right, centered, or decimal tab. You can even specify that a tab have dot leaders.

1. Select the **paragraphs** to be modified. The paragraphs will be highlighted.

2. Click on **Format**. The Format menu will appear.

3. Click on **Tabs**. The Tabs dialog box will open.

A list of custom tabs for the selected paragraphs is displayed.

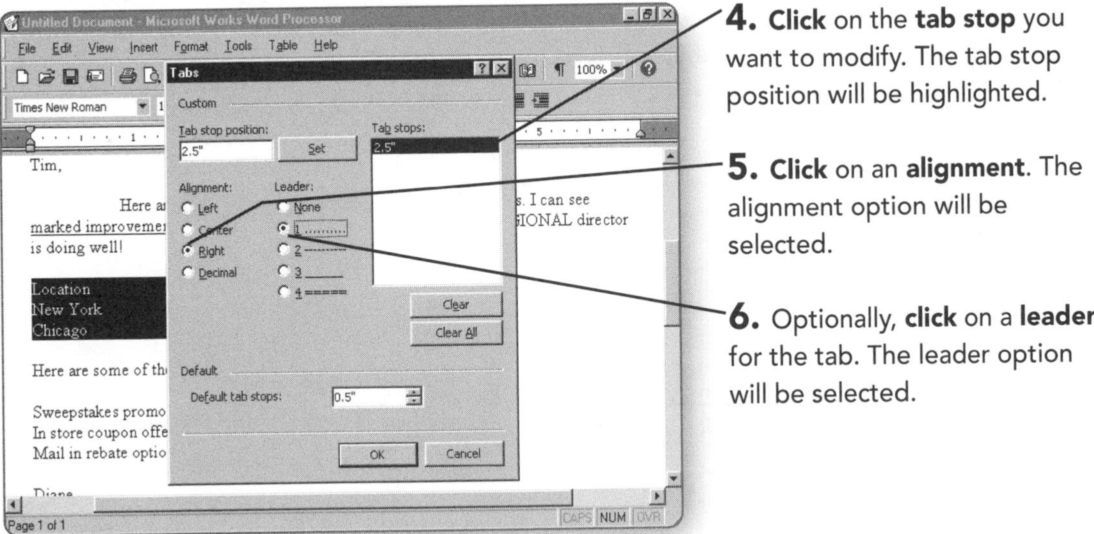

4. **Click** on the **tab stop** you want to modify. The tab stop position will be highlighted.

5. **Click** on an **alignment**. The alignment option will be selected.

6. Optionally, **click** on a **leader** for the tab. The leader option will be selected.

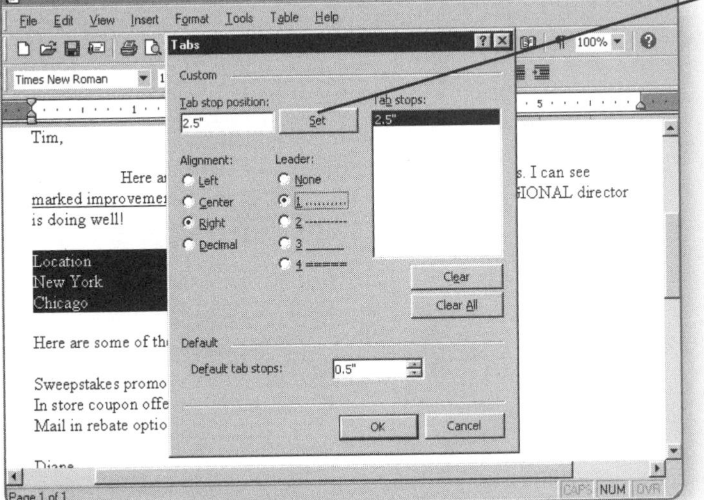

7. **Click** on **Set**. The changes will be recorded to the tab.

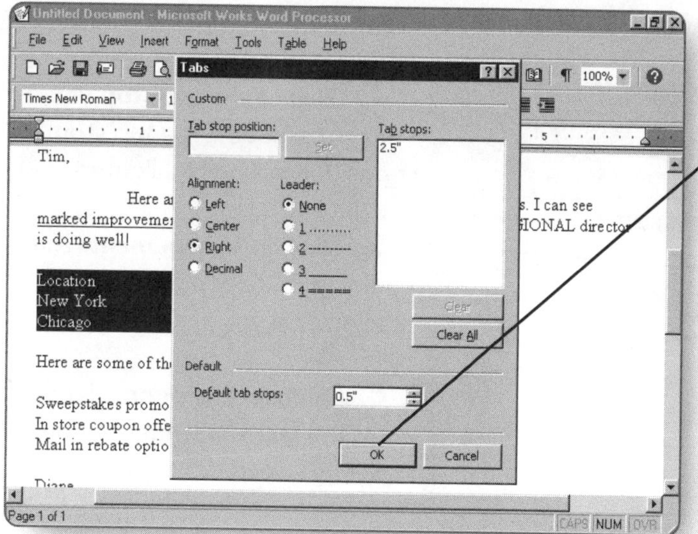

8. **Repeat steps 4–7** for each tab that you want to modify.

9. **Click** on **OK**. The Tabs dialog box will close.

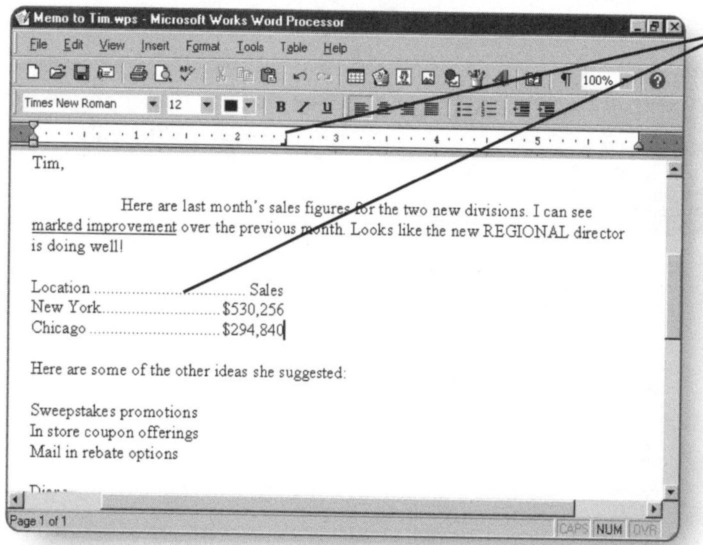

The tab changes will be applied to the selected paragraphs.

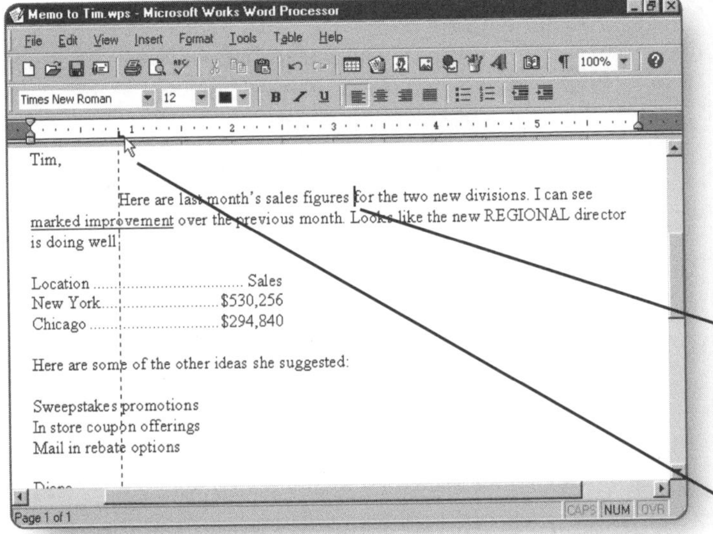

Deleting Tabs

Delete any tabs placed in error or no longer wanted in the paragraph. Make sure your insertion point is in the paragraph that contains the tab you want to delete.

1. **Click** the **mouse** in the paragraph to be modified. The blinking insertion point will appear in the paragraph.

2. **Drag** the **unwanted tab** off the ruler anywhere into the body of the document. The tab will be removed.

Working with Bullets

Works makes it easy to create a bulleted paragraph.

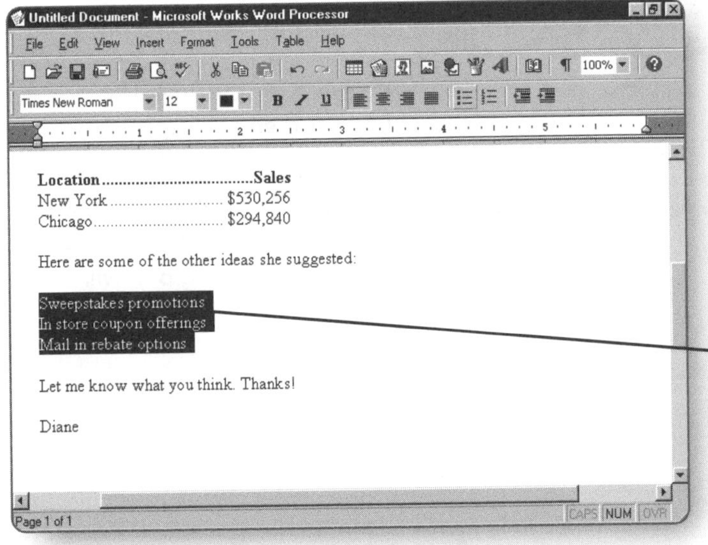

Adding a Bullet

Often, indenting a paragraph or group of paragraphs is not enough to draw attention to it, so you might want to add a symbol in front of it. This is known as a *bullet*.

1. **Select** the **paragraphs** to bullet. The paragraphs will be highlighted.

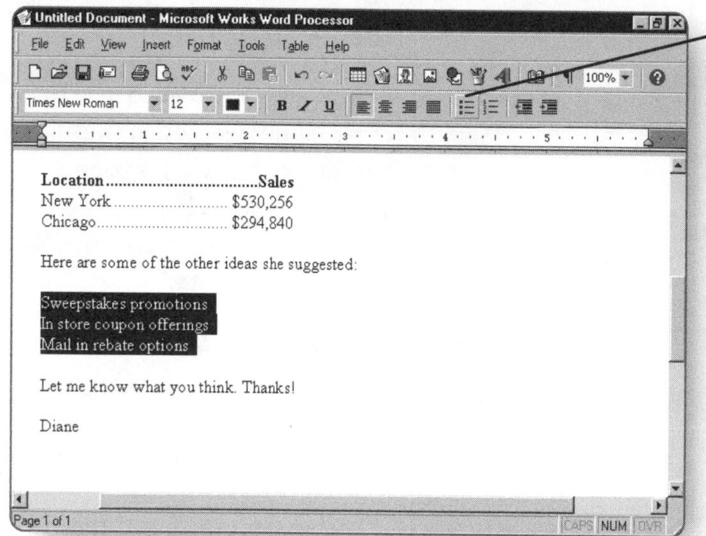

2. Click on the **Bullet button**. The paragraph will be immediately bulleted and indented.

> **TIP**
>
> Repeat steps 1 and 2 to remove the bullet from a paragraph.

Changing a Bullet Style

Choose from a collection of bullet styles ranging from small, black, filled circles to check marks to funny little icons.

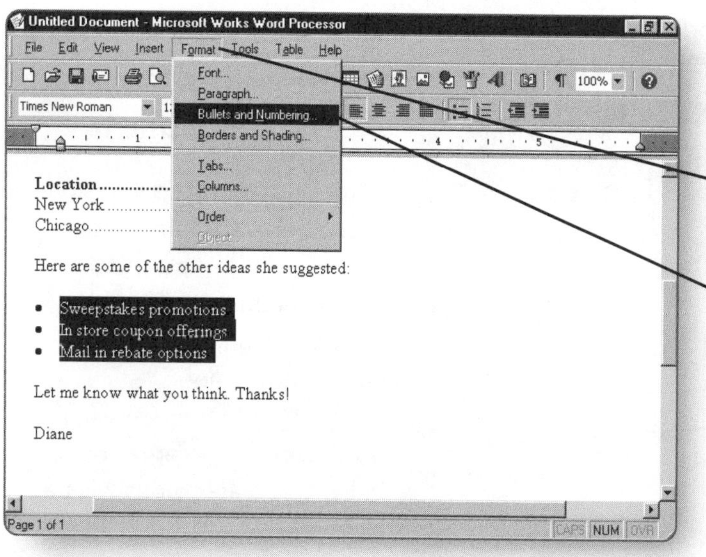

1. Select the **paragraphs** to modify the bullet. The paragraphs will be highlighted.

2. Click on **Format**. The Format menu will appear.

3. Click on **Bullets and Numbering**. The Bullets and Numbering dialog box will open.

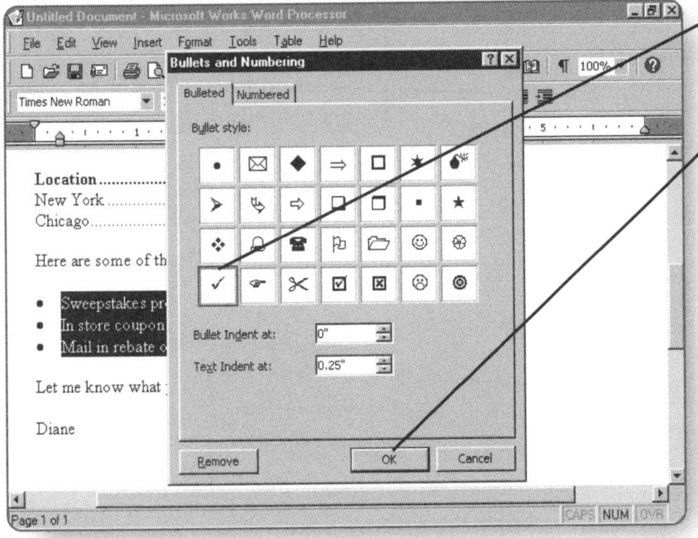

4. Click on a **bullet style**. The bullet style will be highlighted.

5. Click on **OK**. The Format Bullets dialog box will close, and the bulleted paragraphs will reflect the newly selected bullet style.

Creating a Numbered List

New to Works 2000 is the numbered list feature. Creating a numbered list is preferred to just typing numbers because as an item from the list is deleted or moved, all the remaining items are automatically renumbered.

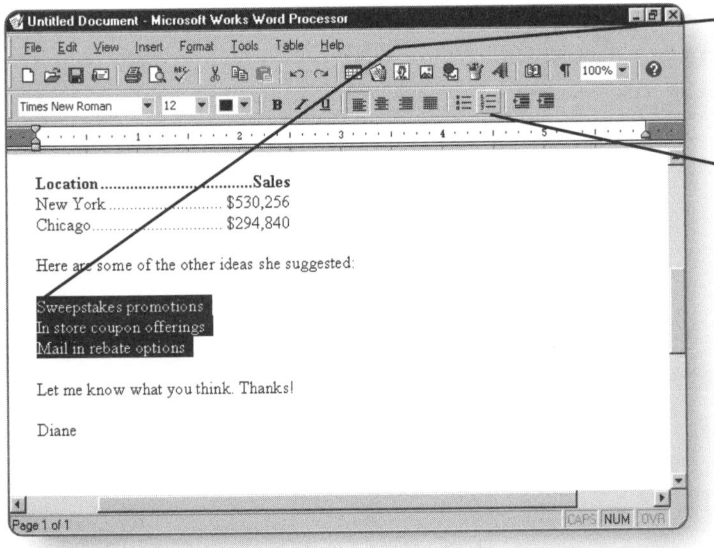

1. Select the **paragraphs** to be numbered. The paragraphs will be highlighted.

2. Click on the **Numbering button**. The paragraphs will be immediately numbered.

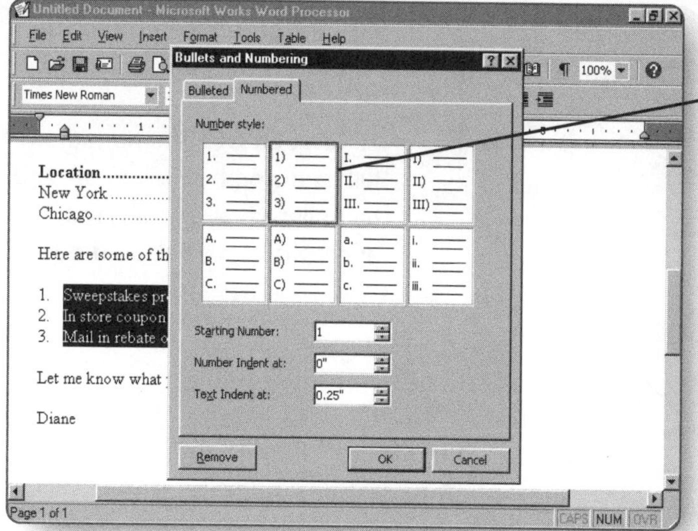

TIP

Click on Format, Bullets and Numbering to open the Bullets and Numbering dialog box. From there you can select a different style for your numbered list.

5 Working with Tables

Prior to tables, a typist had to spend a lot of time pressing the Tab key or spacebar to line up text in columns. Tables have greatly simplified this process. Tables have columns and rows, making it easy to enter columnar text. In this chapter, you'll learn how to:

- Create a table
- Modify a table size
- Format a table

Creating a Table

New to Works 2000 is a menu specifically designed for working with tables.

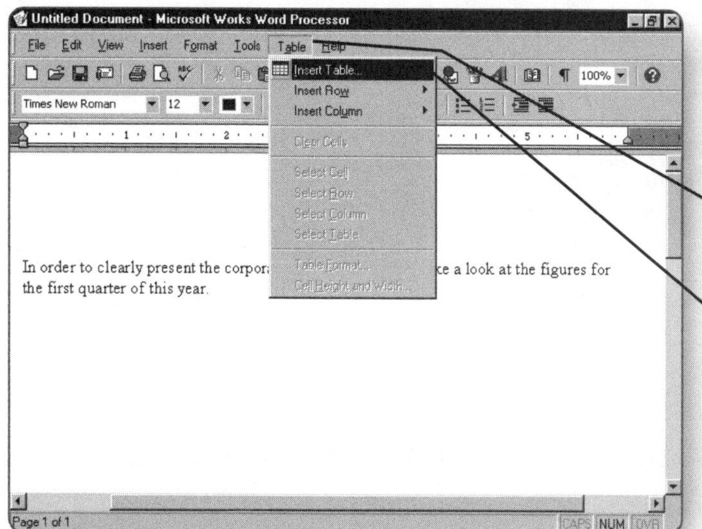

1. Click the **mouse** where you want the table to appear. The blinking insertion point will appear.

2. Click on **Table**. The Table menu will appear.

3. Click on **Insert Table**. The Insert Table dialog box will open.

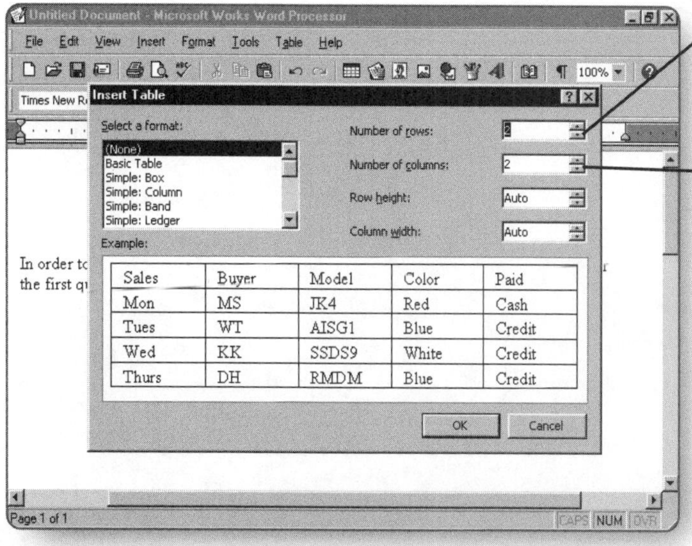

4. Click on the **up and down arrows** (⬍) to indicate the number of rows for the table.

5. Click on the **up and down arrows** (⬍) to indicate the number of columns for the table.

The number of rows and columns can be modified later.

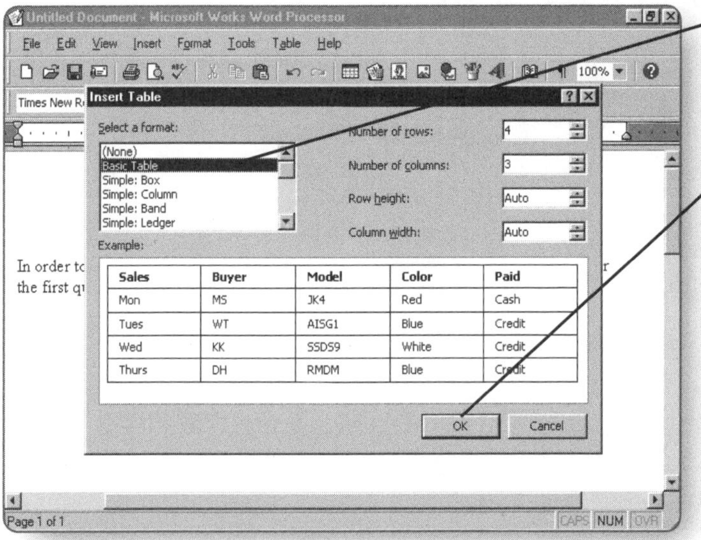

6. **Click** on a predefined **format** for the table. A sample will appear in the Example: box.

7. **Click** on **OK**. The table will be inserted into your document.

Entering Text into a Table

Text typed into a table cell is restricted by the boundaries of each table cell. Use the Tab key to move from one cell to the next, and use Shift+Tab to move the insertion point back to the previous cell. You can also use your arrow keys to move from cell to cell.

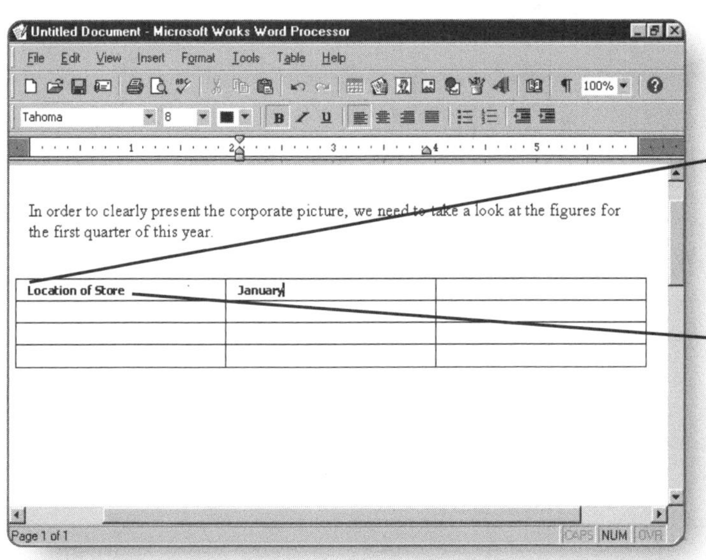

1. **Click** on the **cell** where you want to enter data. The blinking insertion point will appear in the cell.

2. **Type** some **text**. The text will appear in the cell.

3. **Press** the **Tab** key. The insertion point will move to the next cell.

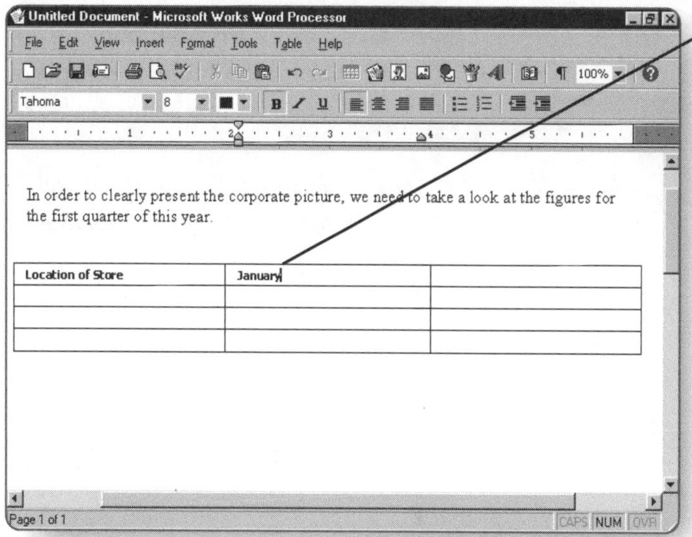

4. **Type** some **text**. The text will appear in the next cell.

5. **Repeat steps 1–4** to enter your data.

Selecting Table Cells

To modify a table, you'll need to select the cells you want to change. Pay close attention to the mouse pointer when attempting to select cells. The mouse pointer must be in the shape of a white arrow.

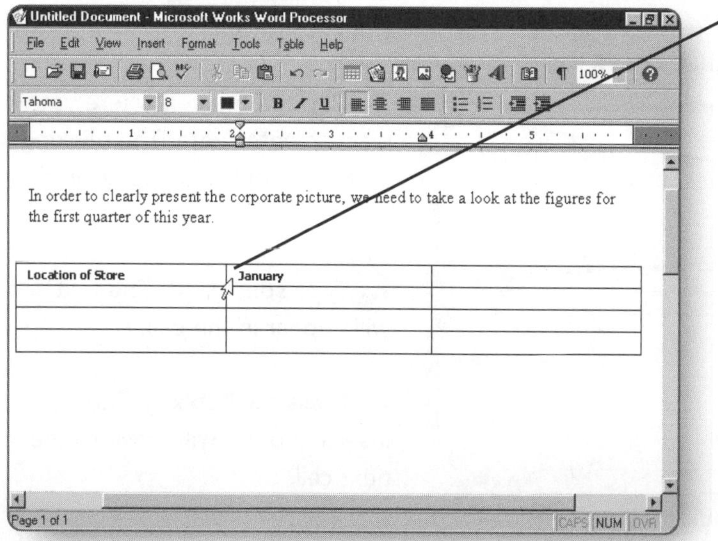

- To select a single cell, click on a cell.

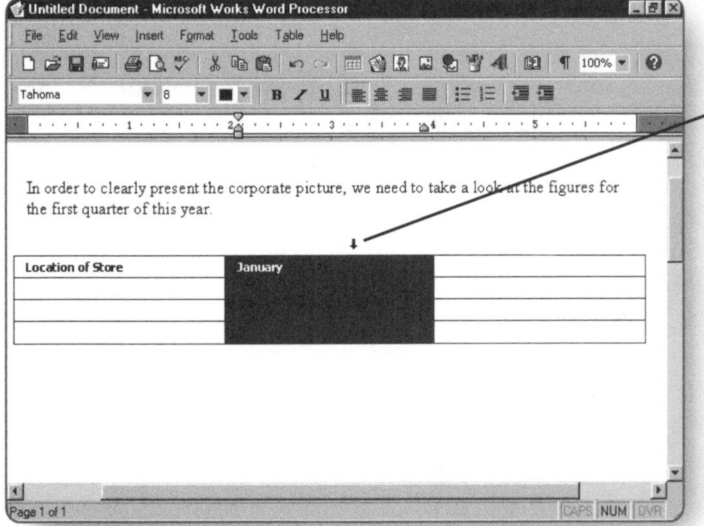

When selected, cells appear onscreen as all black.

- To select an entire column, position the mouse at the top of a column where the mouse turns into a black arrow pointing downward and then click.

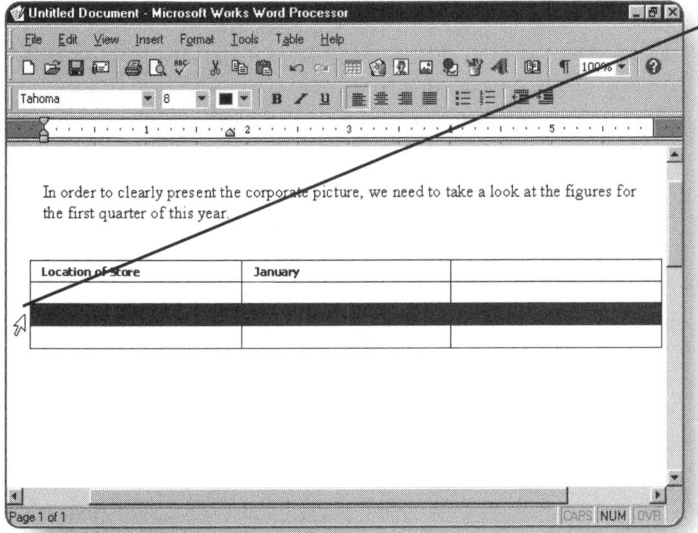

- To select an entire row, position the mouse at the left of a row where the mouse turns into a white arrow and then click.

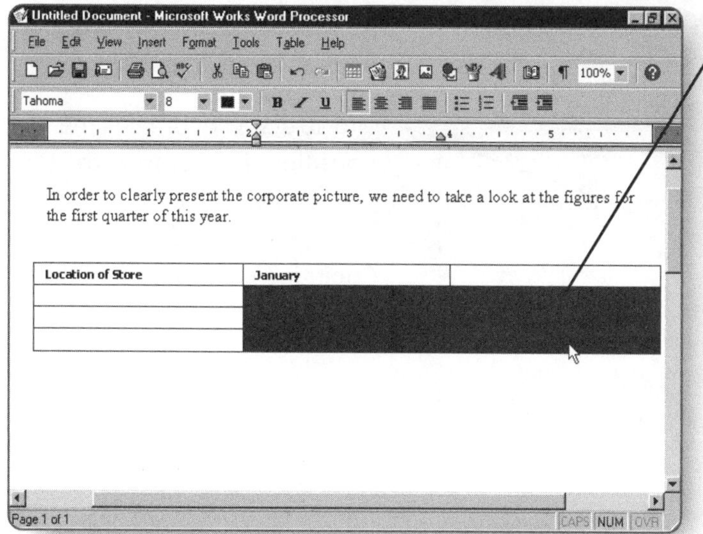

- To select a block of cells, click on the beginning cell, hold down the mouse button, and drag across the additional cells. Then release the mouse button.

Modifying Table Size

After you start working with a table, you may find that you need to add rows and columns, or you may want to make a column narrower or wider based on the text in that column.

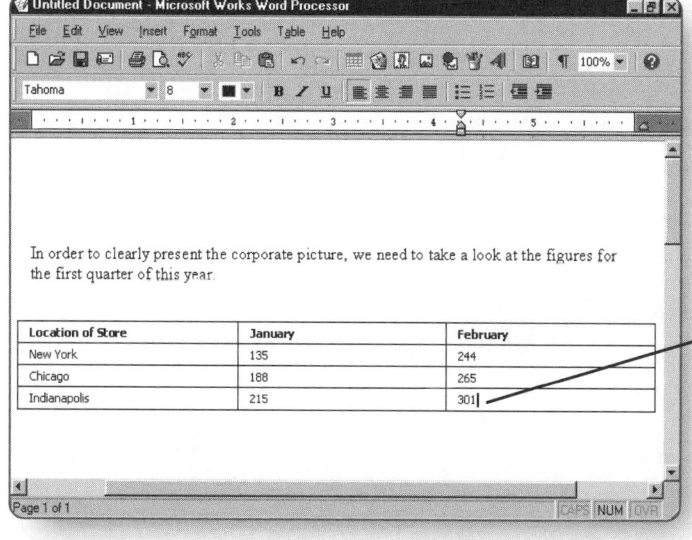

Adding Rows at the End

If you need additional rows when you reach the end of your table, Works can quickly add them for you.

1. **Click** in the last **cell** of the table. The blinking insertion point will appear.

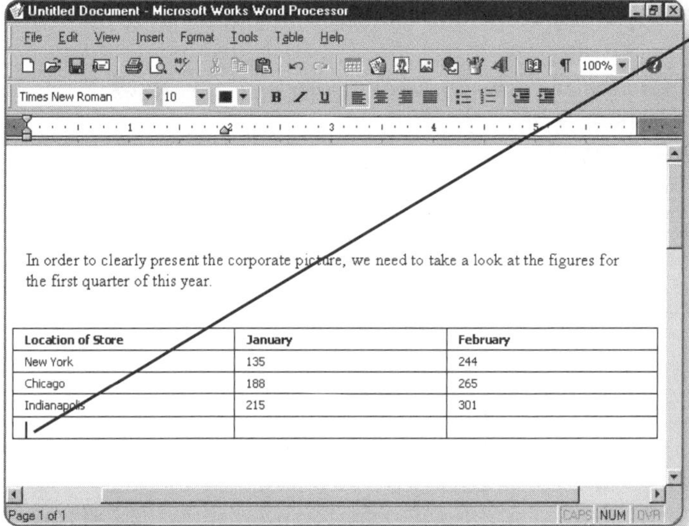

2. Press the **Tab key**. An additional row will be added to the table.

3. Repeat steps 1 and **2** for as many additional rows as needed.

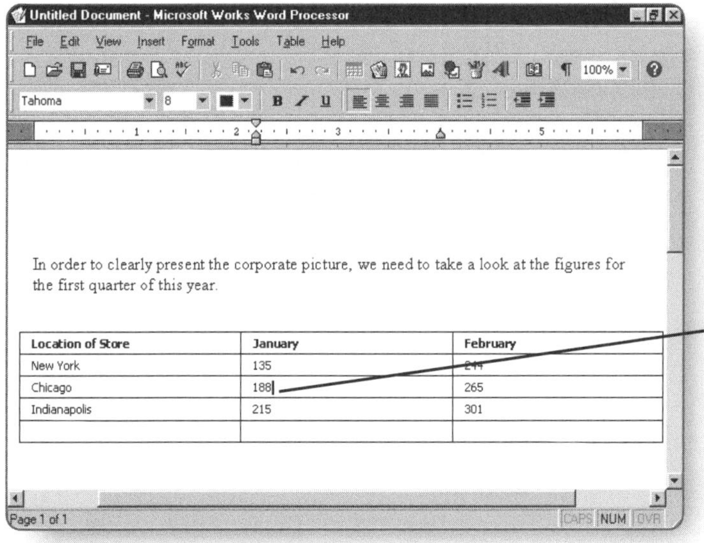

Adding Rows in the Middle

When you add rows in the middle of a table, all existing rows below the new row are moved down.

1. Click anywhere in the **row** where you want the new row to appear. The blinking insertion point will appear or a cell in that row will be selected.

2. **Click** on **Table**. The Table menu will appear.

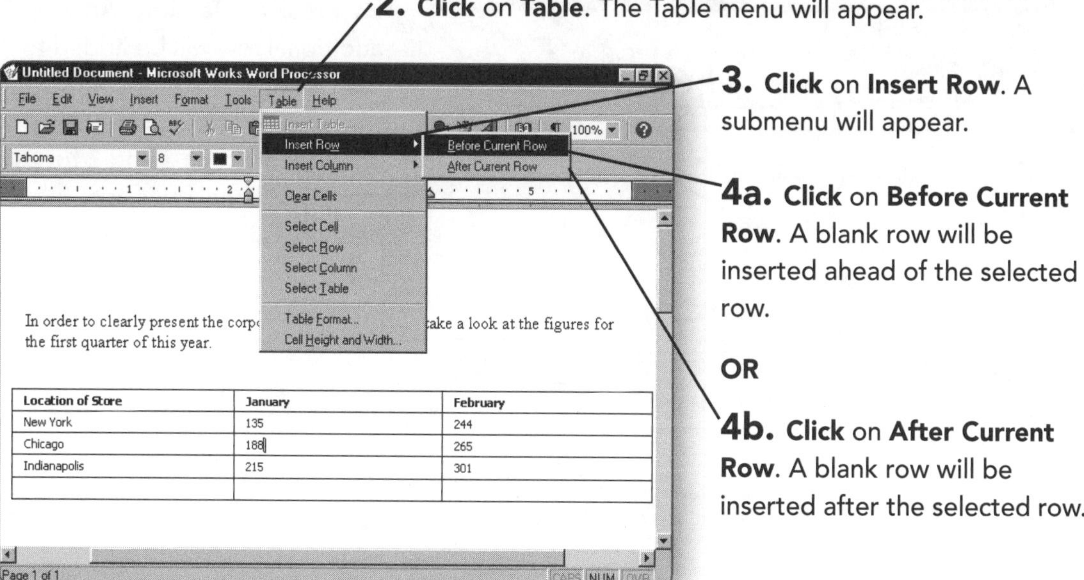

3. **Click** on **Insert Row**. A submenu will appear.

4a. **Click** on **Before Current Row**. A blank row will be inserted ahead of the selected row.

OR

4b. **Click** on **After Current Row**. A blank row will be inserted after the selected row.

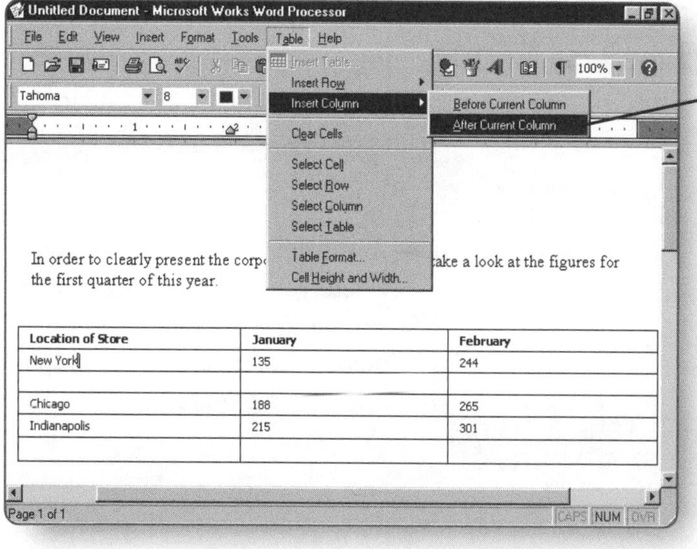

TIP

To add columns, choose Insert Columns from the Table menu. Columns can be added before or after the currently selected column. Existing columns are moved to the right of a new column.

Deleting Rows or Columns

If a row or column is no longer necessary, you can delete it.

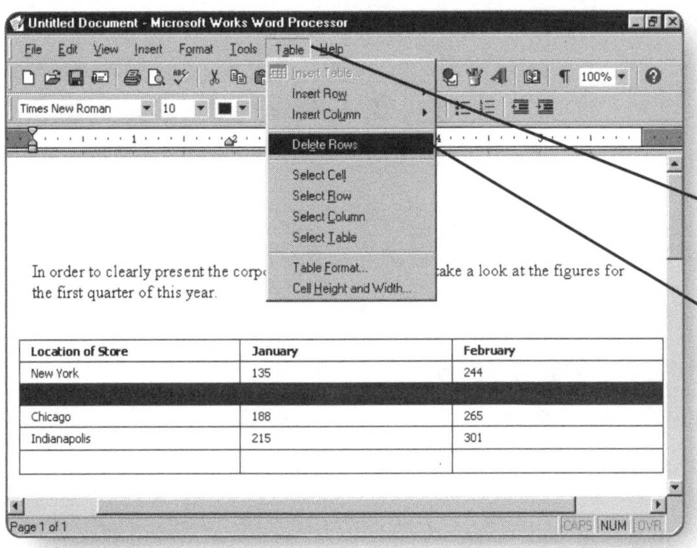

1. **Select** the **columns** or **rows** you want to delete. The entire column or row will be highlighted.

2. **Click** on **Table**. The Table menu will appear.

3. **Click** on **Delete Rows** or **Delete Columns**. The selected row or columns will be deleted.

> **NOTE**
>
> The Table menu choices will change depending on your selection.

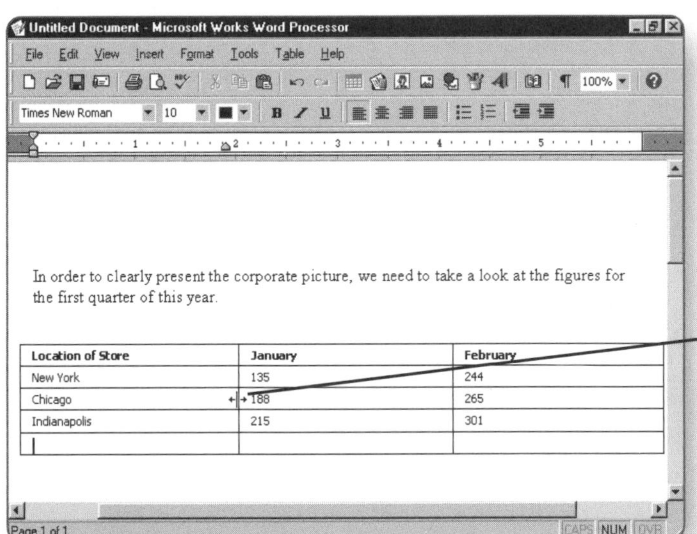

Changing Column Width

By default, all columns are equally spaced, and a table expands across the entire width of the document margins.

1. **Position** the **pointer** over the right border of a column. The pointer will change to a black double-headed arrow.

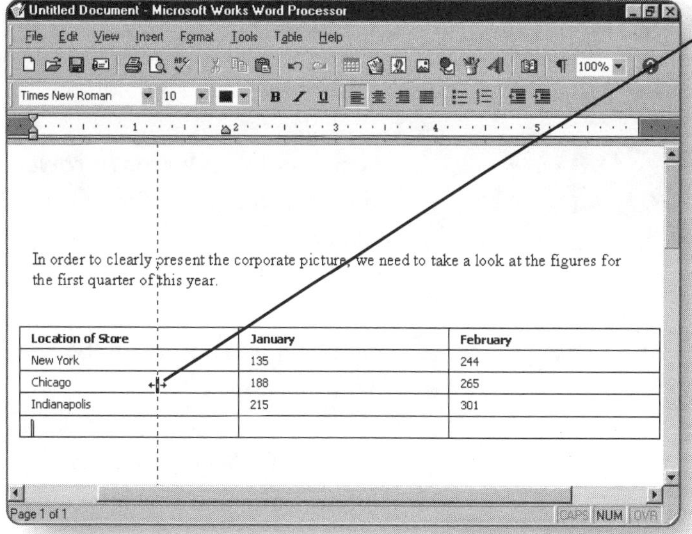

2. **Press the mouse button** and **drag** the **border** until the column is the desired size. A dotted line will indicate the new column size.

3. **Release** the **mouse button**. The column will be resized.

6

Working with Page Layout

In the world of word processing documents, one size doesn't always fit all. You may need to adjust the size of the text area of a document. Headers and footers are often used to repeat key information on each page of a document such as a company's name or the page number. These types of page layout features give your document a professional look. In this chapter, you'll learn how to:

- Set margins
- Change page size
- Change page orientation
- Add a header or footer

Setting Margins

The size of the text area is determined by the page margins. You can set left, right, top, and bottom margins. By setting the margins, you control the amount of text area available. The default margin setting is 1 inch for the top and bottom margins and 1.25 inch for the left and right margins.

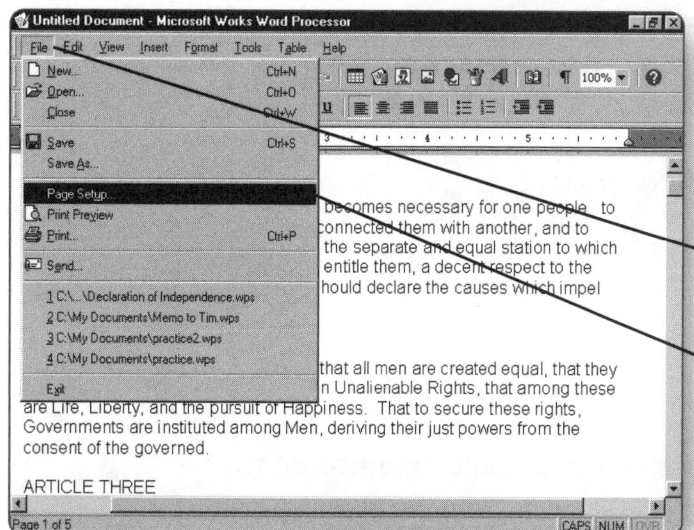

1. Click on **File**. The File menu will appear.

2. Click on **Page Setup**. The Page Setup dialog box will open.

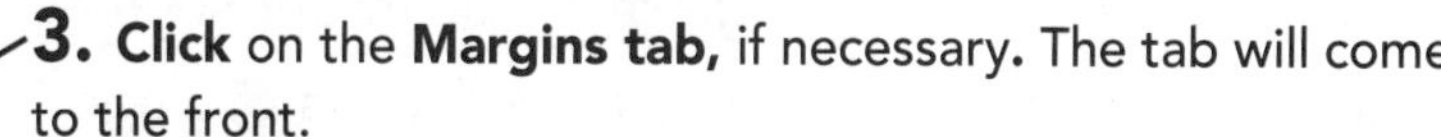

3. Click on the **Margins tab,** if necessary. The tab will come to the front.

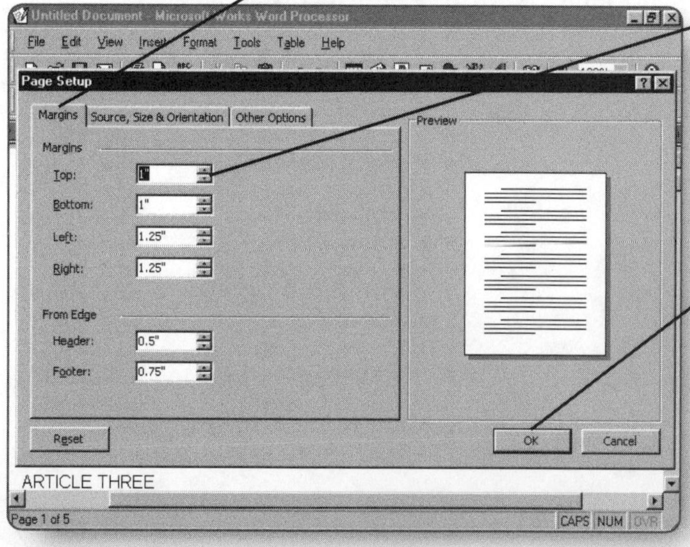

4. Click on the **up and down arrows** (⬍) for each margin in the Top margin, Bottom margin, Left margin, and Right margin spin boxes. The value in these boxes is measured in inches.

5. Click on **OK**. The Page Setup dialog box will close.

Changing Page Size

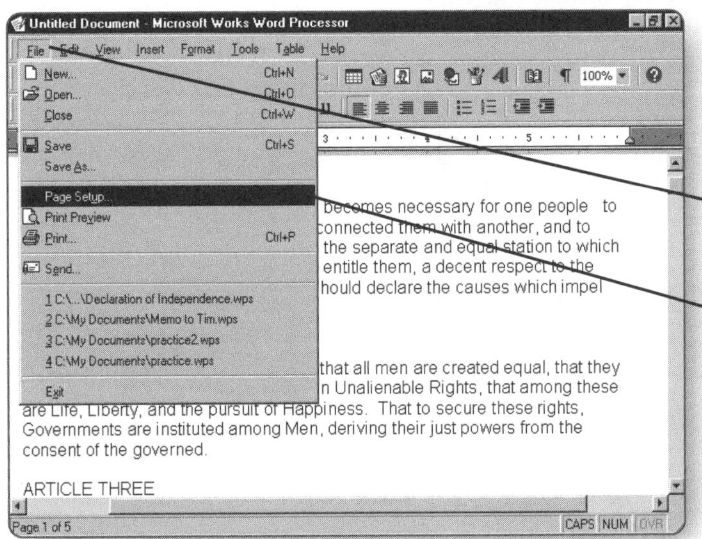

Works lets you select from several page size options, which are based on the page size settings of your printer.

1. Click on **File**. The File menu will appear.

2. Click on **Page Setup**. The Page Setup dialog box will open.

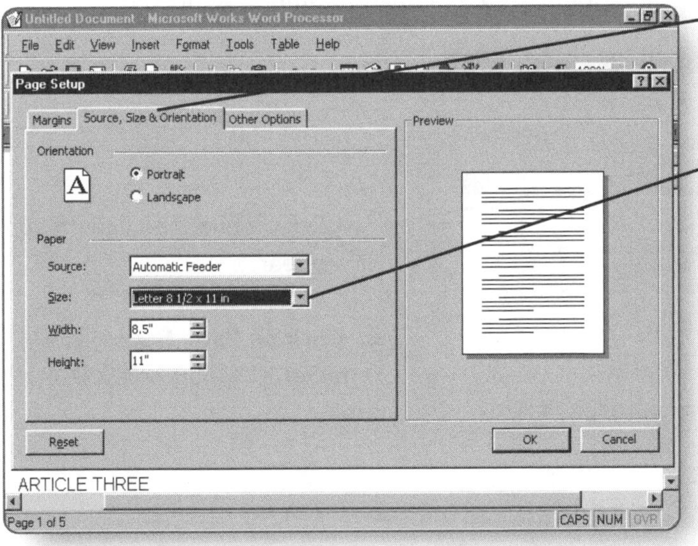

3. Click on the **Source, Size & Orientation tab.** The tab will come to the front.

4. Click on the **down arrow** (▼) at the right of the Size: list box. The list of available page size options will appear.

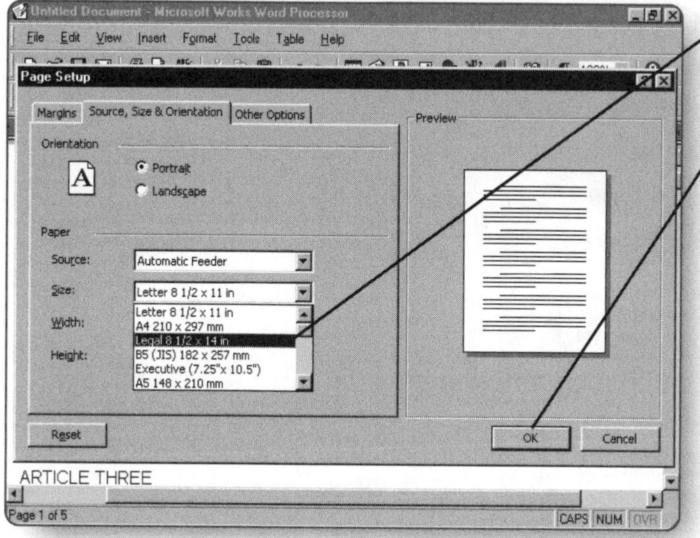

5. Click on a **page size**. The page size will be selected.

6. Click on **OK**. The Page Setup dialog box will close.

Changing Page Orientation

Works lets you print a document using either a portrait or landscape orientation. Portrait orientation prints the document in a vertical layout, whereas landscape orientation prints horizontally across the page.

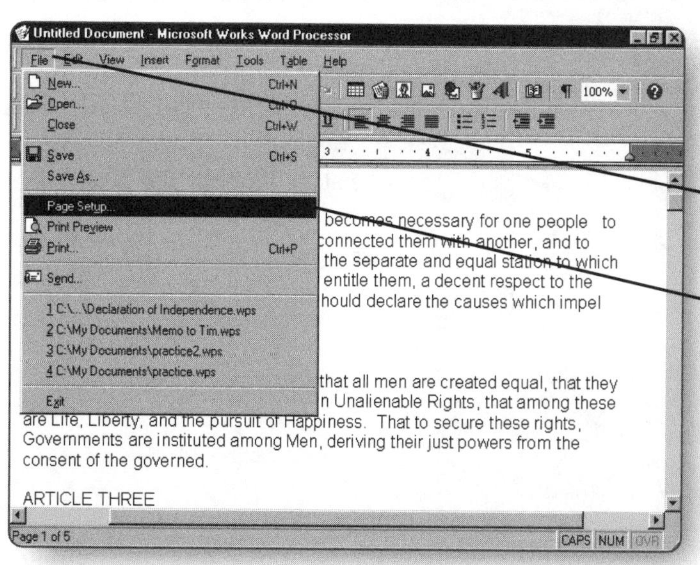

1. Click on **File**. The File menu will appear.

2. Click on **Page Setup**. The Page Setup dialog box will open.

3. Click on the **Source, Size & Orientation tab.** The tab will come to the front.

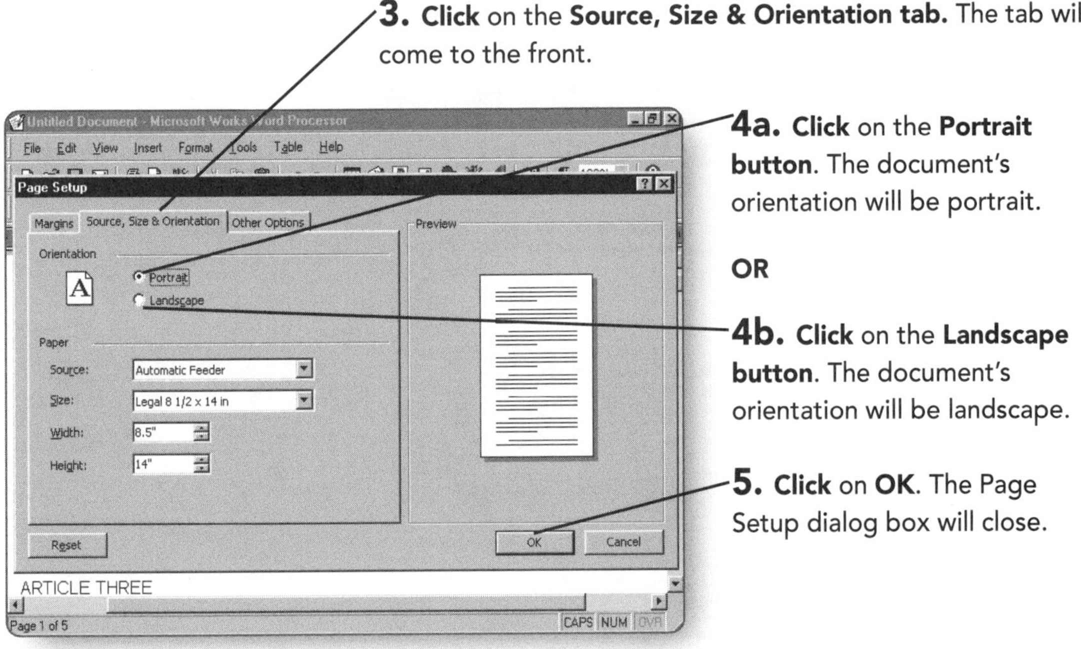

4a. Click on the **Portrait button**. The document's orientation will be portrait.

OR

4b. Click on the **Landscape button**. The document's orientation will be landscape.

5. Click on **OK**. The Page Setup dialog box will close.

Adding a Header or Footer

Two areas in a document are reserved for repeating text. When this text is at the top of a page, it is called a *header*. When this text is at the bottom of a page, it is called a *footer*. The header or footer area is displayed as a box with an outline at the top or bottom of the document.

Creating a Header or Footer

Examples of text you may want to place in a header or footer are the date the document was created, the document name, your company's name, or the current page number. The header and footer area are automatically created when you create a new document.

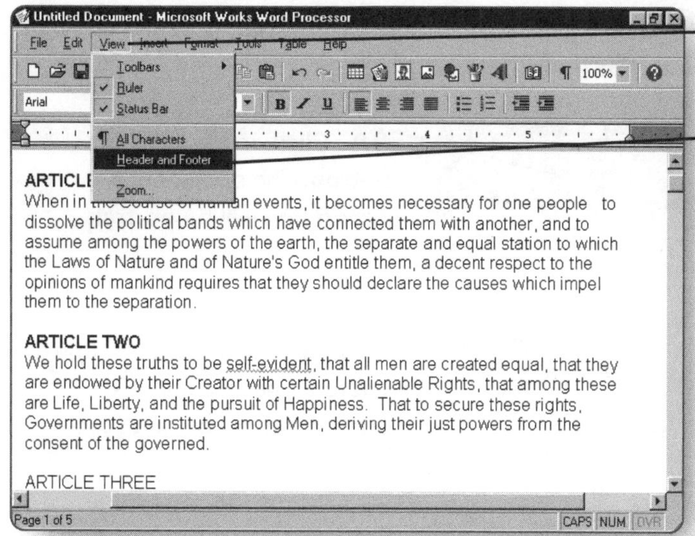

1. Click on **View**. The View menu will appear.

2. Click on **Header and Footer**. The header area of your document will appear.

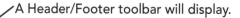

A Header/Footer toolbar will display.

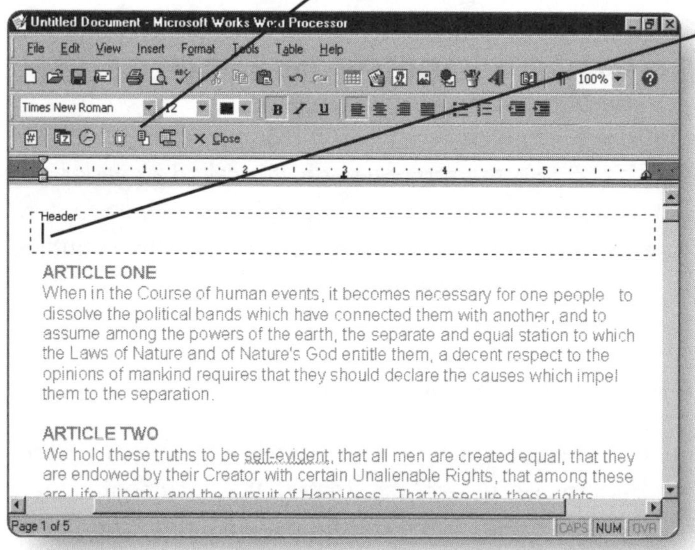

The insertion point will be located in the header area of the document.

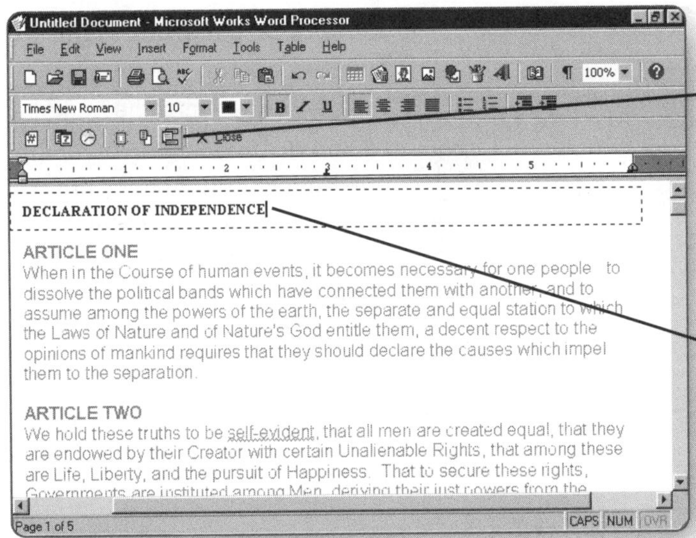

TIP

Click on the Switch Between Header and Footer button to move the insertion point to the document footer.

3. Type the header or footer **text**. The text will be added to the header or footer.

TIP

Format header or footer text using the same methods used to format the document body text. Formatting text was discussed in Chapter 4, "Formatting a Document."

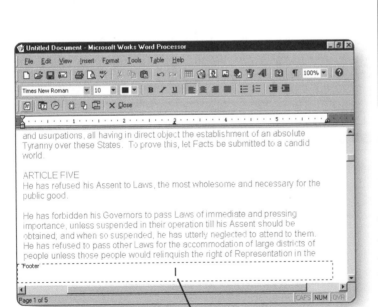

Inserting a Page Number in a Header or Footer

When creating a header or footer, do not type a number for the page number because Works requires a special field to increment them.

1. Position the **insertion point** at the location in the header or footer where you want the page number to be printed. The insertion point will be located in the header or footer area of the document.

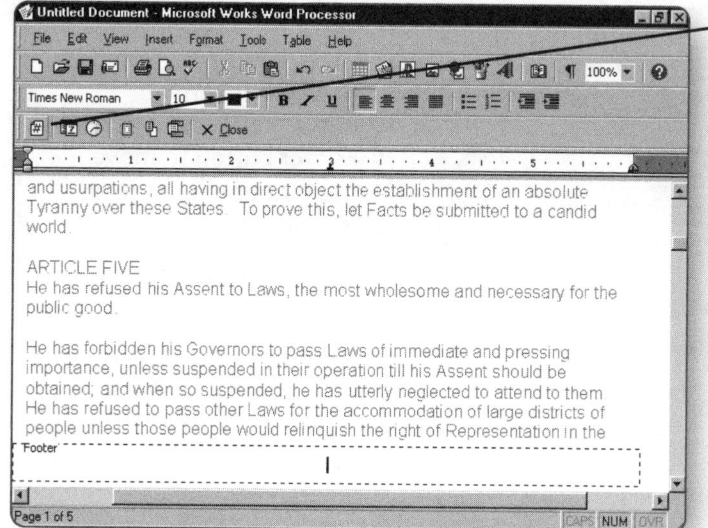

2. Click on the **Insert Page Number button**. The number will be inserted into the header or footer. This number is, however, a programming code for the current page number. Works will change the numbers as you move along in the document.

TIP

If you want the page number to be preceded by text, such as the word "Page," type the text in front of the page numbering field.

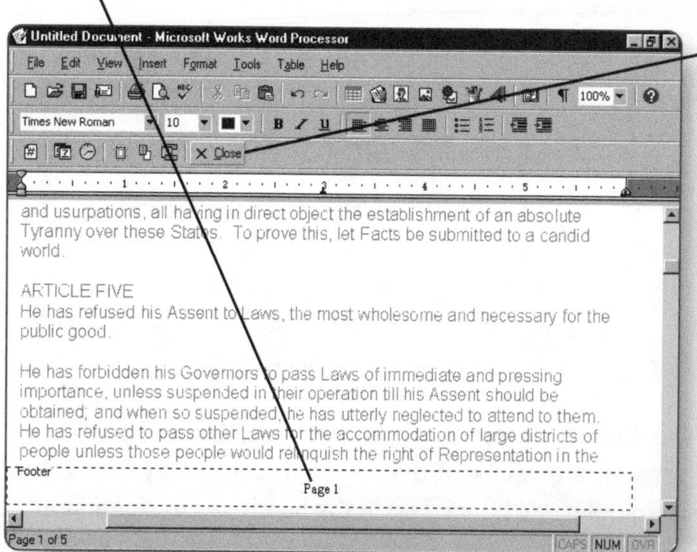

3. Click on the **Close button**. The document will return to the main editing screen.

7

Creating Reports

Reports are second only to letters in popularity and use. Whether you are a student, consultant, or other professional, you will have many uses for reports. Students often must do reports as part of their class work; professionals often do reports for a variety of reasons ranging from cost and project justifications to recommendations and strategic directions. In this chapter, you'll learn how to:

- Add page breaks
- Add page borders
- Add footnotes

Inserting Page Breaks

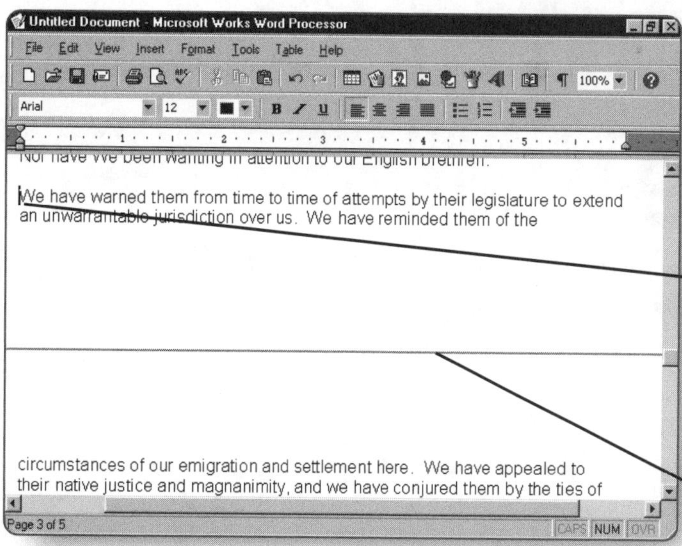

When a page is full of text, Works automatically begins a new page. Sometimes, however, you want a new page to begin at a specific location. This is called a *page break*.

1. **Click** the **mouse** at the position where you want the new page to begin. The blinking insertion point will appear at that position.

Existing page breaks appear as a black line across the screen.

2. **Click** on **Insert**. The Insert menu will appear.

3. **Click** on **Break**. A submenu will appear.

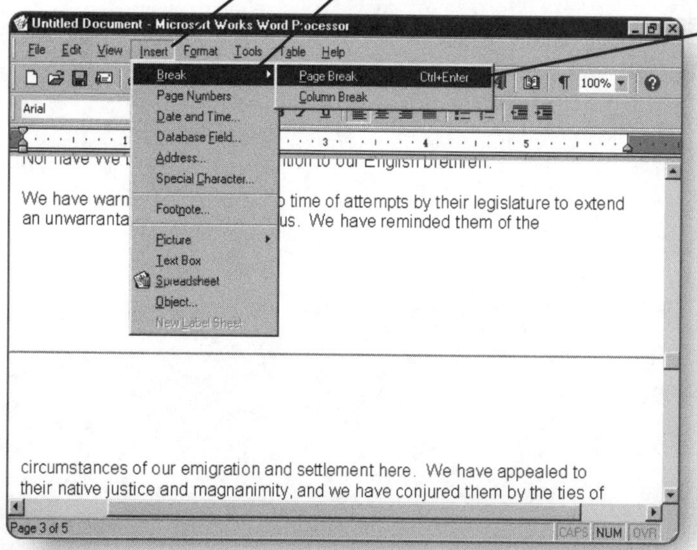

4. **Click** on **Page Break**. The insertion point will appear at the beginning of a new page.

Adding Borders

Decorate your document with a border. Works offers a variety of borders that you can use around a selected paragraph or the current page.

Applying a Paragraph Border

Add prominence to part of a page by placing a border around it.

1a. Click the **mouse pointer** in the paragraph to have a border. The blinking insertion point will appear.

OR

1b. Highlight multiple **paragraphs** to have borders applied. The paragraphs will be highlighted.

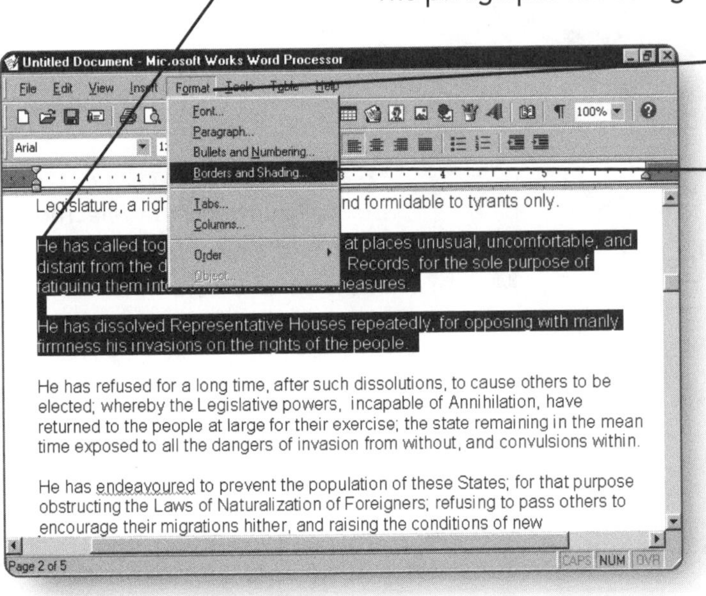

2. Click on **Format**. The Format menu will appear.

3. Click on **Borders and Shading**. The Borders and Shading dialog box will open.

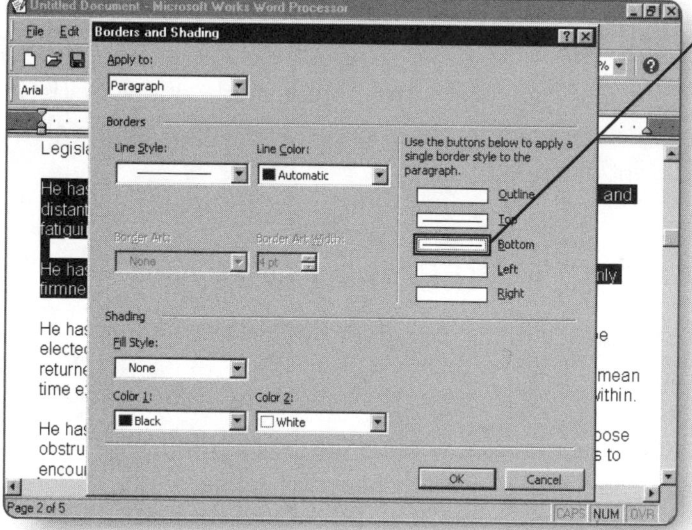

4. Click on the **placement buttons** to indicate where you want the paragraph border. For example, if you only want a line across the bottom of the paragraph, click on the Bottom button. If you want lines around the entire paragraph, choose the Outline button. A line style will appear in the selected choices.

There are many different line styles to choose from: single lines, double lines, thick or thin lines; even dashed or dotted lines.

5. Click on the **Line Style: down arrow (▼)**. A list of available line styles will appear.

6. Click on a **line style**. A black box will surround the selected style, and a sample will appear in the sample box.

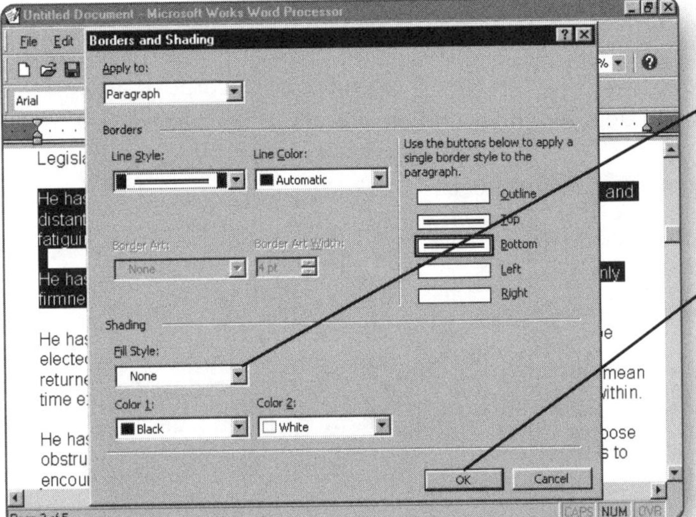

TIP

Optionally, choose a shading pattern from the Fill Style: drop-down list.

7. **Click** on **OK**. The Borders and Shading dialog box will close.

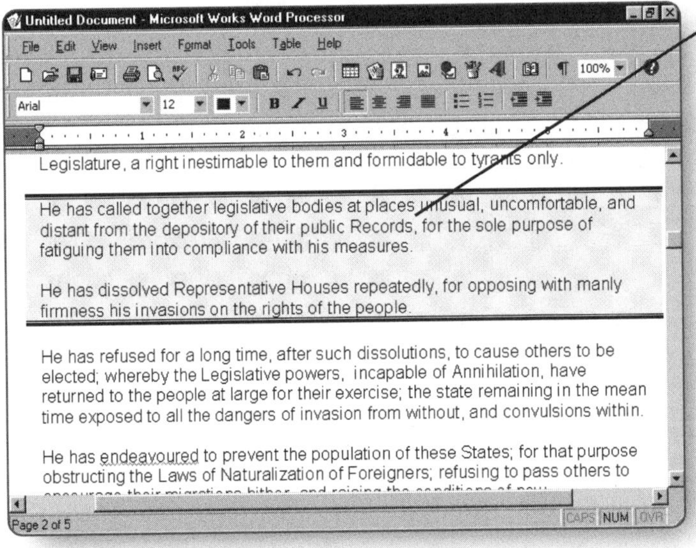

The paragraph border and fill selections will be applied to the current or selected paragraphs.

Bordering Pages

Works includes more than 150 pieces of decorative artwork that can be applied around each page of your document. Choose from simple lines, to stars, hearts or leaves.

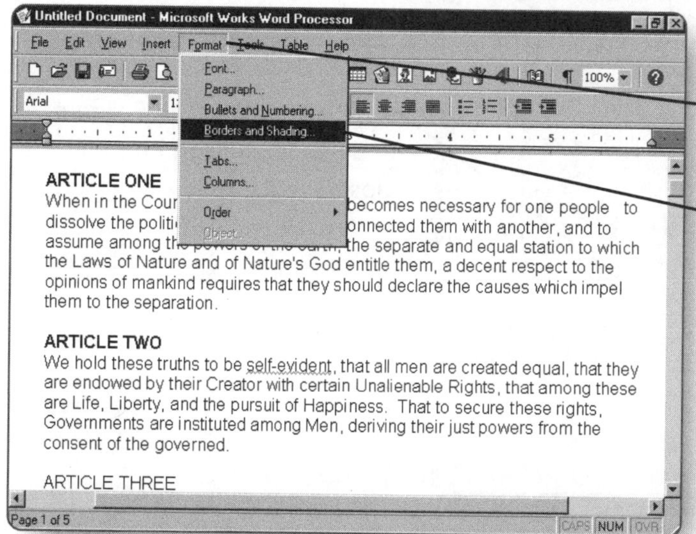

1. **Click** on **Format**. The Format menu will appear.
2. **Click** on **Borders and Shading**. The Borders and Shading dialog box will open.

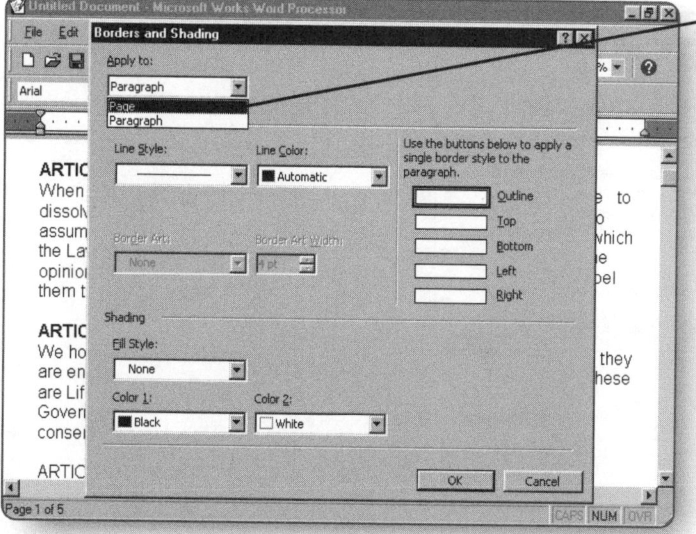

3. **Click** on the **Page option** from the Apply to: drop-down list. The Border Art selections will become available.

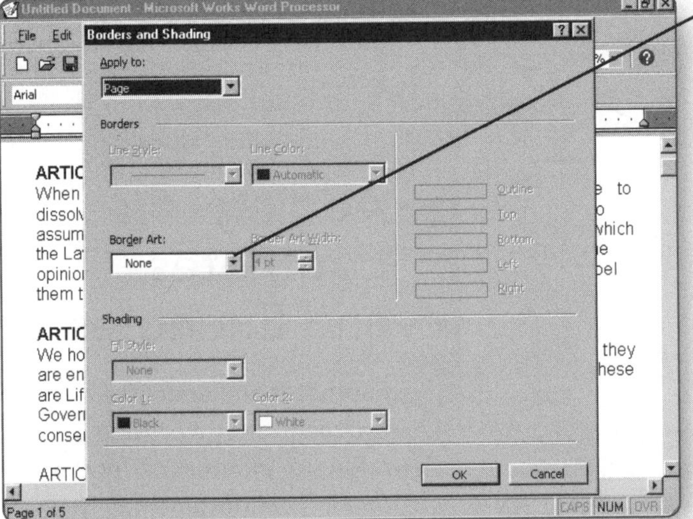

4. Click on the **Border Art: drop-down list**. A selection of available styles will appear.

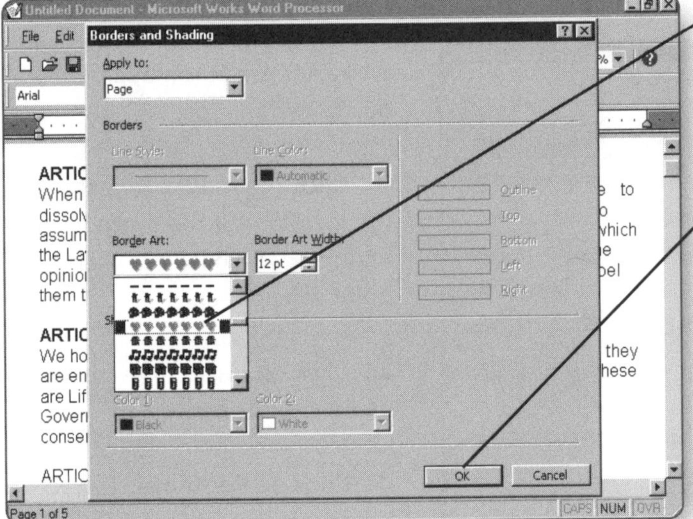

5. Click on a **Border Art: style**. The selected option will appear in the Border Art: drop-down box.

6. Click on **OK**. The Borders and Shading dialog box will close.

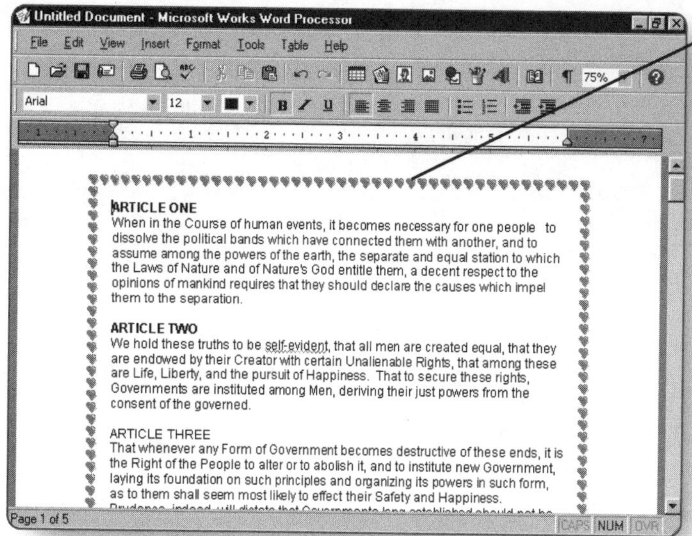

Each page of the entire document will have a decorative border.

Adding Footnotes and Endnotes

Footnotes and endnotes comment on and provide reference information for the text in your document. Footnotes appear at the bottom of the current page, whereas endnotes appear on a separate page at the end of the document. Footnotes and endnotes are automatically numbered for you.

1. **Click** the **mouse pointer** at the location for the footnote or endnote. The blinking insertion point will appear.
2. **Click** on **Insert**. The Insert menu will appear.
3. **Click** on **Footnote**. The Footnote and Endnote dialog box will open.

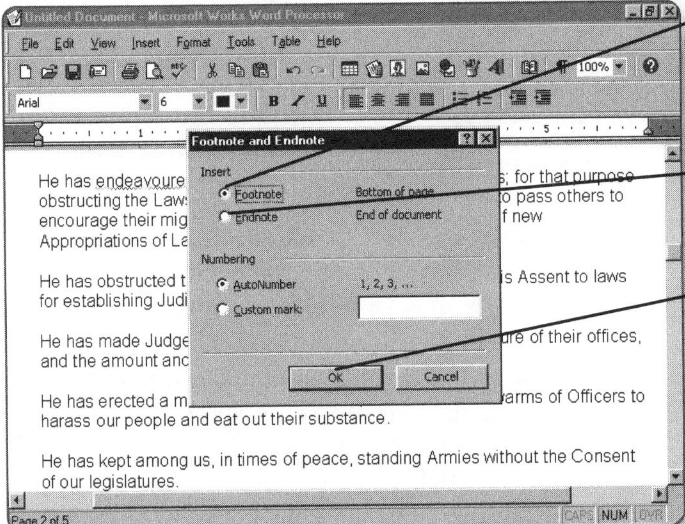

4a. Click on **Footnote**. The option will be selected.

OR

4b. Click on **Endnote**. The option will be selected.

5. Click on **OK**. The footnote or endnote reference will be added to the document, and the insertion point will be placed in the footnote or endnote area of the document.

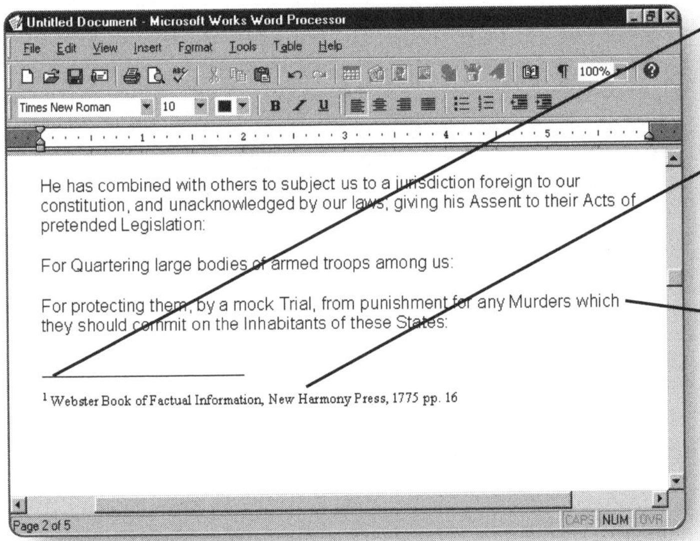

Works automatically includes a separator line for your footnotes.

6. Type the **text** of the note. The text will be entered for this note.

7. Click in the **document body**. You will return to the main text of the document.

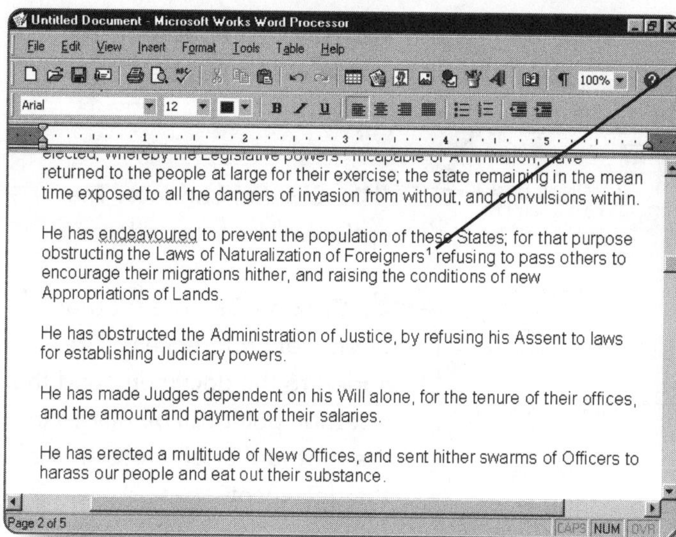

The superscripted reference number is displayed in the document body.

> **TIP**
>
> To delete a footnote or endnote, highlight the reference number and press the Delete key. The corresponding text will also be deleted.

8

Improving Your Writing

One goal of Microsoft Works is to make document creation as easy as possible. To reach this goal, several features have been included to improve your writing. For example, the Spell Correct feature of Works can catch many misspellings for you, and if you can't think of the exact word you want to use, the Thesaurus can help you out. These and other features, such as Find and Replace, can be used to improve your writing style. In this chapter, you'll learn how to:

- Use the Find and Replace features
- Check your spelling and grammar
- Use the Thesaurus feature

Using Find to Locate Text

Do you have a long document that you created, but you can't remember where you used a particular word or phrase? Use the Find feature to search for words or phrases in a document.

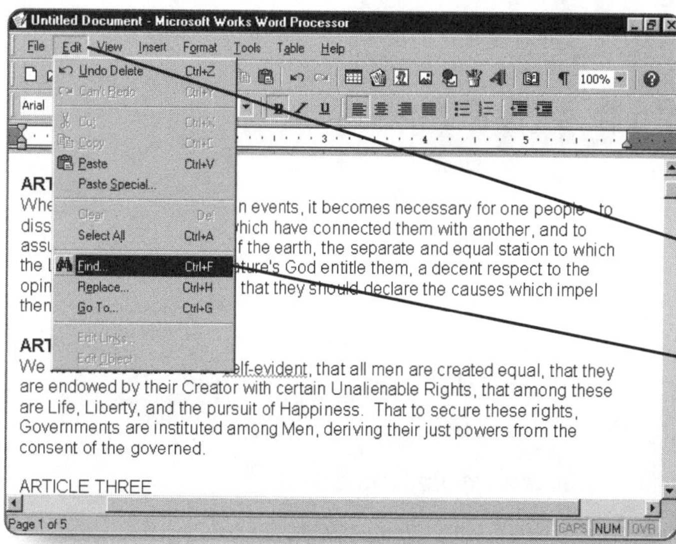

1. **Click** the **mouse** at the location to begin the search—usually the beginning of the document. The insertion point will appear at that location.

2. **Click** on **Edit**. The Edit menu will appear.

3. **Click** on **Find**. The Find and Replace dialog box will open.

> **TIP**
>
> Another way to access the Find feature is to press Ctrl+F.

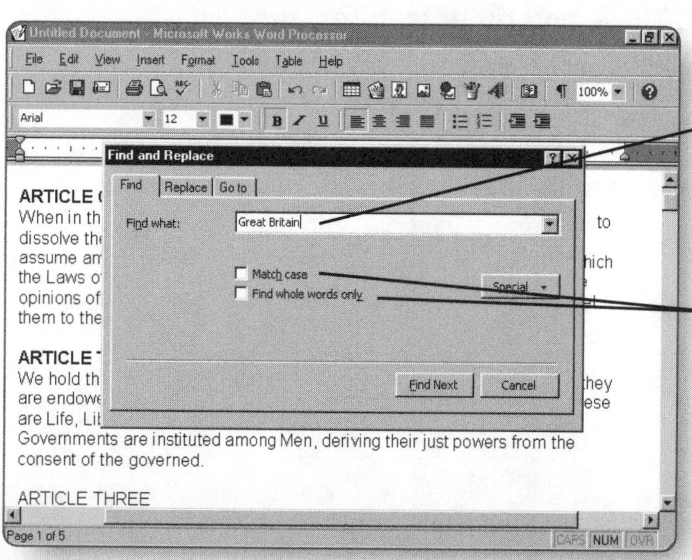

4. **Type** the **word** or **phrase** you want to locate. The text will appear in the Find what: text box.

5. Optionally, **click** on **Find whole words only** or **Match case**. These items will be selected.

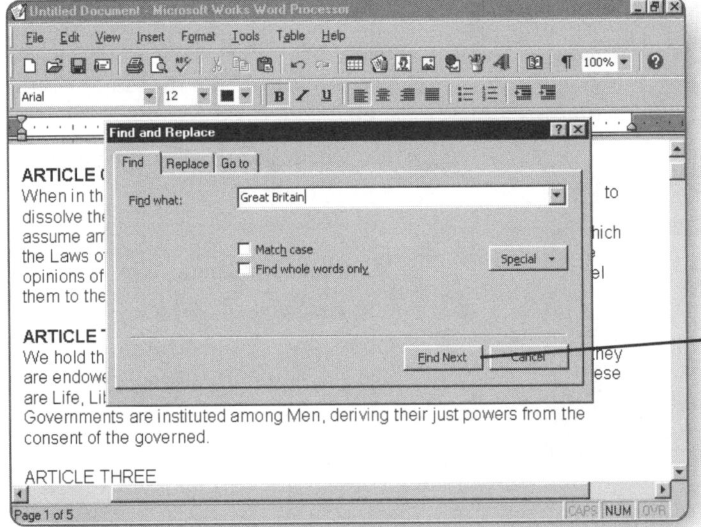

For example, if you type "and" in the Find box and select Find whole words only, Works will not find the words "Anderson," "candy," or "band." If you choose Match case, Works would only find "and." It would not find "AND" or "And."

6. **Click** on **Find Next**. The first occurrence of the found text will be highlighted.

> **NOTE**
>
> Occasionally, the found text is hidden under the dialog box. You may have to move the Find dialog box by clicking and dragging on the title bar at the top of the dialog box.

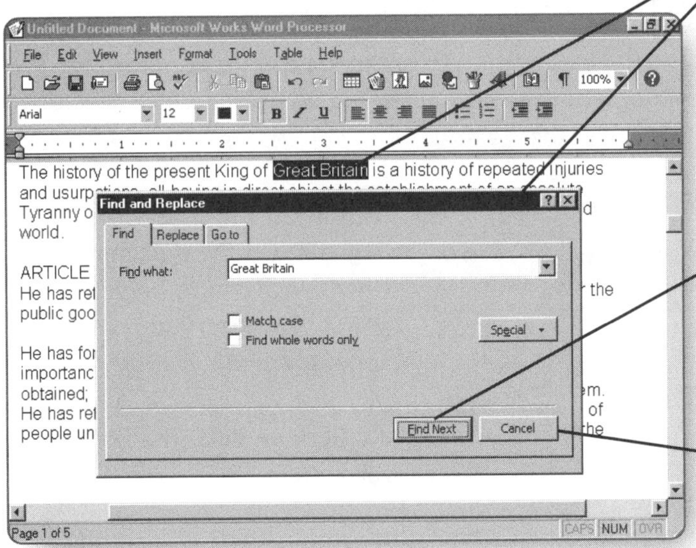

7a. **Click** on **Find Next**. Works will locate the next occurrence of the found text.

OR

7b. **Click** on **Cancel**. The Find dialog box will close, and the found text remains highlighted.

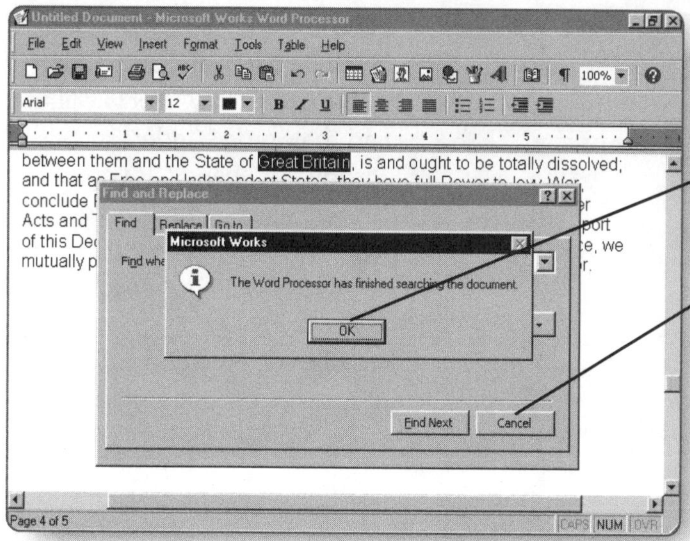

When the entire document has been searched, Works will advise you with a message box.

8. **Click** on **OK**. The message box will close.

9. **Click** on **Cancel**. The Find and Replace dialog box will close, and the last found text will premain highlighted.

Replacing Text

Use the Replace feature to exchange a word or phrase for something else. You can replace some or all occurrences of the text with other text.

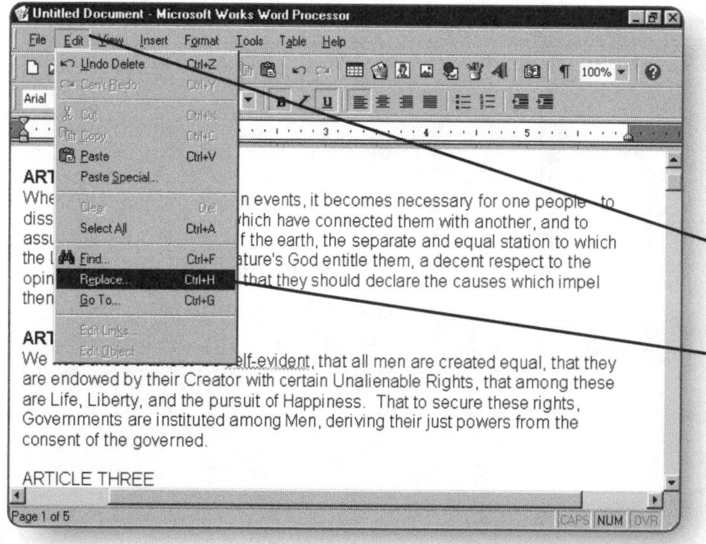

1. **Click** the **mouse** at the beginning of the document or where you want to begin the search. The insertion point will appear at that location.

2. **Click** on **Edit**. The Edit menu will appear.

3. **Click** on **Replace**. The Replace dialog box will open.

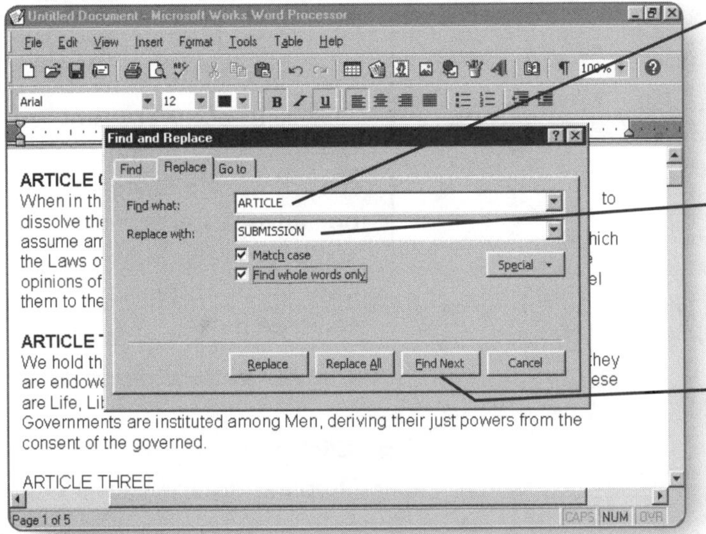

4. **Type** the **text** that you want to find in the Find what: text box. The text will appear in the box.

5. **Type** the **text** in the Replace with: text box that will replace the Find text in step 4. The text will appear in the box.

6. **Click** on **Find Next**. The first location of the Find text will be highlighted.

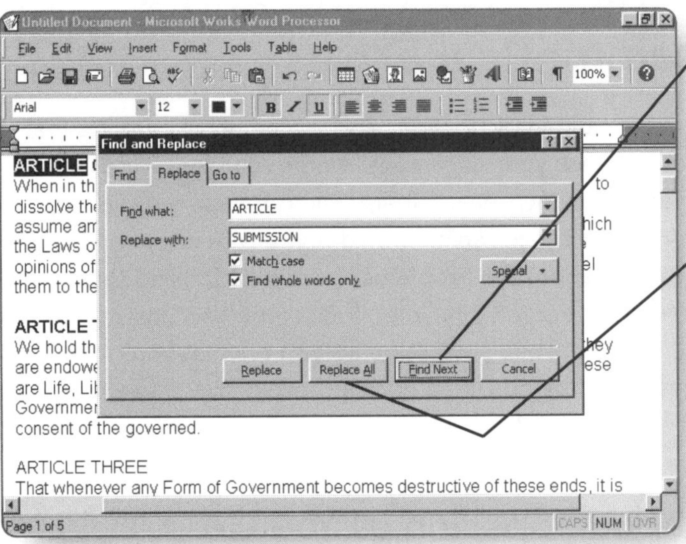

7a. **Click** on **Find Next**. Works will leave the found text alone and go to the next occurrence.

OR

7b. **Click** on **Replace**. The replacement text will be placed in the document, and Works will search for the next occurrence of the text.

> **NOTE**
>
> If the Replace box is left blank and you click on Replace, Works deletes the Find word or phrase.

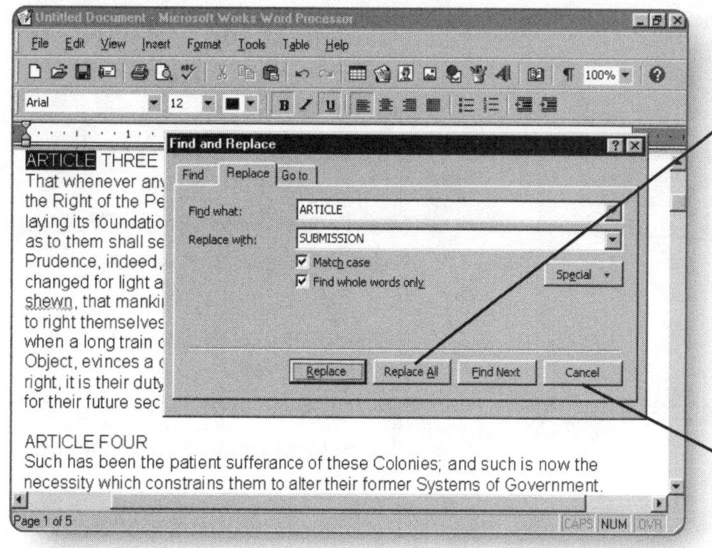

TIP

Click on Replace All to replace all occurrences of the search text at the same time. A message box advises you of the number of replacements. Click on OK to close the message box.

8. Click on **Cancel**. The Find and Replace dialog box will close.

Correcting Spelling and Grammatical Errors

Works has built-in dictionaries and grammatical rule sets that it uses to check your document. Works can identify possible problems as you type, and it also can run a special spelling and grammar check, which provides you with more information about the problems and tools for fixing them. These features aren't infallible; if you type "air" instead of "err," Works probably won't be able to tell that you're wrong. However, combined with a good proofreading, these tools can be very helpful.

Checking Spelling as You Go

By default, Works identifies problems right in your document as you type. Spelling errors have a red wavy line underneath them.

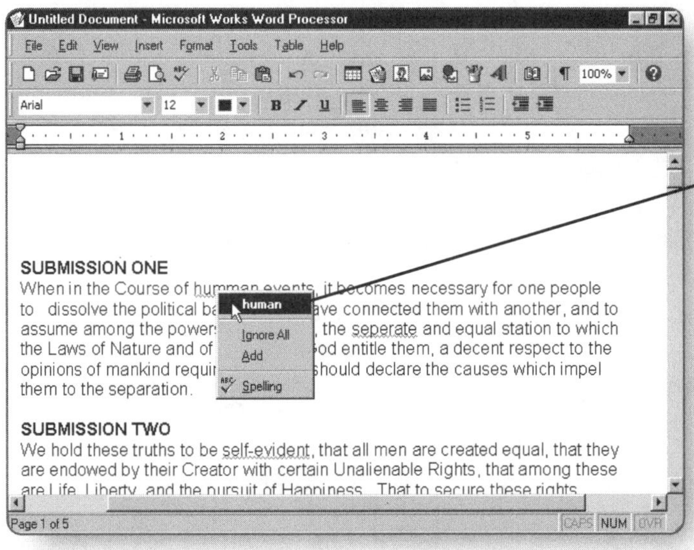

1. Right-click on the **word.** The shortcut menu will appear with suggested corrections.

2. Click on the **correct spelling**. The questionable word will be replaced with your selection.

Running a Spelling and Grammar Check

New to Works 2000 is the capability to check your grammar. A spelling and grammar check can be run at the same time.

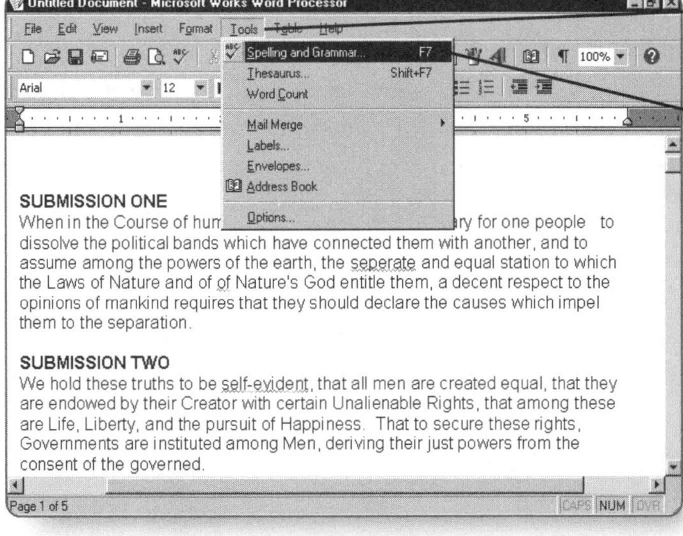

1. Click on **Tools**. The Tools menu will appear.

2. Click on **Spelling and Grammar**. The Spelling and Grammar dialog box will open.

> **TIP**
>
> Alternatively, click on the Spelling and Grammar button.

The first error encountered, whether spelling or grammar, will be displayed. If the error is in spelling, it is identified in the Not in dictionary: text box. In the Suggestions: text box, there are possible correct spellings for the word. In this example, the correct spelling is already highlighted.

3. Click on **one** of the following options:

- **Change.** Choose this to change just this incident of the spelling mistake.
- **Change All.** Choose this if you think you could have made the mistake more than once.

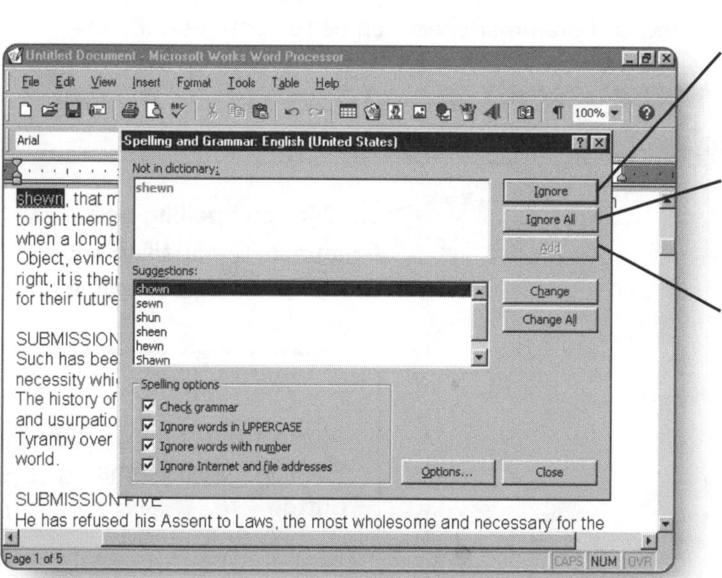

- **Ignore.** Choose this if you don't want to correct this instance of the spelling.
- **Ignore All.** Choose this if you don't want to correct any instances of the spelling.
- **Add.** Choose this to add a word, such as a proper name or legal term, to Works' built-in dictionary so that it won't be flagged as an error in the future. This feature is not available for all words.

After you choose one of these actions, the check will proceed to the next possible error.

If Works finds a grammatical error, it will display it in the top text box, with a suggested revision or explanation of the error in the Suggestions: text box.

4. **Click** on **one** of the following:

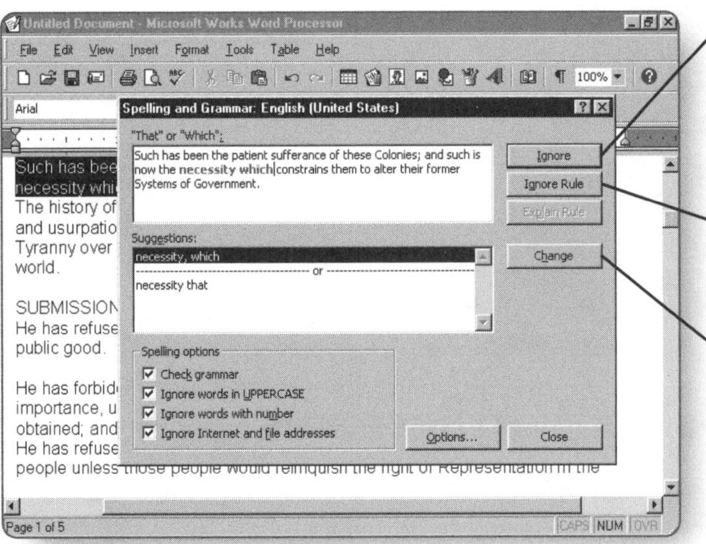

- **Ignore.** Choose this if you don't want to change this instance of the grammatical problem or if you want to modify it at a later time.
- **Ignore Rule.** Choose this to ignore all instances of the grammatical problem.
- **Change.** Choose this to make the suggested change.

> **NOTE**
>
> Sometimes, Works cannot give a grammatical suggestion. In those cases, you'll need to correct the error yourself.

> **TIP**
>
> Do *not*, repeat do *NOT*, rely on the Spell Check and Grammar features to catch all your errors. They are far from perfect and can miss many items. They can also flag errors when your text is really okay and can suggest wrong things to do to fix both real problems and false error reports. You alone know what you want your document to say. Proofread it yourself!

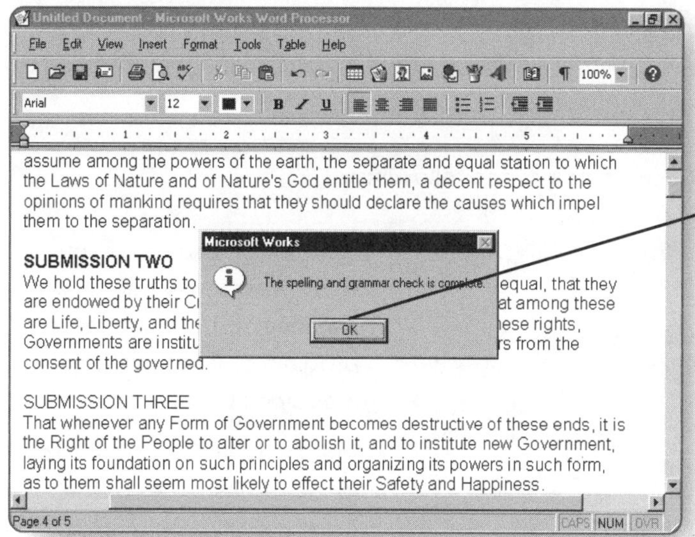

When all mistakes have been identified, Works will notify you that the spelling and grammar check is complete.

5. **Click** on **OK**. The message box will close.

Using the Thesaurus

The Works Thesaurus gives you an easy way to find just the right words to use in your document.

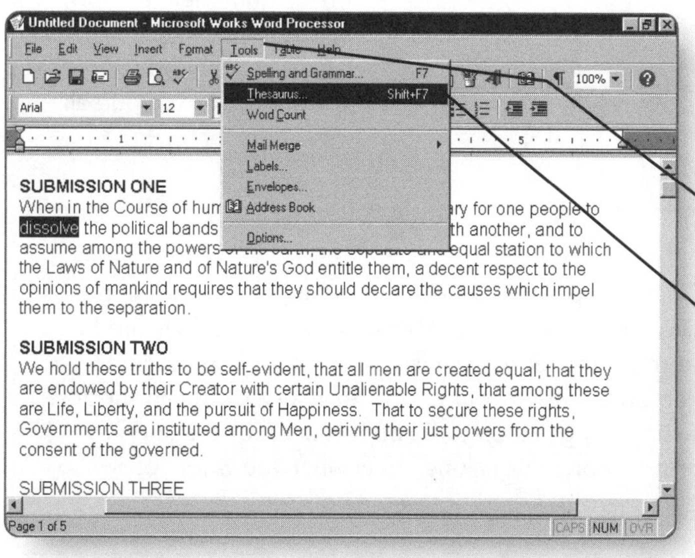

1. **Highlight** or **Click** in the **word** you want to replace. The blinking insertion point will appear in the word.

2. **Click** on **Tools**. The Tools menu will appear.

3. **Click** on **Thesaurus**. The Thesaurus dialog box will open.

4. Click on a **meaning** in the Meanings: list box. A list of synonyms for that meaning will appear.

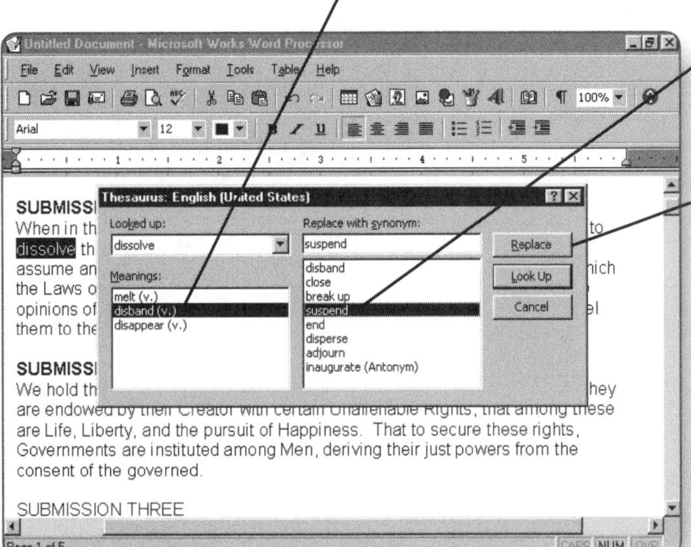

5. Click on a **word** from the Replace with synonym: list box. The word will be highlighted.

6. Click on **Replace**. The Thesaurus dialog box will close.

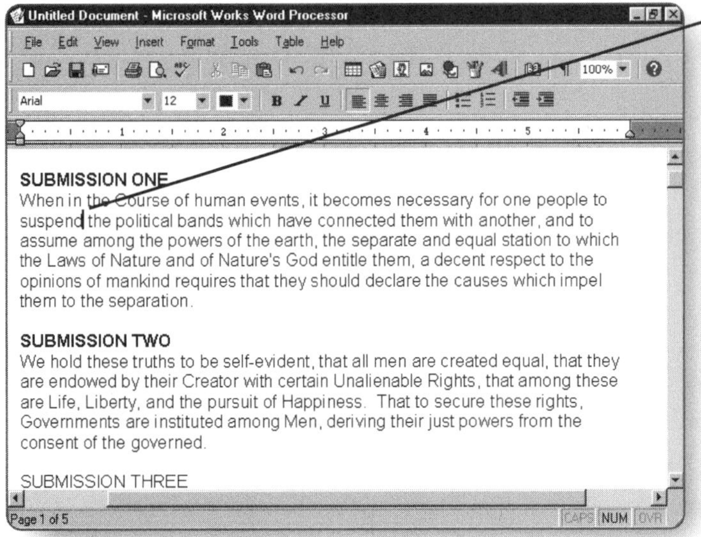

The word will be replaced in the document.

9

Completing Your Document

Your work on the document is coming to an end. The final steps include printing the document and then closing it. In this chapter, you'll learn how to:

- Print a document
- Create an envelope
- Open and close a document

Printing a Document

The Works word processor is a what-you-see-is-what-you-get (WYSIWYG) program, which means that text and other elements, such as graphics, appear onscreen the same way they will look when printed to paper.

Using Print Preview

Before you print your document, preview it full-screen. Previewing a document gives you an idea of how document layout settings, such as margins, will look on the printed document.

1. **Click** on the **Print Preview button**. The document will be sized so that an entire page is visible on the screen. You won't be able to edit the document from this screen.

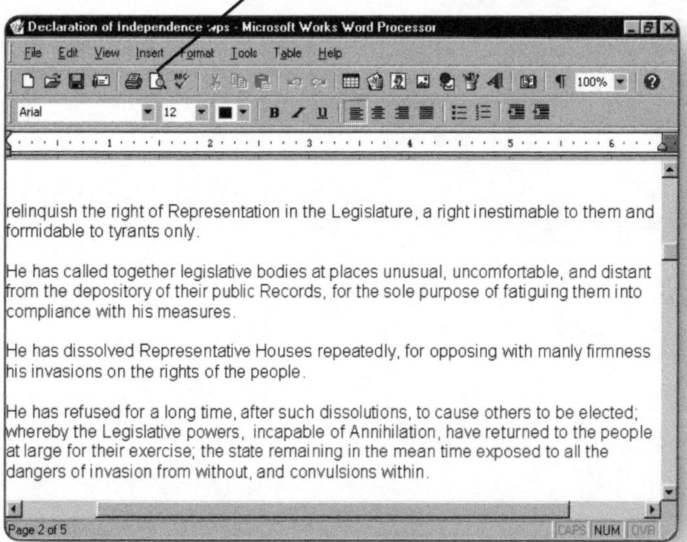

2. Click on the **Next button**. The next page of the document will appear.

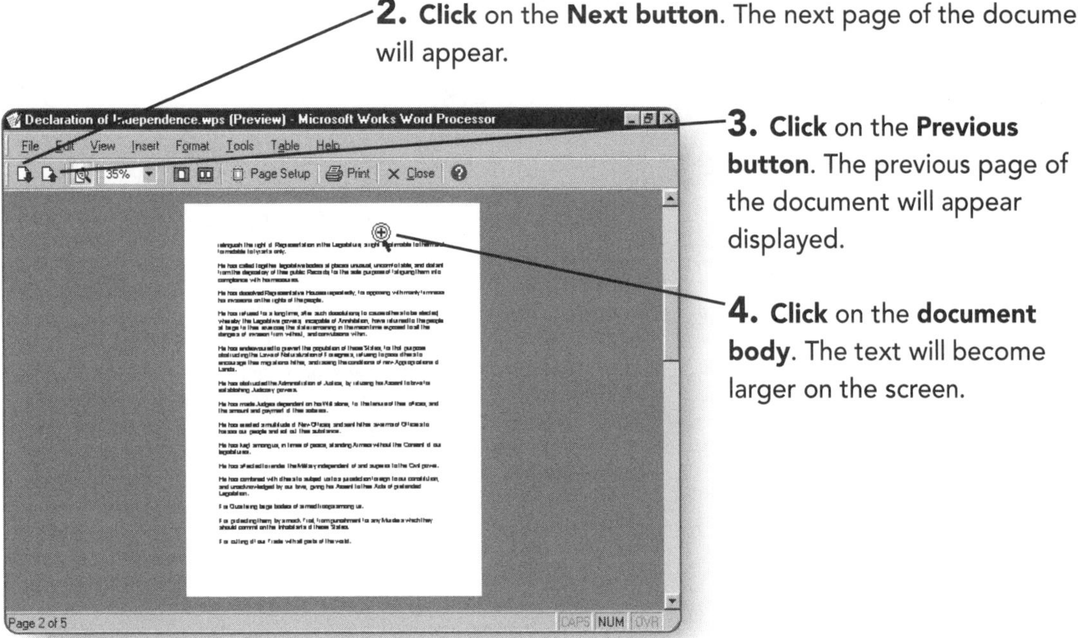

3. Click on the **Previous button**. The previous page of the document will appear displayed.

4. Click on the **document body**. The text will become larger on the screen.

5. Click on the **document body** again. The text will become smaller on the screen.

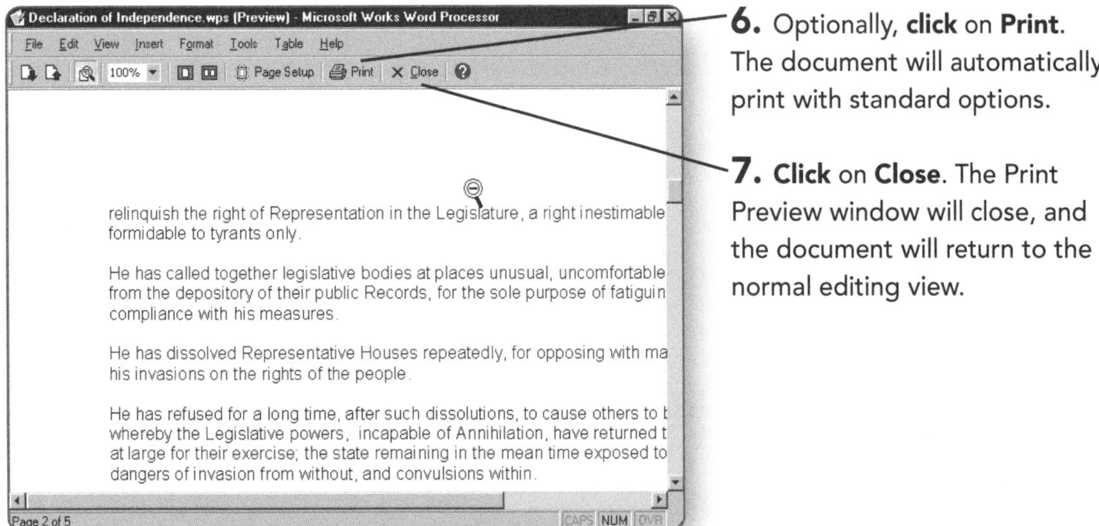

6. Optionally, **click** on **Print**. The document will automatically print with standard options.

7. Click on **Close**. The Print Preview window will close, and the document will return to the normal editing view.

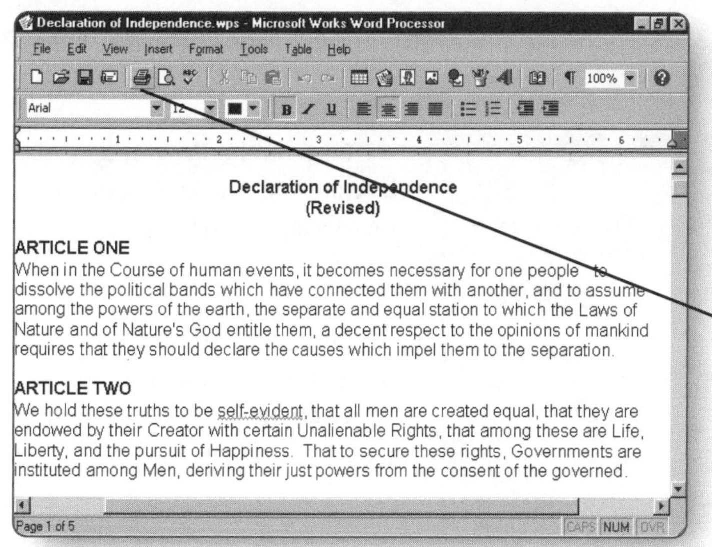

Printing Your Work

Typically, the end result of creating a document in Works is getting text onto paper. Works gives you a quick and easy way to get that result.

1a. Click on the **Print button**. The document will print with standard options.

OR

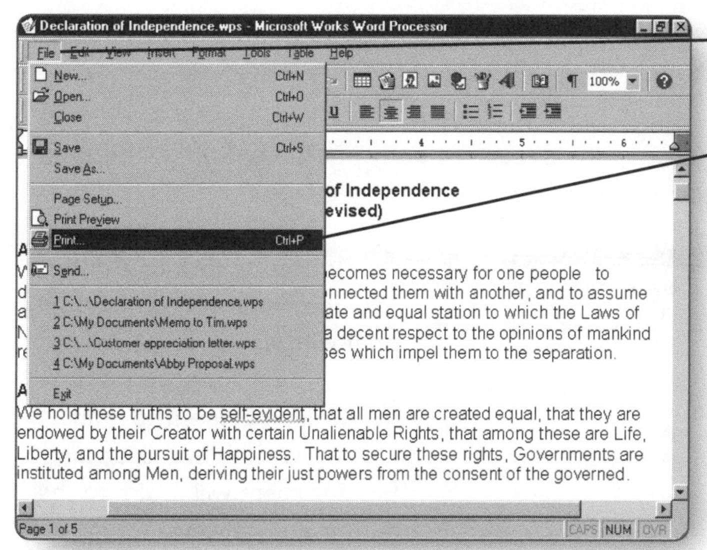

1b. Click on **File**. The File menu will appear.

2. Click on **Print**. The Print dialog box will open.

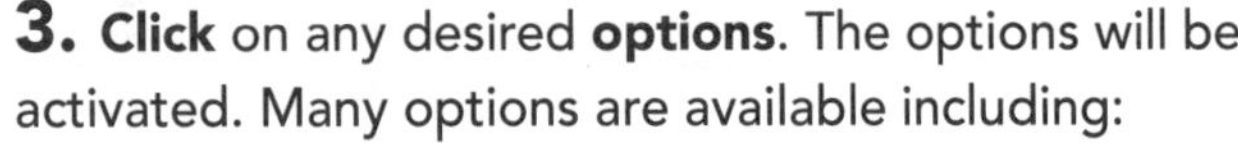

3. Click on any desired **options**. The options will be activated. Many options are available including:

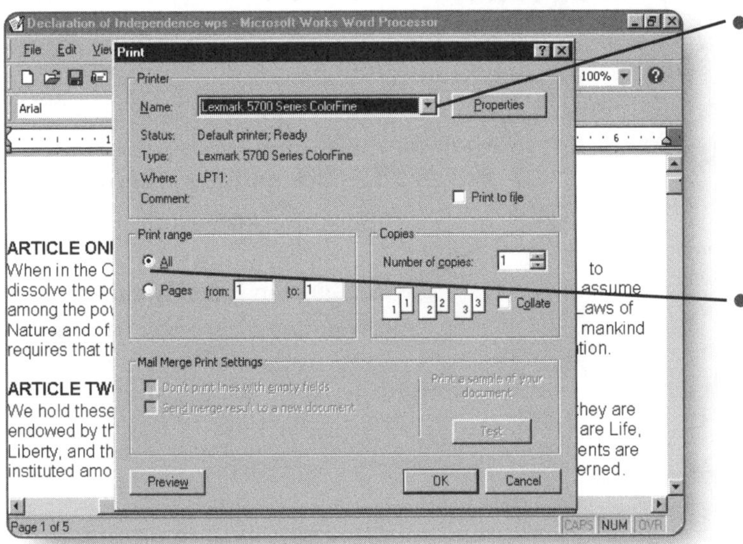

- **Name.** If you are connected to more than one printer, you can choose which one to use for this print job. Click on the down arrow (▼) in the Name: drop-down list box and make a selection.
- **Print range**. You can choose which pages of your document to print with the Print range options.

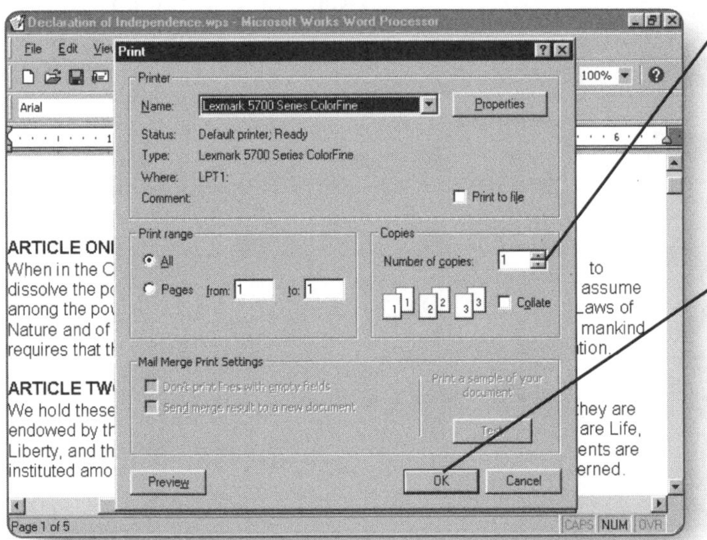

- **Number of copies**. Choose the number of copies to be printed by clicking on the up/down arrows (⬍) at the right of the Number of copies: list box.

4. Click on **OK**. The document will be sent to the printer.

Creating an Envelope

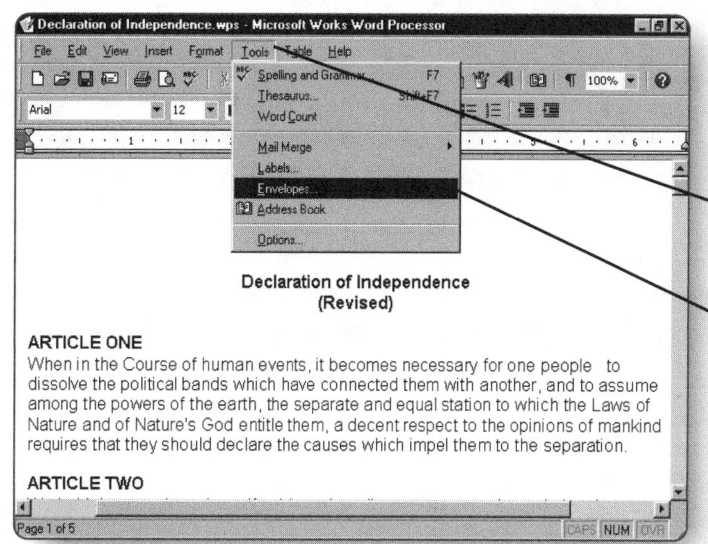

With a laser or inkjet printer and Microsoft Works, you can easily print a professional-looking envelope.

1. **Click** on **Tools**. The Tools menu will appear.

2. **Click** on **Envelopes**. The Envelopes dialog box will open.

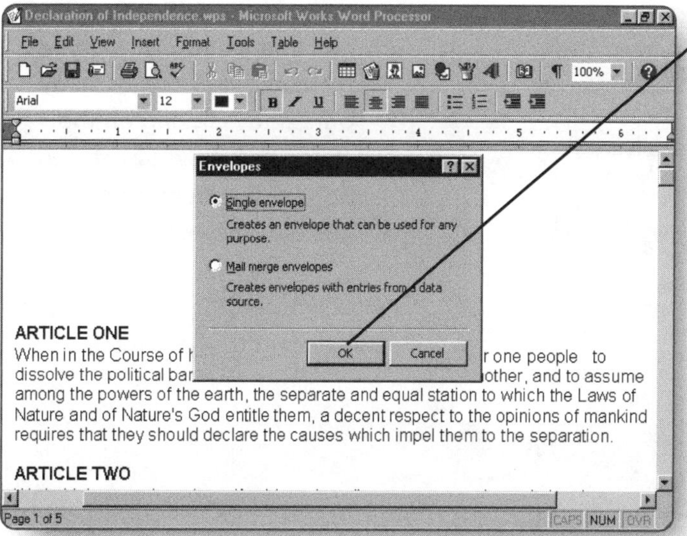

3. **Click** on **OK**. The Envelopes Settings dialog box will open.

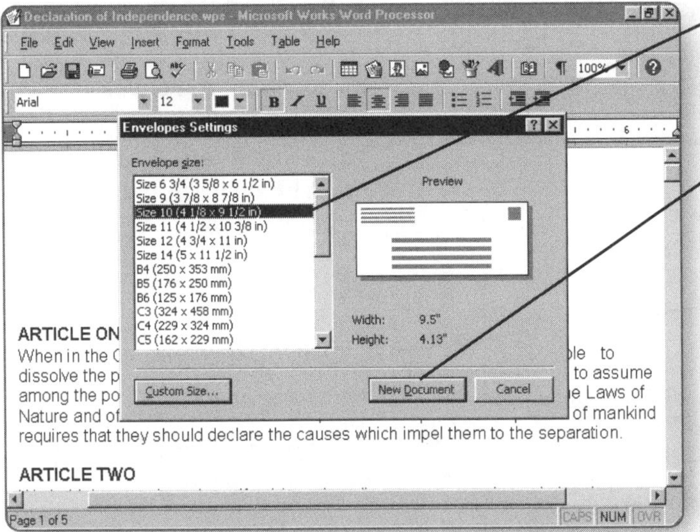

4. Click on an **envelope size**. The selection will be highlighted.

5. Click on **New Document**. Works will create an envelope document containing the settings you specified.

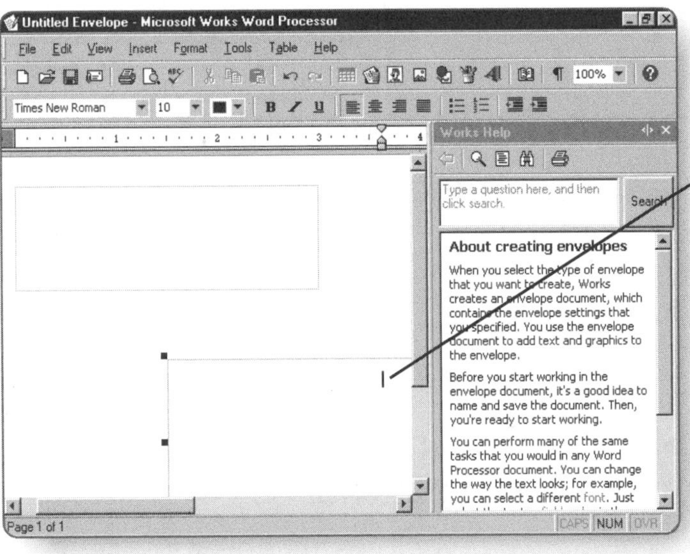

The blinking insertion point will appear in the mailing address text box.

6. Type the **mailing address**. Use any formatting techniques you learned in earlier chapters. The mailing address will appear in the mailing address text box.

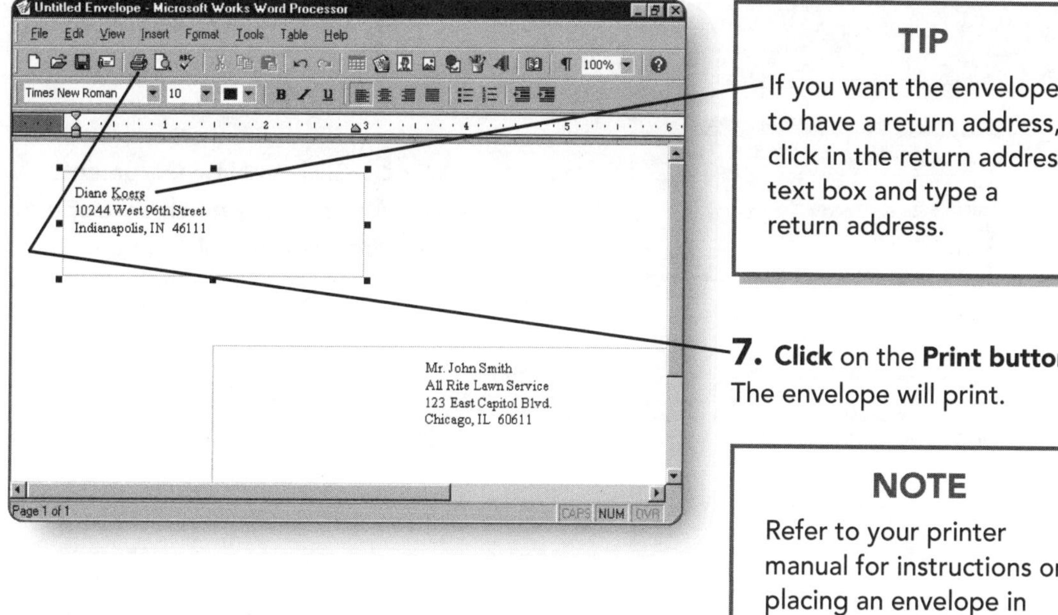

TIP

If you want the envelope to have a return address, click in the return address text box and type a return address.

7. Click on the **Print button**. The envelope will print.

NOTE

Refer to your printer manual for instructions on placing an envelope in your printer.

Opening a Document

Opening a document places a copy of that file into the computer's memory and onto your screen so that you can work on it. If you make any changes, be sure to save the file again. See Chapter 3, "Creating a Simple Document," if you need assistance on how to save a file.

Opening a Document from the Task Launcher

You can open a document from the Works Task Launcher that appears when you first start the Works program.

1. Click on **History**. A listing of previously opened Works documents will appear.

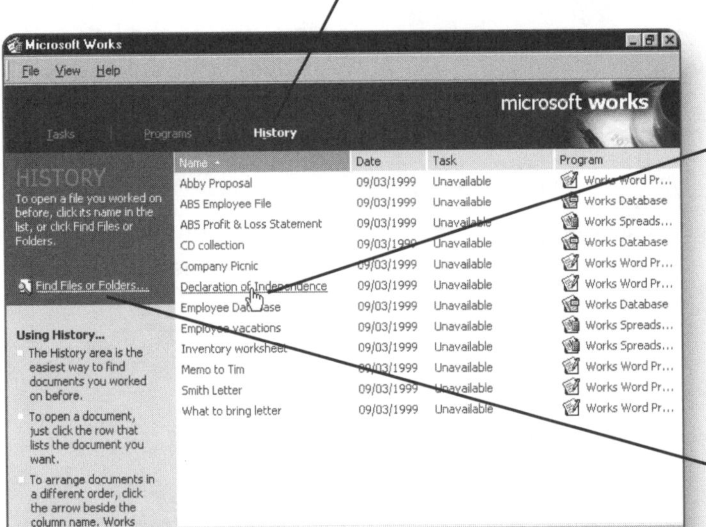

If the document you want to open is listed:

2. Click on the **filename** that you want to open. The filename will be highlighted, and the file will appear on your screen, ready for you to edit.

If the document you want to open is not listed:

3. Click on **Find Files or Folders**. The Find: All Files dialog box will open.

4. Type the **filename** to open. If you don't know the entire filename, type any portion of it. The text will appear in the Named: text box.

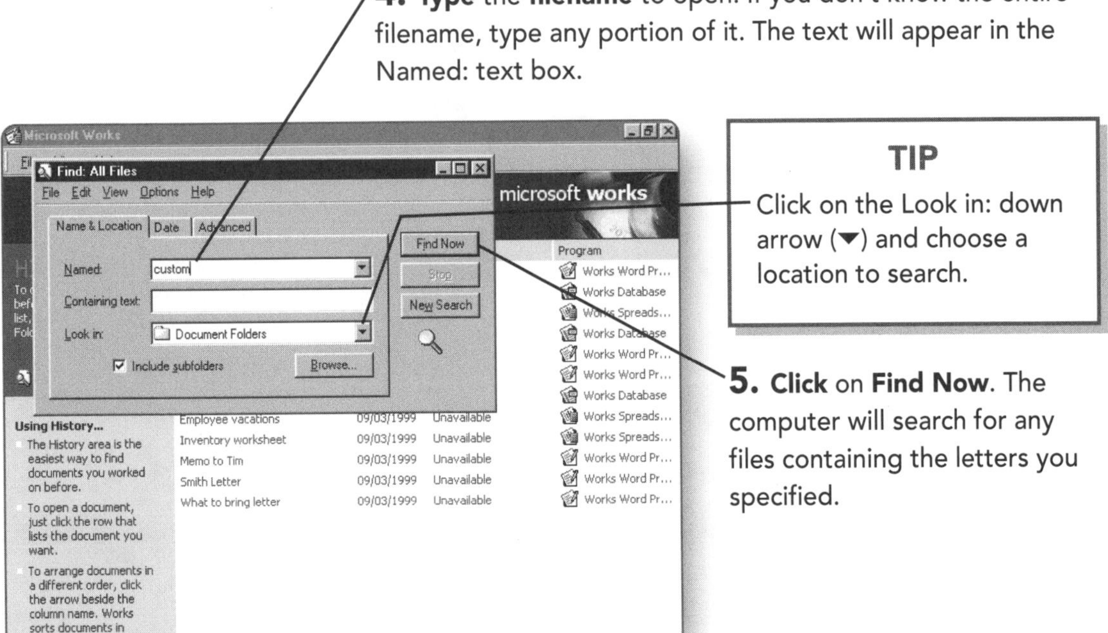

TIP

Click on the Look in: down arrow (▼) and choose a location to search.

5. Click on **Find Now**. The computer will search for any files containing the letters you specified.

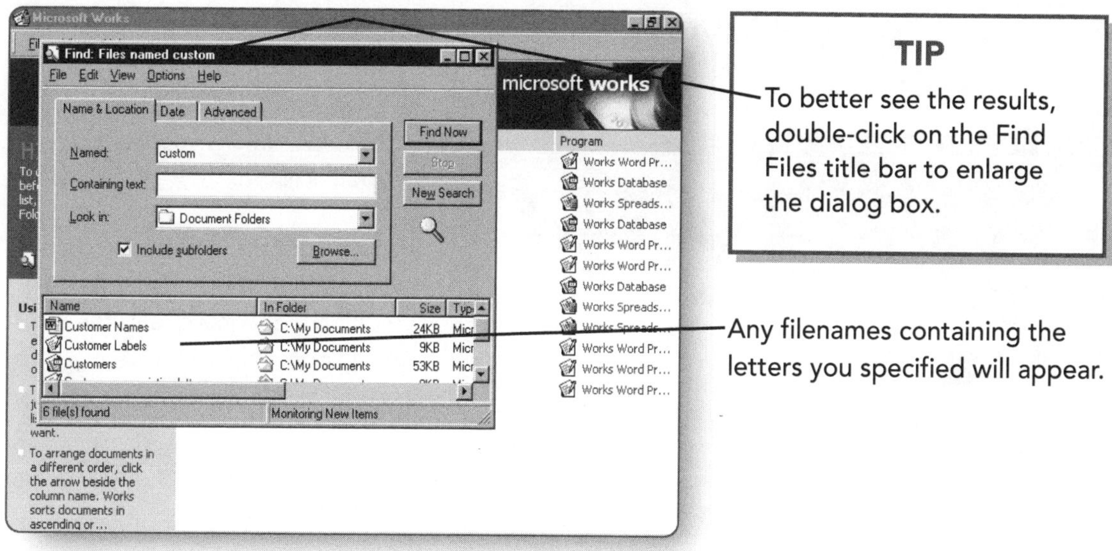

TIP

To better see the results, double-click on the Find Files title bar to enlarge the dialog box.

Any filenames containing the letters you specified will appear.

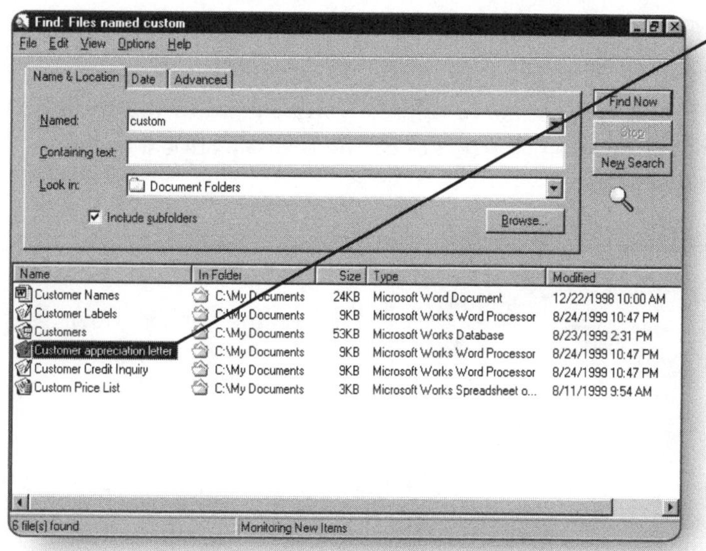

4. Double-click on the **filename** you want to open. The file will be placed on your screen, ready for you to edit.

Opening Multiple Documents

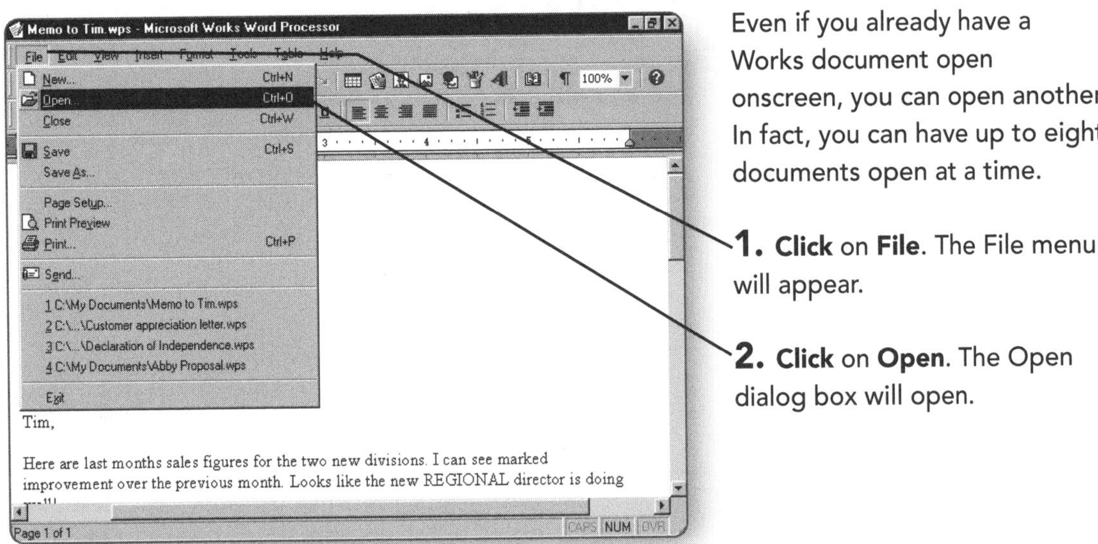

Even if you already have a Works document open onscreen, you can open another. In fact, you can have up to eight documents open at a time.

1. Click on **File**. The File menu will appear.

2. Click on **Open**. The Open dialog box will open.

3. Click on the **filename** you want to open. The filename will be highlighted and appear in the File name: text box.

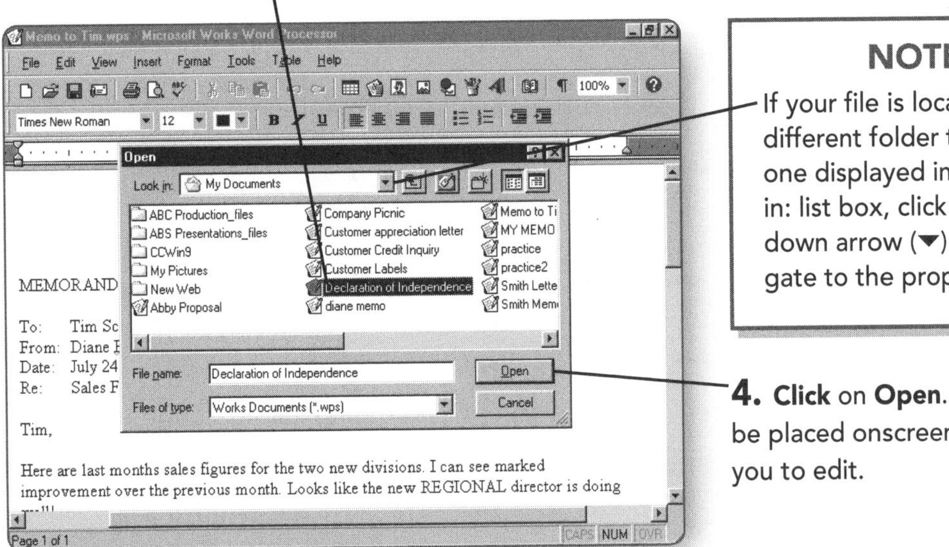

> **NOTE**
>
> If your file is located in a different folder than the one displayed in the Look in: list box, click on the down arrow (▼) to navigate to the proper folder.

4. Click on **Open**. The file will be placed onscreen, ready for you to edit.

Working with Multiple Documents

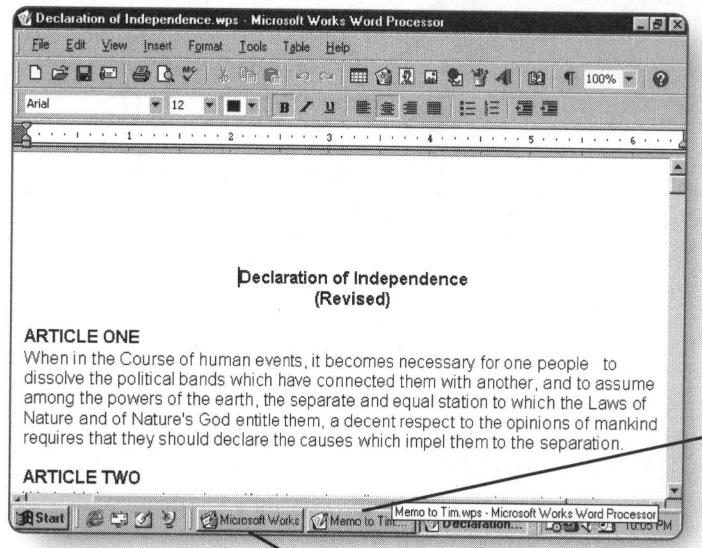

Although multiple documents can be open, only one document can be edited at a time. Use the Windows Taskbar to locate and switch to a different open document. When more than one document is open at a time, one document will be displayed on top of all the others.

1. **Click** the **name of the document** that you want to edit. The document appears on top of the stack of open documents.

Click on the Microsoft Works icon to activate the Works Task Launcher.

Closing a Document

When you are finished working on a document, you should close it. Closing is the equivalent of putting it away for later use. When you close a document, you are putting only the document away—not the program. Works is still active and ready to work for you.

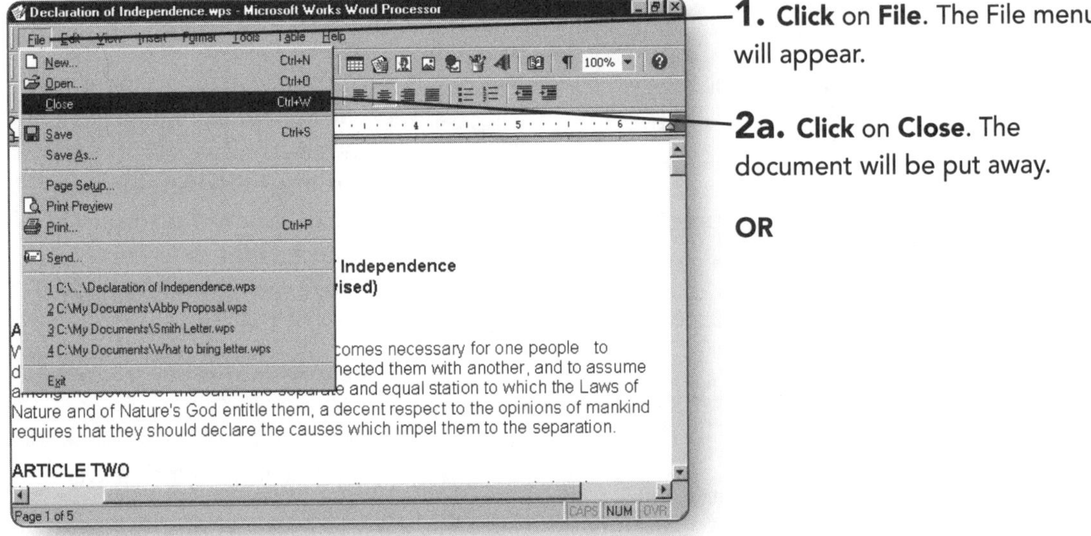

1. Click on **File**. The File menu will appear.

2a. Click on **Close**. The document will be put away.

OR

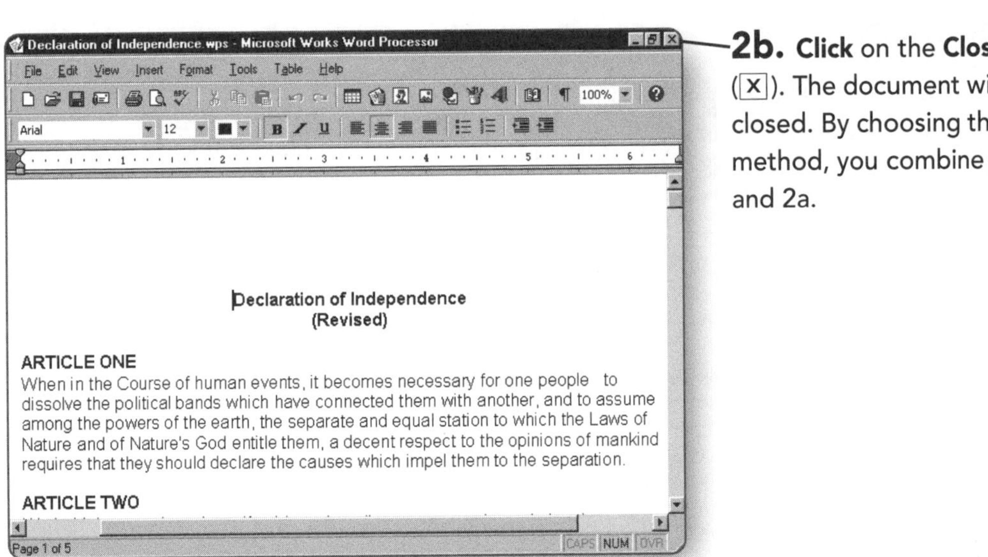

2b. Click on the **Close button** ([X]). The document will be closed. By choosing this method, you combine steps 1 and 2a.

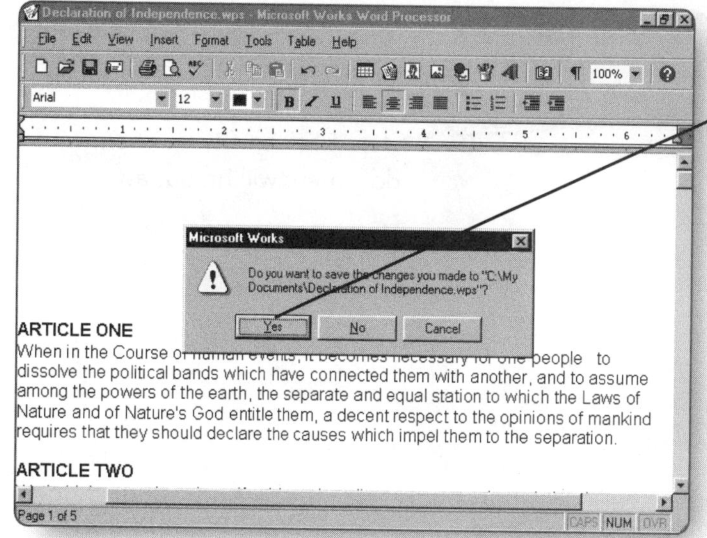

NOTE

If you close a document with changes that have not been saved, Works prompts you with a dialog box. Choose Yes to save the changes or No to close the file without saving the changes.

If you have no other documents open, the Task Launcher will reappear.

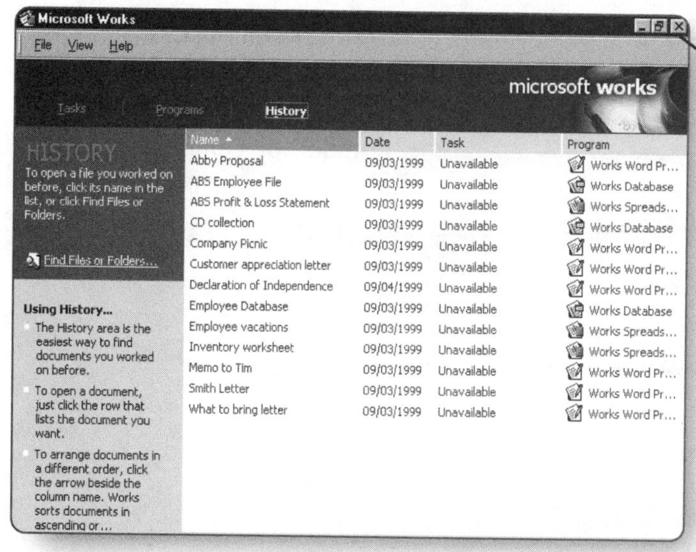

TIP

The Works program will not close until you click on the Close button (X) to close the Works Task Launcher.

Part II Review Questions

1. What two keys can you press to quickly move to the beginning of a document? *See "Moving Around Using the Keyboard" in Chapter 3*
2. What feature will reverse the last step you performed? *See "Undoing Mistakes" in Chapter 3*
3. How often should you save a document? *See "Resaving a Document" in Chapter 3*
4. What are the four types of text alignment? *See "Setting Paragraph Alignment" in Chapter 4*
5. What should you display if you are going to be working with tabs? *See "Displaying the Ruler" in Chapter 4*
6. In a table, what key is used to move the insertion point from one cell to the next? *See "Entering Text into a Table" in Chapter 5*
7. What two areas of a document are reserved for repeating text? *See "Adding a Header or Footer" in Chapter 6*
8. Around which parts of your document can borders be placed? *See "Adding Borders" in Chapter 7*
9. When using Spell Check, what is the difference between the options Ignore and Ignore All? *See* "Running a Spelling and Grammar Check" *in Chapter 8*
10. What screen on the Task Launcher is used to open a previously created document? *See "Opening a Document from the Task Launcher" in Chapter 9*

PART III

Using Spreadsheets

10

Creating a Spreadsheet

Works has a full-featured spreadsheet program that you can use to make calculations, create charts, and even sort data. In this chapter, you'll learn how to:

- Create a new spreadsheet
- Explore and move around in the spreadsheet screen
- Enter and edit labels and values
- Undo mistakes
- Save a spreadsheet

Opening a New Spreadsheet

Create a new spreadsheet from the Works Task Launcher.

1. **Click** on **Programs**. A list of Works programs will appear.

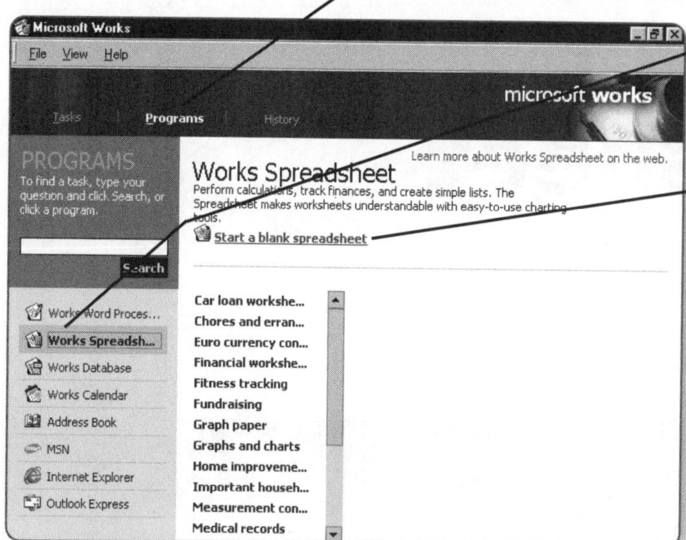

2. **Click** on **Works Spreadsheet**. A list of spreadsheet tasks will appear.

3. **Click** on **Start a blank spreadsheet**. A blank spreadsheet will appear on your screen.

> **NOTE**
>
> If the Help window is open, you may want to close it to better display your spreadsheet.

Exploring the Spreadsheet Screen

Many items that you see when you open a new spreadsheet are standard to most Windows 95 or Windows 98 programs.

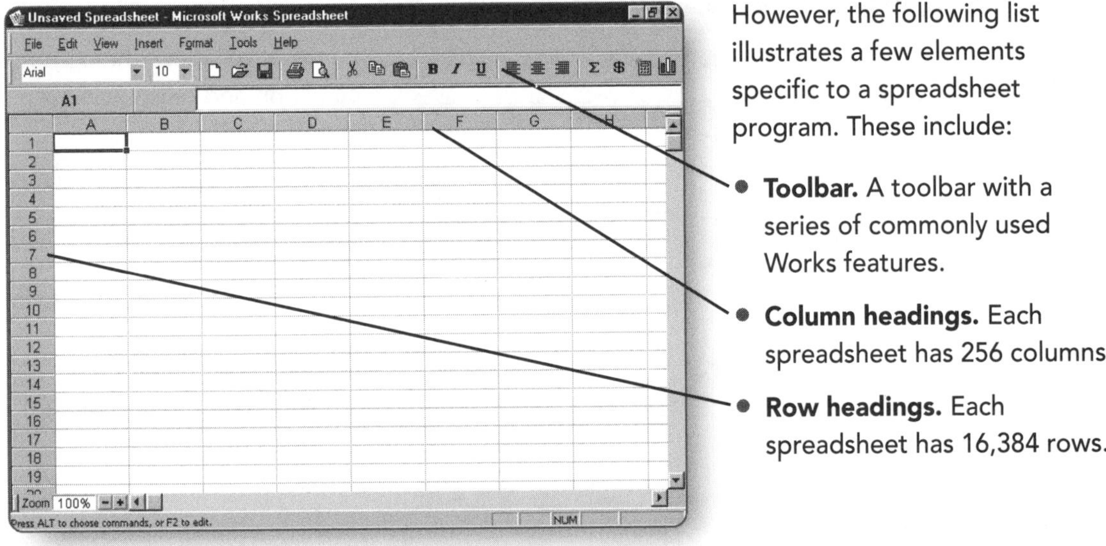

However, the following list illustrates a few elements specific to a spreadsheet program. These include:

- **Toolbar.** A toolbar with a series of commonly used Works features.
- **Column headings.** Each spreadsheet has 256 columns.
- **Row headings.** Each spreadsheet has 16,384 rows.

- **Edit line.** This line consists of several parts:

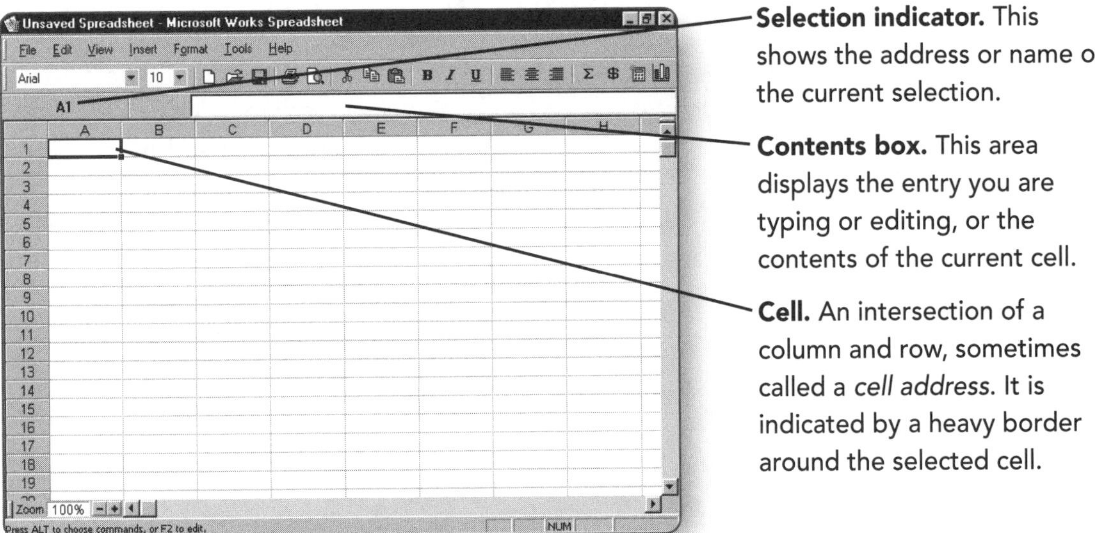

Selection indicator. This shows the address or name of the current selection.

Contents box. This area displays the entry you are typing or editing, or the contents of the current cell.

Cell. An intersection of a column and row, sometimes called a *cell address*. It is indicated by a heavy border around the selected cell.

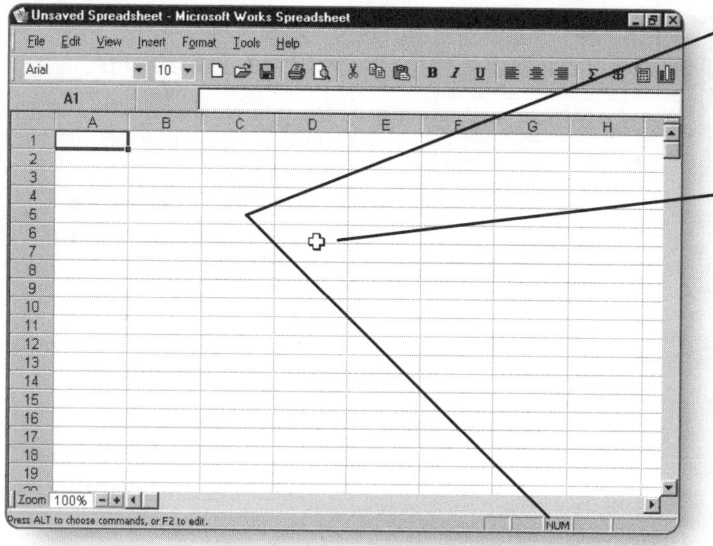

- **Status bar.** Gives you information about the current selection and tells you what Works is doing.
- **Mouse pointer**. Often, while you're using a spreadsheet, the mouse pointer will look like a white cross. You'll see in Chapter 11, "Editing a Spreadsheet," where the mouse pointer may change its shape.

Moving Around the Spreadsheet Screen

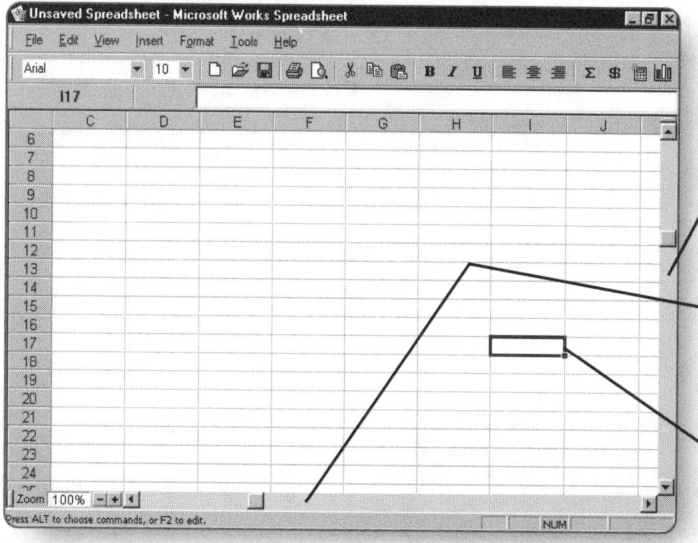

You can use your mouse or keyboard to quickly move around in a spreadsheet.

1. **Click** on the **vertical scroll bar** until the row you are looking for is visible.
2. **Click** on the **horizontal scroll bar** until the column you are looking for is visible.
3. **Click** on the **desired cell**. It will become the current cell.

The following table describes keyboard methods for moving around in your spreadsheet:

Keystroke	Result
Arrow keys	Move one cell at a time up, down, left, or right
Page Down	Moves one screen down
Page Up	Moves one screen up
Home	Moves to column A of the current row
Ctrl+Home	Moves to cell A1
F5	Displays the GoTo dialog box, which enables you to specify a cell address

Entering Data

Spreadsheet data is made up of three components: labels, values, and formulas. *Labels* are traditionally descriptive pieces of information, such as names, months, or types of products.

Entering Labels into Cells

Works identifies a cell as a label if it begins with a letter or a prefix character.

1. Click on the **cell** where you want to place the label. A border will appear around the selected cell.

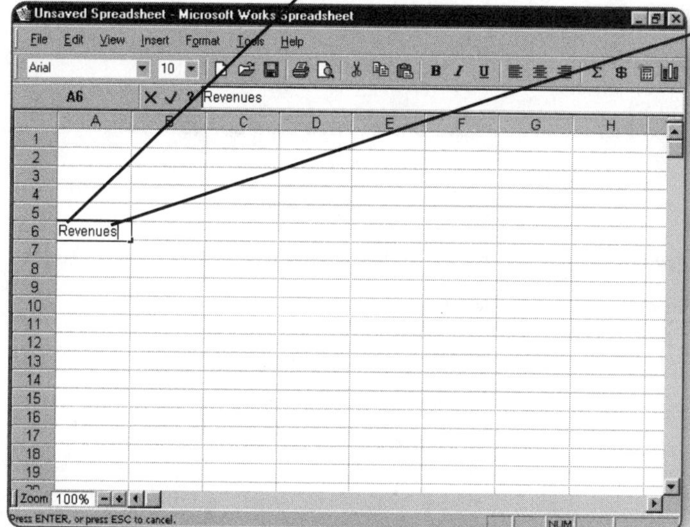

2. Type text. A blinking insertion point will appear.

> **TIP**
>
> If you make a mistake and you have not yet pressed Enter, press the Backspace key to delete characters and type a correction, or press the Escape key to cancel the typing.

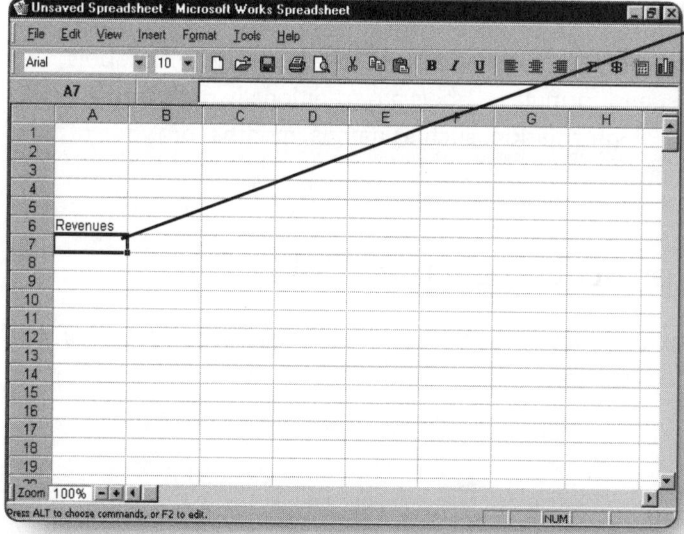

3. Press Enter to accept the label. The text will be entered and will align along the left edge of the cell. The next cell down will be selected.

4. Repeat steps 1 through **3** for each label you want to enter.

> **NOTE**
>
> Optionally, you could press an arrow key instead of the Enter key. This not only accepts the cell you were typing in but also moves to the next cell in the direction of the arrow key at the same time.

Entering Values into Cells

Values are the raw numbers that you track in a spreadsheet. There is no need to enter commas or dollar signs. Let Works do that for you later.

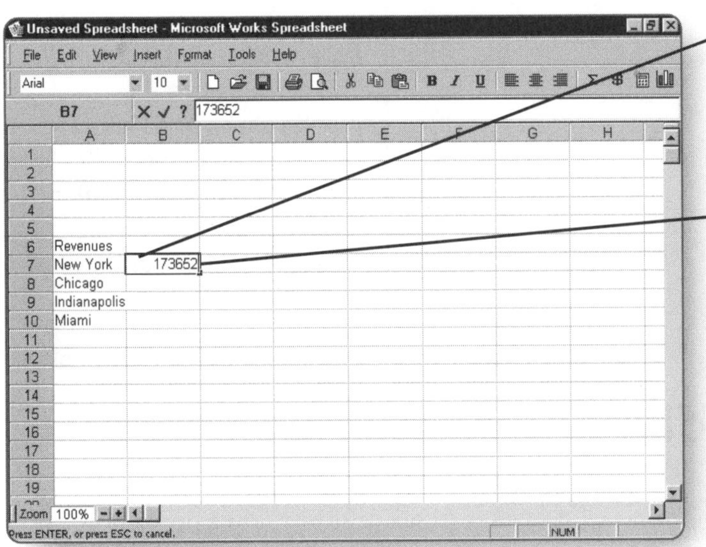

1. **Click** on the **cell** where you want to place the value. A border will appear around the selected cell.

2. **Type** the numerical **value**. A blinking insertion point will appear.

3. **Press Enter** to accept the value. The number will be entered into the cell, and the selection will move to the next cell down.

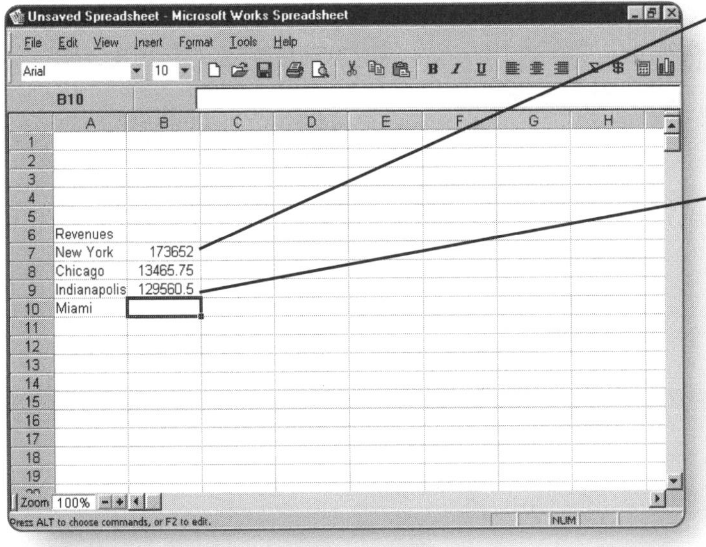

Notice how values are aligned along the right edge of the cell.

> **NOTE**
>
> If you entered a number such as 39.95, that is exactly what will be displayed in the cell; however, if you entered 39.50, the spreadsheet will display 39.5 (without the trailing zero). Don't worry; nothing is lost. You will change the appearance later.

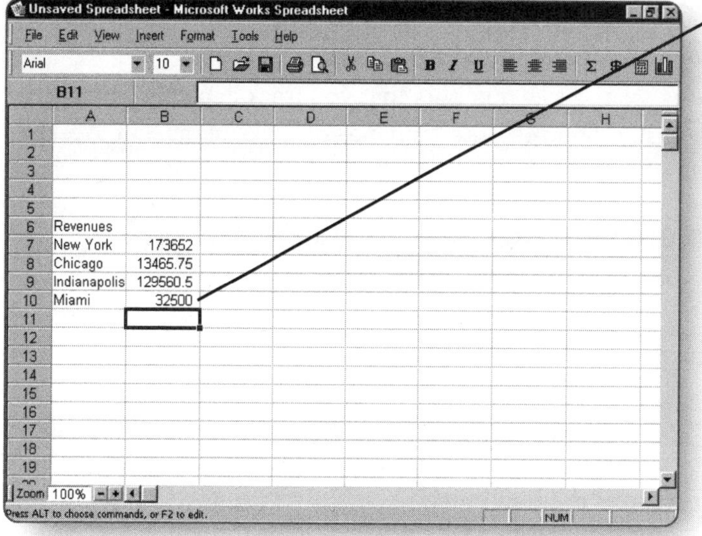

4. Repeat steps 1 through **3** for each value you want to enter.

> **TIP**
>
> To enter a value as a label, type a quotation (") character before the number, such as "1997. The quotation character tells Works that the information is a label. The quotation character will not display in your spreadsheet.

Editing Data

You can edit your data in a variety of ways. You may need to change the contents of a cell, or you may want to move the data to another part of the spreadsheet.

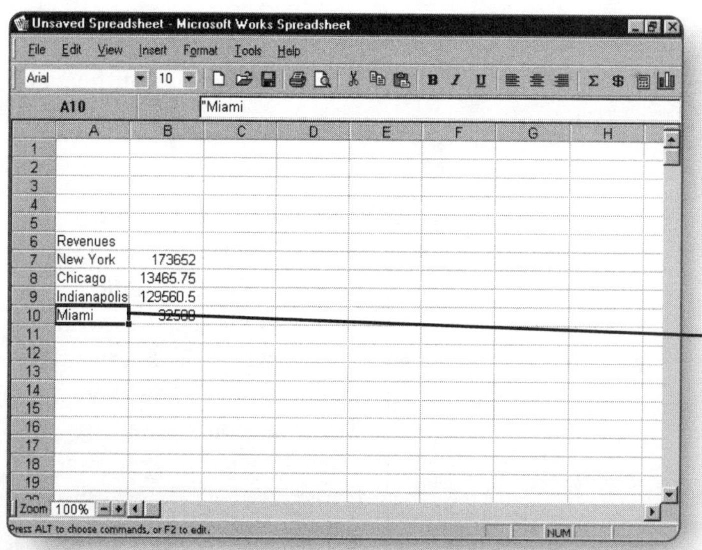

Replacing the Contents of a Cell

You can make changes to the contents of a cell in two ways. One is by typing over the contents of a cell.

1. Click on a **cell**. The cell and its contents will be selected.

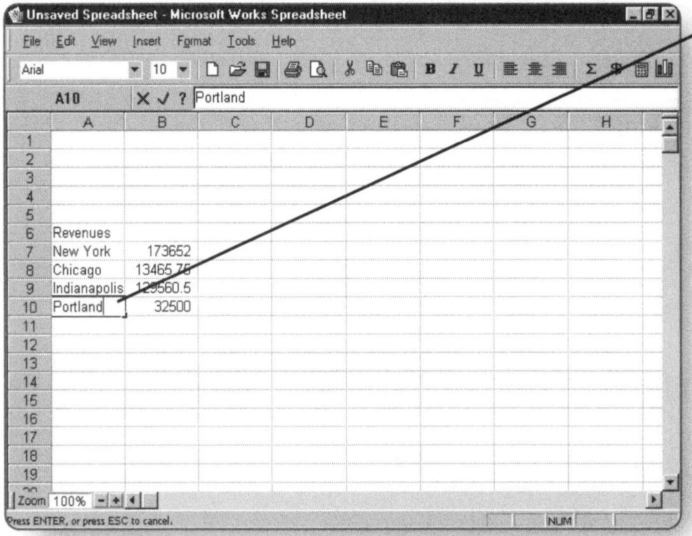

2. Type new **text**. The new text will appear in the cell.

3. Press Enter. The text will be entered in the selected cell.

Editing the Contents of a Cell

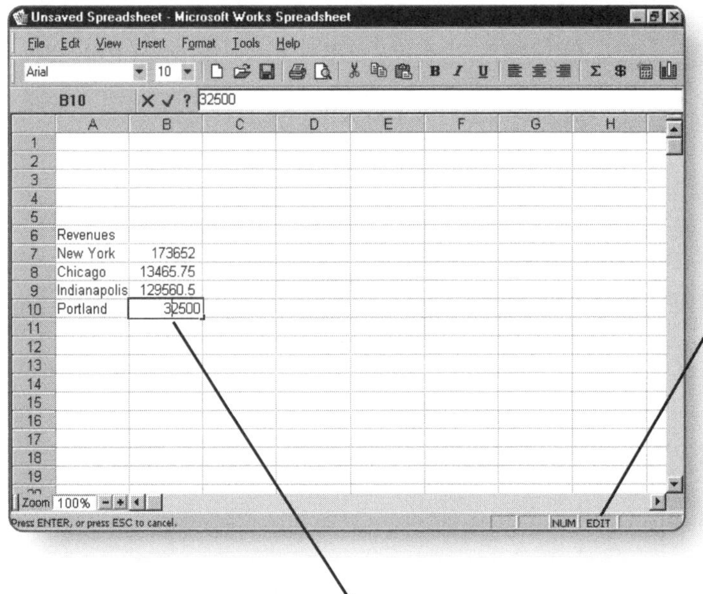

The other method to make changes to the contents of a cell is by using the Edit feature.

1. Double-click on the **cell** to be edited. The insertion point will blink within the cell.

Edit mode is indicated on the status bar.

> **TIP**
>
> You can also press the F2 key to edit the contents of a cell.

2. Press the **left arrow key**. The insertion point will be relocated within the current cell.

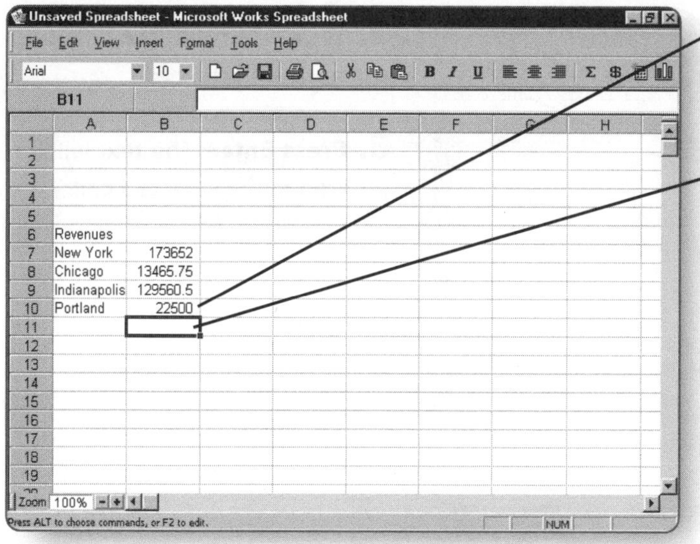

3. Type the **changes**. The changes will appear in the current cell.

4. Press Enter. The changes will be entered into the current cell and the selection will move to the next cell.

Undoing Mistakes

If you make a mistake while working in a spreadsheet, STOP! Don't go any farther. Works can reverse the last step you took.

1. Click on **Edit**. The Edit menu will appear.

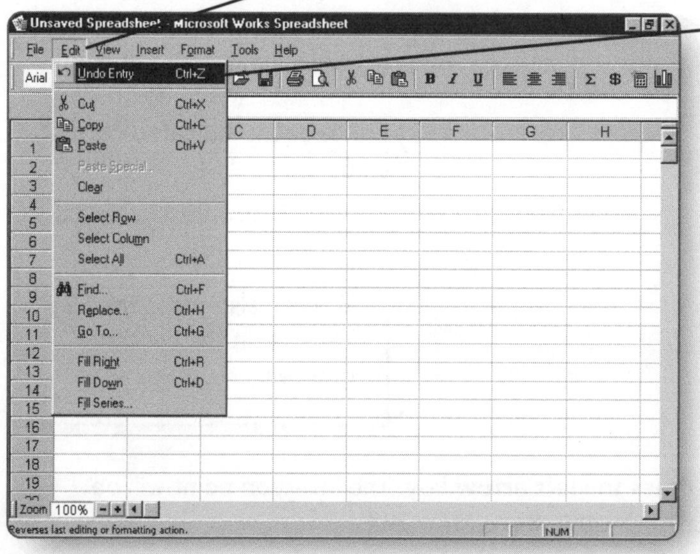

2. Click on **Undo Entry**. The last step you took will be reversed.

Saving a Spreadsheet

As you create a spreadsheet in Works, it is stored temporarily in the computer's memory. That memory is erased when you exit Works or when you turn off the computer. To prevent losing your work, you need to save it.

Saving a Spreadsheet the First Time

When you first create a spreadsheet, it is untitled. To save the spreadsheet for use again at a later date, you must give it a name. When you have saved a spreadsheet, the name appears at the top of the screen in the title bar.

1. **Click** on **File**. The File menu will appear.

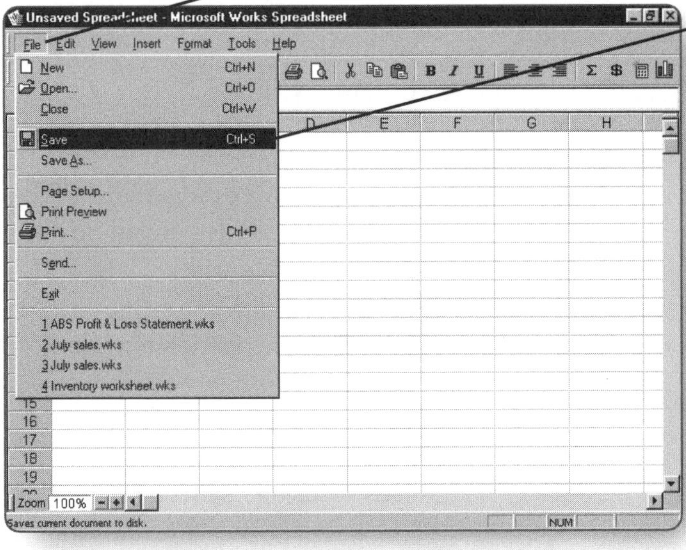

2. **Click** on **Save**. The Save As dialog box will open.

TIP

If you want to save the spreadsheet with a different name or in a different folder, click on File, then choose Save As. The Save As dialog box prompts you for the new name or folder. The original document remains as well as the new one.

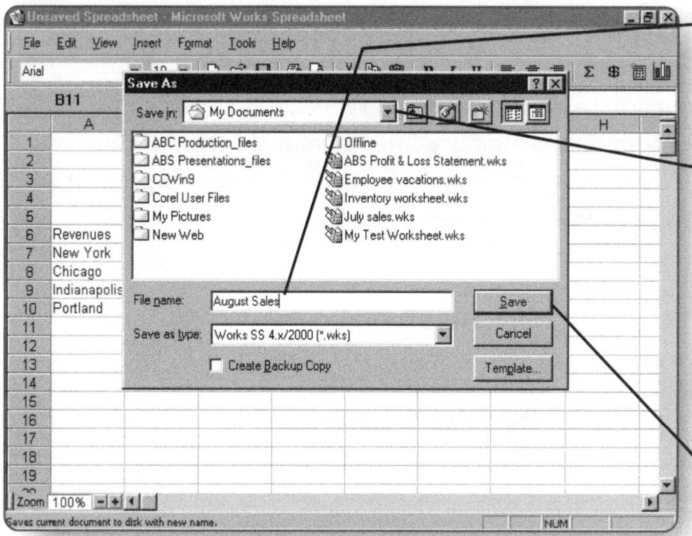

3. Type a **name** for your file in the File name: text box. The file name will be displayed.

The Save in: drop-down list box shows the folder where the file will be saved. The default folder that appears is My Documents. If you want to save to a different folder or disk, you can select another one. Click on the down arrow (▼) to browse.

4. Click on **Save**. Your spreadsheet will be saved, and the name you specified will appear in the title bar.

Resaving a Spreadsheet

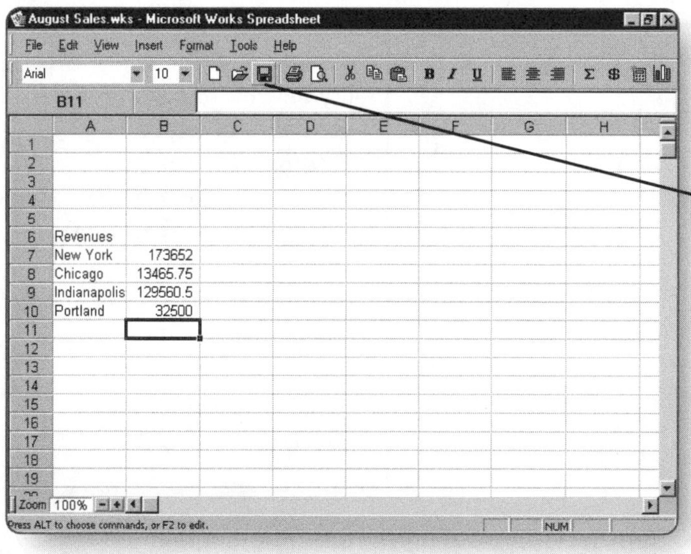

You should resave your spreadsheet every ten minutes or so to ensure that you do not lose any changes.

1. Click on the **Save button**. The spreadsheet will be resaved with any changes. No dialog box will appear because the spreadsheet is being resaved with the same name and in the same folder as previously specified.

11

Editing a Spreadsheet

Frequently after data is entered into a spreadsheet, you'll need to change the location of the data. You can insert or delete rows or columns as needed or just move the data to a new location. In this chapter, you'll learn how to:

- Select cells, rows, and columns
- Insert and delete rows and columns
- Move data
- Use the Fill feature

Learning Selection Techniques

TIP

Make sure that the mouse pointer is a white plus before attempting to select cells.

To move, copy, delete, or change the formatting of data in the spreadsheet, the cells to be modified must first be selected. When cells are selected, they appear black onscreen—just the reverse of unselected text. An exception to this is if a block of cells is selected. In this case, the first cell will not be black—it will have a black border around it. The following table describes some of the different selection techniques.

To Select	Do This
A A cell	Click on the desired cell.
B A column	Click on the column letter at the top of the screen.
C A row	Click on the row number on the left side of the screen.
D A sequential block of cells	Click on the first cell and drag to highlight the rest of the cells.

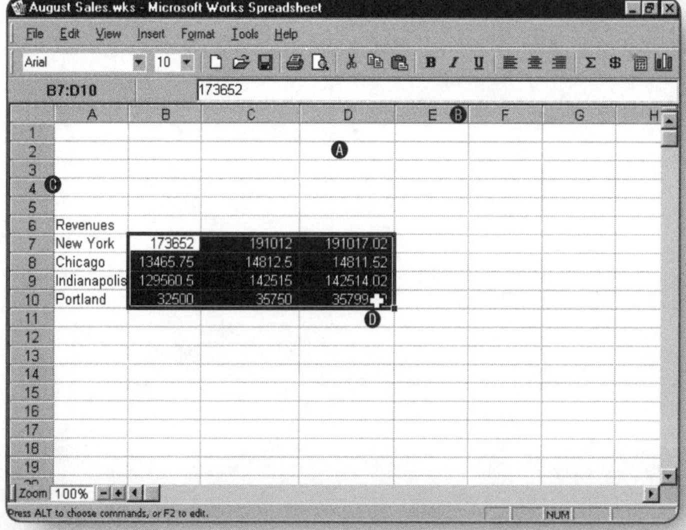

NOTE

Microsoft Works does not allow for a group of nonsequential cells to be selected.

TIP

To deselect a block of cells, click the mouse in any other cell.

Inserting Rows and Columns

Occasionally, you need a column or a row to be inserted into the middle of information that you have already entered. Each worksheet always has 256 columns and 16,384 rows.

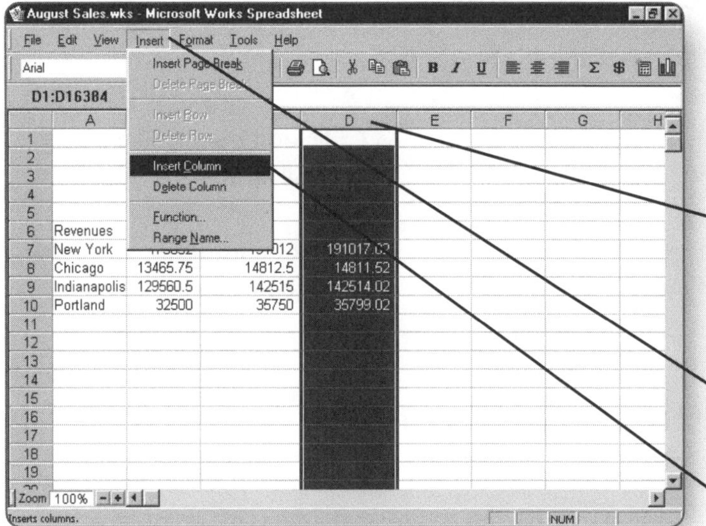

Inserting Columns

Inserting a column moves existing data to the right of the new column.

1. **Click** on the **Column Heading letter** where you want to insert the new column. The entire column will be selected.
2. **Click** on **Insert.** The Insert menu will appear.
3. **Click** on **Insert Column**. A new column will be inserted.

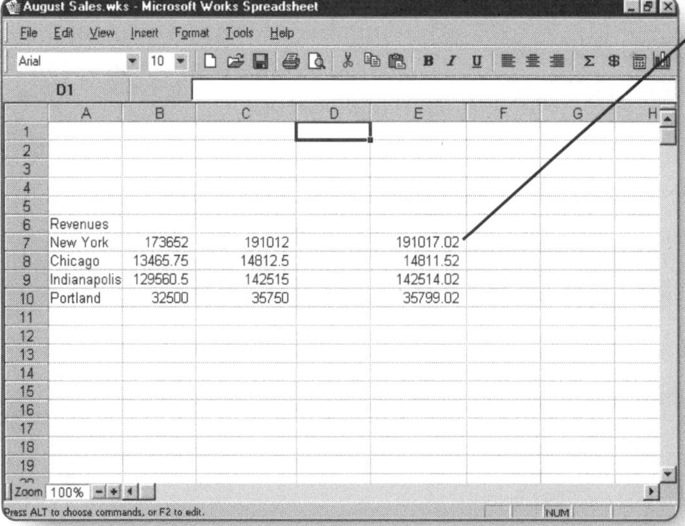

Existing columns move to the right.

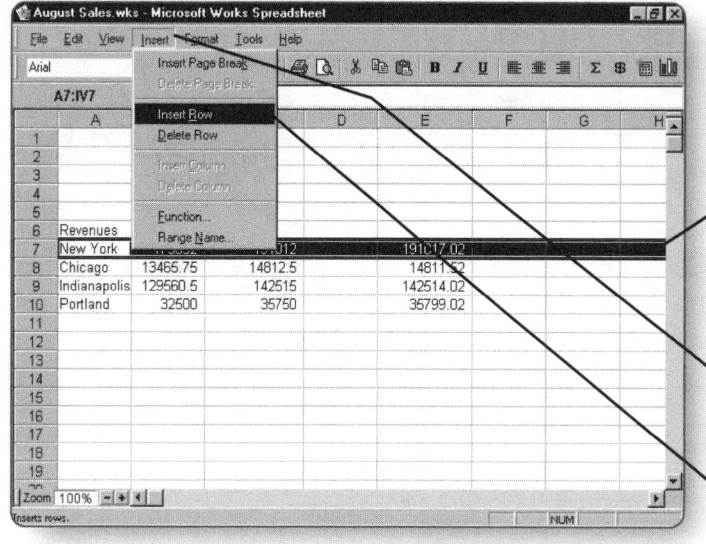

Inserting Rows

Inserting a row moves existing data down one row.

1. Click on the **Row Heading number** where you want to insert the new row. The entire row will be selected.

2. Click on **Insert.** The Insert menu will appear.

3. Click on **Insert Row**. A new row will be inserted.

Deleting Rows and Columns

Use caution when deleting a row or column. Deleting a row deletes it across all 256 columns; deleting a column deletes it down all 16,384 rows.

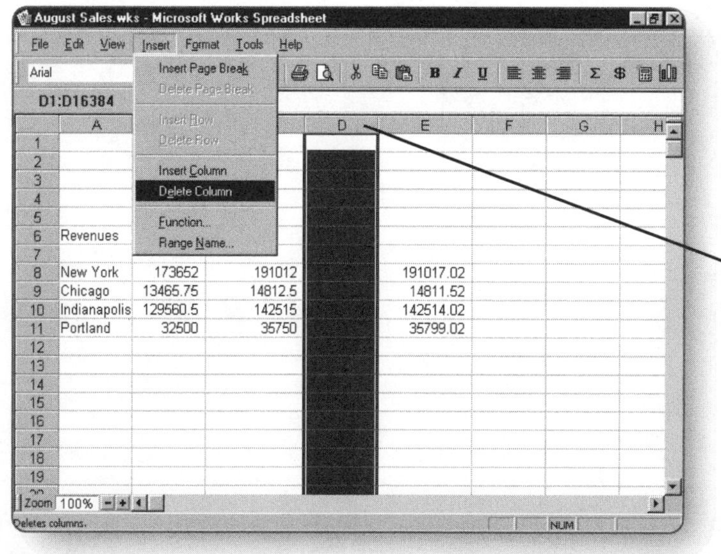

1a. Select the **Row Heading number** of the row that you want to delete. The row will be highlighted.

OR

1b. Select the **Column Heading letter** of the column that you want to delete. The column will be highlighted.

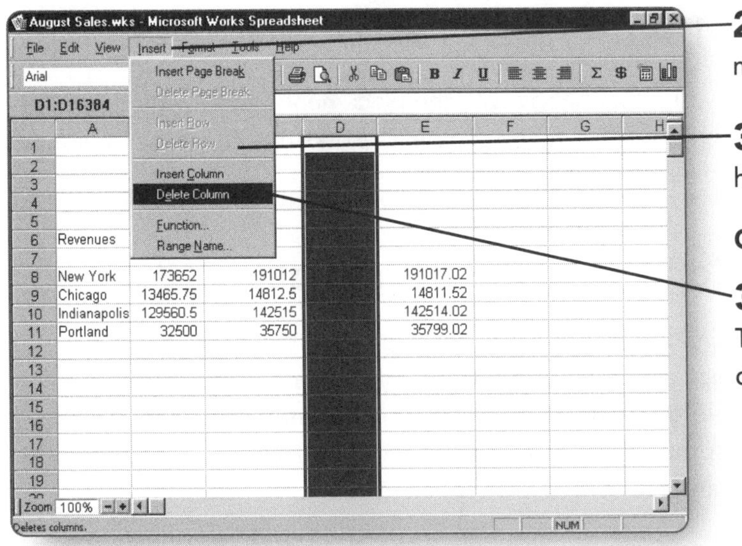

2. Click on **Insert**. The Insert menu will appear.

3a. Choose Delete Row. The highlighted row will be deleted.

OR

3b. Choose Delete Column. The highlighted column will be deleted.

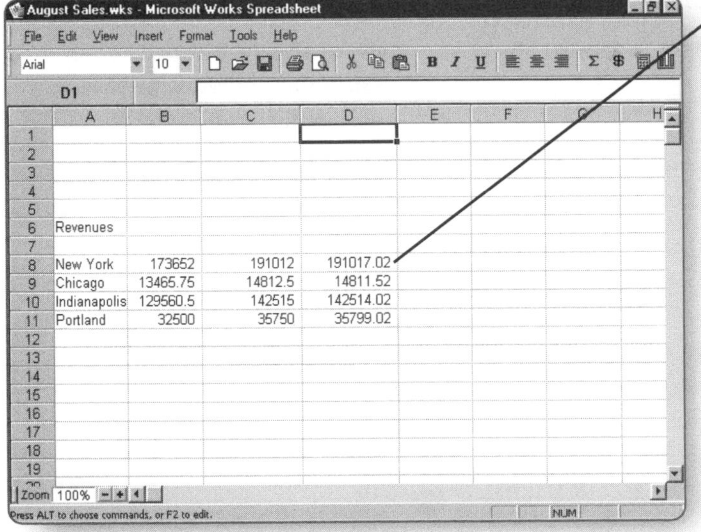

Remaining columns move to the left; remaining rows move up.

Moving Data Around

If you're not happy with the placement of data, you don't have to delete it and retype it. Works makes it easy for you to move it around.

Copying and Pasting Cells

Windows comes with a feature called the Clipboard. The Clipboard temporarily holds information in memory. It is helpful if you want to transfer information from one place to another. To copy information, Works uses the Copy and Paste features.

1. **Select** some **cells** to be duplicated. The cells will be highlighted.

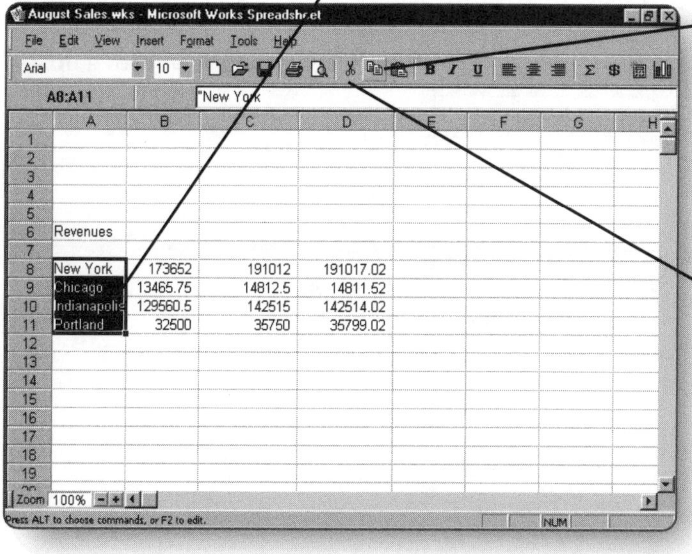

2. **Click** on the **Copy button**. It won't look like anything happened; however, the text will be duplicated to the Clipboard.

> **TIP**
>
> If you want to move the information from one cell to another, click on the Cut button instead.

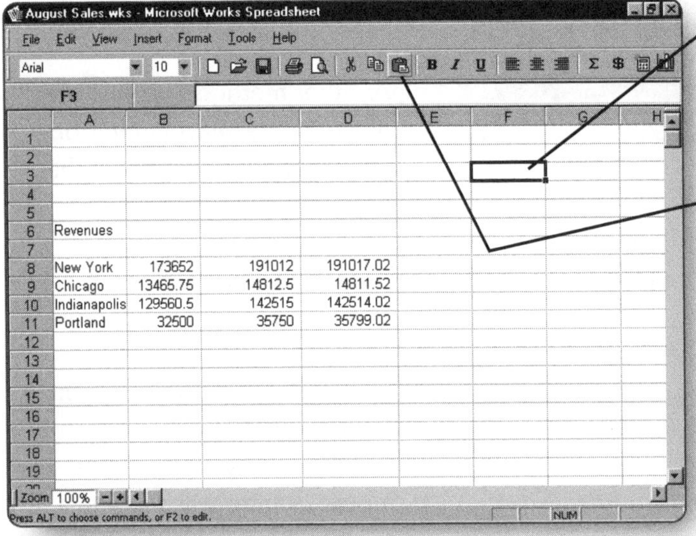

3. Click on the beginning **cell** where you want to place the duplicated information. The cell will be highlighted.

4. Click on the **Paste button**. The information will be copied to the new location.

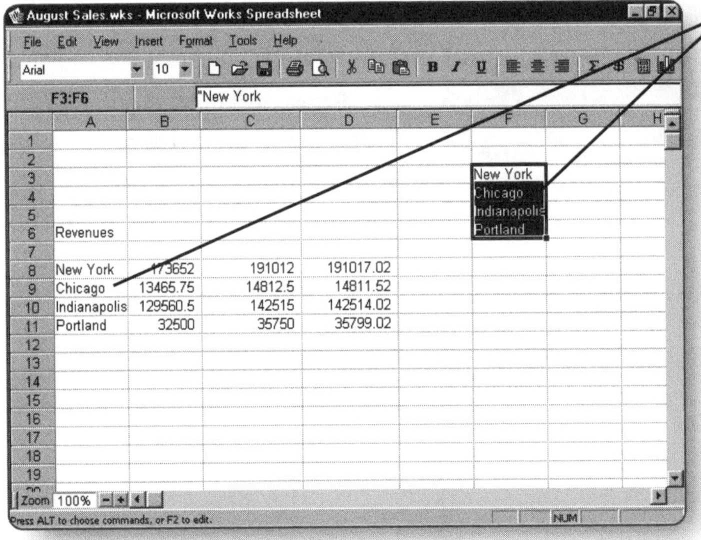

When using the Copy command, the original cells retain the information you copied.

TIP

If you pasted the cells in the wrong area, click on the Edit menu and choose Undo Paste to reverse the step.

Using Drag and Drop to Move Cells

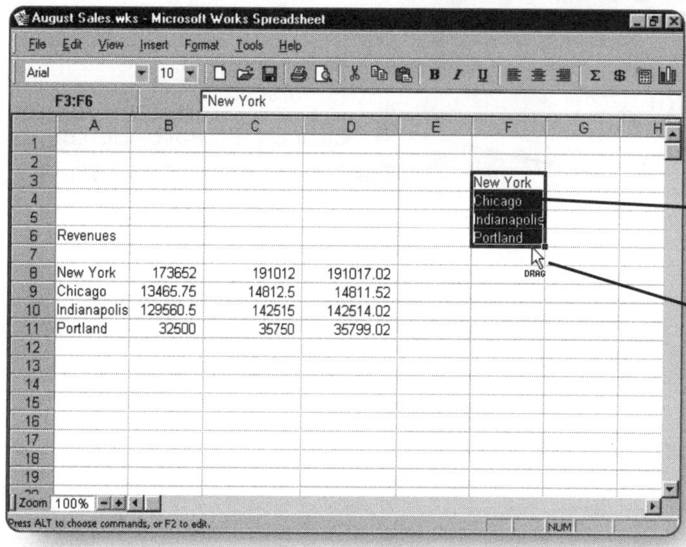

Another method that you can use to move information from one location to another is the drag-and-drop method.

1. Select some **cells** to move. The cells will be highlighted.

2. Position the **mouse pointer** around one of the outside edges of the selection. The mouse pointer will become a small white arrow with the word "DRAG" displayed.

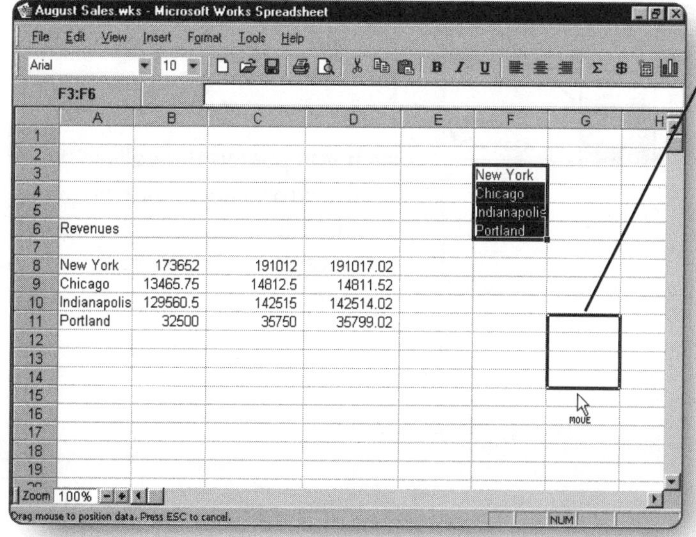

3. Press and **hold** the **mouse button** and **drag** the **cell** to a new location. The "DRAG" command changes to "MOVE." The second box represents where the moved cells will be located.

4. Release the **mouse button**. The cells will be moved.

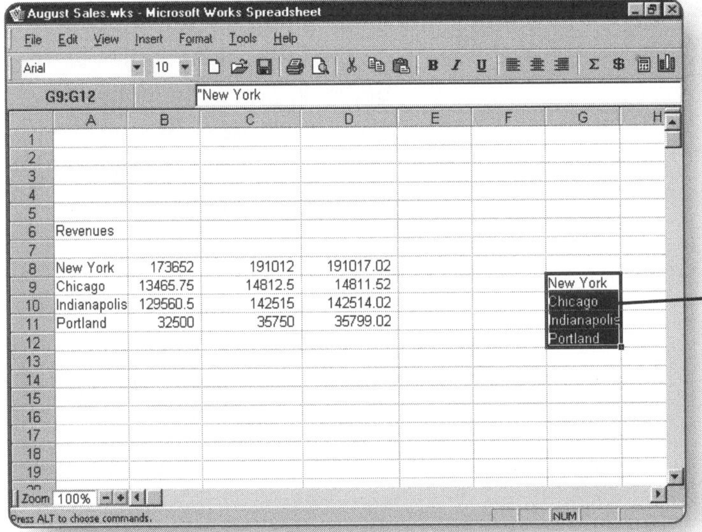

Clearing Cell Contents

If you have data that you no longer want in cells, you can easily delete the data.

1. Select some **cells** to be cleared. The cells will be highlighted.

2. Press the **Delete key**. The contents of the cells will be removed.

Using the Fill Feature

Works has a great built-in time-saving feature called Fill. If you give Works the beginning month, day, season, or numbers, it can fill in the rest of the pattern for you. For example, if you type January, Works fills in February, March, April, and so on.

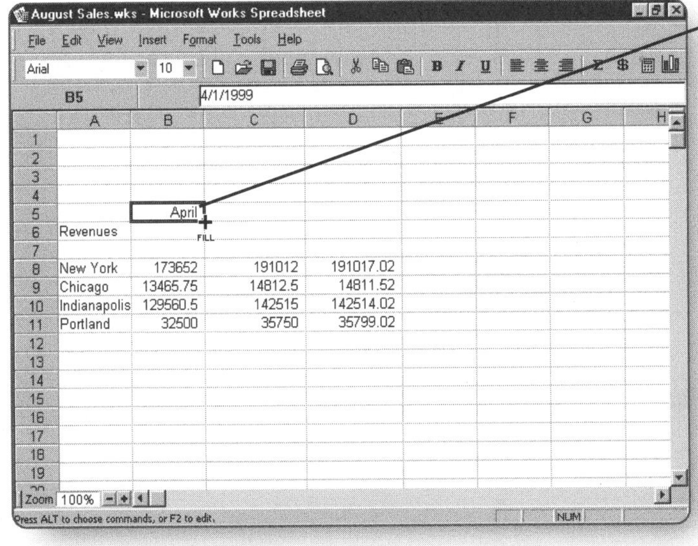

1. Type the **beginning month, day, or season** in the beginning cell. The text will be displayed in the cell.

If you want Works to fill in numbers, you must first give it a pattern. For example, enter the value of "1" in the first cell and then enter "2" in the second cell.

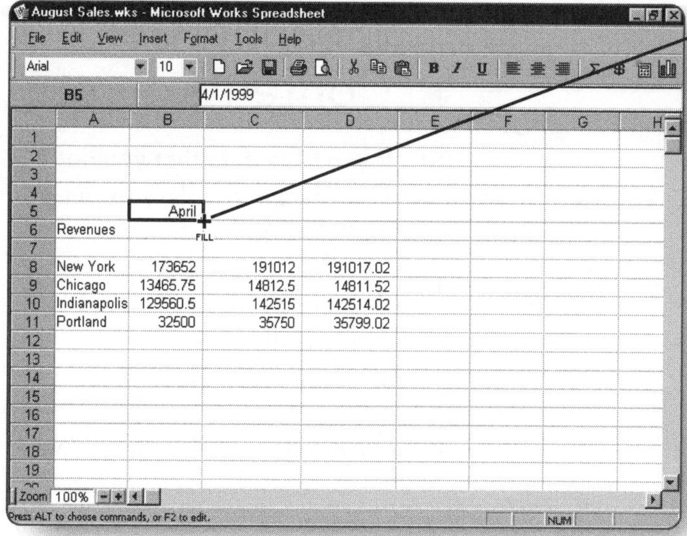

2. **Position** the **mouse pointer** on the lower-right corner of the beginning cell. The mouse pointer will become a small black cross with the word "FILL" displayed.

> **TIP**
>
> For numbers, select both the first and second cells before proceeding to step 3.

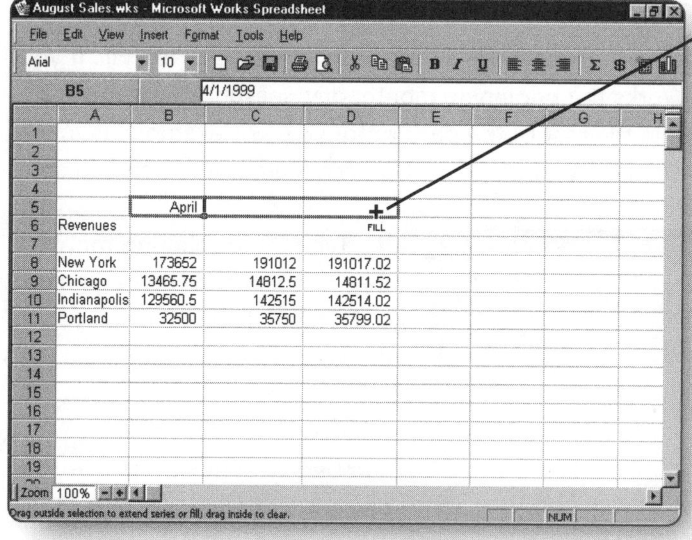

3. **Press** and **hold** the **mouse button** and **drag** to select the next cells to be filled in. The cells will have a gray border surrounding them.

4. **Release** the **mouse button**. The pattern will be repeated.

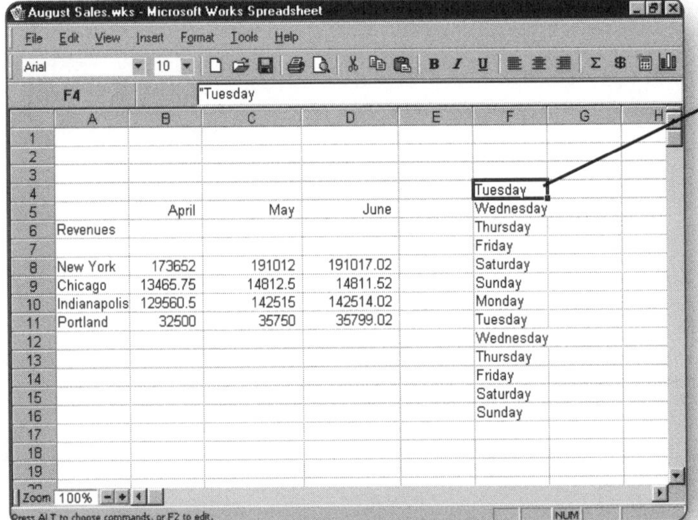

TIP

A pattern will begin with wherever you start and will repeat if necessary. For example, if you fill up the cells with Tuesday, Wednesday, Thursday all the way through Monday, and still have cells to fill, Works will begin with Tuesday again.

12

Working with Functions and Formulas

Formulas in a Works spreadsheet do calculations for you. For example, by referencing a cell address in a formula, if the data in the cell changes, so will the formula answer. In this chapter, you'll learn how to:

- Create simple and compound formulas
- Copy formulas
- Create an absolute reference
- Use functions

Creating Formulas

All formulas must begin with the equal (=) sign, regardless of whether the formula consists of adding, subtracting, multiplying, or dividing.

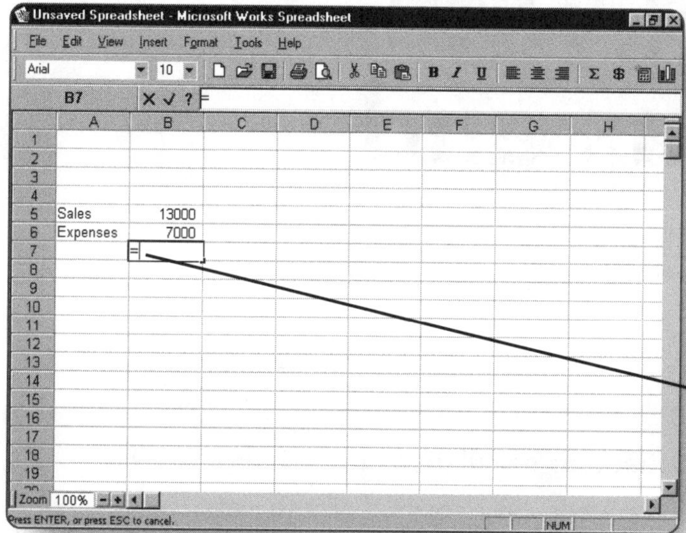

Creating a Simple Formula

An example of a simple formula might be =B5–B6.

1. Click on the **cell** in which you want to place the formula answer. The cell will be selected.

2. Type an **equal sign (=)** to begin the formula. The symbol will appear in the cell.

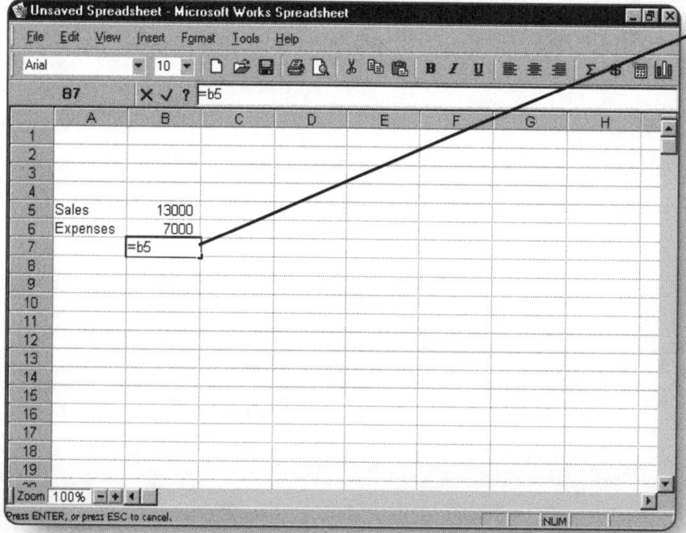

3. Type the **cell address** of the first cell to be included in the formula. This is called the cell *reference*. In this example, the cell reference B5 is referring to the value of 13000.

> **NOTE**
>
> Spreadsheet formulas are not case sensitive. For example, B5 is the same as b5.

A formula needs an *operator* to suggest the next action to be performed.

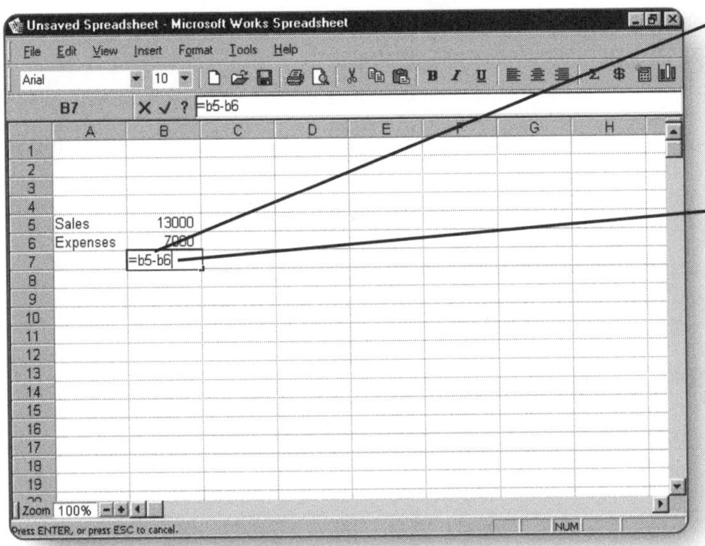

4. Type the **operator**: plus (+), minus (–), multiply (*), or divide (/). The operator will appear in the formula.

5. Type the **reference** to the second cell of the formula. The reference will appear in the cell.

6. Press Enter. The result of the calculation will appear in the cell.

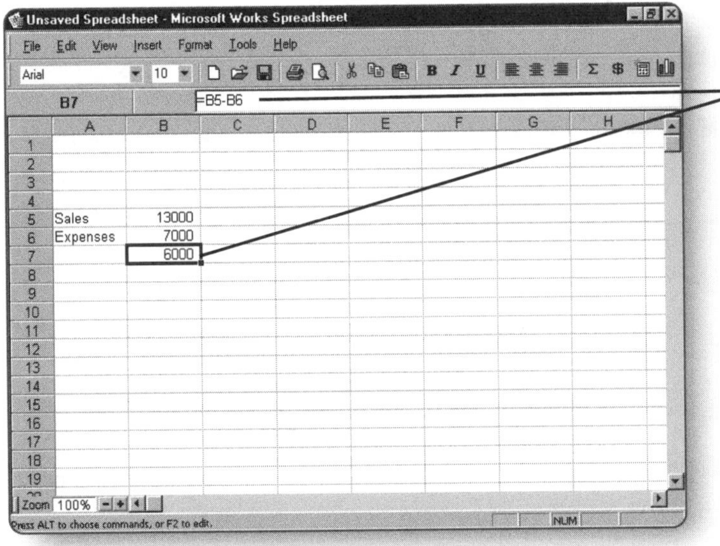

NOTE

Notice how the result appears in the cell, but the actual formula, =B5–B6, appears in the Contents box of the Edit line.

Creating a Compound Formula

You use compound formulas when you need more than one operator. Examples of a compound formula might be =B7+B8+B9+B10 or =B11–B19*A23.

> **NOTE**
>
> When you have a compound formula, Works does the multiplication and division first and then the addition and subtraction. If you want a certain portion of the formula to be calculated first, put it in parentheses. Works does whatever is in the parentheses before calculating the rest of the formula. The formula =B11–B19*A23 gives a totally different answer than =(B11–B19)*A23.

1. **Click** on the **cell** in which you want to place the formula answer. The cell will be selected.

2. **Type** an **equal sign (=)** to begin the formula. The symbol will appear in the cell.

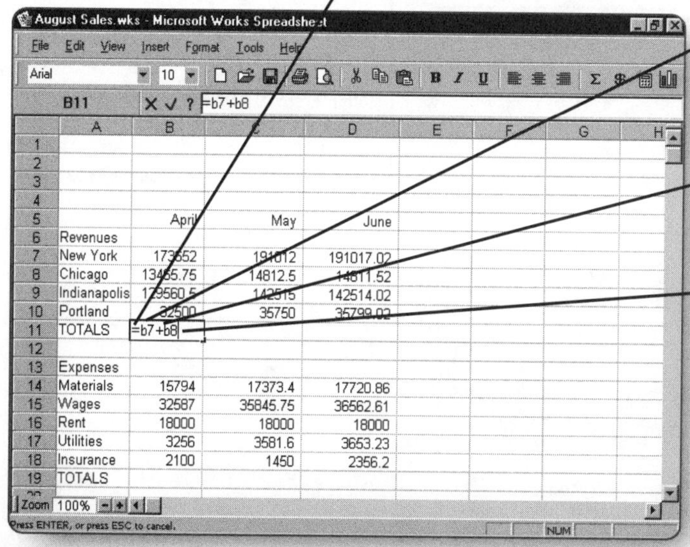

3. **Type** the **reference to the first cell** of the formula. The reference will appear in the cell.

4. **Type** the **operator**. The operator will appear in the cell.

5. **Type** the **reference to the second cell** of the formula. The reference will appear in the cell.

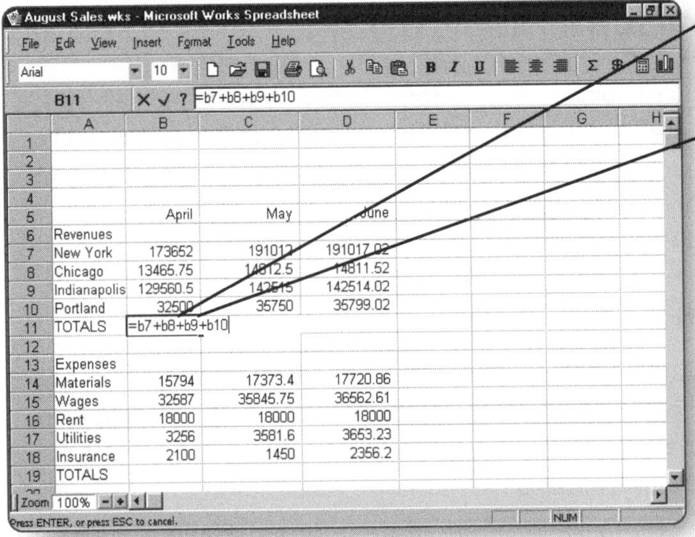

6. Type the **next operator**. The operator will appear in the cell.

7. Type the **reference to the third cell** of the formula. The reference will appear in the cell.

8. Repeat steps 6 and **7** until the formula is complete, adding the parentheses wherever necessary.

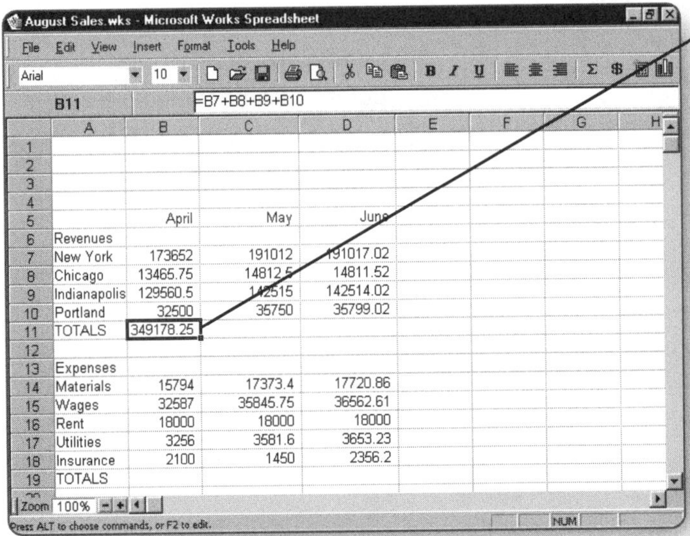

9. Press Enter to accept the formula. The calculation answer will appear in the cell, and the formula will appear in the content bar.

Try changing one of the values you originally typed in the spreadsheet and watch the answer to the formula change.

Copying Formulas

If you're going to copy a formula to a surrounding cell, you can use the Fill method. If the cells are not sequential, you can use Copy and Paste. Fill and Copy and Paste were discussed in Chapter 11, "Editing a Spreadsheet."

Copying Formulas Using Fill

Similar to filling a pattern of days, months, or seasons as you learned in the previous chapter, Works can also fill cells with the pattern of a formula.

1. **Click** on the **cell** that has the formula. The cell will be selected.

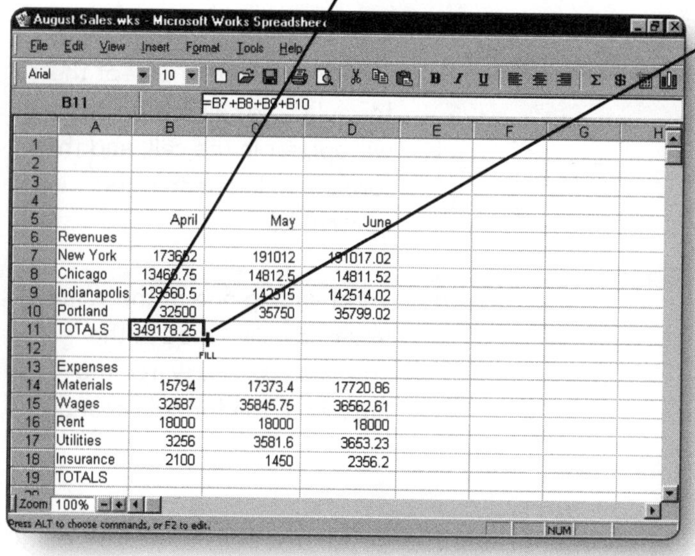

2. **Position** the **mouse pointer** on the lower-right corner of the beginning cell. The mouse pointer will become a black cross with the word "FILL" below it.

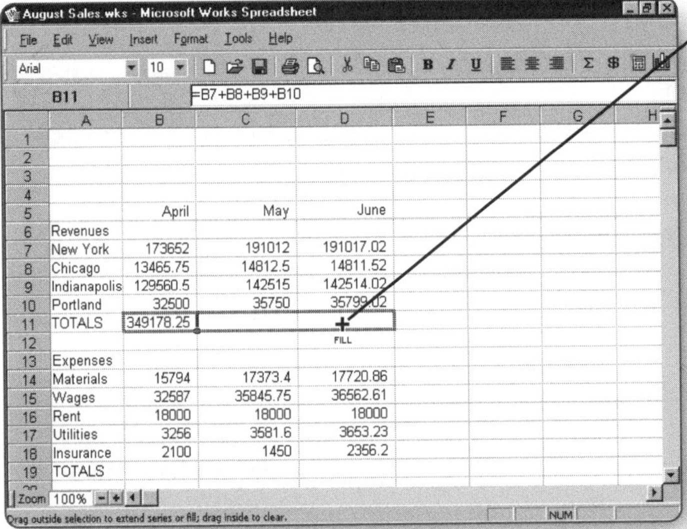

3. **Press** and **hold** the **mouse button** and **drag** to select the next cells to be filled in. The cells will be selected.

4. **Release** the **mouse button**. The formula will be copied.

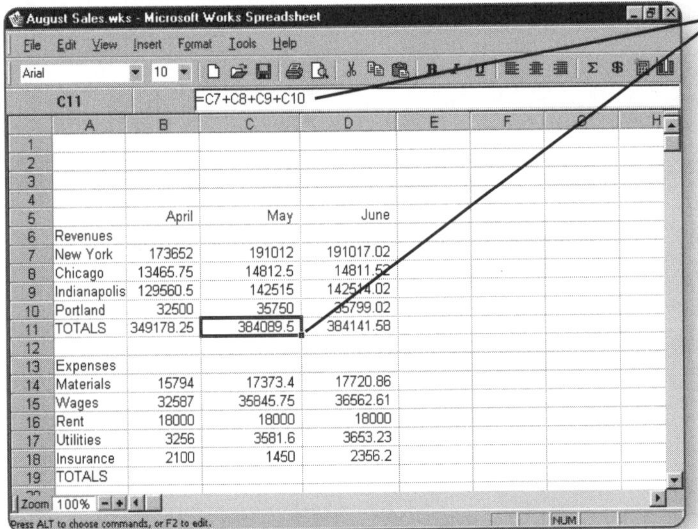

When Works copies a formula, the references change as the formula is copied. If the original formula was =B11–B19 and you copied it to the next cell to the right, the formula would read =C11–C19. Then, if you copied it to the next cell to the right, it would be =D11–D19, and so on.

The reason is that when a formula is copied, the concept behind it is actually copied, not the formula itself. For example, if the original formula is B5+B6 and the answer is to be placed in cell B7, Works is actually theorizing to add the two cells above the answer. When you copy that formula to cell C7, it's still theorizing to add the two cells above it, which would be C5 and C6.

Copying Formulas with Copy and Paste

Another time saving method to duplicate formulas is to use the Windows copy and paste commands.

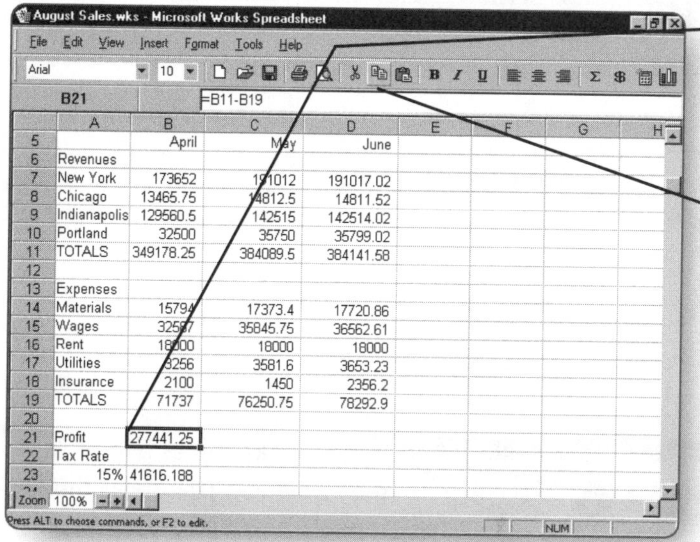

1. **Select** the **cell or cells** with the formula that you want to duplicate. The cells will be selected.

2. **Click** on the **Copy button**. The formulas will be copied to the Clipboard.

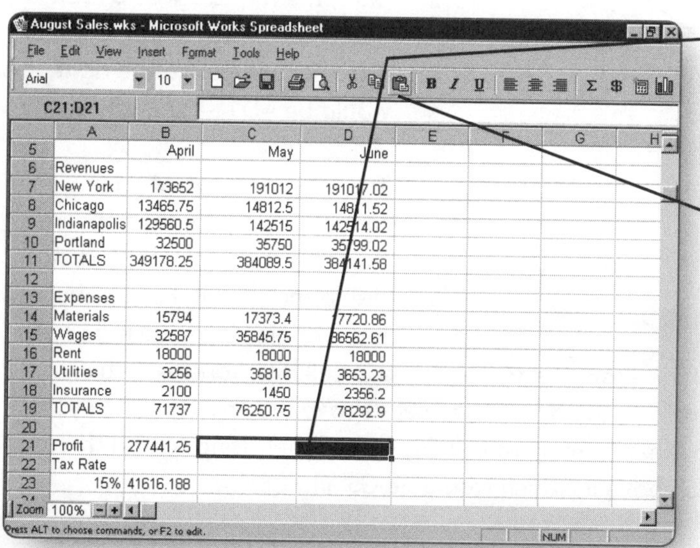

3. **Highlight** the **cells** in which you want to place the duplicated formula. The cells will be selected.

4. **Click** on the **Paste button**. The information will be copied to the new location.

Creating an Absolute Reference in a Formula

Occasionally when you copy a formula, you do not want one of the cell references to change. That's when you need to create an absolute reference. You use the dollar sign ($) to indicate an absolute reference.

It's called an *absolute reference* because when you copy it, it absolutely and positively stays that cell reference and never changes. An example of a formula with an absolute reference might be =B21*B23. The reference to cell B23 will not change when copied.

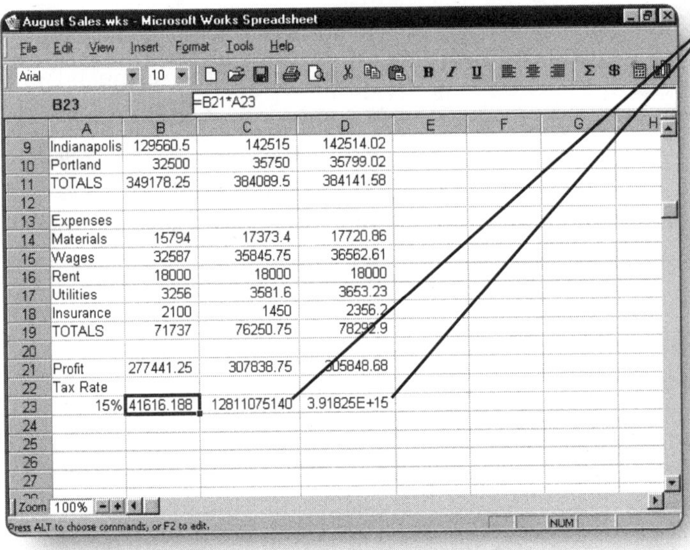

Notice the values in cells C23 and D23. The original formula was intended to take the profit figure of $277,441.25 in cell B21 and multiply it times the tax rate of 15% in cell A23. That formula is fine for cell B23, but when copied to C23 and D23, the answers appear to be in error. Works read the copied formula in cell C21 to read C21 times B23 instead of A23.

1. **Click** on the **cell** in which you want to place the formula answer. The cell will be selected.

2. **Type** an **equal sign (=)** to begin the formula.

3. **Type** the **reference to the first cell** of the formula. If this reference is to be an absolute reference, add dollar signs ($) in front of both the column reference and the row reference. In the example shown, the first cell does not need to be an absolute reference.

4. **Type** the **operator**.

5. **Type** the **reference to the second cell** of the formula. If this reference is to be an absolute reference, add dollar signs ($) in front of both the column reference and the row reference.

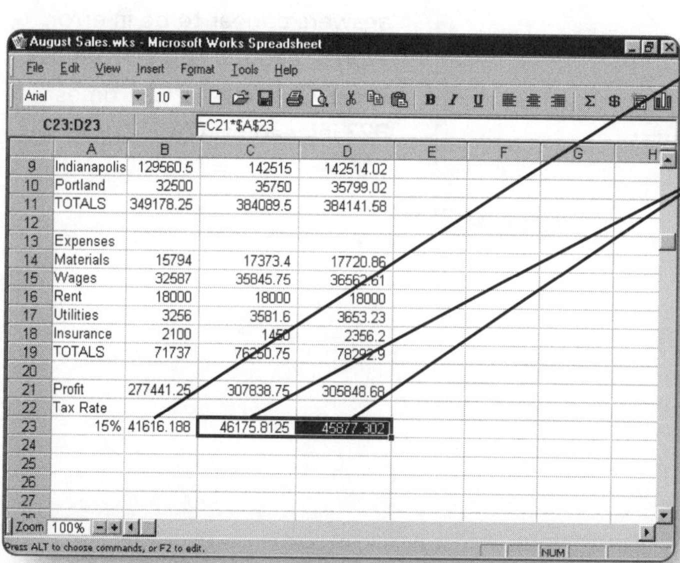

6. **Press Enter** to complete the formula.

7. **Copy** the **formula** to the adjacent cells using one of the methods in the preceding sections.

NOTE

Compound formulas can also have absolute references.

Using Functions

Sometimes, formulas can be complex and time consuming to build. Works has more than 70 different functions to assist you with your calculations. All Works functions begin with the equal (=) sign and have the basis (arguments) for the formula in parentheses.

Using the SUM Function

The SUM function totals a range of values. The syntax for this function is =SUM(*range of values to total*). An example might be =SUM(B7:D7).

> **NOTE**
>
> There are two ways to reference a range of values. If the cells to be included are sequential, they are separated by a colon (:). If the range is nonsequential, the cells are separated by a comma (,). For example, the range (B7:D7) would include cells B7, C7, and D7; the range (B7:D7,F4) would include cells B7, C7, D7, and F4.

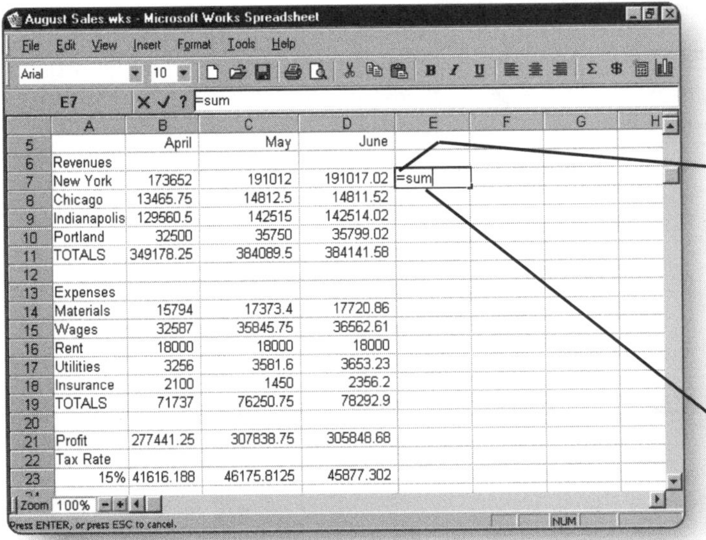

	A	B	C	D	E
5		April	May	June	
6	Revenues				
7	New York	173652	191012	191017.02	=sum
8	Chicago	13465.75	14812.5	14811.52	
9	Indianapolis	129560.5	142515	142514.02	
10	Portland	32500	35750	35799.02	
11	TOTALS	349178.25	384089.5	384141.58	
12					
13	Expenses				
14	Materials	15794	17373.4	17720.86	
15	Wages	32587	35845.75	36562.61	
16	Rent	18000	18000	18000	
17	Utilities	3256	3581.6	3653.23	
18	Insurance	2100	1450	2356.2	
19	TOTALS	71737	76250.75	78292.9	
20					
21	Profit	277441.25	307838.75	305848.68	
22	Tax Rate				
23	15%	41616.188	46175.8125	45877.302	

1. **Click** on the **cell** in which you want to place the sum of values. The cell will be selected.

2. **Type** the **equal (=) sign**. The symbol will appear in the cell. Remember that functions are complex formulas and all formulas must begin with the equal (=) sign.

3. **Type** the function name **sum.** The characters will appear in the cell.

4. Type the **open parentheses** symbol. The symbol will appear in the cell.

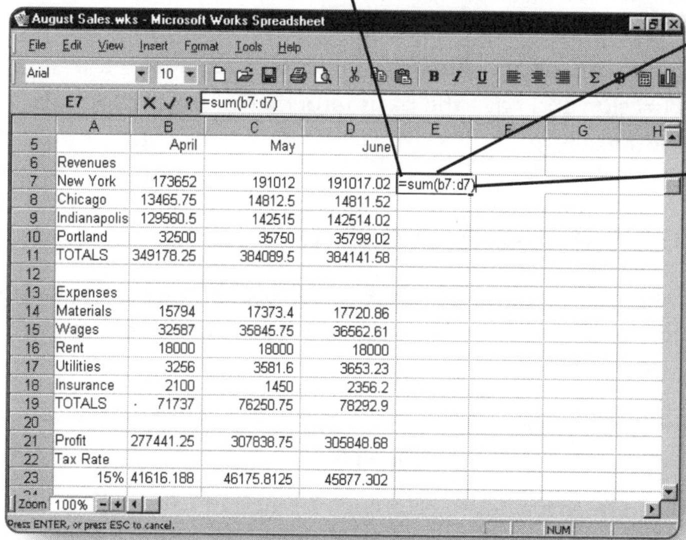

5. Type the **range** to be totaled. The range will appear in the cell.

6. Type the **close parentheses** symbol. The symbol will appear in the cell.

7. Press Enter. The total of the range will appear in the selected cell.

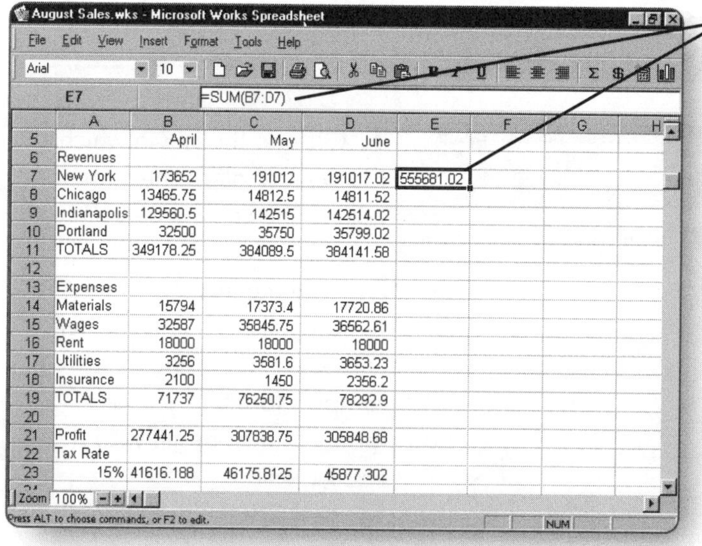

Again, while the result displays in the selected cell, the formula appears in the contents box.

Using the AutoSum Button

Works includes the SUM function as a button on the toolbar. This makes creating a simple addition formula a mouse click away.

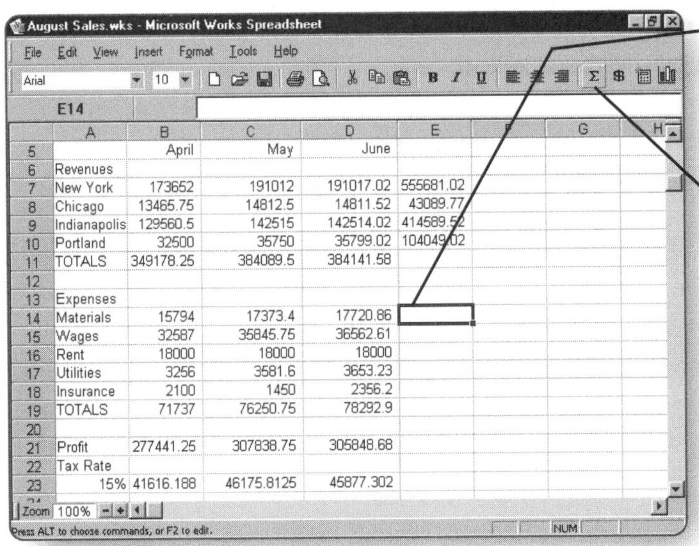

1. **Click** on the **cell** below or to the right of the values to be totaled. The cell will be selected.

2. **Click** on the **AutoSum button**. The cells to be totaled will be highlighted.

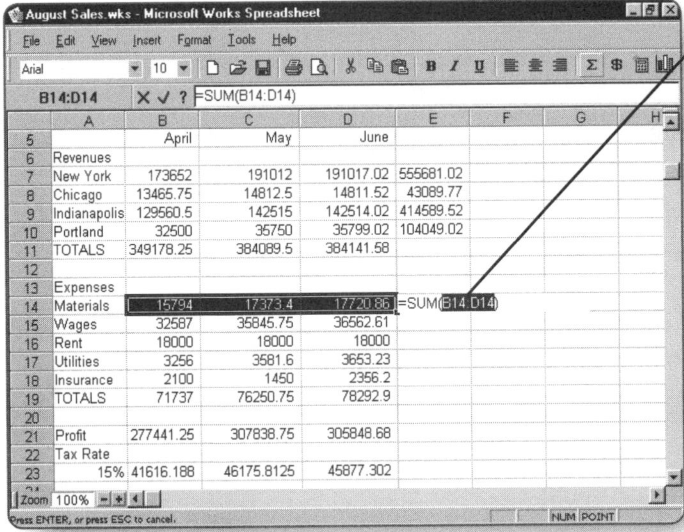

3. **Press Enter**. The sum of the values will appear above the selected cell or to the left of it.

> **NOTE**
>
> Works will sum the values directly above the selected cell first. If no values are above it, Works will look for values in the cells to the left.

Using the AVG Function

The AVG function finds an average value of a range of cells. The syntax for this function is =AVG(*range of values to average*). An example might be =AVG(B7:D7).

1. Click on the **cell** in which you want to place the average. The cell will be selected.

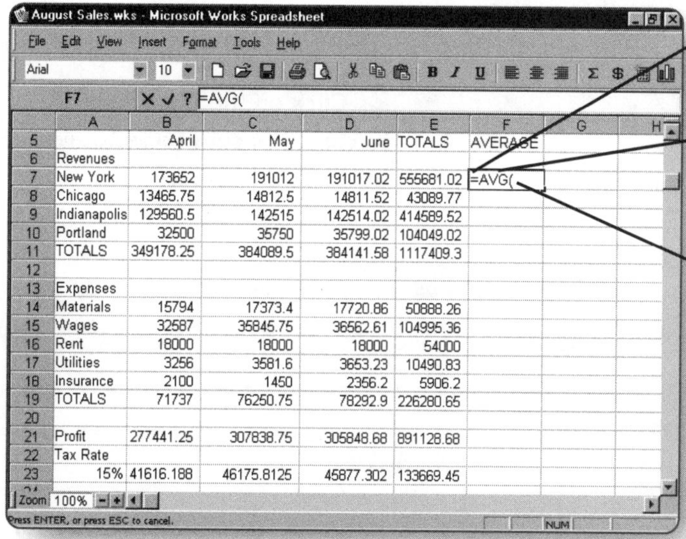

	A	B	C	D	E	F
5		April	May	June	TOTALS	AVERAGE
6	Revenues					
7	New York	173652	191012	191017.02	555681.02	=AVG(
8	Chicago	13465.75	14812.5	14811.52	43089.77	
9	Indianapolis	129560.5	142515	142514.02	414589.52	
10	Portland	32500	35750	35799.02	104049.02	
11	TOTALS	349178.25	384089.5	384141.58	1117409.3	
12						
13	Expenses					
14	Materials	15794	17373.4	17720.86	50888.26	
15	Wages	32587	35845.75	36562.61	104995.36	
16	Rent	18000	18000	18000	54000	
17	Utilities	3256	3581.6	3653.23	10490.83	
18	Insurance	2100	1450	2356.2	5906.2	
19	TOTALS	71737	76250.75	78292.9	226280.65	
20						
21	Profit	277441.25	307838.75	305848.68	891128.68	
22	Tax Rate					
23	15%	41616.188	46175.8125	45877.302	133669.45	

2. Type the **equal (=)** sign. The symbol will appear in the cell.

3. Type the function name **AVG**. The characters will appear in the cell.

4. Type the **open parentheses** symbol. The symbol will appear in the cell.

> **TIP**
>
> Instead of typing the range as noted in step 4, you can highlight the range with the mouse. Works fills in the cell references for you.

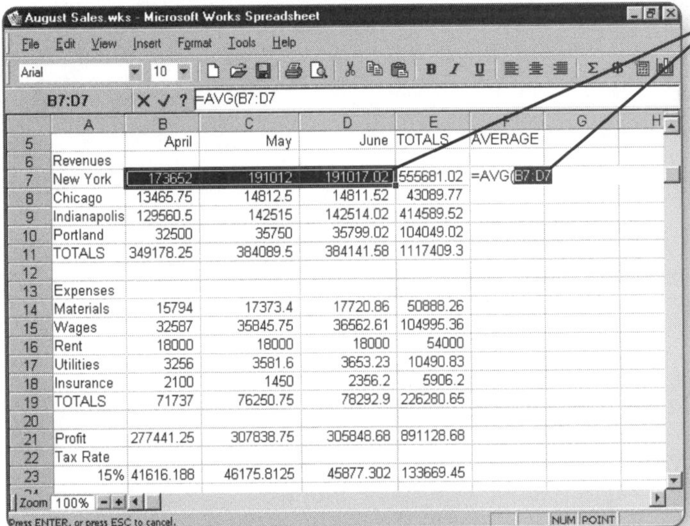

5. Type or **highlight** the **range** to be averaged. The range will appear in the cell.

6. Type the **close parentheses** symbol. The symbol will appear in the cell.

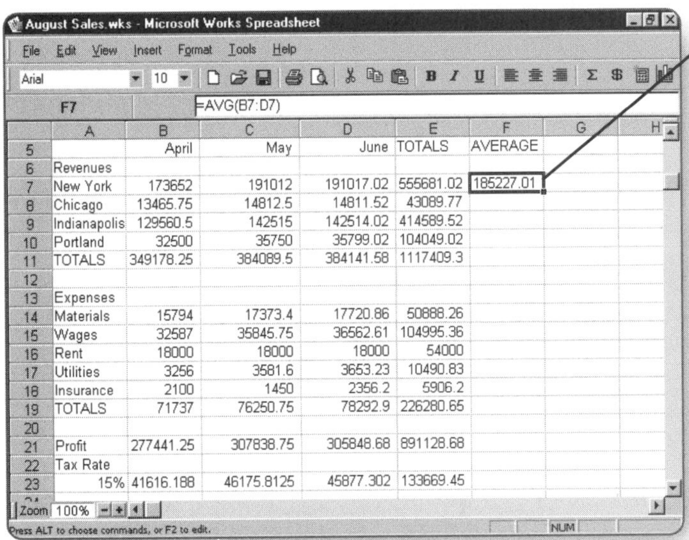

7. Press Enter. Works will average the values in the selected range.

> **NOTE**
>
> Other similar functions are the =MAX, =MIN, and =COUNT functions. The =MAX function finds the largest value in a range of cells. The =MIN function finds the smallest value in a range of cells. The =COUNT function counts the nonblank cells in a range of cells. Examples might include =MAX(B7:B15) or =COUNT(B7:B15).

13

Formatting Worksheets

The days of the dull spreadsheet are gone. Liven up your spreadsheet by changing its appearance. In this chapter, you'll learn how to:

- Set number formatting
- Change alignment and column width
- Select fonts and cell borders
- Use AutoFormat
- Adjust the view of the spreadsheet

Formatting Numbers

By default, values are displayed as general numbers. Values can be displayed as currency, percentages, fractions, dates, and many other formats.

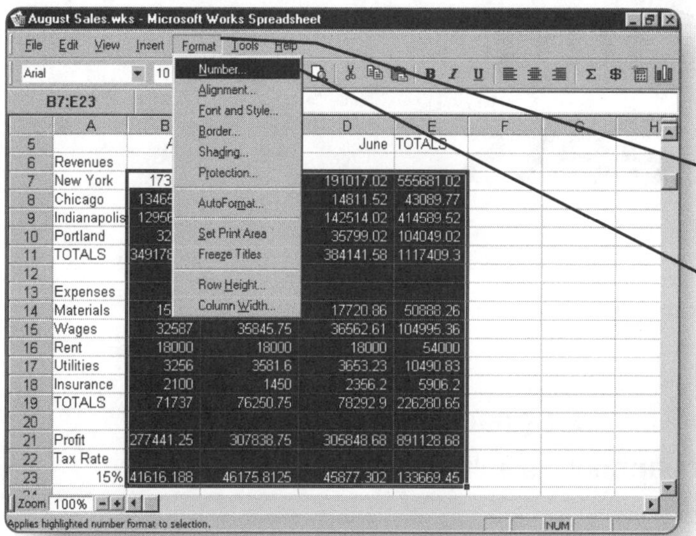

1. **Select** some **cells** to be formatted. The cells will be highlighted.

2. **Click** on **Format**. The Format menu will appear.

3. **Click** on **Number**. The Format Cells dialog box will open with the Number tab in front.

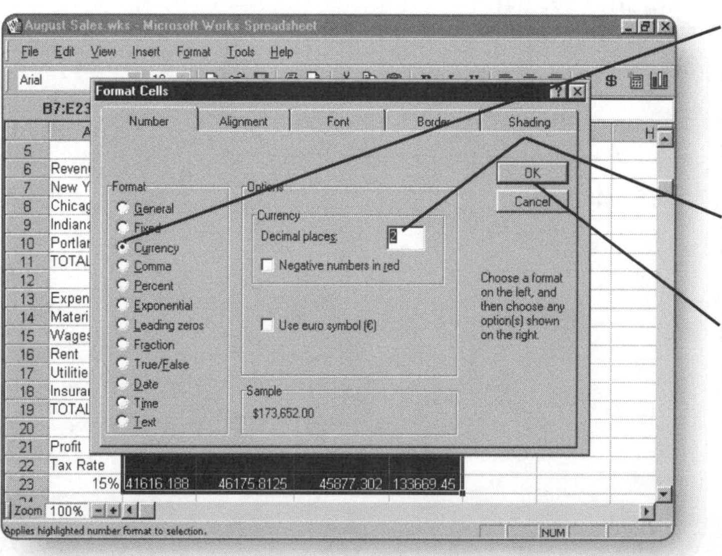

4. **Click** on the **format** of your choice. The format will be selected, and any available options will appear.

5. **Change** any desired **option**. The option will be selected.

6. **Click** on **OK**. The Format Cells dialog box will close.

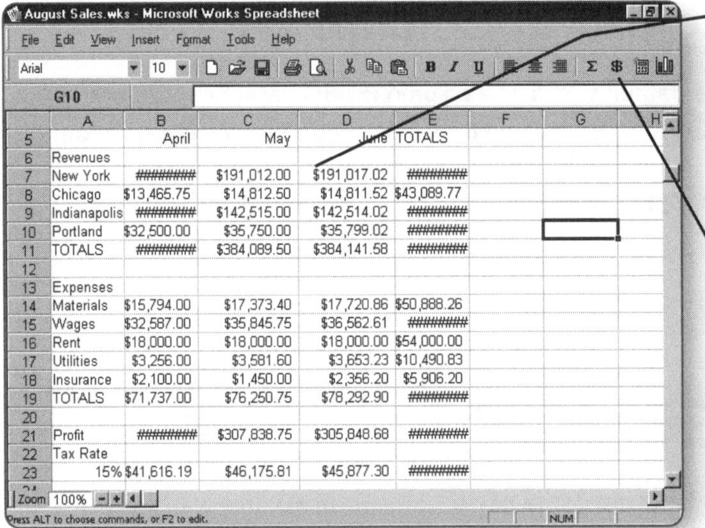

	A	B	C	D	E	F	G	H
5		April	May	June	TOTALS			
6	Revenues							
7	New York	########	$191,012.00	$191,017.02	########			
8	Chicago	$13,465.75	$14,812.50	$14,811.52	$43,089.77			
9	Indianapolis	########	$142,515.00	$142,514.02	########			
10	Portland	$32,500.00	$35,750.00	$35,799.02	########			
11	TOTALS	########	$384,089.50	$384,141.58	########			
12								
13	Expenses							
14	Materials	$15,794.00	$17,373.40	$17,720.86	$50,888.26			
15	Wages	$32,587.00	$35,845.75	$36,562.61	########			
16	Rent	$18,000.00	$18,000.00	$18,000.00	$54,000.00			
17	Utilities	$3,256.00	$3,581.60	$3,653.23	$10,490.83			
18	Insurance	$2,100.00	$1,450.00	$2,356.20	$5,906.20			
19	TOTALS	$71,737.00	$76,250.75	$78,292.90	########			
20								
21	Profit	########	$307,838.75	$305,848.68	########			
22	Tax Rate							
23	15%	$41,616.19	$46,175.81	$45,877.30	########			

The new number format will be applied to the selected cells. Notice the dollar signs and two decimal points. These cells had the currency style applied to them.

TIP

A quick way to apply currency style is to select the cells and click on the currency button.

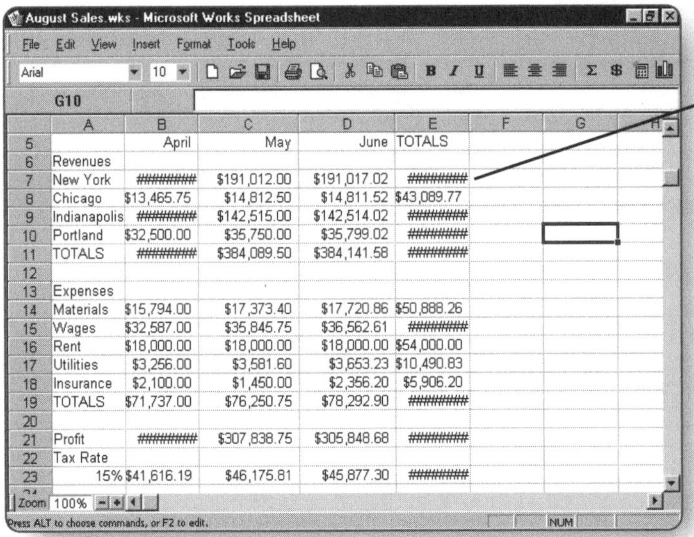

	A	B	C	D	E	F	G	H
5		April	May	June	TOTALS			
6	Revenues							
7	New York	########	$191,012.00	$191,017.02	########			
8	Chicago	$13,465.75	$14,812.50	$14,811.52	$43,089.77			
9	Indianapolis	########	$142,515.00	$142,514.02	########			
10	Portland	$32,500.00	$35,750.00	$35,799.02	########			
11	TOTALS	########	$384,089.50	$384,141.58	########			
12								
13	Expenses							
14	Materials	$15,794.00	$17,373.40	$17,720.86	$50,888.26			
15	Wages	$32,587.00	$35,845.75	$36,562.61	########			
16	Rent	$18,000.00	$18,000.00	$18,000.00	$54,000.00			
17	Utilities	$3,256.00	$3,581.60	$3,653.23	$10,490.83			
18	Insurance	$2,100.00	$1,450.00	$2,356.20	$5,906.20			
19	TOTALS	$71,737.00	$76,250.75	$78,292.90	########			
20								
21	Profit	########	$307,838.75	$305,848.68	########			
22	Tax Rate							
23	15%	$41,616.19	$46,175.81	$45,877.30	########			

NOTE

Don't be alarmed if some of the cells display a series of number signs (######) or are in scientific format (1E+08) instead of your values. This is because the column width is too small. You learn how to change this in the next section.

Adjusting Column Width

The default width of a column is ten characters, but each individual column can be from one to 240 characters wide.

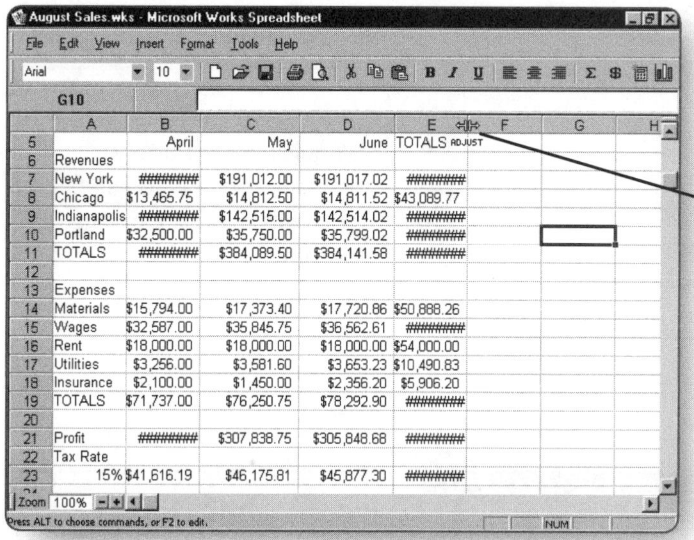

	A	B	C	D	E
5		April	May	June	TOTALS
6	Revenues				
7	New York	########	$191,012.00	$191,017.02	########
8	Chicago	$13,465.75	$14,812.50	$14,811.52	$43,089.77
9	Indianapolis	########	$142,515.00	$142,514.02	########
10	Portland	$32,500.00	$35,750.00	$35,799.02	########
11	TOTALS	########	$384,089.50	$384,141.58	########
12					
13	Expenses				
14	Materials	$15,794.00	$17,373.40	$17,720.86	$50,888.26
15	Wages	$32,587.00	$35,845.75	$36,562.61	########
16	Rent	$18,000.00	$18,000.00	$18,000.00	$54,000.00
17	Utilities	$3,256.00	$3,581.60	$3,653.23	$10,490.83
18	Insurance	$2,100.00	$1,450.00	$2,356.20	$5,906.20
19	TOTALS	$71,737.00	$76,250.75	$78,292.90	########
20					
21	Profit	########	$307,838.75	$305,848.68	########
22	Tax Rate				
23	15%	$41,616.19	$46,175.81	$45,877.30	########

A line located at the right edge of each column heading divides the columns. You use this line to change the column width.

1. Position the **mouse pointer** on the right column line for the column you want to change. The mouse pointer will become a double-headed white arrow with the word "ADJUST" displayed under it.

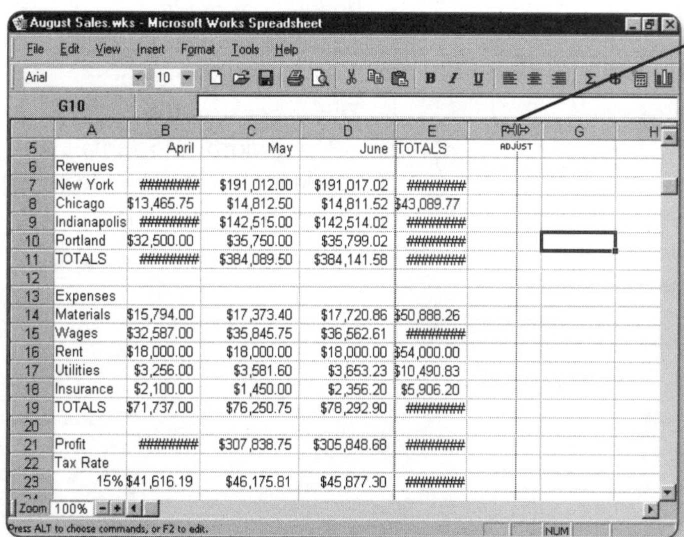

	A	B	C	D	E
5		April	May	June	TOTALS
6	Revenues				
7	New York	########	$191,012.00	$191,017.02	########
8	Chicago	$13,465.75	$14,812.50	$14,811.52	$43,089.77
9	Indianapolis	########	$142,515.00	$142,514.02	########
10	Portland	$32,500.00	$35,750.00	$35,799.02	########
11	TOTALS	########	$384,089.50	$384,141.58	########
12					
13	Expenses				
14	Materials	$15,794.00	$17,373.40	$17,720.86	$50,888.26
15	Wages	$32,587.00	$35,845.75	$36,562.61	########
16	Rent	$18,000.00	$18,000.00	$18,000.00	$54,000.00
17	Utilities	$3,256.00	$3,581.60	$3,653.23	$10,490.83
18	Insurance	$2,100.00	$1,450.00	$2,356.20	$5,906.20
19	TOTALS	$71,737.00	$76,250.75	$78,292.90	########
20					
21	Profit	########	$307,838.75	$305,848.68	########
22	Tax Rate				
23	15%	$41,616.19	$46,175.81	$45,877.30	########

2. Press and **hold** the **mouse button** and **drag** the column line. If you drag it to the right, the column width will increase; if you drag it to the left, the column width will decrease.

3. Release the **mouse button**. The column width will be changed.

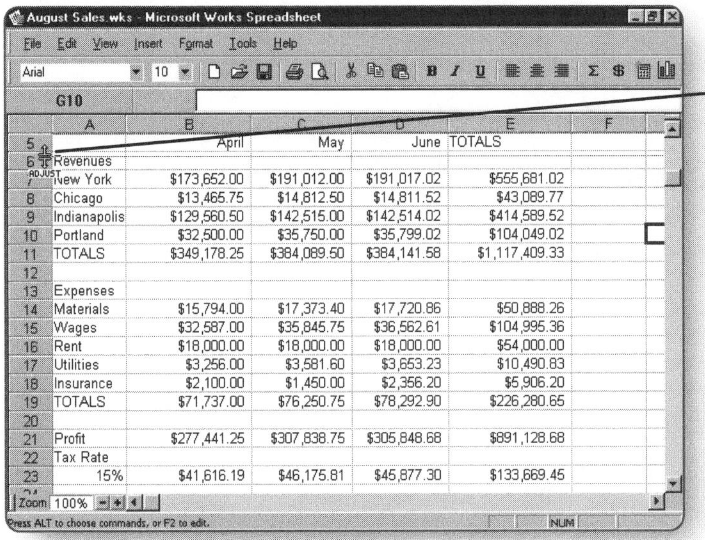

TIP

Row height can be adjusted in a similar manner. Position the mouse pointer on the bottom edge of the row heading. Again, the mouse will change to a double-headed white arrow. Drag the line down to increase row height or up to decrease row height.

Setting Worksheet Alignment

Labels are left aligned, and values are right aligned by default; however, you can change the alignment of either one to be left, right, centered, or full justified. Also by default, both are vertically aligned to the bottom of the cell.

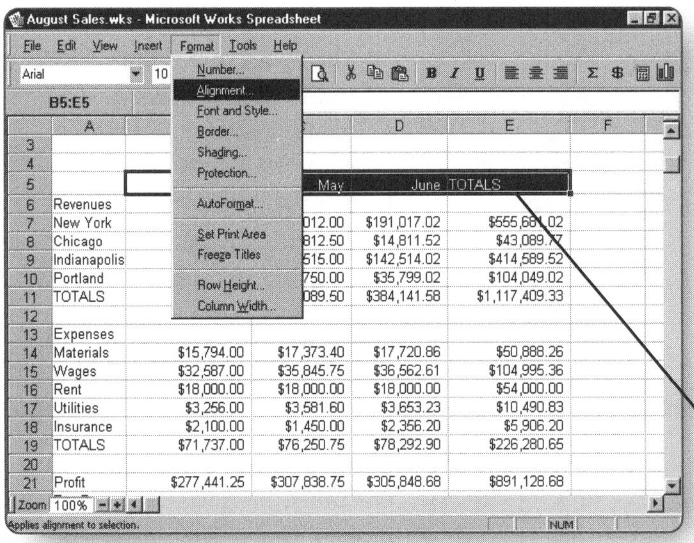

Wrapping text in cells is useful when text is too long to fit in one cell, and you don't want it to overlap to the next cell.

Adjusting Cell Alignment

Adjust cells individually or adjust a block of cells at once.

1. Select the **cells** to be formatted. The cells will be highlighted.

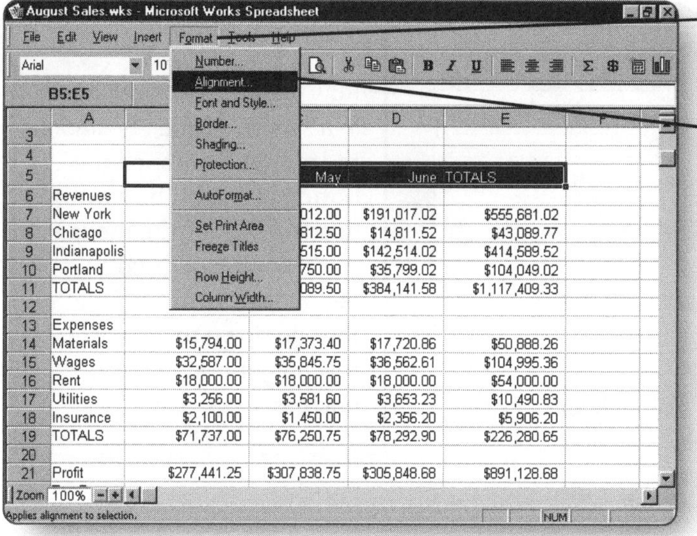

2. Click on **Format**. The Format menu will appear.

3. Click on **Alignment**. The Format Cells dialog box will open with the Alignment tab in front.

4. Click on an **option** under Horizontal alignment. The horizontal alignment of the text in the cell will change.

5. Click on an **option** under Vertical alignment. The vertical alignment of the text in the cell will change.

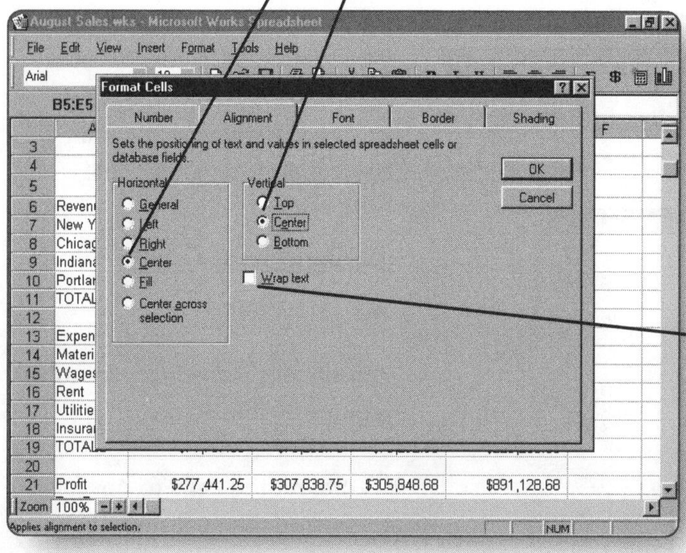

TIP

The Wrap text feature treats each cell like a miniature word processor, with text wrapping around in the cell.

6. Click on the **Wrap text check box**, if desired. A ✔ will appear in the selection box.

7. Click on **OK**. The selections will be applied to the highlighted cells.

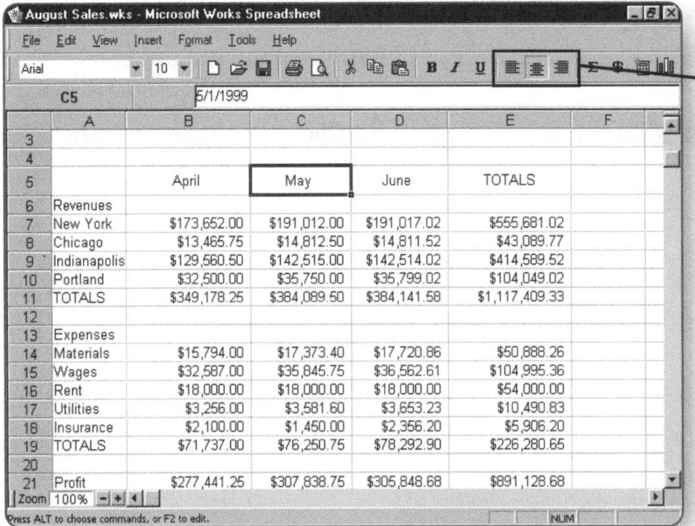

TIP

Optionally, select cells to be aligned and click on one of the three alignment buttons on the toolbar: Left, Center, or Right.

Centering Headings

Text also can be centered across a group of columns to create attractive headings.

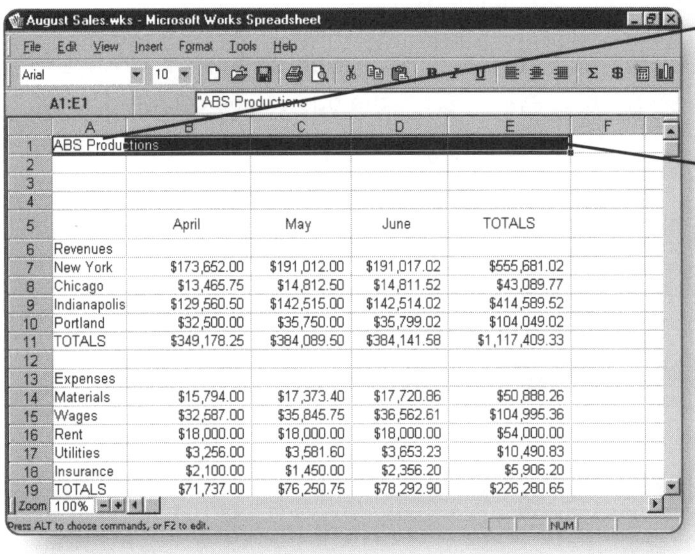

1. **Type** the **heading text** in the first column of the worksheet body. This is usually column A.

2. **Select** the **heading cell** and **the cells to be included** in the heading. The cells will be highlighted.

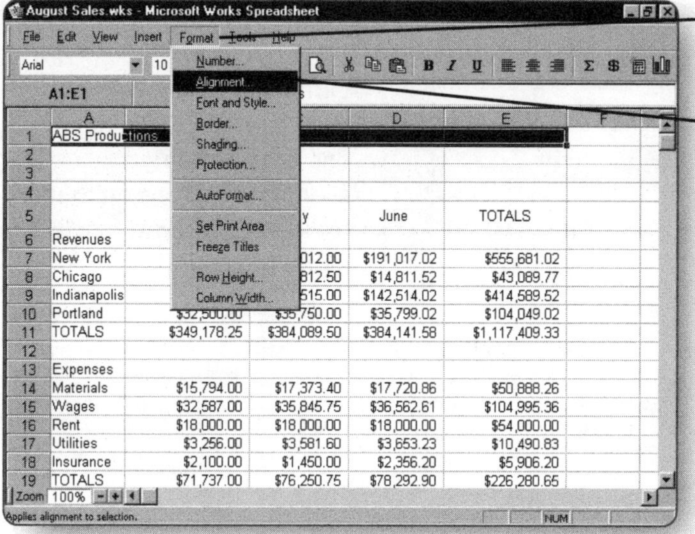

3. **Click** on **Format**. The Format menu will appear.

4. **Click** on **Alignment**. The Format Cells dialog box will open with the Alignment tab in front.

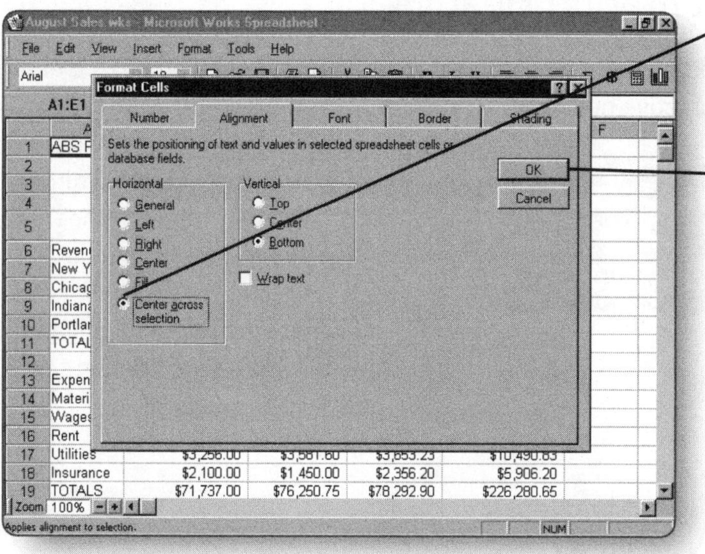

5. **Click** on **Center across selection**. The option will be selected.

6. **Click** on **OK**. The Format Cells dialog box will close, and the title will be centered.

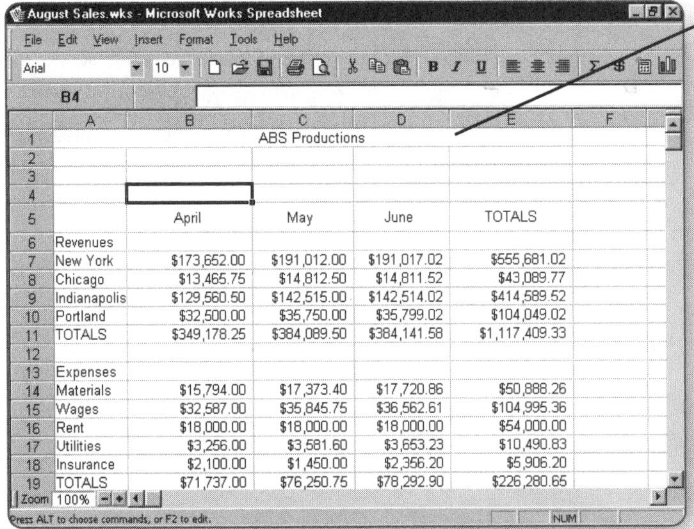

Notice the gridlines have disappeared, and the cells appear to be joined together.

NOTE

In this example, the headings appear to be located in column C; however, the text is still in Column A. If you are going to make other changes, be sure to select column A, not column C.

Formatting with Fonts

The default font in a spreadsheet is Arial 10 points, but both the typeface or size can be easily changed.

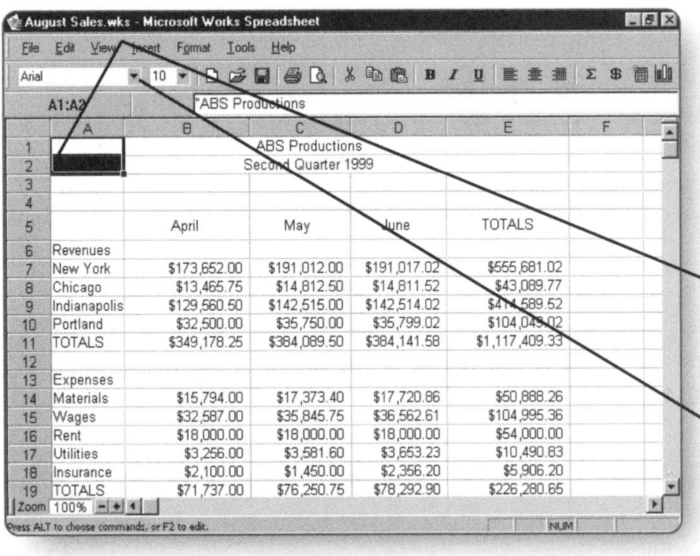

Selecting a Font Typeface

Your font choices vary depending on the software installed on your computer.

1. Select some **cells** in which to change the typeface. The cells will be highlighted.

2. Click on the **Font Name drop-down arrow (▼).** A list of available fonts will appear.

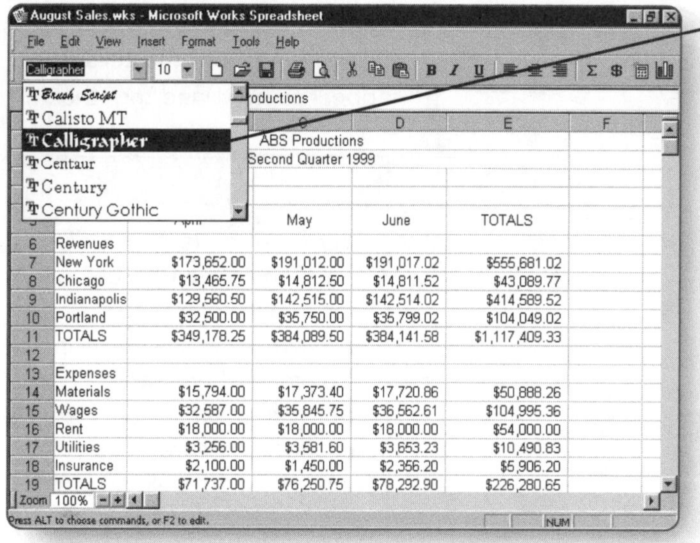

3. Click on the **font** of your choice. The selection list will close, and the new font will be applied to the selected cells.

Selecting a Font Size

The default font size in a Works spreadsheet is 10 points. There are approximately 72 points in an inch, so a 10-point font is slightly less than one-seventh of an inch tall.

1. Select some **cells** in which to change the font size. The cells will be highlighted.

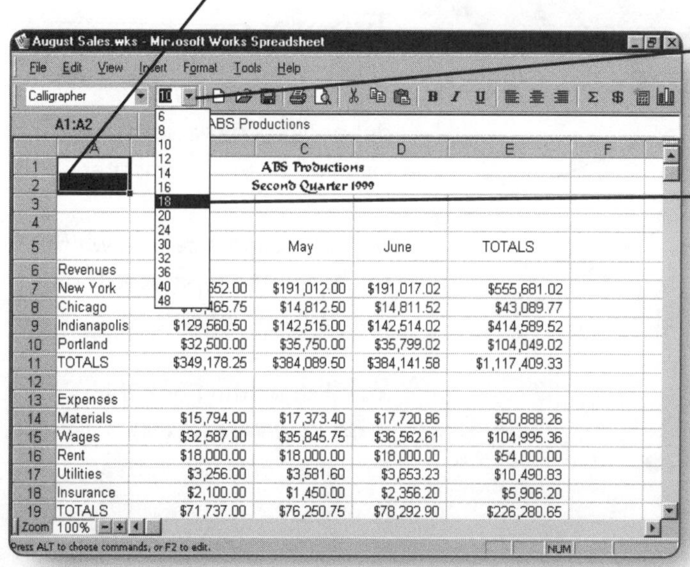

2. Click on the **Font Size drop-down arrow (▼)**. A list of available font sizes will appear.

3. Click on the **size** of your choice. The selection list will close.

> **TIP**
>
> If the size you want is not listed, type in the desired size in the size text box.

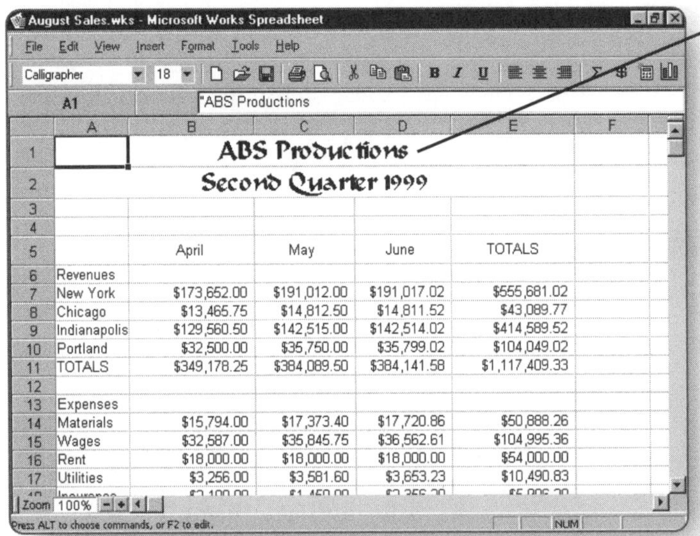

The new font size will be applied to the selected cells.

Selecting a Font Style

Font styles include attributes such as **bold**, *italics*, and underlining.

1. Select some **cells** in which to change the style. The cells will be highlighted.

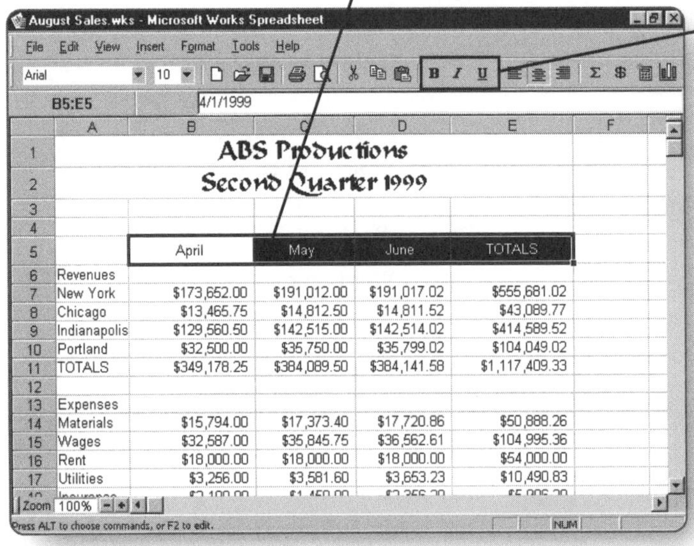

2. Click on any of the following **options**:

- Bold button
- Italics button
- Underline button

The attributes will be applied to the text in the cell.

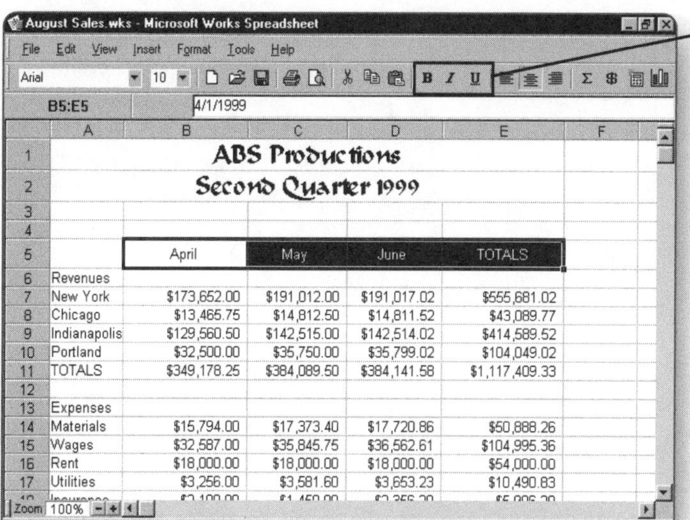

The Bold, Italics, and Underline buttons are like toggle switches. Click on them a second time to turn off the attribute.

TIP

Shortcut keys include Ctrl+B for Bold, Ctrl+I for Italics, and Ctrl+U for Underline.

NOTE

Underlining is not the same as a cell border. Cell borders are discussed in the next section.

Adding Borders

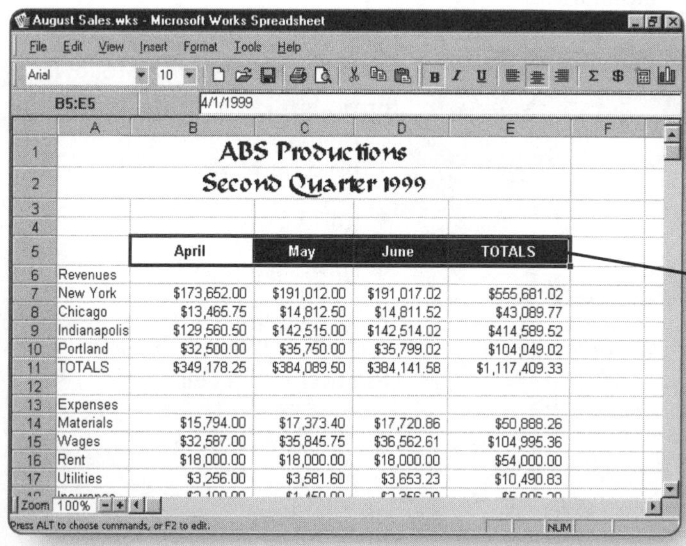

You can add borders or lines to cells to emphasize important data. Borders are different from the gridlines that separate cells in the sheet. You can change the style and color of borders.

1. **Select** the **cells** that you want to have borders or lines. The cells will be highlighted.

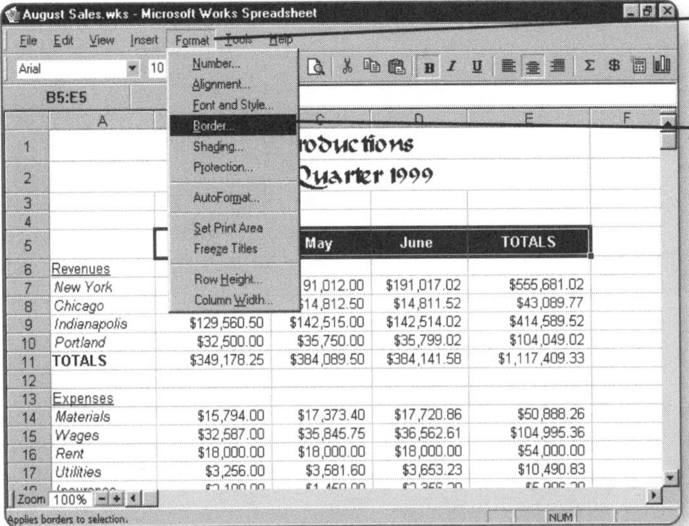

2. Click on **Format**. The Format menu will appear.

3. Click on **Border**. The Format Cells dialog box will open with the Border tab in front.

4. Choose a border **Line style**. The selected style will have a black box around it.

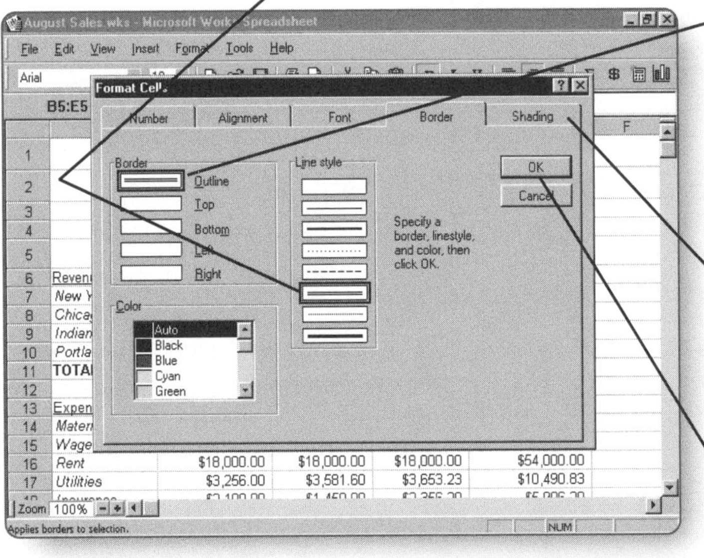

5. Choose from the **Border placement options**. A sample of the chosen line style from step 4 will appear in the selected placement options.

> **TIP**
>
> Click on the Shading tab and select shading options for the selected cells.

6. Click on **OK**. The Format Cells dialog box will close.

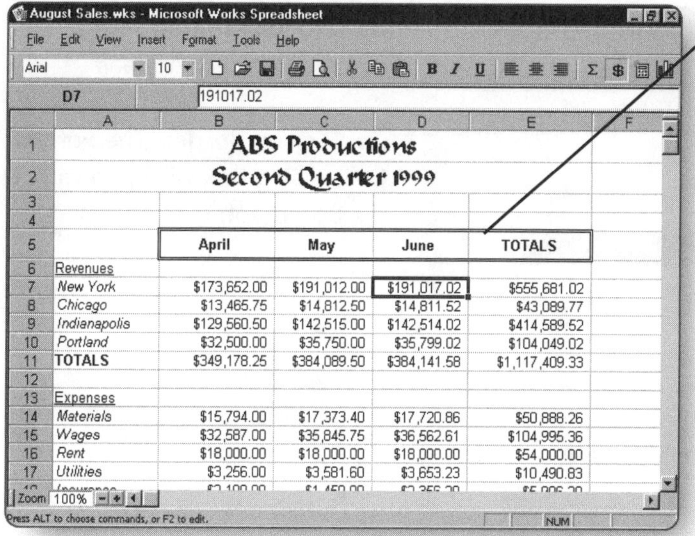

The border choices will be applied to the highlighted cells.

Saving Time with AutoFormat

Save time by letting Works format your spreadsheet using the AutoFormat feature. You can choose from 16 different styles.

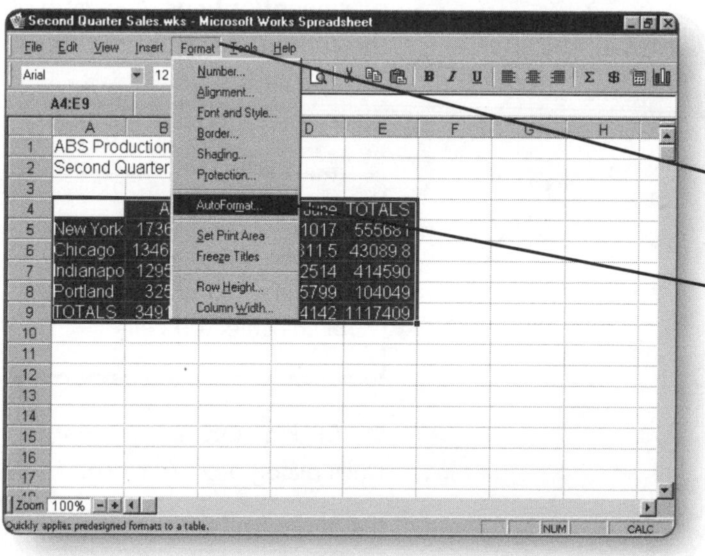

1. **Select** the **cells** to be formatted. The cells will be highlighted.
2. **Click** on **Format**. The Format menu will appear.
3. **Click** on **AutoFormat**. The AutoFormat dialog box will open.

4. Click on a **format** from the Select a format: list. A sample will appear in the Example box.

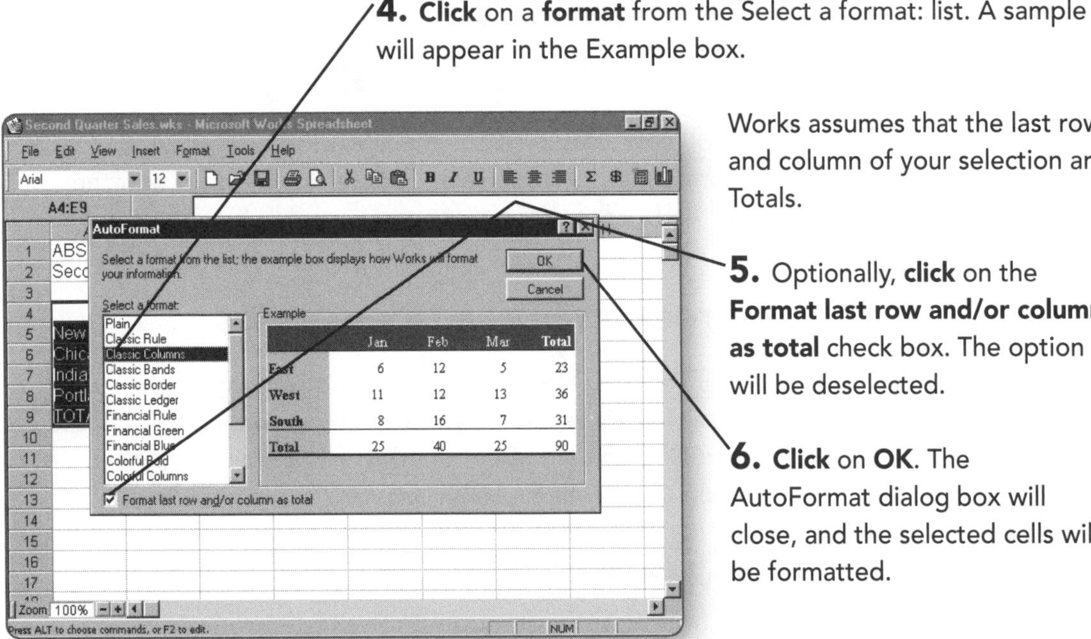

Works assumes that the last row and column of your selection are Totals.

5. Optionally, **click** on the **Format last row and/or column as total** check box. The option will be deselected.

6. Click on **OK**. The AutoFormat dialog box will close, and the selected cells will be formatted.

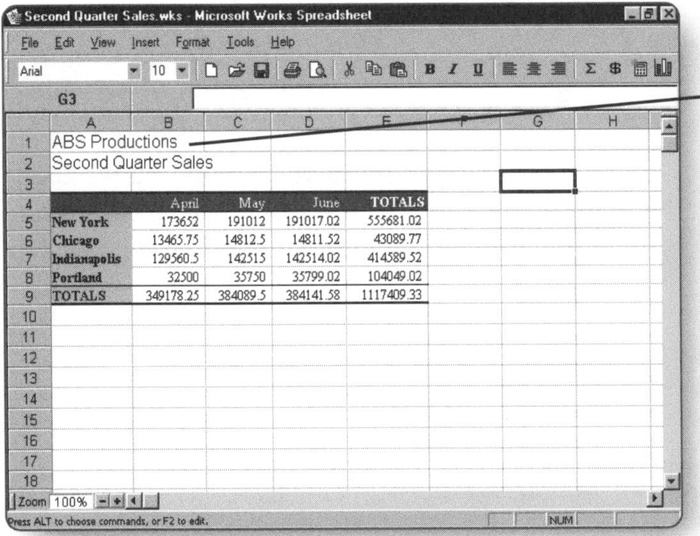

TIP

You can still change any format option (such as numbers or fonts) manually as necessary.

Changing the Spreadsheet Display

Works includes several options to modify the display of your spreadsheet. Most display options do not affect how the spreadsheet prints, only the way you see it on the monitor.

Freezing Spreadsheet Titles

You can freeze columns, rows, or both so that column and row titles remain in view as you scroll through the sheet instead of scrolling off the screen with the rest of the spreadsheet. This is particularly helpful with larger spreadsheets.

1. **Click** the **mouse** on the desired cell:

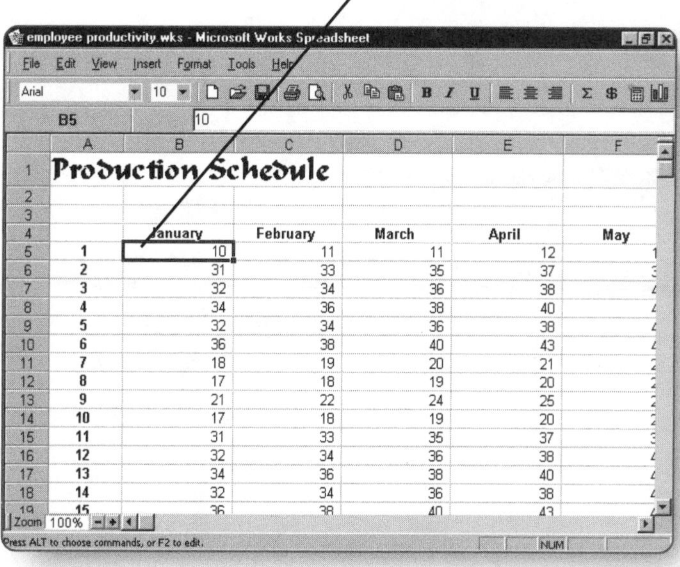

- To freeze columns, position the mouse pointer one cell to the right of the columns you want to freeze.
- To freeze rows, position the cell pointer one cell below the rows you want to freeze.
- To freeze both columns and rows, position the cell pointer in the cell below the rows and to the right of the columns you want to freeze.

2. Click on **Format**. The Format menu will appear.

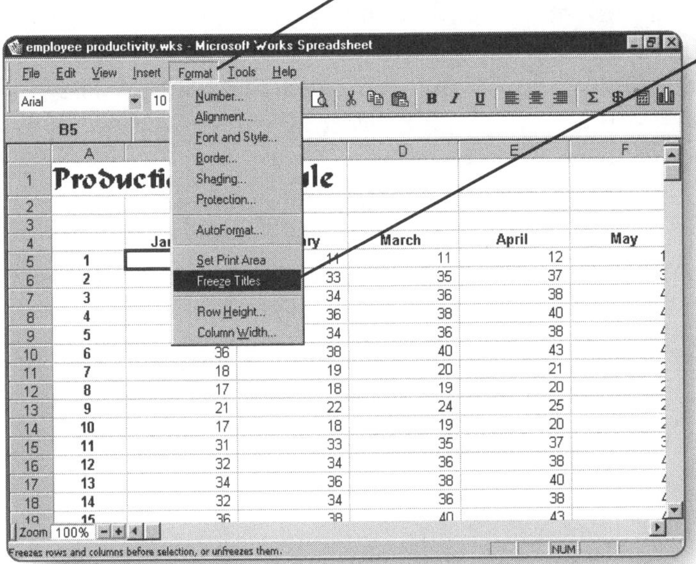

3. Click on **Freeze Titles**. Lines will appear on the document indicating the frozen areas.

As you scroll down or across in your document, the frozen part stays stationary on the screen while the rest of the text moves.

> **TIP**
>
> Repeat steps 2 and 3 to unfreeze the windows.

Using Zoom

Zoom enlarges or shrinks the display of your spreadsheet to allow you to see more or less of it. Zooming in or out does not affect printing. The normal display of your spreadsheet is 100%.

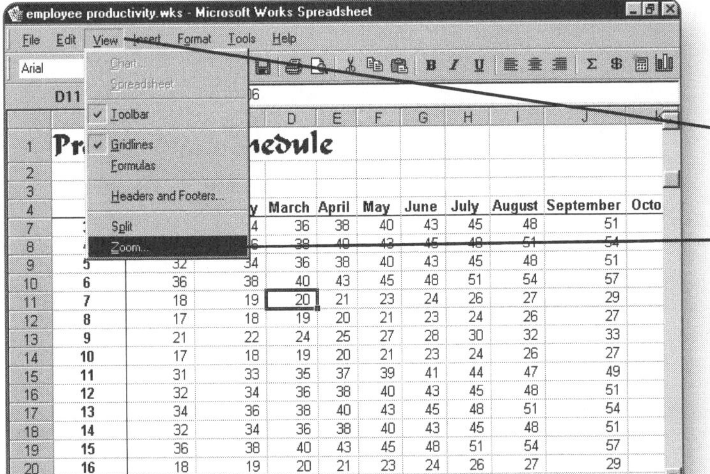

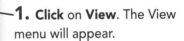

1. Click on **View**. The View menu will appear.

2. Click on **Zoom**. The Zoom dialog box will open.

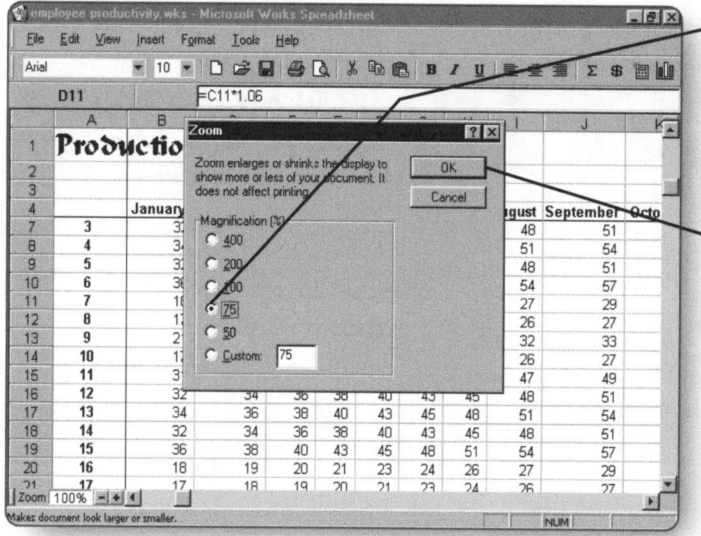

3. Click on a **Magnification (%) choice**. The higher the number, the larger the cells will appear onscreen. The option will be selected.

4. Click on **OK**. The Zoom dialog box will close, and the display of your screen will adjust according to your selection.

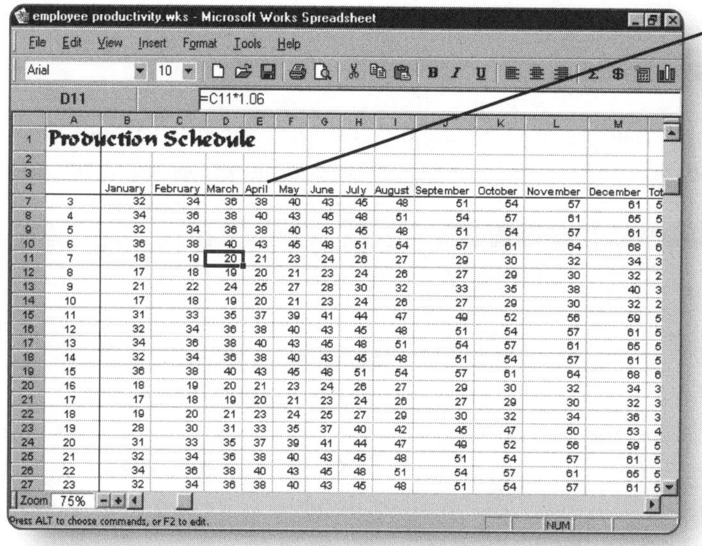

In this example, the zoom was set to 75%, which allowed more of the worksheet to display on the screen.

Hiding Gridlines

Gridlines are the light gray lines displayed on the screen that separate one cell from another. If you do not want the gridlines to display on the screen, you can quickly turn them off.

1. **Click** on **View**. The View menu will appear.

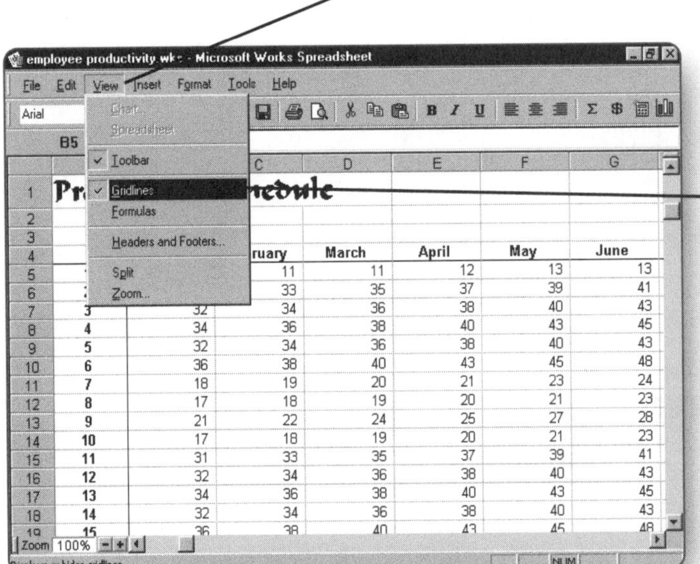

The ✔ beside menu items indicates that these items are currently activated and in use.

2. **Click** on **Gridlines**. The option will be deselected, and the display of gridlines will be turned off.

3. **Repeat steps 1** and **2**. The gridlines will reappear.

By default, gridlines do not print whether or not you have them displayed on the spreadsheet. The option to print them must be selected separately. See Chapter 14, "Printing Your Spreadsheet," for instructions on printing gridlines.

Viewing Formulas

When you create formulas, the result of the formula is displayed in the spreadsheet, not the formula itself. Viewing the formula is a wonderful tool for troubleshooting formula errors in your spreadsheet.

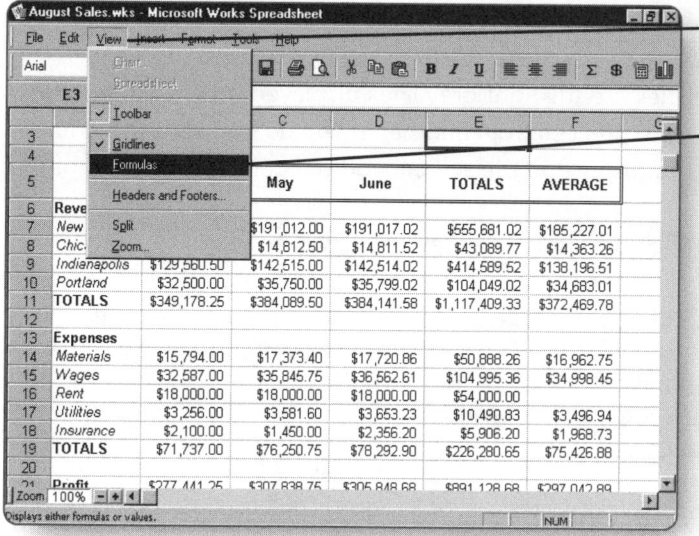

1. **Click** on **View**. The View menu will appear.

2. **Click** on **Formulas**. The option will be selected.

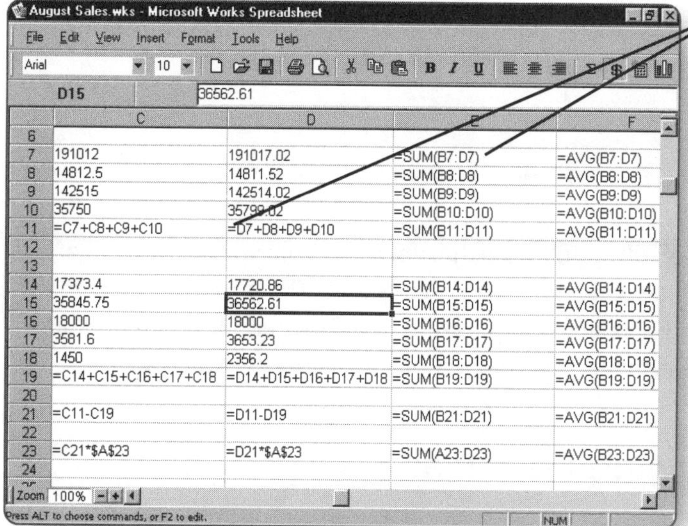

The spreadsheet formulas will be displayed in each cell instead of the result of the formula.

3. **Repeat steps 1** and **2**. The formula results will reappear.

> **NOTE**
>
> If you print the spreadsheet while the formulas are displayed, the formulas will print, but not the formula results.

14

Printing Your Spreadsheet

Now that you have created your spreadsheet with all its text, values, and formulas, you'll want to prepare it for final output. You should proof its appearance as well as specify what area you want to print. In this chapter, you'll learn how to:

- Set page margins and orientation
- Use Print Preview
- Print a spreadsheet

Preparing to Print

Before you print your spreadsheet, you may want to tell Works what size paper you'd like to use, how large the margins should be, and whether to print the gridlines. These options and others are selected from the Page Setup feature of Works.

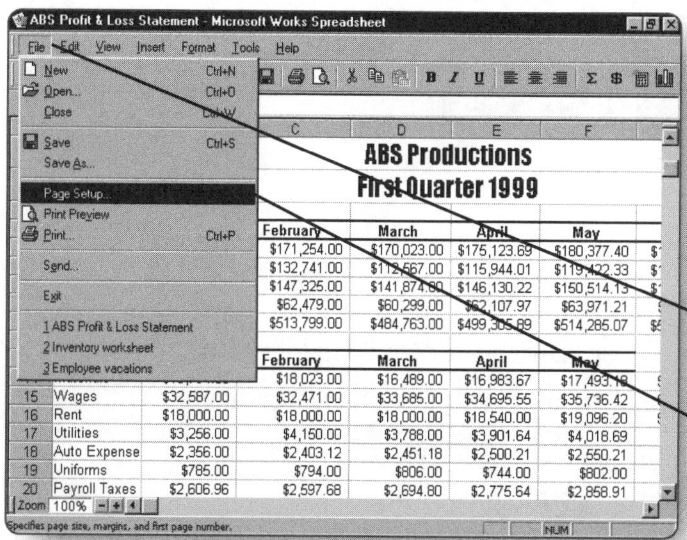

Setting Up Margins

By default, the top and bottom margins are set at 1 inch, and the left and right margins are set at 1.25 inch. You can change these margins.

1. Click on **File**. The File menu will appear.

2. Click on **Page Setup**. The Page Setup dialog box will open.

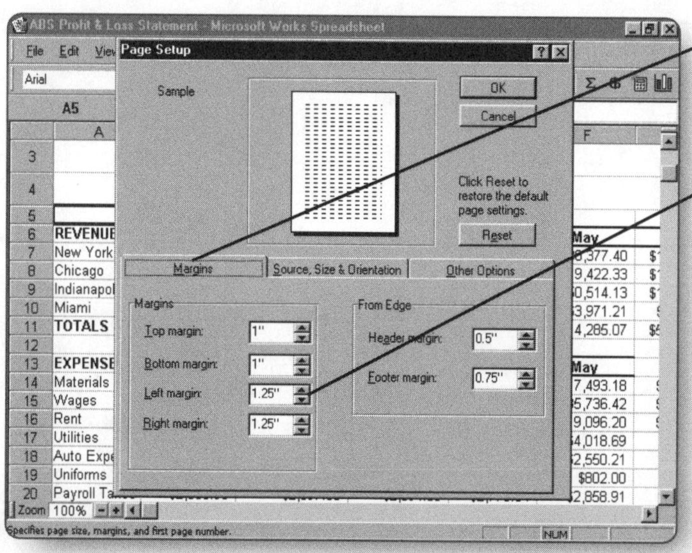

3. If necessary, **click** on the **Margins tab**. The tab will come to the front.

4. Click on the **up/down arrows** (⬍) on each margin you want to change. A sample will appear in the Sample box.

5. Click on **OK**. The Page Setup dialog box will close.

Setting Up Page Orientation and Size

If your spreadsheet uses many columns, you may want to change the orientation or paper size. The default size is 8½-by-11-inch paper in portrait orientation—the short side at the top. Changing to landscape orientation prints with the long edge of the paper at the top.

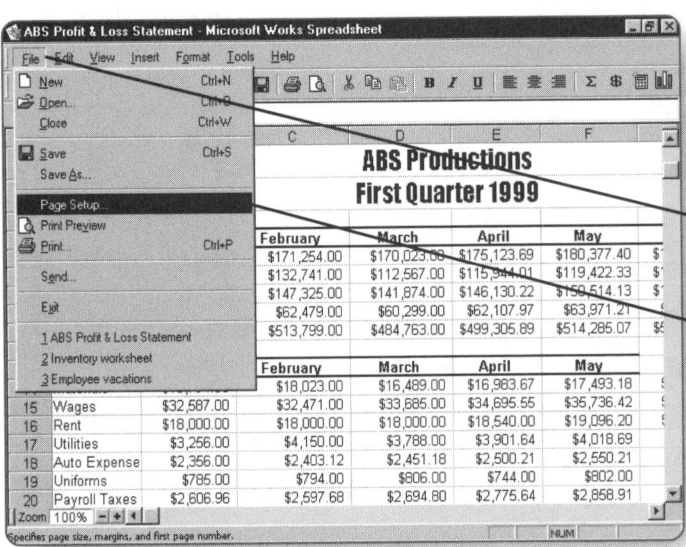

1. **Click** on **File**. The File menu will appear.

2. **Click** on **Page Setup**. The Page Setup dialog box will open.

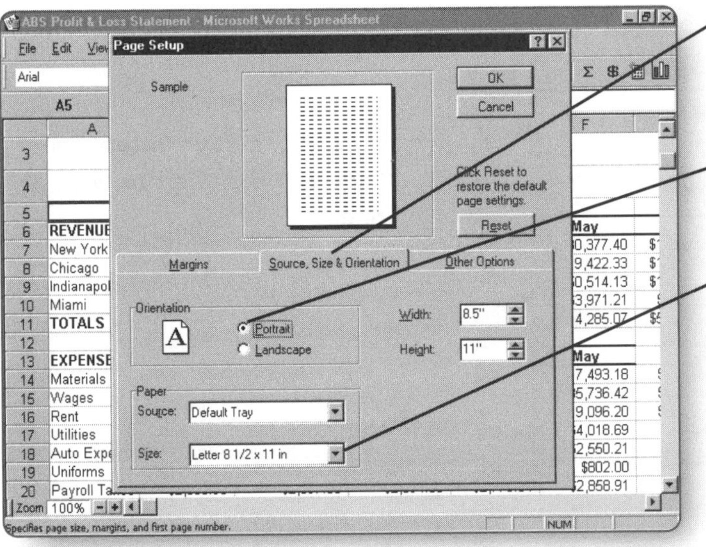

3. If necessary, **click** on the **Source, Size & Orientation tab**. The tab will come to the front.

4. **Click** on an **Orientation**. The option will be selected.

5. **Click** on the **down arrow** (▼) to the right of the Size: list box. The list of available paper size options will appear.

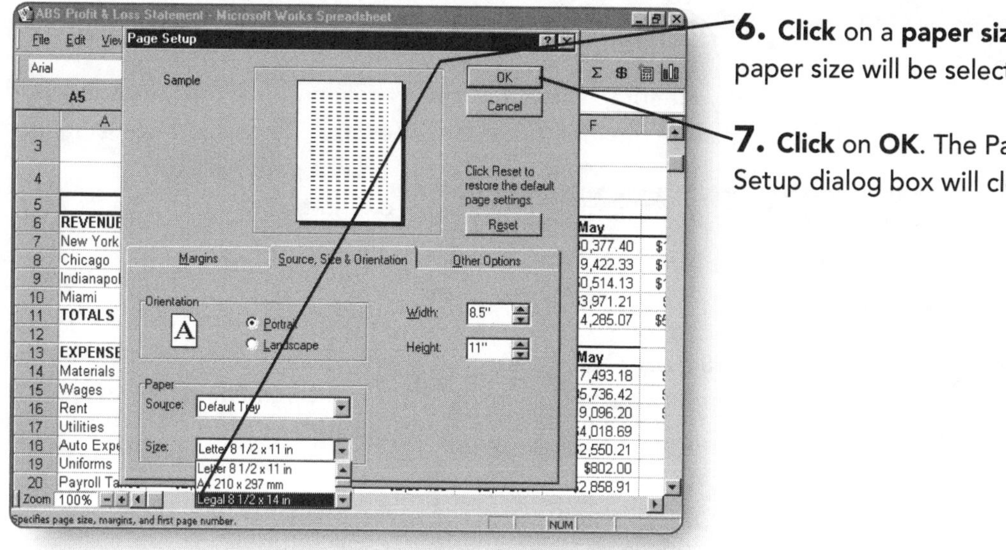

6. **Click** on a **paper size**. The paper size will be selected.

7. **Click** on **OK**. The Page Setup dialog box will close.

Setting Other Printing Options

You may want to consider other options for your worksheet, such as whether to print the gridlines or the row and column headings.

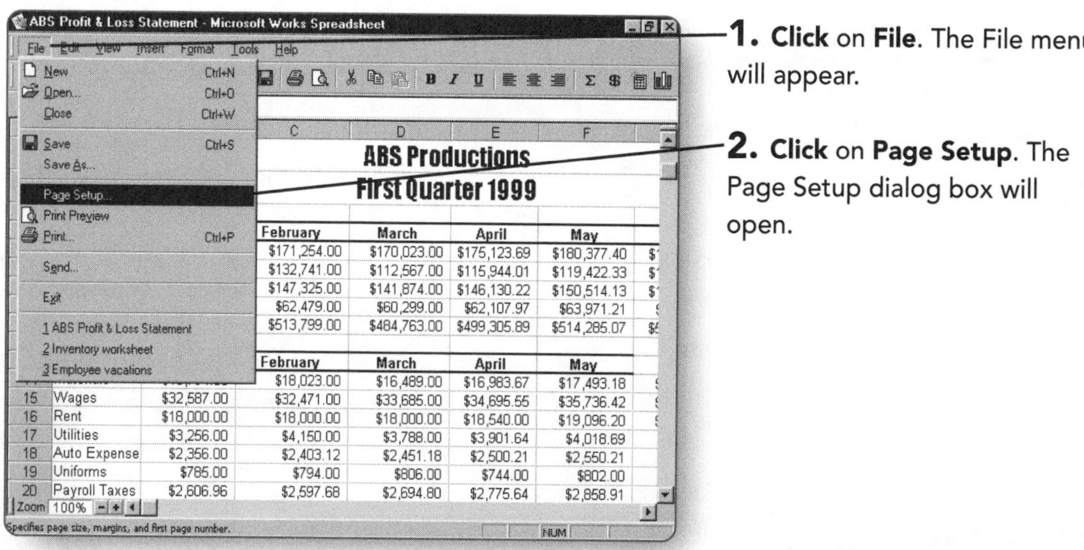

1. **Click** on **File**. The File menu will appear.

2. **Click** on **Page Setup**. The Page Setup dialog box will open.

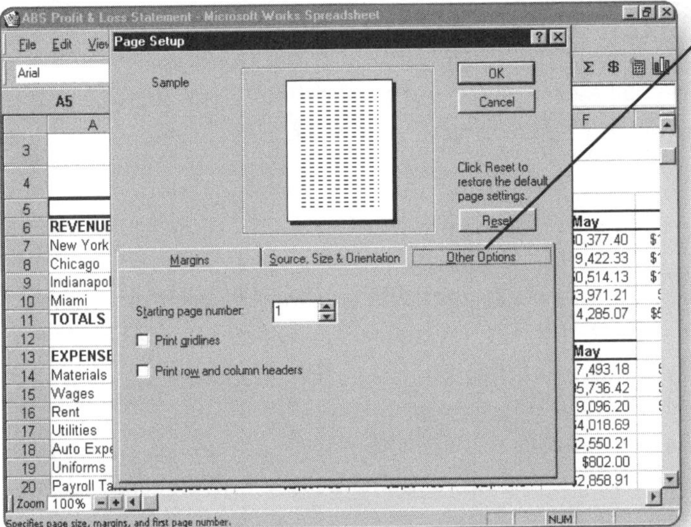

3. If necessary, **click** on the **Other Options tab**. The tab will come to the front.

4. Click on **Print gridlines** if you want to print the gridlines. A ✔ will be placed in the selection box.

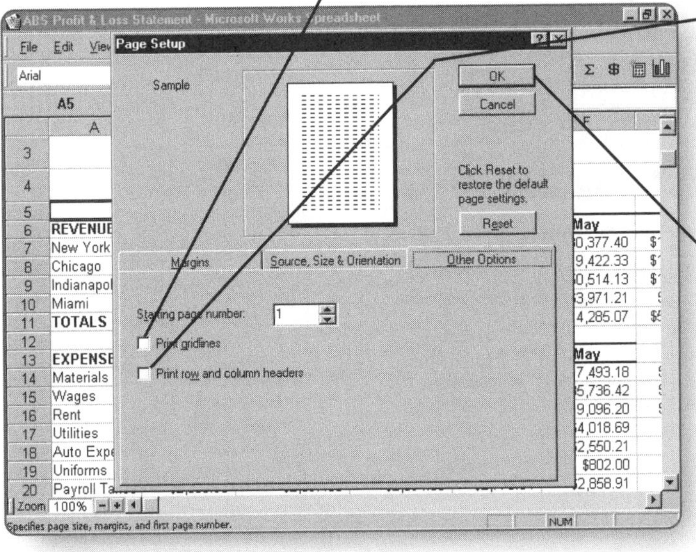

5. Click on **Print row and column headers** if you want the column headings or row headings to print on the spreadsheet. A ✔ will be placed in the selection box.

6. Click on **OK**. The Page Setup dialog box will close.

Printing a Spreadsheet

After you have created your spreadsheet, you can print a hard copy for your records or to send to someone else.

Printing a Range

By default, Works assumes that you want to print the entire spreadsheet. If this is not the case, you need to specify the area you want to print.

1. **Select** the **cells** you want to print if you do not intend to print the entire spreadsheet. The cells will be highlighted.

2. **Click** on **Format**. The Format menu will appear.

3. **Click** on **Set Print Area**. A confirmation dialog box will open.

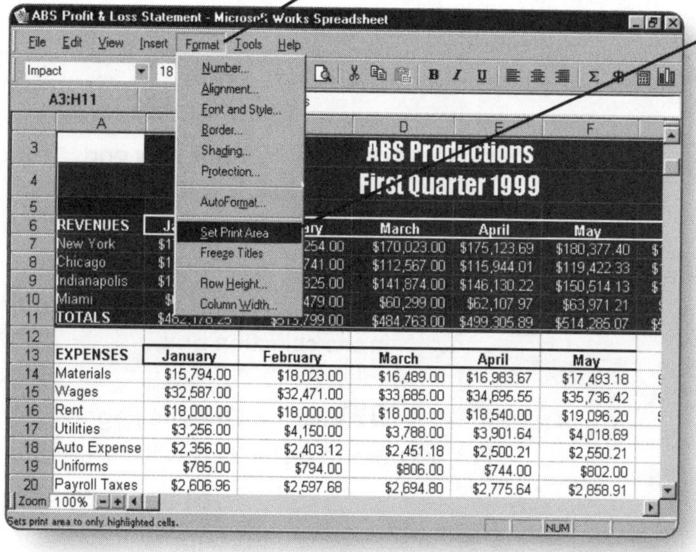

4. Click on **OK**. The dialog box will close.

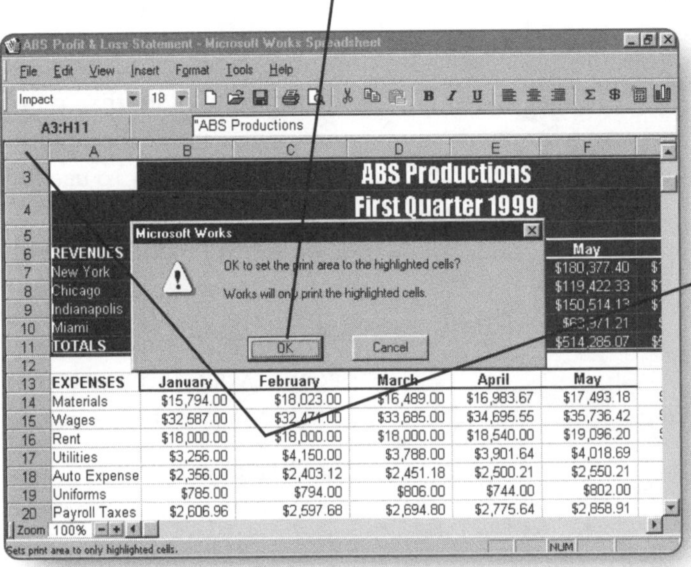

Now when you print your spreadsheet, only the cells you selected in step 1 will print.

> **TIP**
>
> If you later want to print the entire spreadsheet, select the entire spreadsheet by clicking in the small gray box above the row headings and to the left of the column headings; then choose Format, Set Print Area and click on OK.

Printing Your Work

Typically, the end result of creating a Works document is getting text onto paper. Works gives you a quick and easy way to get that result.

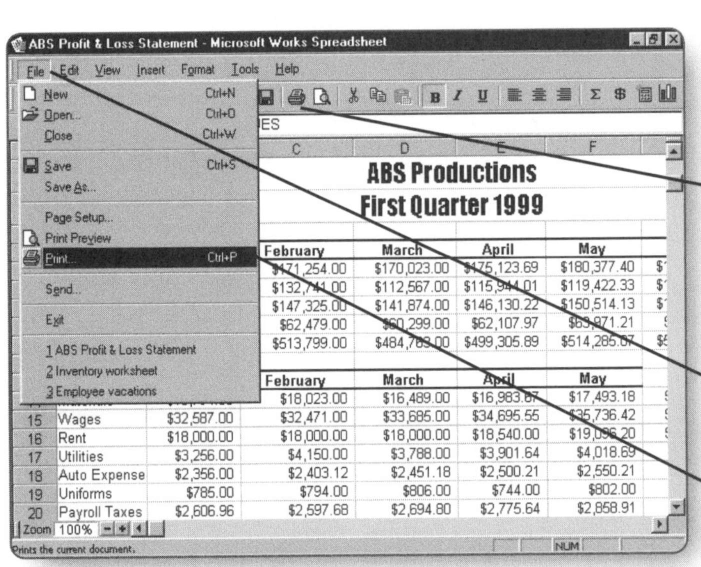

1a. Click on the **Print button**. The spreadsheet will print with standard options.

OR

1b. Click on **File**. The File menu will appear.

2. Click on **Print**. The Print dialog box will open.

Many options are available from the Print dialog box, including:

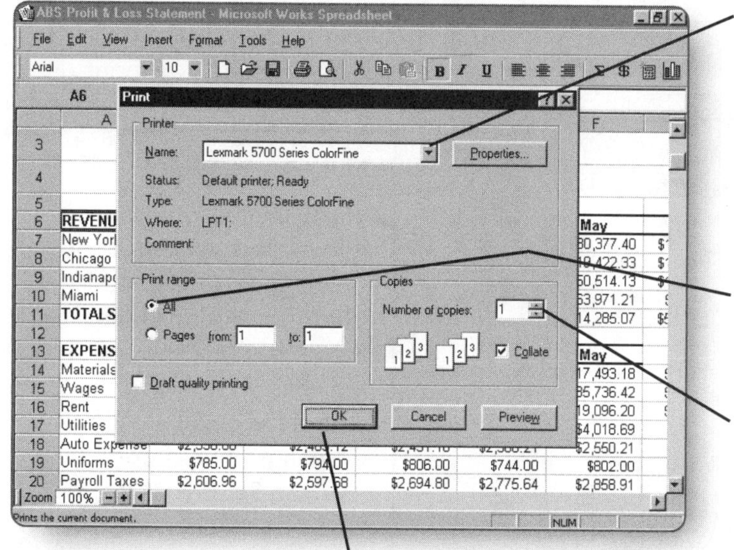

- **Printer name**. If you are connected to more than one printer, you can choose the name of the printer to use for this print job. Click on the down arrow (▼) in the Name: list box and make a selection.
- **Print range**. Choose which pages of your document to print in the Print range box.
- **Number of copies**. Choose the number of copies to be printed by clicking on the up/down arrows (⬍) in the Number of copies: list box.

3. Click on any desired **option.** The option will be selected.

4. Click on **OK** after you have made your selections. The document will be sent to the printer.

15

Creating Charts

A chart is an effective way to illustrate the data in your spreadsheet. It can make relationships between numbers easier to see because it turns numbers into shapes, and the shapes can then be compared to one another. In this chapter, you'll learn how to:

- Create a chart
- Modify a chart
- Delete a chart

Creating a Chart

Creating a chart is a simple process using the Works Chart Wizard. You first decide what you want to chart and how you want it to look.

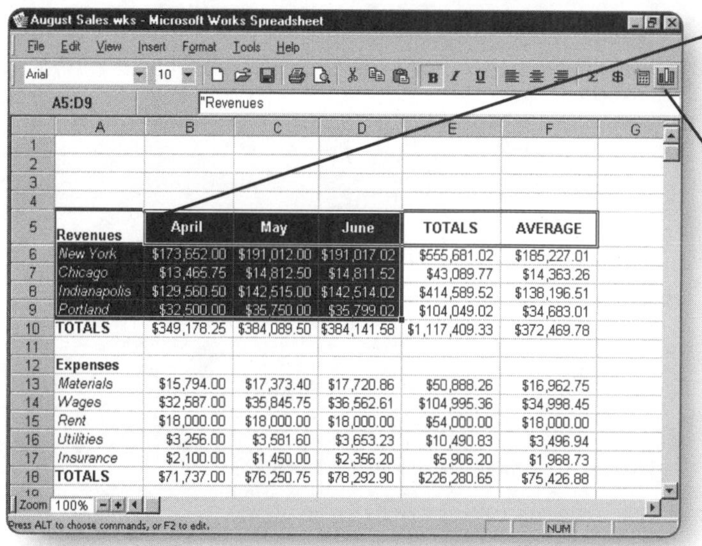

1. **Select** the **range** that you want to chart. The range will be highlighted.

2. **Click** on the **New Chart button**. The New Chart Wizard will display onscreen.

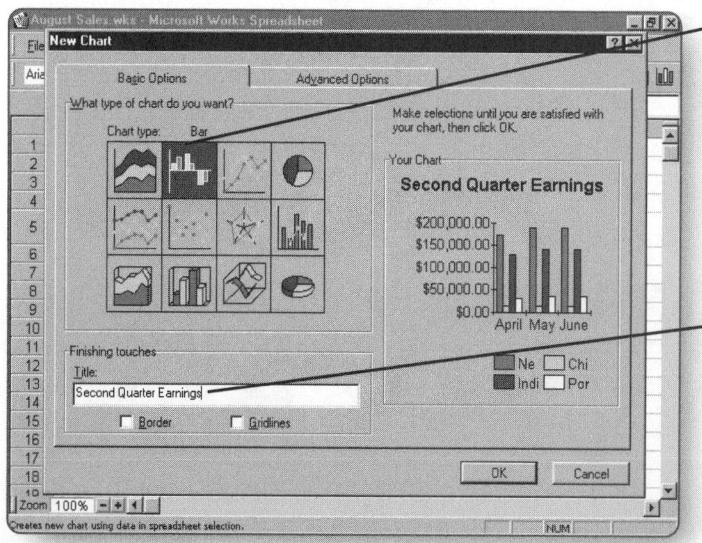

3. **Click** on a **Chart type**. A sample will be displayed in the Your Chart area.

4. **Click** in the **Title: text box**. A blinking insertion point will appear.

5. **Type** a **title** for your chart. The title will appear in the Title: text box.

6. Click on the **Border check box** if you want a border around the entire chart. A ✔ will be placed in the box.

7. Click on the **Gridlines check box** if you want gridlines displayed in your chart. A ✔ will be placed in the box.

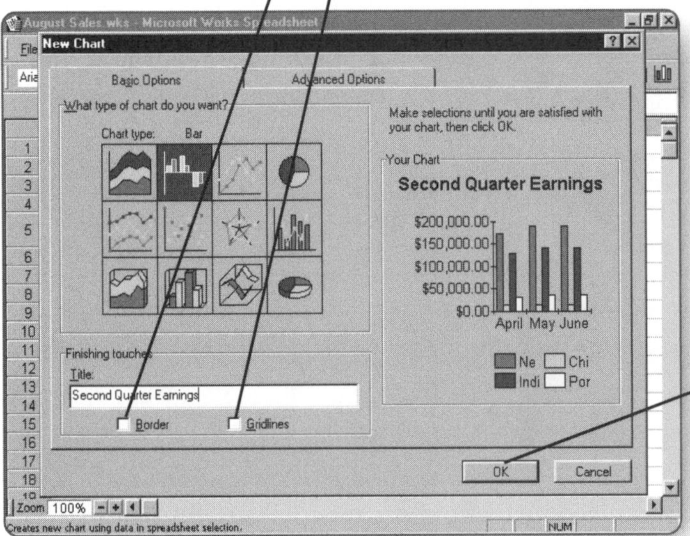

NOTE

If Works does not read the data in the order you expected it, click on the Advanced Options tab and experiment with the options listed.

8. Click on **OK**. The chart will be displayed as a new window.

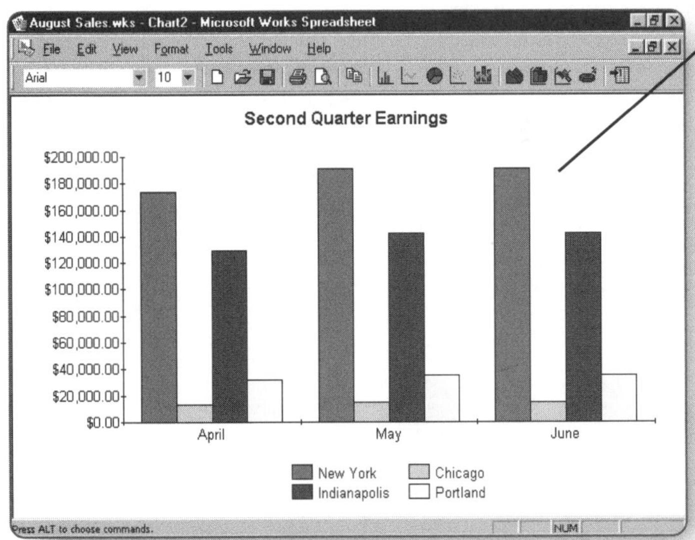

The data from the selected cells of the spreadsheet is plotted out in a chart. If the data in the spreadsheet changes, the chart also changes.

Switching Views

After creating the chart, you may need to return to the spreadsheet window to edit the data.

1. **Click** on **View**. The View menu will appear.

2. **Click** on **Spreadsheet**. The spreadsheet will be displayed.

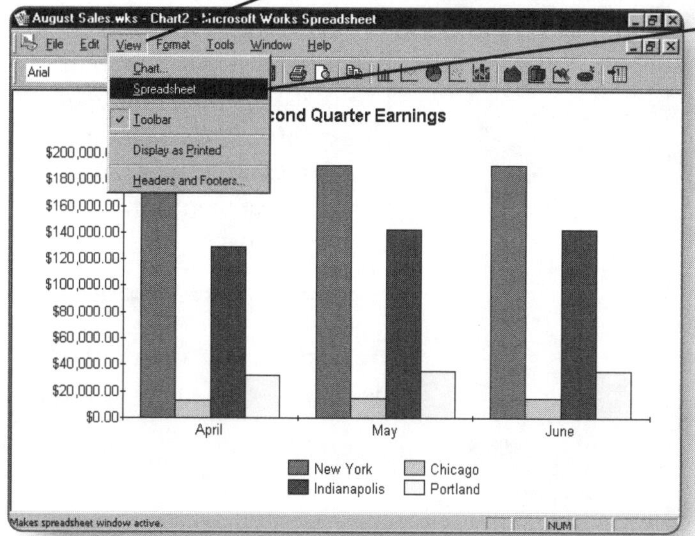

3. **Click** on **View** to return to the chart window. The View menu will appear.

4. **Click** on **Chart**. The View Chart dialog box will open.

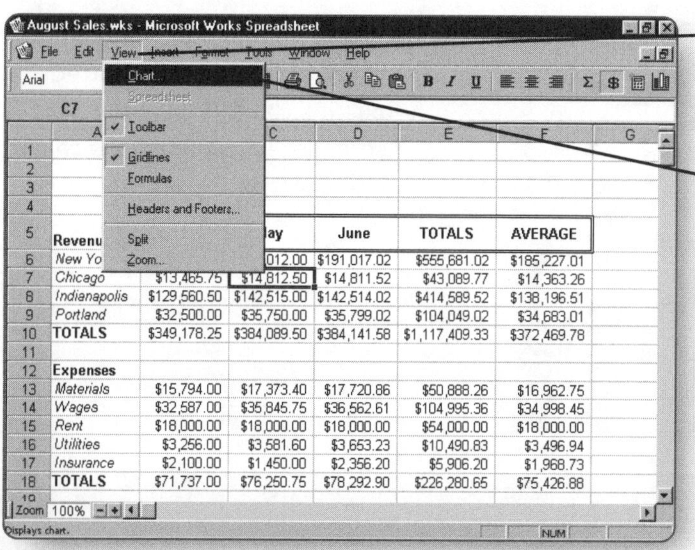

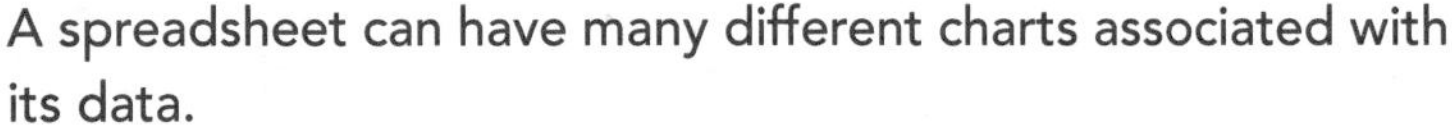

A spreadsheet can have many different charts associated with its data.

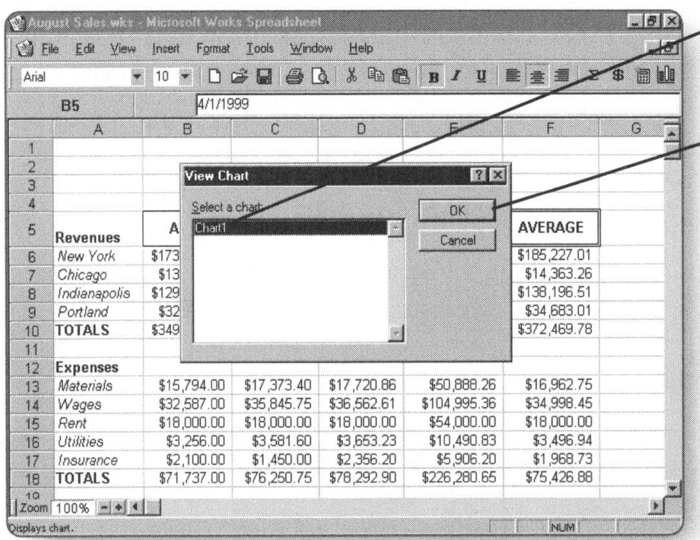

5. Click on the **chart** to display. The option will be highlighted.

6. Click on **OK**. The chart window will be displayed.

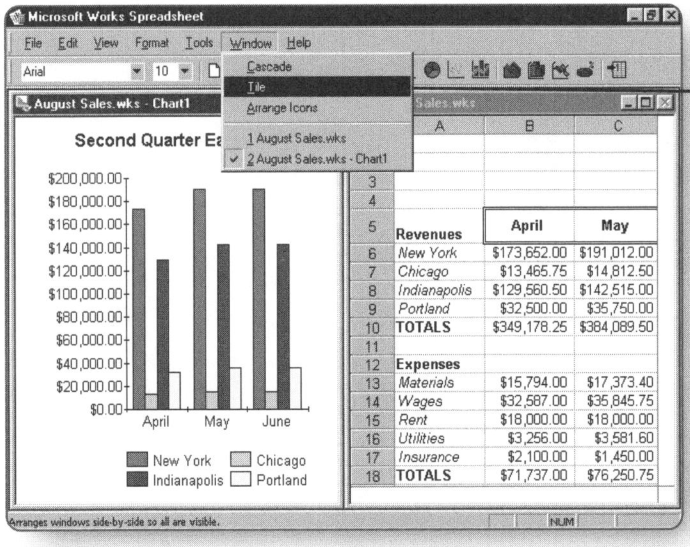

TIP

To view both the spreadsheet and chart at the same time, click on Window and then click on Tile. The two windows will be displayed side by side. Double-click on the title bar of either window to maximize it to a full screen.

Modifying a Chart

Creating a chart is so simple that you probably want to enhance the chart to improve its appearance. You can change the style, make it 3-D, or add titles to the chart to further explain its use.

Changing a Chart Style

If you want to change the style of the chart, you can select a bar, area, pie, or line chart as well as make it 3-D.

1. Display the **chart**. The chart window will be active.

2. Click on **Format**. The Format menu will appear.

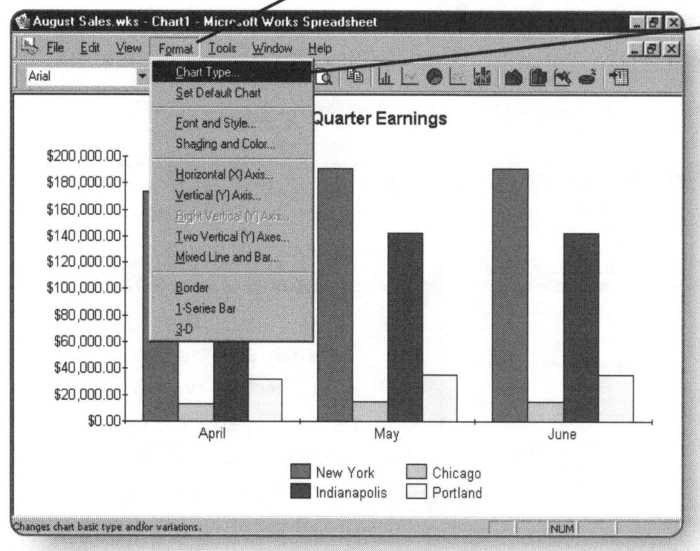

3. Click on **Chart Type**. The Chart Type dialog box will open with the Basic Types tab in front.

4. Click on a **Chart type**. A sample will be displayed.

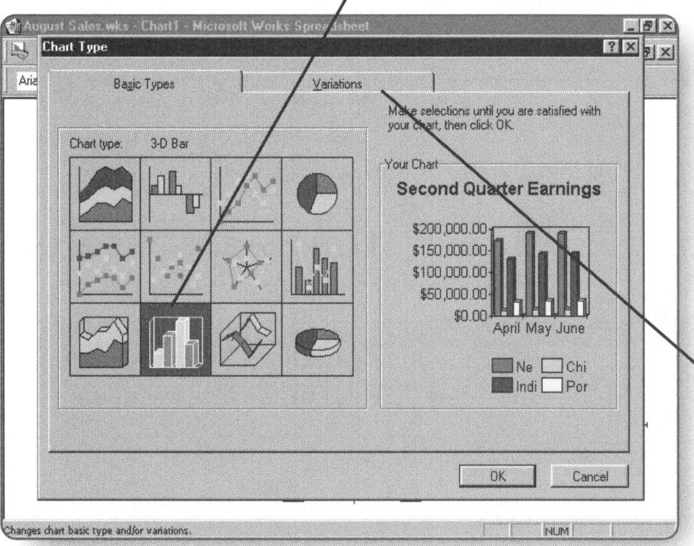

NOTE

Traditionally, bar charts compare item to item, pie charts compare parts of a whole item, and line charts show a trend over a period of time.

5. Click on the **Variations tab**. Options for each chart type will be displayed.

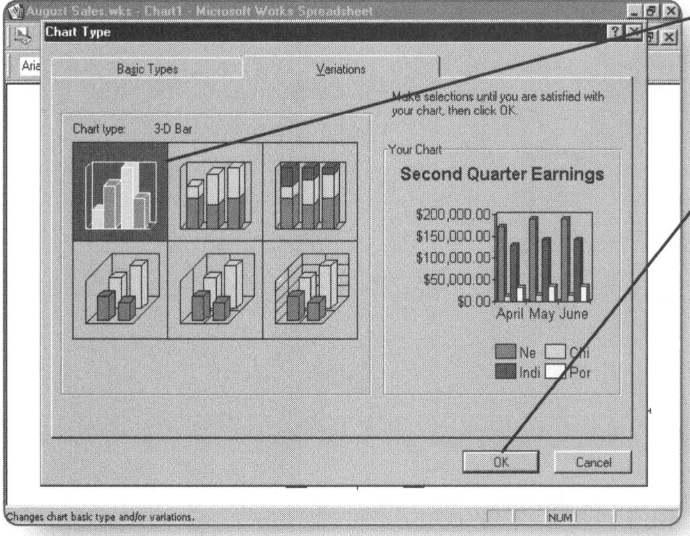

6. Click on any desired **variation**. A sample will be displayed.

7. Click on **OK**. The chart will change to the selected style.

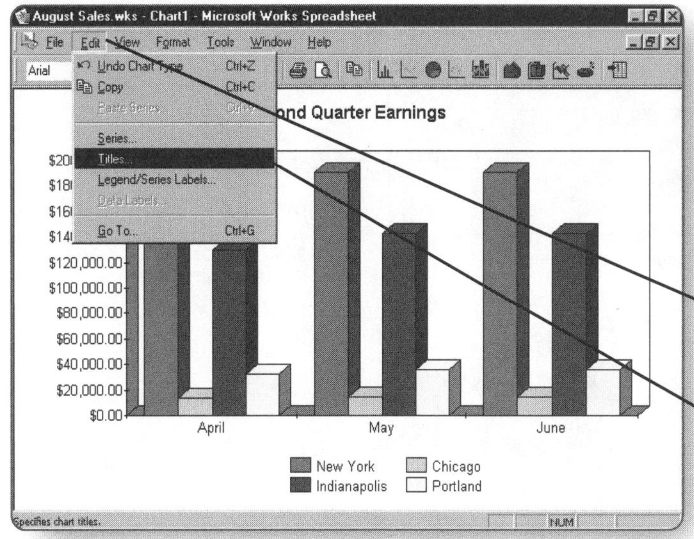

Adding Chart Titles

When you first created the chart, you had an option to give the chart a title. You can edit or delete that title, or assign other types of titles.

1. Click on **Edit**. The Edit menu will appear.

2. Click on **Titles**. The Edit Titles dialog box will open.

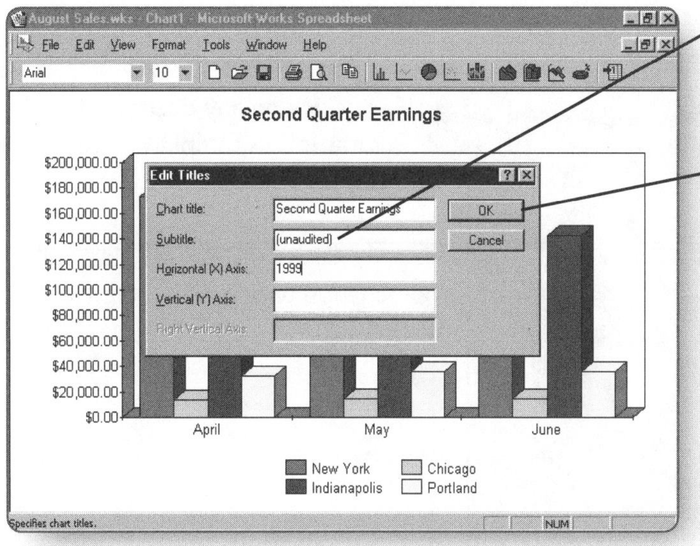

3. Type or modify the **text** for any title. The title will appear in the text box.

4. Click on **OK**. The chart titles will be changed.

Naming a Chart

It's possible to have many charts associated with a single spreadsheet. Identify the charts by assigning them a name other than the default name—Chart1, Chart2, and so on.

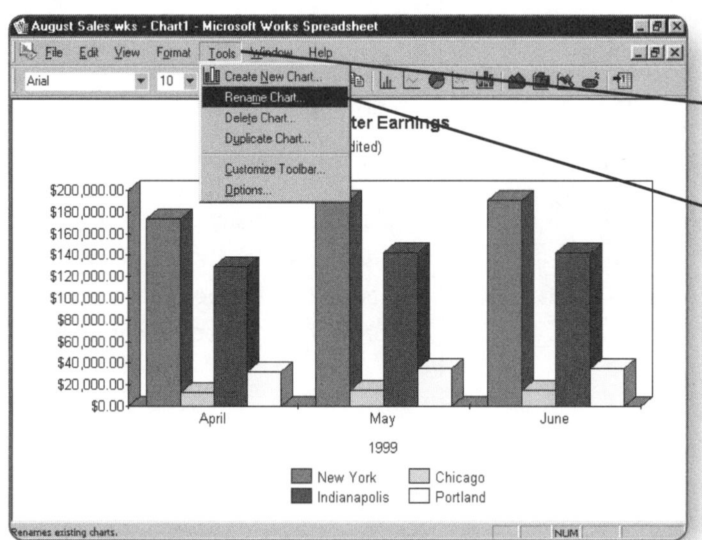

1. **Click** on **Tools**. The Tools menu will appear.

2. **Click** on **Rename Chart**. The Rename Chart dialog box will open.

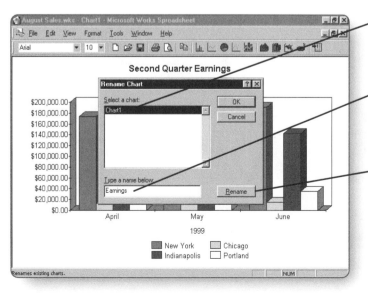

3. **Click** on the **chart** to be renamed. The chart name will be highlighted.

4. **Type** a new **name** in the Type a name below: text box. The new name will be displayed.

5. **Click** on **Rename**. The chart will be renamed.

6. **Click** on **OK**. The Rename Chart dialog box will close.

Changing the Chart Series

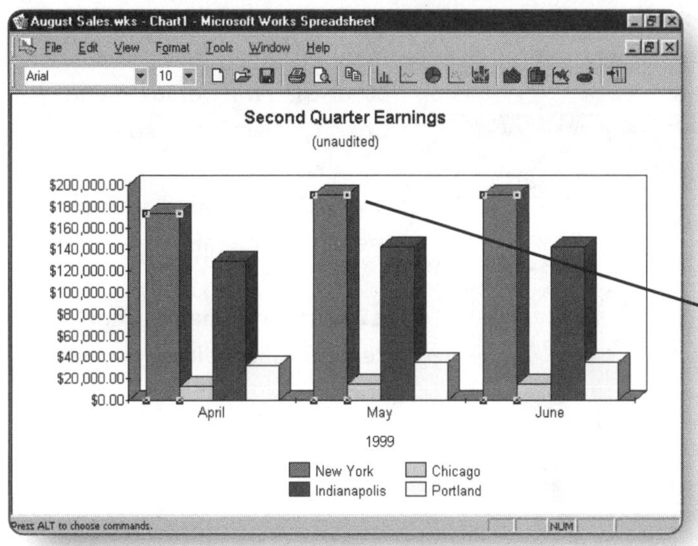

If you do not like the default colors assigned to a chart, you can change them for any series.

1. **Display** the **chart** to be modified. The chart will be displayed.

2. **Click** on any colored **bar, line, or series** item. Four white handles will appear around all items in the selected series.

3. **Click** on **Format**. The Format menu will appear.

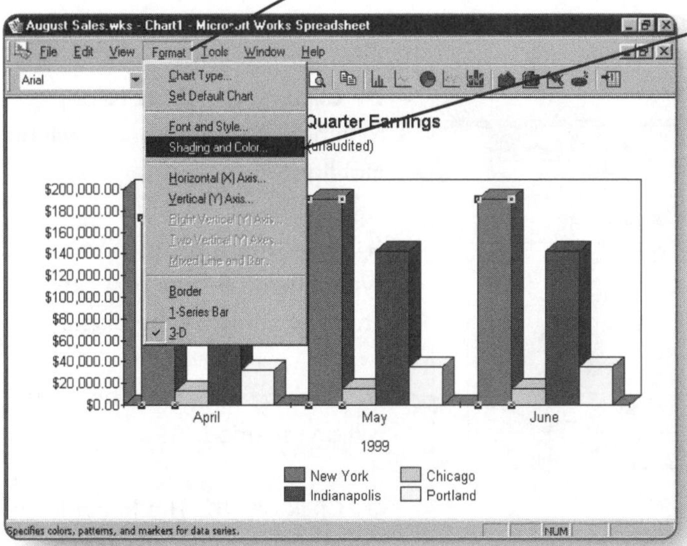

4. **Click** on **Shading and Color**. The Format Shading and Color dialog box will open.

> **TIP**
>
> Alternatively, double-click on any bar, line, or series item to open the Format Shading and Color dialog box.

5. Click on a **color** for the selected series. The color will be highlighted.

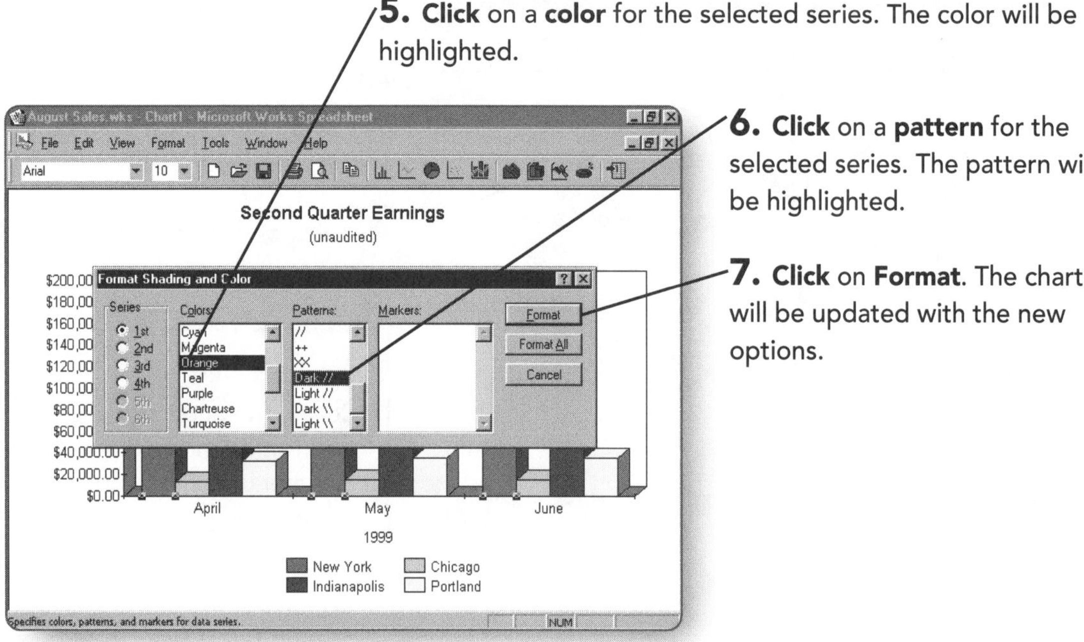

6. Click on a **pattern** for the selected series. The pattern will be highlighted.

7. Click on **Format**. The chart will be updated with the new options.

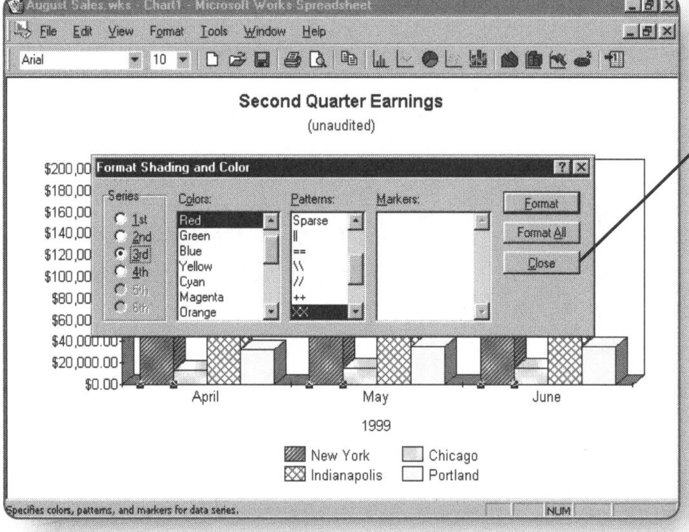

8. Repeat steps 3 through **5** for each series to be changed.

9. Click on **Close**. The Format Shading and Color dialog box will close.

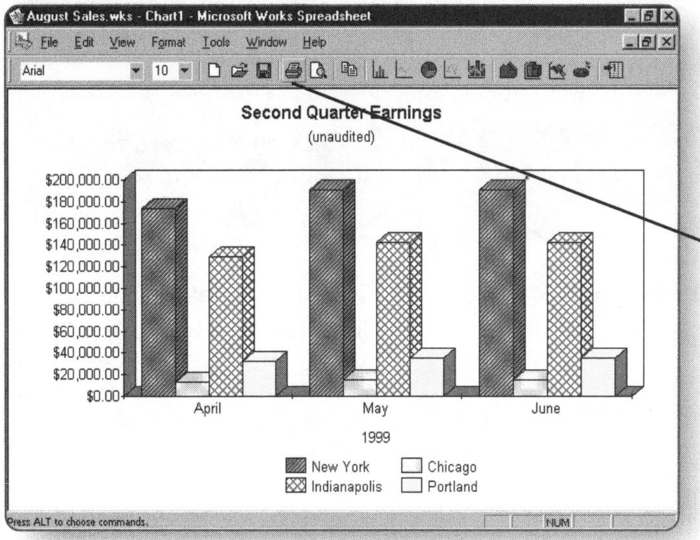

Printing a Chart

Printing a chart is generally a little slower than other types of documents. Be patient.

1. Click on the **Print button**. The chart will print.

> **TIP**
>
> Set up the page size and orientation through the File menu and the Page Setup dialog box.

Deleting a Chart

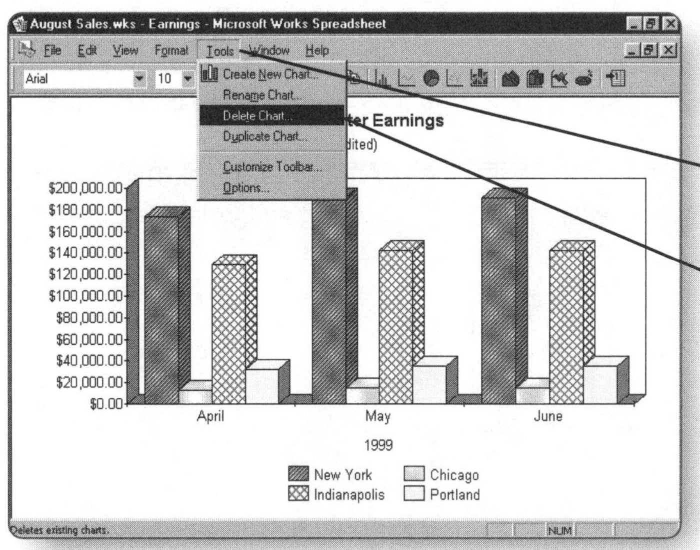

If you no longer want the chart created from your spreadsheet, you can delete it.

1. Click on **Tools**. The Tools menu will appear.

2. Click on **Delete Chart**. The Delete Chart dialog box will open.

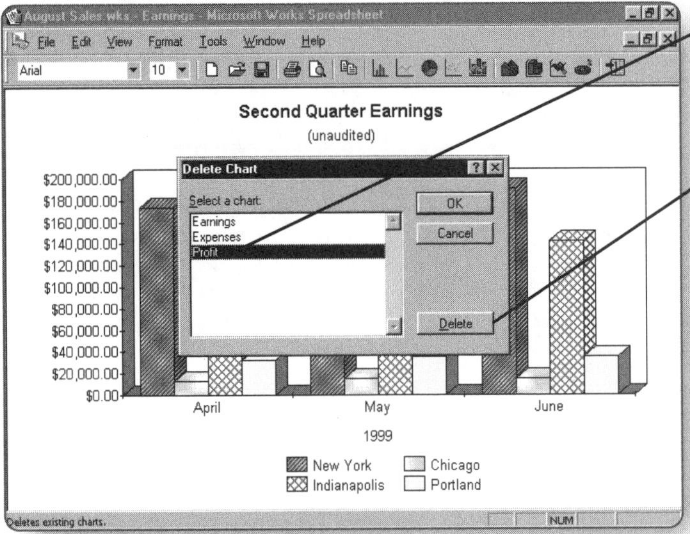

3. Click on the **chart** that you want to delete. The chart name will be highlighted.

4. Click on **Delete**. The chart will be deleted from the dialog box.

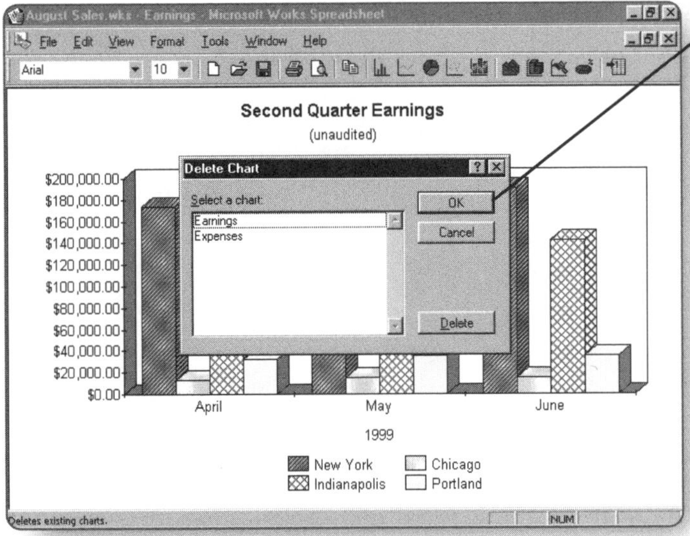

5. Click on **OK**. A confirmation message will appear.

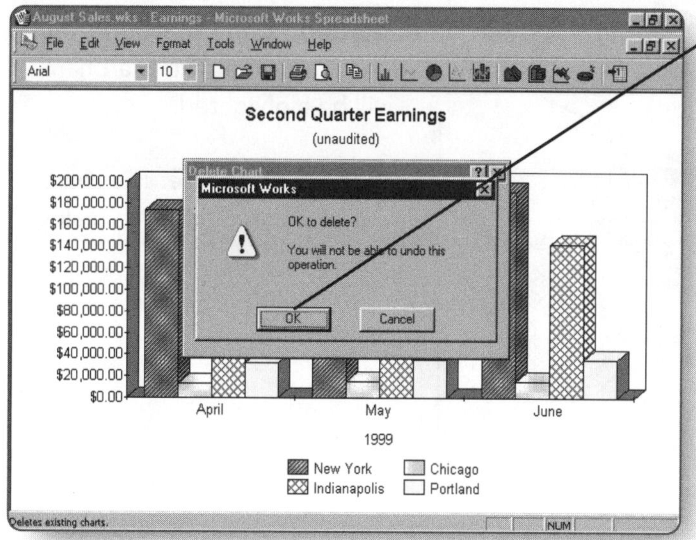

6. Click on **OK**. The chart will be permanently deleted.

> **NOTE**
>
> All charts are saved with their corresponding spreadsheet.

Part III Review Questions

1. Spreadsheet data is made up of what three components? *See "Entering Data" in Chapter 10*
2. What character should you type first to enter a value as a label? *See "Entering Values" in Chapter 10*
3. What function key can be pressed to edit the contents of a cell? *See "Editing the Contents of a Cell" in Chapter 10*
4. When deleting a spreadsheet column, where do the remaining columns move? *See "Deleting Rows and Columns" in Chapter 11*
5. What does the Fill feature do when you type the word January in a cell and drag across to other cells? *See "Using the Fill Feature" in Chapter 11*
6. With what character must all spreadsheet formulas begin? *See "Creating Formulas" in Chapter 12*
7. What character is used in a formula to designate an absolute reference? *See "Creating an Absolute Reference in a Formula" in Chapter 12*
8. How can you center heading text across a group of columns? *See "Centering Headings" in Chapter 13*
9. How do you tell Works you want to print a specific area of the spreadsheet? *See "Printing a Range" in Chapter 14*
10. What styles of charts can Works create? *See "Changing a Chart Style" in Chapter 15*

PART IV

Using a Database

16

Creating a Database

You use databases every day—whether or not you realize it. Your phone book is a database; your television show listing is a database; even a cookbook is a database. A database in its simplest form is an organized list of information. Works provides a simple database application that allows you to create and manage your own databases. In this chapter, you'll learn how to:

- Understand fields and records
- Create a new database
- Look at different database views
- Move, add, or delete fields
- Save a database

Understanding Fields and Records

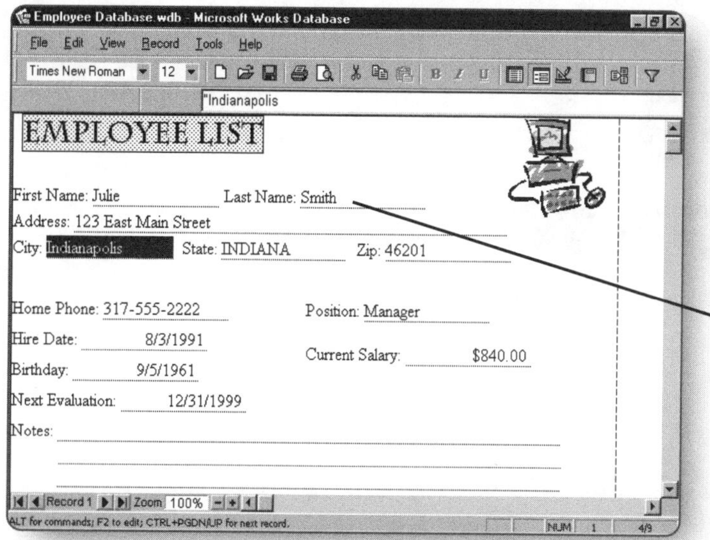

Information in a database is grouped into records and fields.

- A *record* is all the information about one person, product, event, and so on. Every record in a database contains the same fields.
- A *field* is one item in a record, such as a name or address. You can enter text, numbers, dates, or formulas in a field.

Creating a New Database

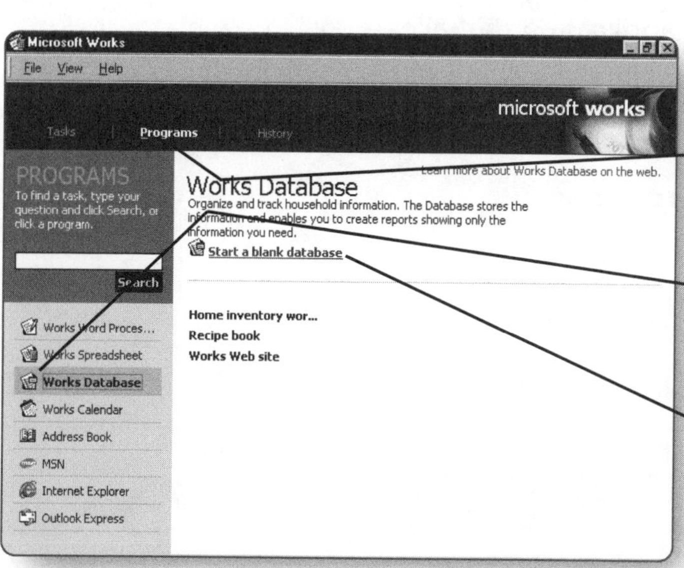

Create a new database by using the Works Task Launcher.

1. **Click** on **Programs**. A listing of the Works components will appear.

2. **Click** on **Works Database**. A listing of database tasks will appear.

3. **Click** on **Start a blank database**. The Create Database dialog box will open.

Adding Fields

The first thing you must do when creating a new database is name your fields. If you are creating an address database, you might include fields such as name, address, phone number or birth date. If you are creating a database to track your CD collection, you might include fields such as title, artist, or date purchased.

1. **Type** a **name** for the first field. The text will appear in the Field name: text box. Field names can be a maximum of 15 characters.

Fields can be in a variety of formats such as General, Number, or Date. Items such as name, address, or telephone number would be a General (text) format, whereas data such as age might be a Number format, and a hire date might be a Date format.

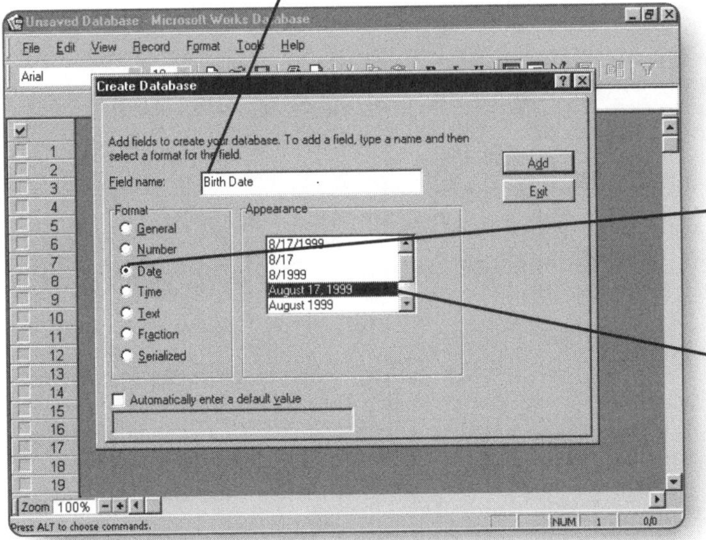

2. **Click** on a **format type** for the field. The option will be selected.

3. **Select** any **Appearance options**. The option will be selected.

Works can automatically enter field data. For example, if you are creating an address book where most records reside in Indiana, Works can automatically enter IN or Indiana. It is then easy to change it for the few records who do not reside in Indiana.

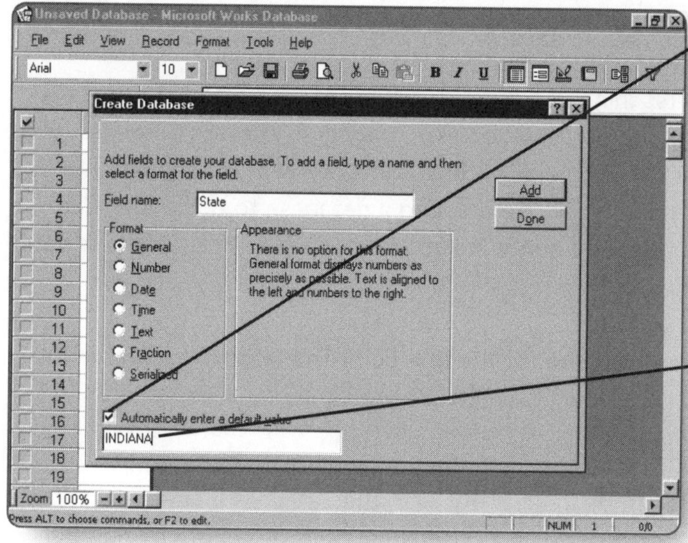

4. Optionally, **click** on **Automatically enter a default value**. A ✔ will be placed in the box.

5. **Click** in the **default value text box**. A blinking insertion point will appear.

6. **Enter** the **default value**. The text will appear in the default value text box.

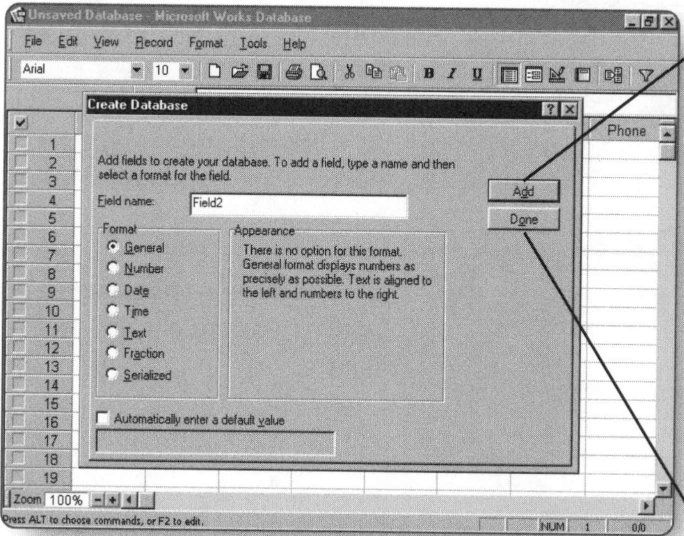

7. **Click** on **Add**. The field will be added, and you will be prompted for the name of the next field.

8. **Repeat steps 1** through **7** until all fields have been added.

> **TIP**
>
> You can edit fields, add fields, or delete unwanted fields later.

9. **Click** on **Done**. The Create Database dialog box will close.

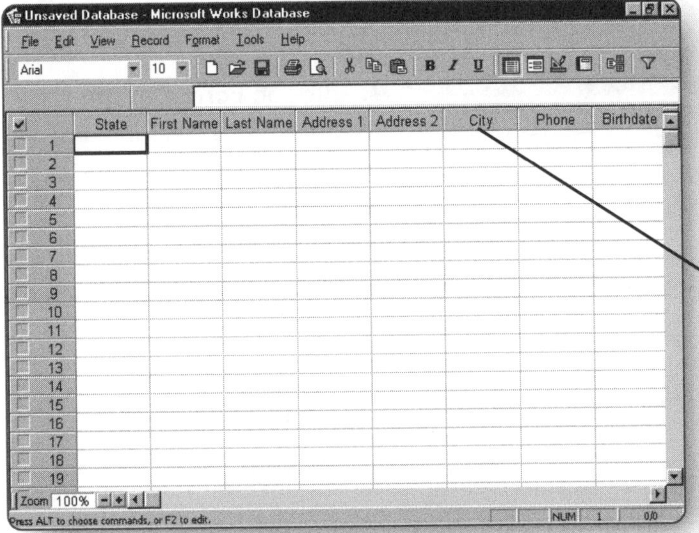

Looking at the Different Views

When the database is first displayed, it is shown in List view.

List view is similar to looking at a spreadsheet. The field names are entered as column headings. As you enter each record, the information displays in the rows. In List view, you can see multiple records at the same time.

1. **Click** on **View**. The View menu will appear.

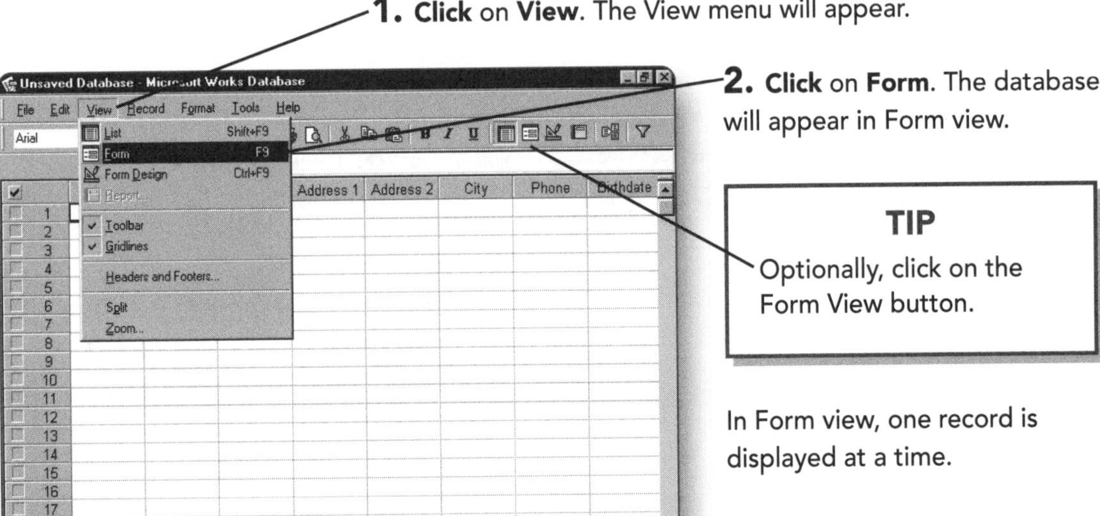

2. **Click** on **Form**. The database will appear in Form view.

TIP

Optionally, click on the Form View button.

In Form view, one record is displayed at a time.

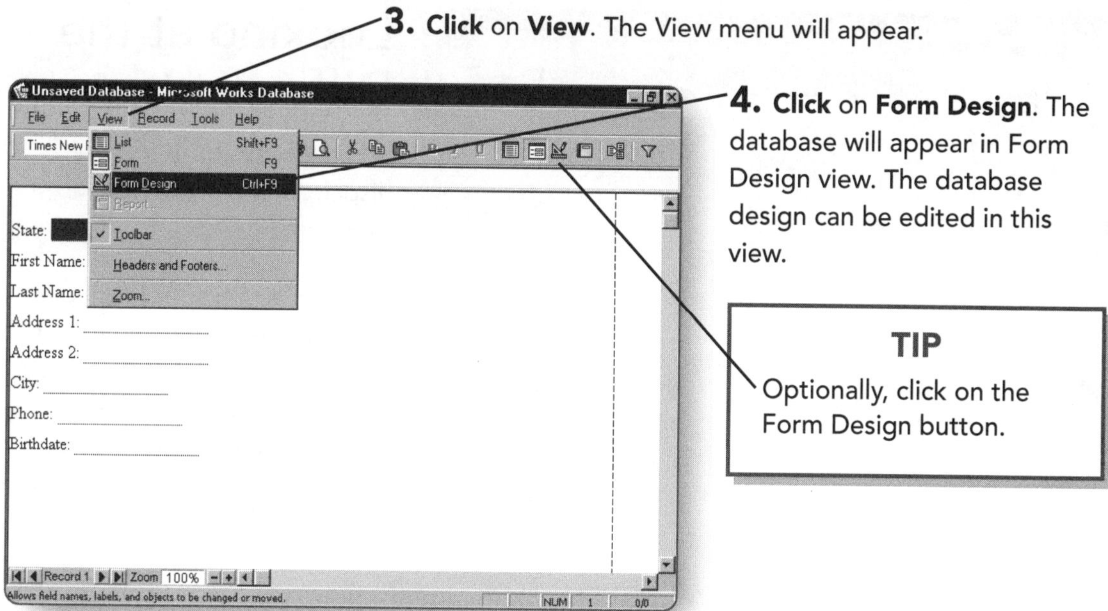

3. **Click** on **View**. The View menu will appear.

4. **Click** on **Form Design**. The database will appear in Form Design view. The database design can be edited in this view.

> **TIP**
>
> Optionally, click on the Form Design button.

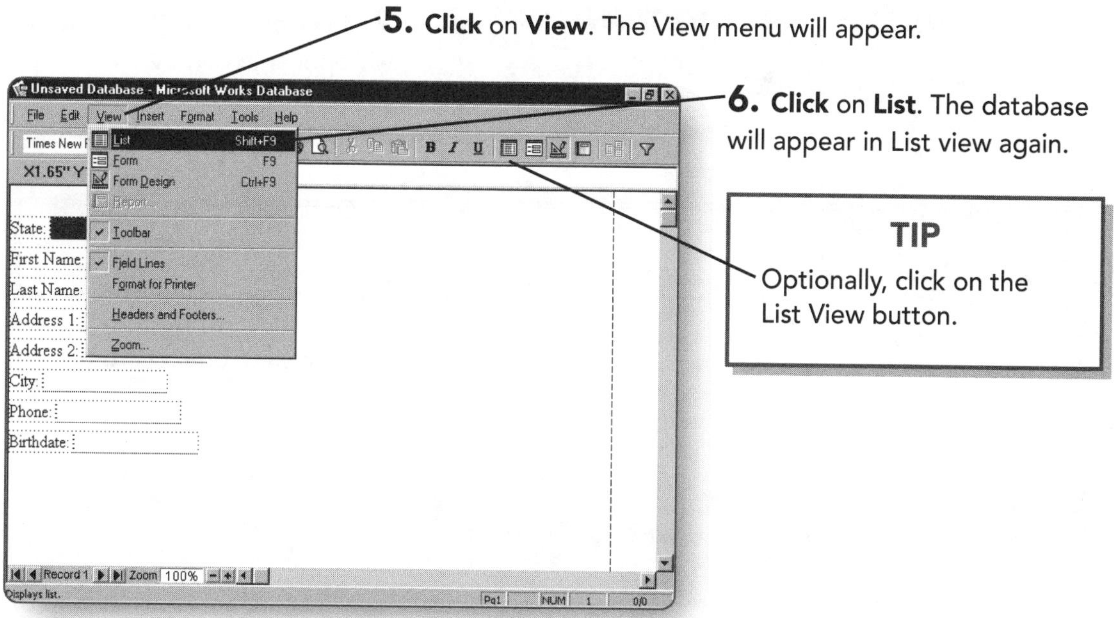

5. **Click** on **View**. The View menu will appear.

6. **Click** on **List**. The database will appear in List view again.

> **TIP**
>
> Optionally, click on the List View button.

Moving a Field

If you place a field in the wrong position, you can move it.

Moving a Field in Form Design View

Enhance the display of the fields by placing them in easy-to-read positions on the screen. All changes to the display design must be made in Form Design view.

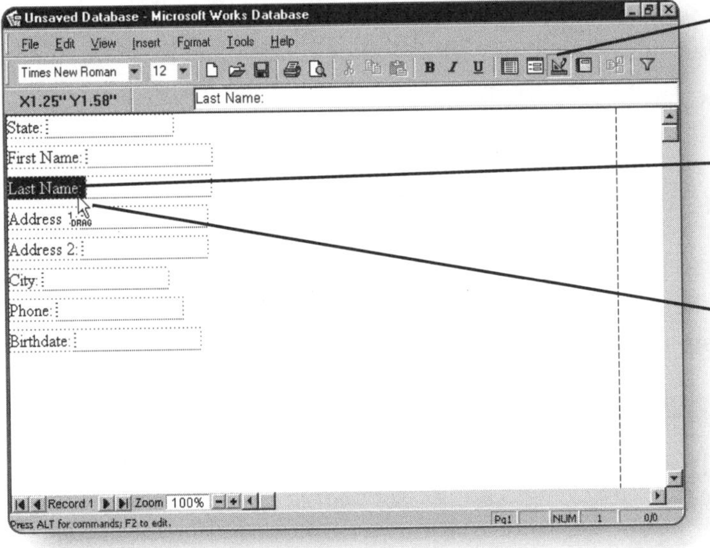

1. **Click** on the **Form Design button.** The database will appear in Form Design view.

2. **Click** on the **field name** to be moved. The field name will be highlighted.

3. **Position** the **mouse pointer** over the highlighted field. The mouse pointer will display the word "DRAG."

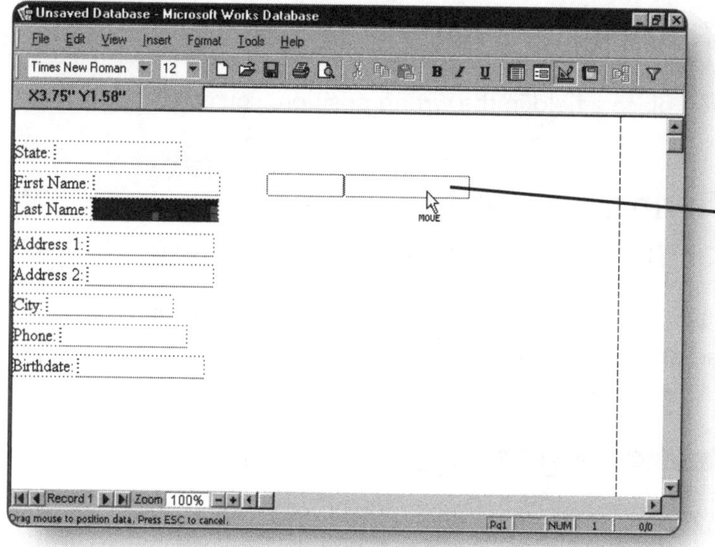

4. **Press and hold** the **mouse button** over the highlighted field. The mouse pointer will display the word "MOVE."

5. **Drag** the **field name** to the desired position. A box will indicate the new position.

6. **Release** the **mouse button**. The field name and field contents will be moved.

Moving a Field in List View

If you move a field in Form view, it does not change the order of the fields in List view. You can use the Windows Copy and Paste commands to change the order in List view.

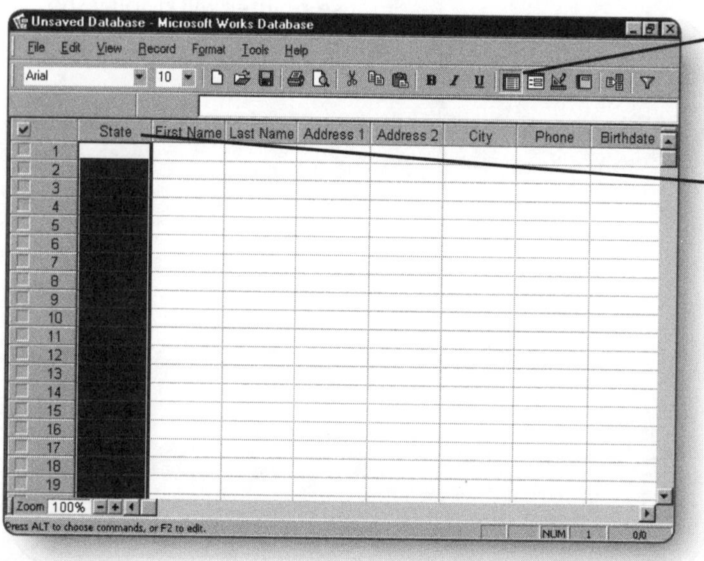

1. **Click** on the **List View button**. The database will appear in List view.

2. **Click** on the **field name** to be moved. The column will be highlighted.

3. Click on **Edit**. The Edit menu will appear.

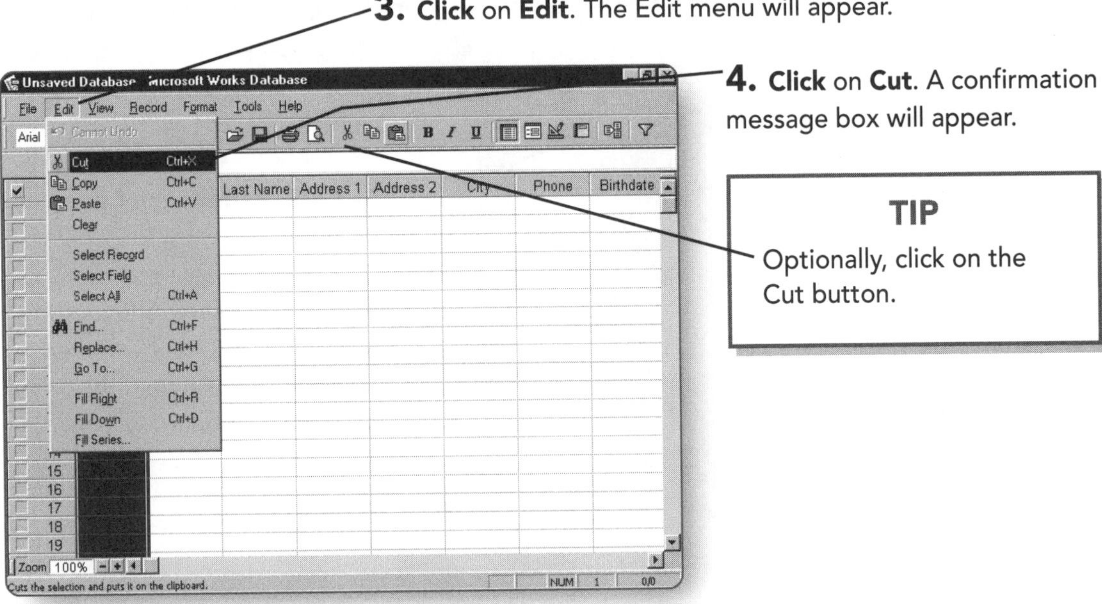

4. Click on **Cut**. A confirmation message box will appear.

TIP

Optionally, click on the Cut button.

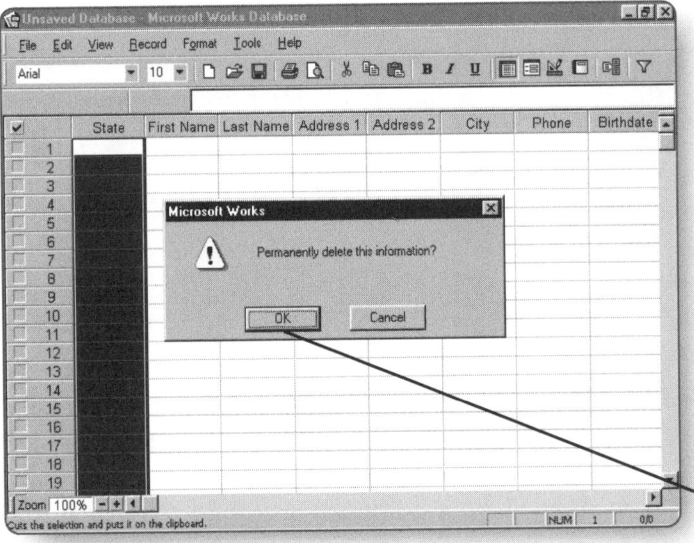

NOTE

This message box says "Permanently delete this information?" Don't be alarmed. You are not going to *permanently* delete the information. You are going to temporarily place the information on the Windows Clipboard.

5. Click on **OK**. The column/field will be deleted.

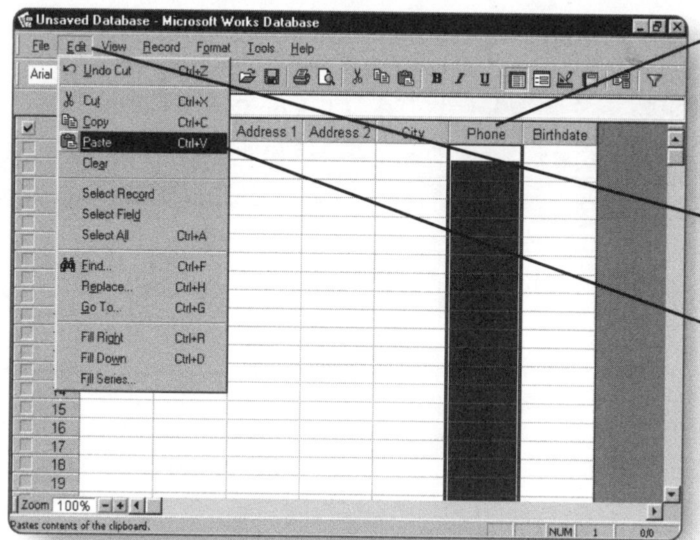

6. **Click** on the **field heading** where you want the field to be positioned. The current field will be highlighted.

7. **Click** on **Edit**. The Edit menu will appear.

8. **Click** on **Paste**. The existing field (and data) will be moved to the right, and the field that you put in the Clipboard will be inserted.

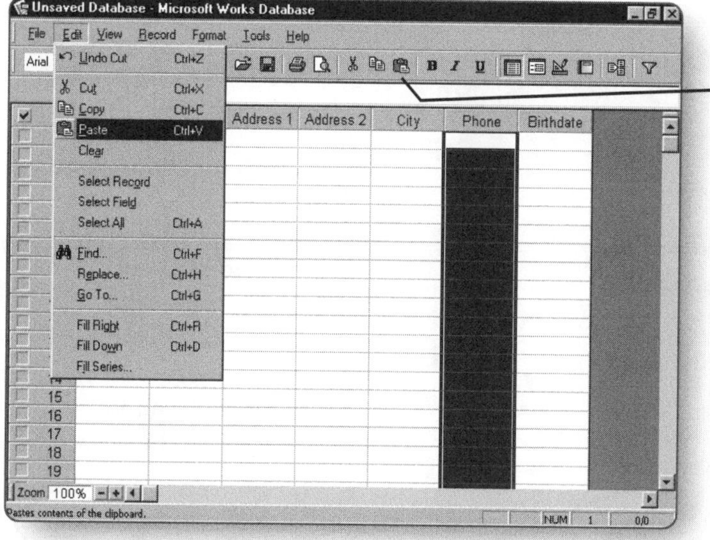

TIP

Optionally, click on the Paste button.

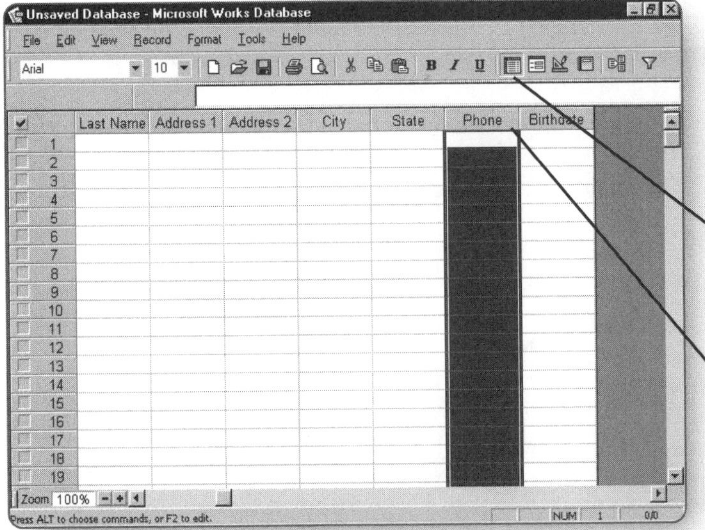

Adding Fields

Add as many fields as you need. The easiest method to add fields is using List view.

1. If necessary, **click** on the **List View button**. The database will appear in List view.

2. Click on the **field heading** located at the position where you want the new field. The field column will be highlighted.

3. Click on **Record**. The Record menu will appear.

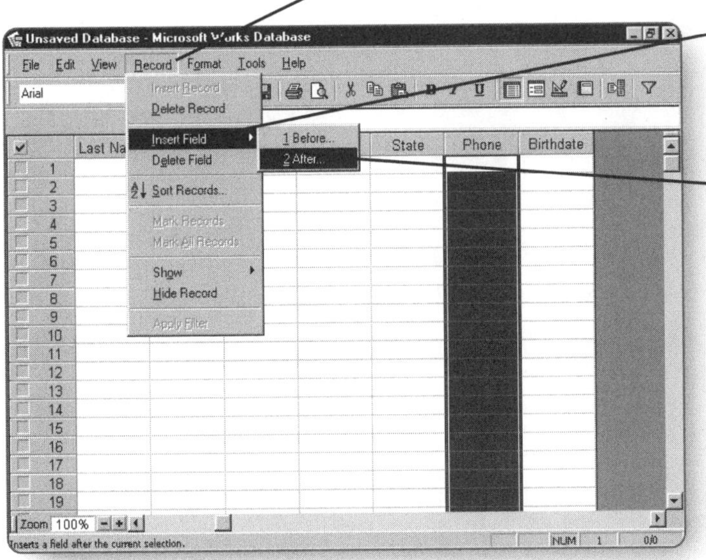

4. Click on **Insert Field**. The Insert Field submenu will appear.

5. Click on **Before or After**. The Insert Field dialog box will open.

6. **Type** a **name** in the Field name: text box. The text will appear in the text box.

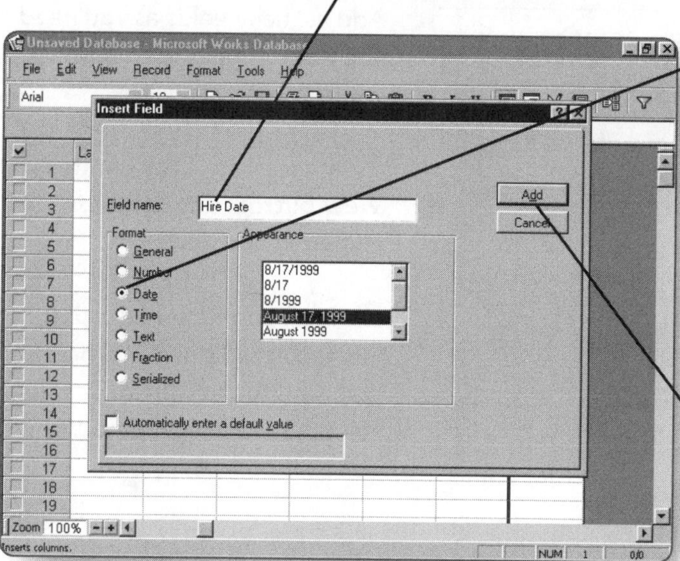

7. **Click** on a **Format** type. The option will be selected.

> **TIP**
>
> Optionally, click on Automatically enter a default value and enter the default value in the text box.

8. **Click** on **Add**. The field will be added.

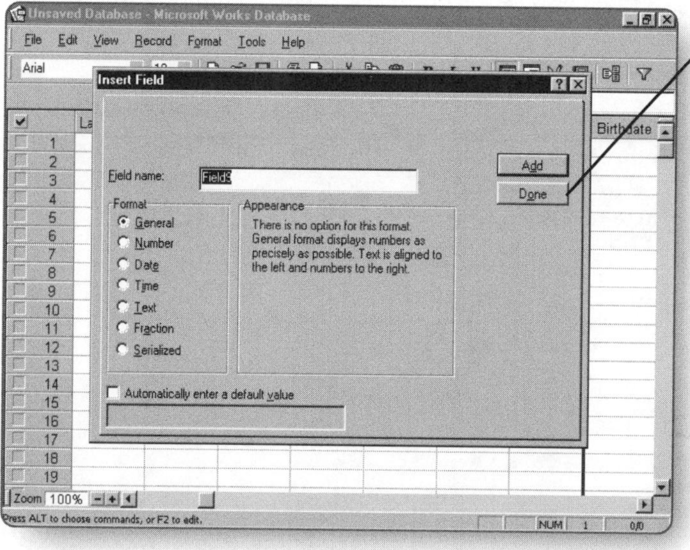

9. **Click** on **Done**. The Insert Field dialog box will close.

Deleting a Field

If a field is no longer needed, you can delete it. When you delete a field, any data for that field is also deleted.

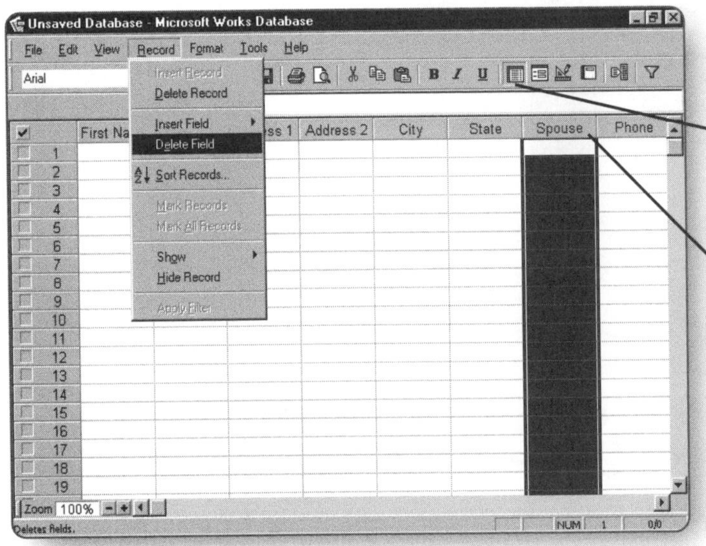

The easiest method to delete a field is using List view.

1. If necessary, **click** on the **List View button**. The database will appear in List view.

2. **Click** on the **field heading** to be deleted. The column will be highlighted.

3. **Click** on **Record**. The Record menu will appear.

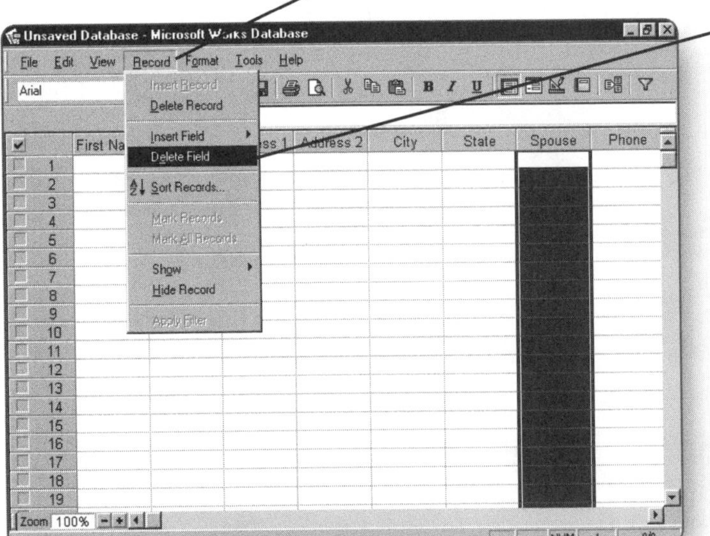

4. **Click** on **Delete Field**. A confirmation message will appear.

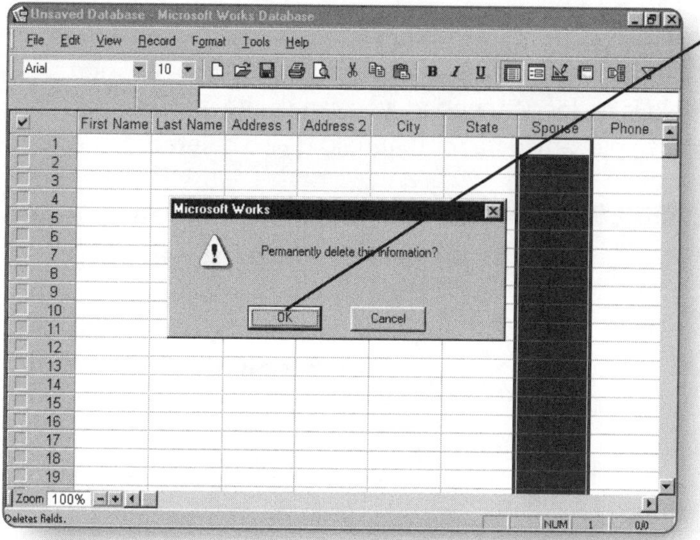

5. Click on **OK**. The field will be deleted.

Saving a Database

As with the other components of Microsoft Works, when you create a file, you should save it for future use.

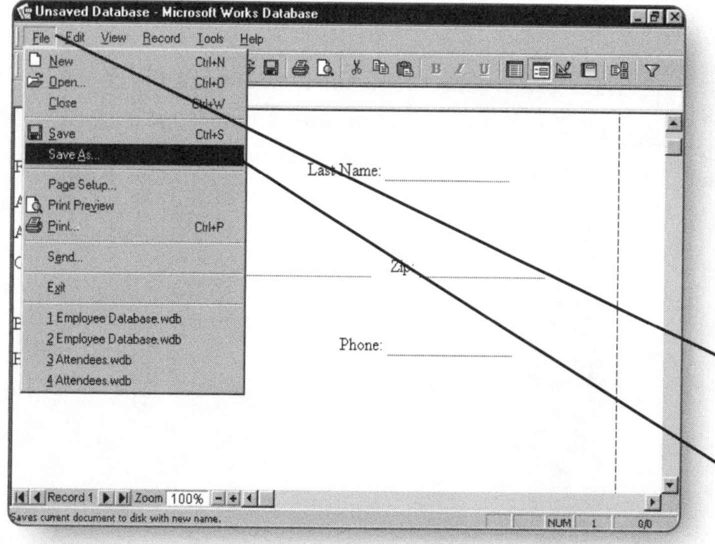

Saving a Database the First Time

When you first create a document, it has no name. If you want to use that document later, it must have a name so that Works can find it.

1. Click on **File**. The File menu will appear.

2. Click on **Save As.** The Save As dialog box will open.

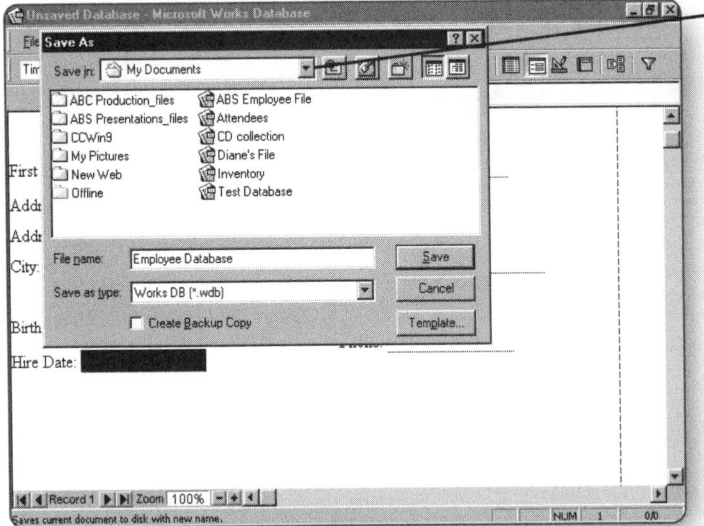

The Save in: drop-down list box lists the folder where the file will be saved. The default folder that appears is My Documents. If you don't want to save to this folder or if you want to save your database to another disk, you can select another one. Click on the down arrow (▼) to browse.

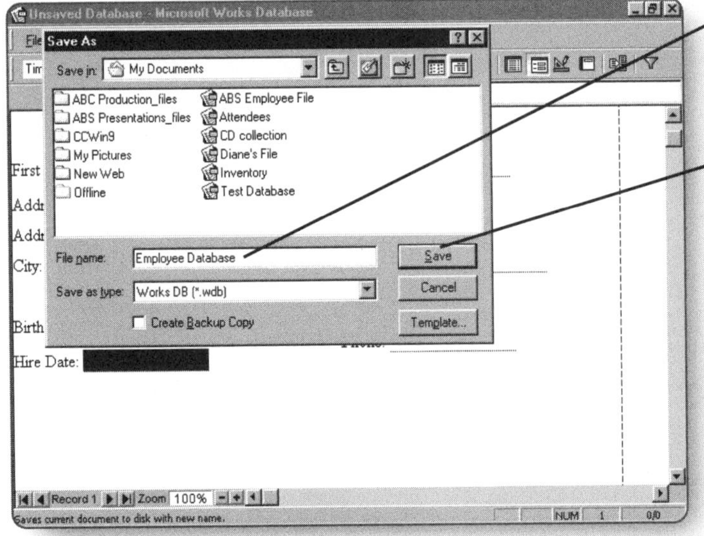

3. **Type** a **name** for your file in the File name: text box. The file name will be displayed.

4. **Click** on **Save**. Your database will be saved, and the name you specified will appear in the title bar.

Resaving a Database

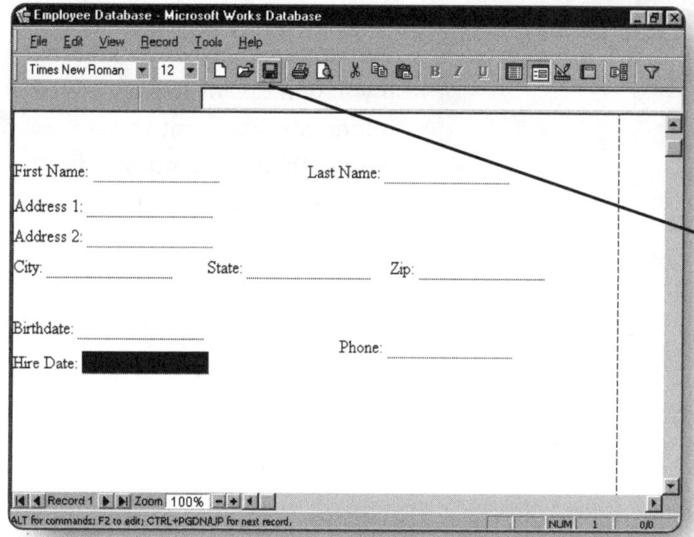

As you continue to work on your database, you should resave your database every ten minutes or so. This ensures that you do not lose any changes.

1. Click on the **Save button**. The database will be resaved with any changes. No dialog box will open because the database is resaved with the same name and in the same folder as previously specified.

17

Working with Data

After you create the database and form, you are ready to add and work with the data for your database. In this chapter, you'll learn how to:

- Enter data
- Move around the database
- Edit records
- Find and sort records
- Delete records

Working with Data

Record data can be entered in either List view or Form view. The number of records that can be entered is limited only by the size of your hard drive.

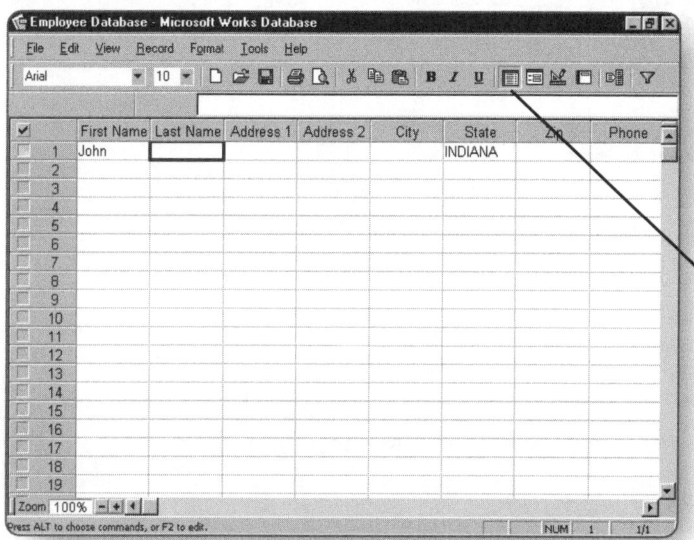

Entering Data in List View

If you are working in List view, you'll see all the records together as you enter them.

1. **Click** on the **List View button**. The database will appear in List view.

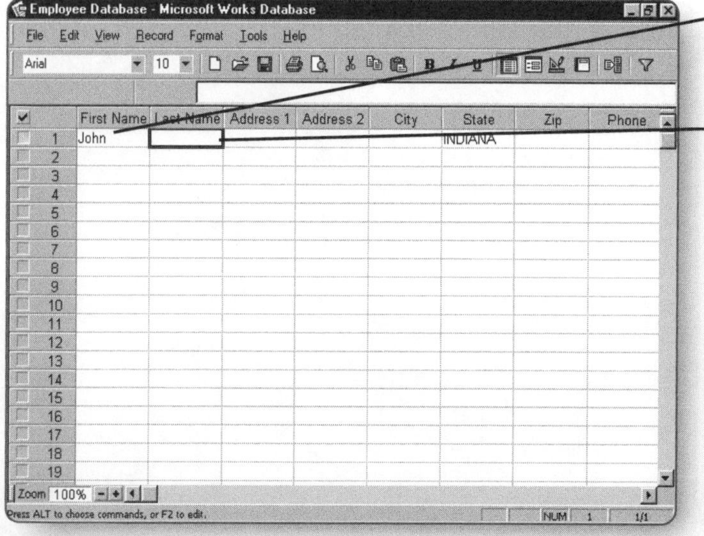

2. **Type** the **data** for the first field. The data will be entered.

3. **Press** the **Tab key**. The next field will be selected.

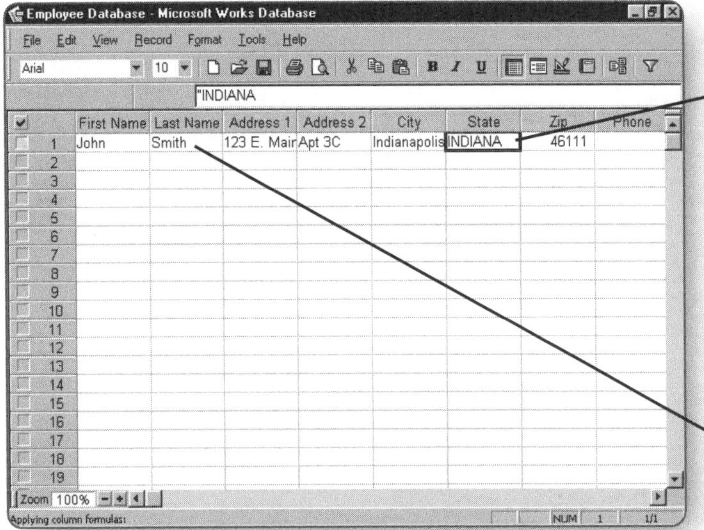

NOTE

When you enter a new record, any fields that you designed with a default value will be automatically entered for you. If you need a different value, highlight the default value and enter the new one.

4. **Type** the **data** for the next field. That data will be entered.

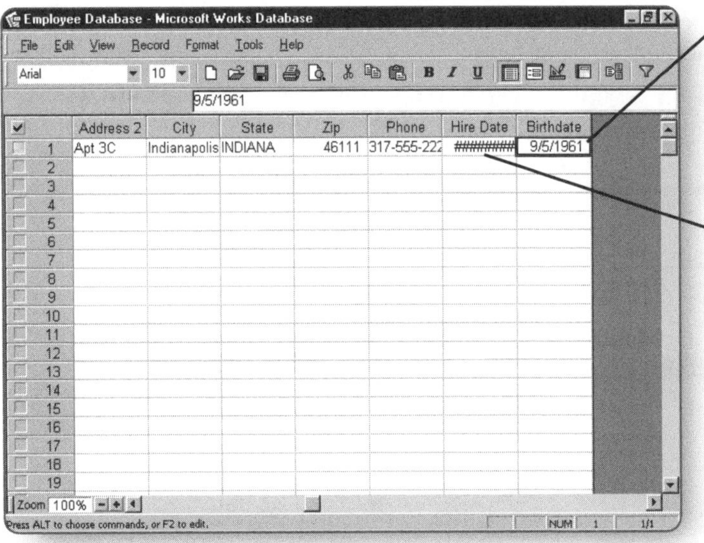

5. **Repeat steps 3** and **4** until you have entered data for the current record.

NOTE

If the data you are typing is larger than the field size, you may not see all the data displayed or you may see #### displayed. In Chapter 18, "Formatting a Database," you'll learn how to change the size of a field.

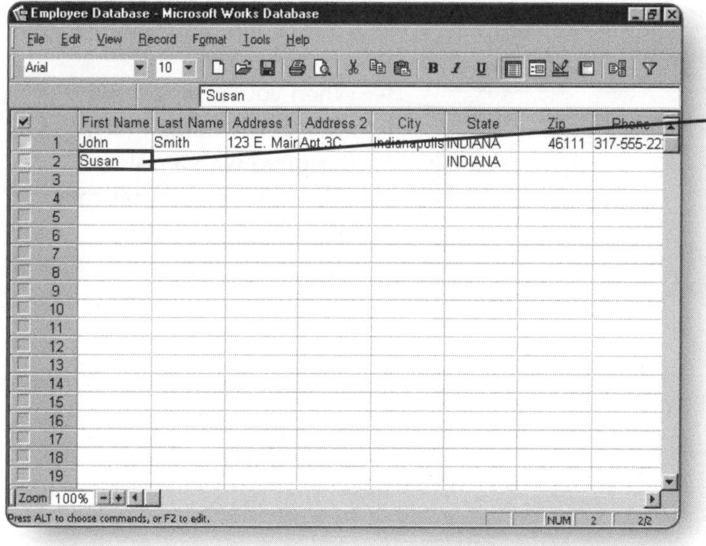

When you are ready to add another record:

6. While in the last field, **press** the **Tab** key. Works will automatically move to the first field of the next record.

Entering Data in Form View

When entering data in Form view, one record at a time will be displayed. Form view is usually the easiest view to use if you have many fields in your database.

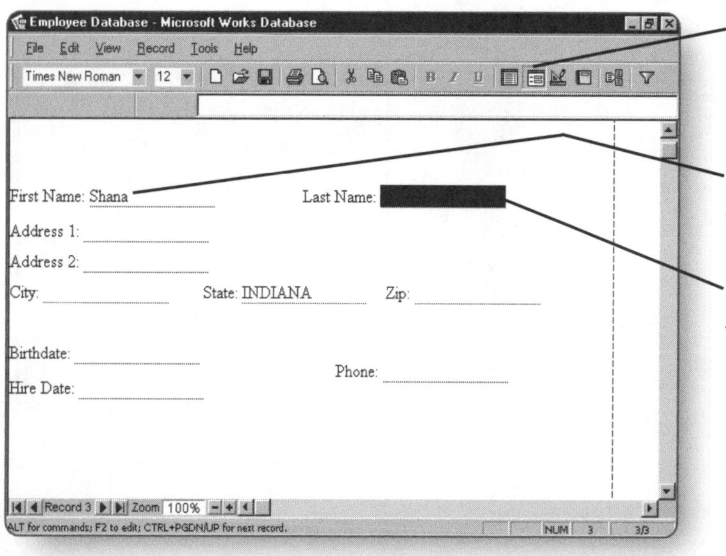

1. Click on the **Form View button**. The database will appear in Form view.

2. Type the **data** for the first field. The data will be entered.

3. Press the **Tab key**. The next field will be selected.

> **NOTE**
>
> If the data you are typing is larger than the field size, you may not see all the data displayed or you may see a series of #### displayed. In Chapter 18, "Formatting a Database," you'll learn how to change the size of a field.

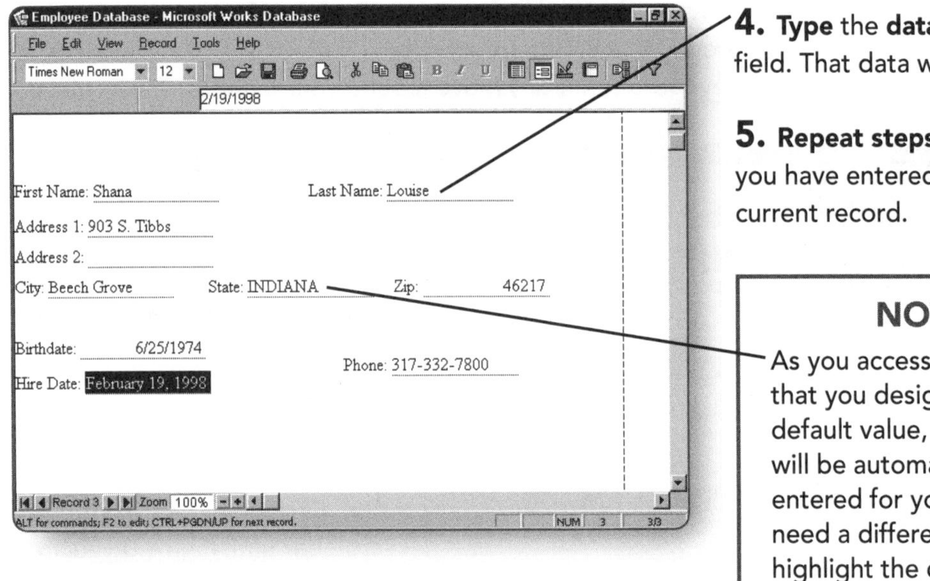

4. **Type** the **data** for the next field. That data will be entered.

5. **Repeat steps 3** and **4** until you have entered data for the current record.

> **NOTE**
>
> As you access any fields that you designed with a default value, the value will be automatically entered for you. If you need a different value, highlight the default value and enter the new one.

When you are ready to add another record:

6. **Press** the **Tab** key. Works automatically displays a blank record, ready for entering data.

Moving Around in the Database

After several records are in the database, you may need to return to a specific record to review it.

Moving Around in List View

Moving around the database in List view is similar to moving around in a Works spreadsheet. You can use your mouse or keyboard to quickly move around your database in List view.

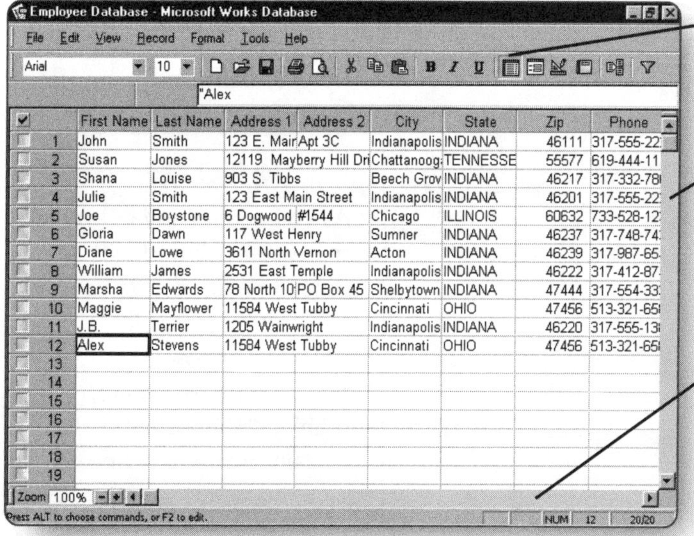

1. Click on the **List View button**. The database will appear in List view.

2a. Click on the **vertical scroll bar** until the record you are looking for is visible.

OR

2b. Click on the **horizontal scroll bar** until the field you are looking for is visible.

3. Click anywhere on the **desired record**. The field within that record will be selected.

The following table describes keyboard methods for moving around in your database in List view:

Keystroke	Result
Up/Down arrow keys	Moves one record at a time up or down
Left/Right arrow keys	Moves one field at a time left or right
Page Down	Moves one screen of records down
Page Up	Moves one screen of records up
Home	Moves to the first field of the current record
Ctrl+Home	Moves to the first field of the first record
F5	Displays the Go To dialog box

Moving Around in Form View

If you are working in Form view, you can display different records one at a time. A movement bar is displayed at the bottom of the Form view window.

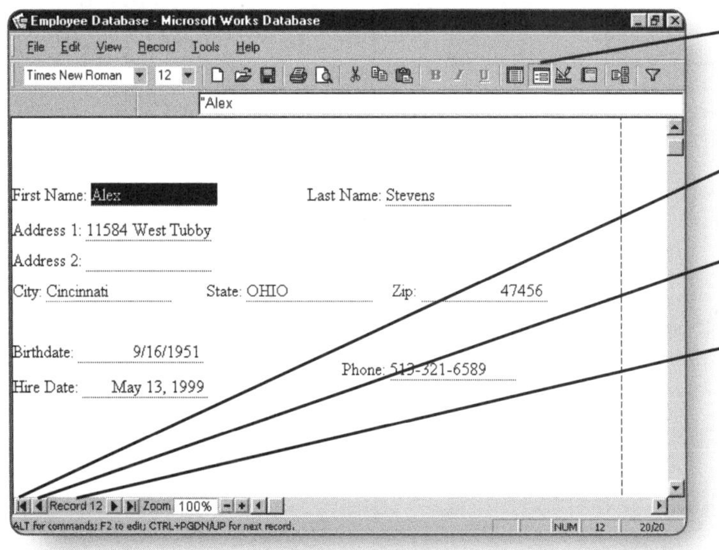

1. Click on the **Form View button**. The database will appear in Form view.

- **First**. Click here to go to the first record.
- **Previous**. Click here to go to the previous record.
- **Current**. Double-click here to display the Go To dialog box. Using the Go To dialog box is discussed in the next section.

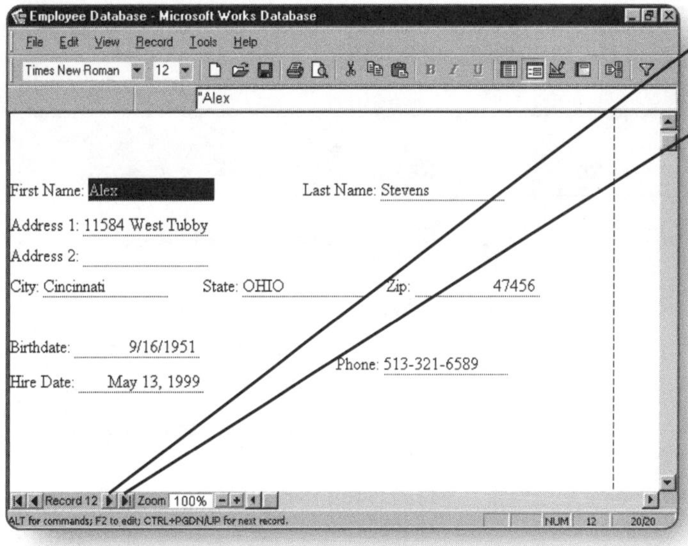

- **Next**. Click here to go to the next record.
- **Last**. Click here to go to the last record.

Using the Go To Dialog Box

Use the Go To dialog box to quickly jump to a specific record or field.

1. Open the **Go To dialog box**. The Go To dialog box will open.

> **TIP**
>
> Other methods to display the Go To dialog box include pressing Ctrl+G, pressing the F5 key, or clicking on the Edit menu and selecting Go To.

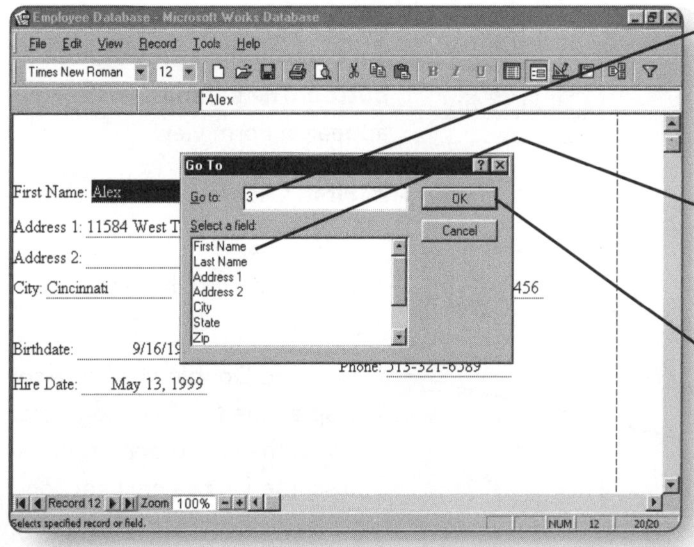

2a. Enter a **record number**. The number will appear in the Go To: text box.

OR

2b. Click on a **field name**. The field name will appear in the Go To: text box.

3. Click on **OK**. The Go To dialog box will close, and the specified record or field will appear.

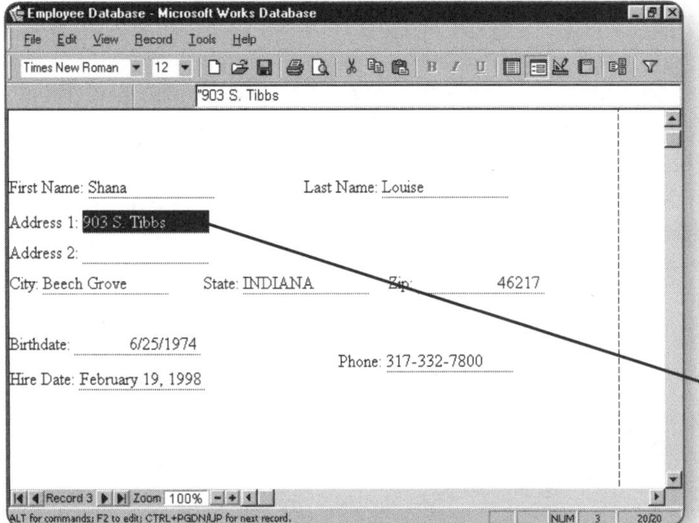

Editing Records

Editing data is the same whether you are in Form view or List view.

1. Locate the **record** to be edited. The current record will appear.

2. Click on the **data** to be edited. The data will be highlighted.

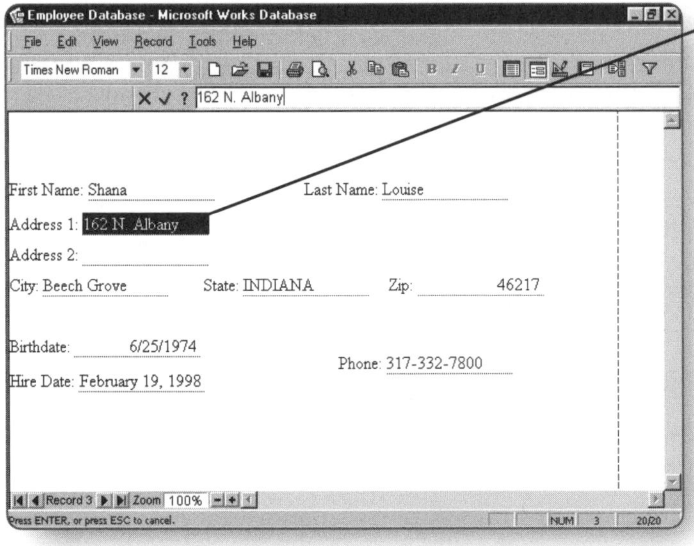

3. Type the **corrected information**. The new data will appear in the field.

4. Press Enter. The existing data will be replaced with the new data.

Finding Records

Need to locate a specific record? Let Works do the searching for you. An example might be to search for anyone who lives in Chicago. Finding records is slightly different from filtering records, which you learn to do in Chapter 20, "Using Reports."

List view is easy to work with when finding specific records.

1. **Click** on the **List View button**. The database will appear in List view.

2. **Click** on **Edit**. The Edit menu will appear.

3. **Click** on **Find**. The Find dialog box will open.

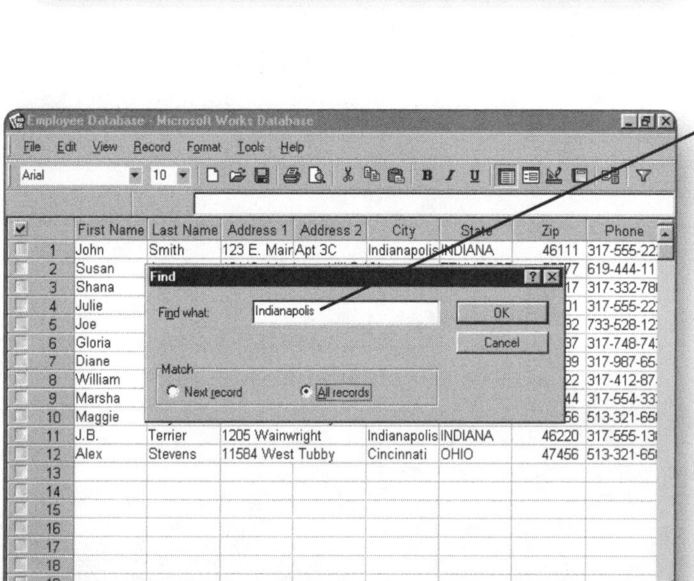

4. **Type** the **characters** you want to locate. The text will appear in the Find what: text box.

5. **Click** on one of the following Match **options**:

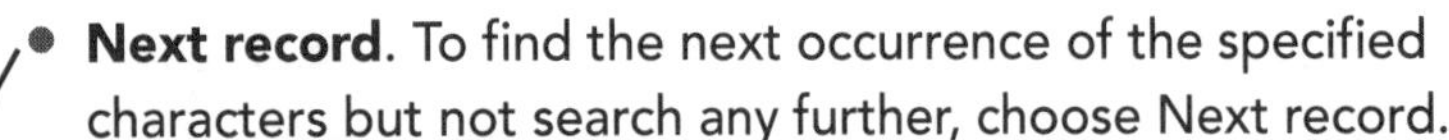

- **Next record**. To find the next occurrence of the specified characters but not search any further, choose Next record.

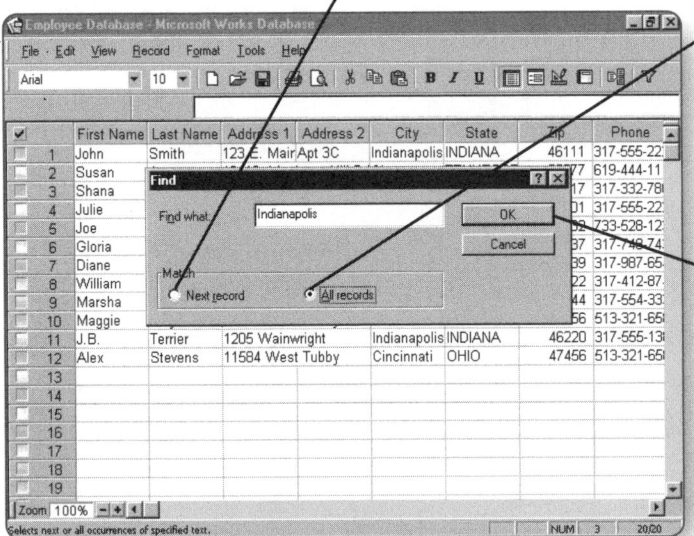

- **All records**. To find all records in the database that contain the specified characters and display those records only, choose All records.

6. **Click** on **OK**. If you selected Next record, the next field that contains the specified text will be highlighted. If you chose All records, only the records matching the criteria will appear.

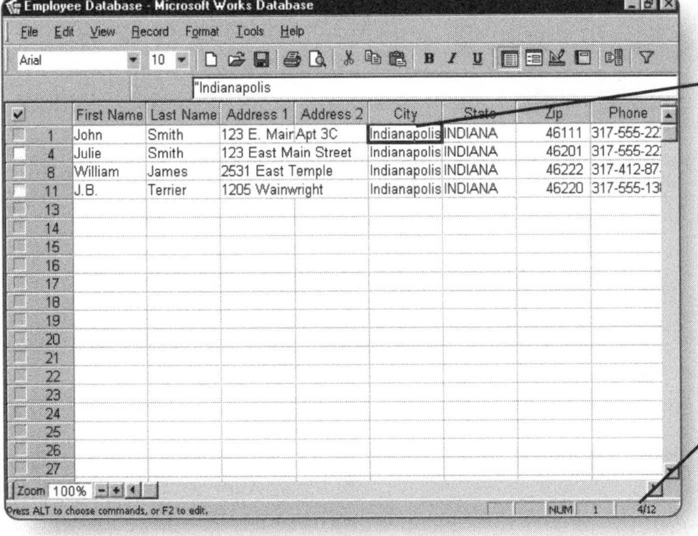

NOTE

Notice in this example, out of the 12 records originally entered, only records 1, 4, 8, and 11 match the criteria.

TIP

In both List view and Form view, Works specifies how many records matched the specified criteria.

Redisplaying Records

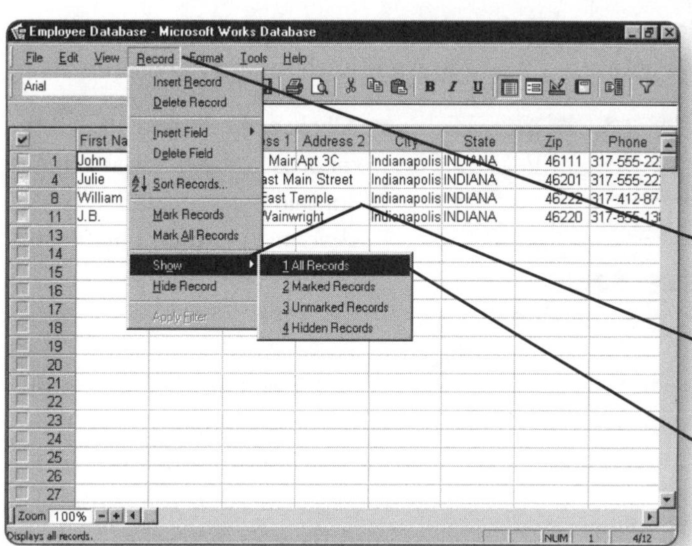

If you chose to find All records, only the records that matched your selection are displayed. You can easily redisplay all records.

1. **Click** on **Record**. The Record menu will appear.
2. **Click** on **Show**. The Show submenu will appear.
3. **Click** on **All Records**. All records in the database will appear.

Sorting Records

By default, the records are listed in the order that you entered them. You can sort them by any field. If multiple records have the same data in the specified field, you also can specify a second or third sorting method.

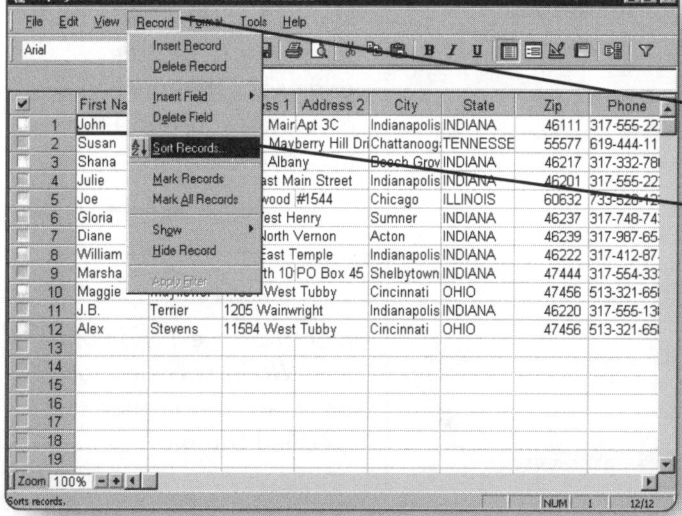

1. **Click** on **Record**. The Record menu will appear.
2. **Click** on **Sort Records**. The Sort Records dialog box will open.

> **NOTE**
>
> Records can be sorted in either List view or Form view.

3. Click on the **down arrow (▼)** in the Sort by list box. A list of fields will appear.

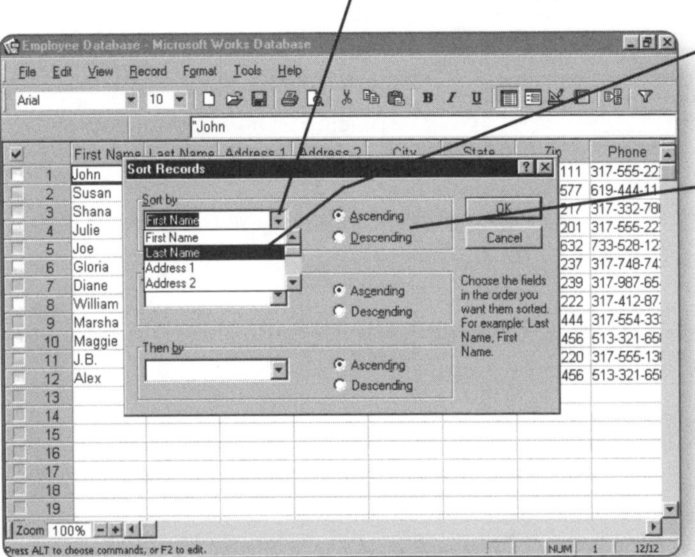

4. Click on the first **field** to sort by. The field name will appear in the Sort by list box.

5. Click on **Ascending or Descending**. The option will be selected.

> **NOTE**
>
> Ascending order will sort from A to Z if the field is alphabetical or from smallest to largest if the field is numerical.

If multiple records have the same data in the specified field, you can also specify a second or third sorting method.

6. Click on the **down arrow (▼)** in the first Then by list box. A list of fields will appear.

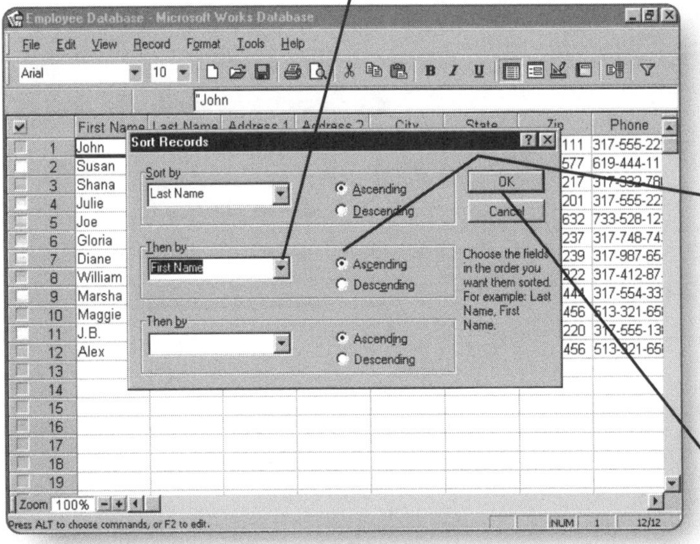

7. Click on the second **field** to sort by. The field name will appear in the first Then by list box.

8. Click on **Ascending or Descending**. The option will be selected.

9. Optionally, **repeat steps 6** through **8** for the second Then by list box.

10. Click on **OK**. The Sort dialog box will close.

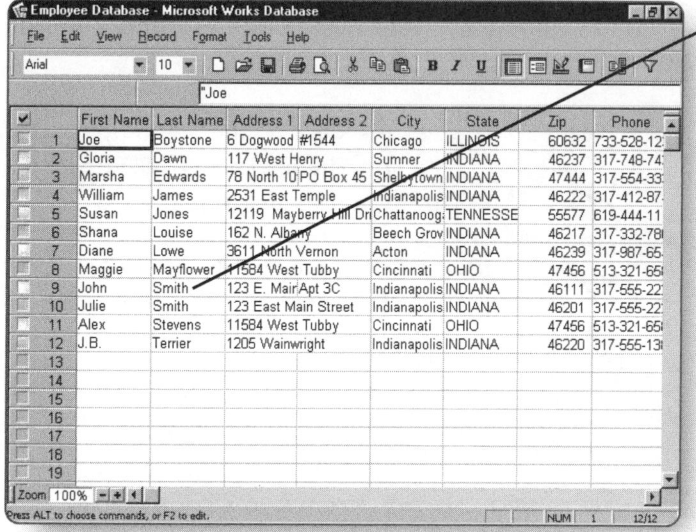

The records will be sorted and displayed in the order specified. Notice in this example that the records are sorted by Last name and then by First name, thereby placing John Smith ahead of Julie Smith.

Deleting Records

It is simple to delete a record. Deleting a record erases all data from all fields of the selected record only. The procedure for deleting a record is the same in List view or Form view.

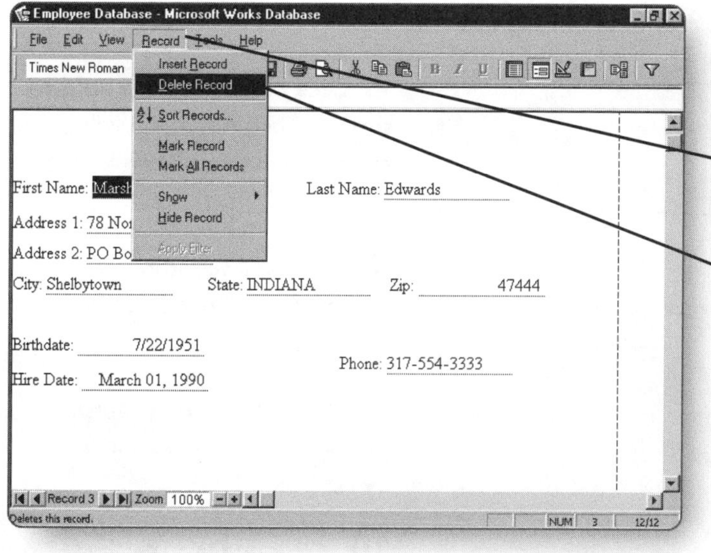

1. **Click** anywhere **on the record** to be deleted. The selected record will appear.
2. **Click** on **Record**. The Record menu will appear.
3. **Click** on **Delete Record**. The selected record will be deleted.

> **TIP**
>
> If you delete a record in error, immediately go to the Edit menu and click on Undo.

18

Formatting a Database

You've learned how to create database fields and enter the records. You can use Works to make your database more noticeable. You can modify and enhance its appearance by changing the look or size of fields or even adding a company logo. In this chapter, you'll learn how to:

- Change the field type
- Change the alignment or size of a field
- Rename a field
- Add non-field text
- Add artwork to a database

Formatting Fields

When you format fields, you change the appearance of your field data. Options for formatting include the type of contents in a field as well as the alignment, font, border, or shading options of field data.

Changing the Field Type

When you first created your database, you were given several options to set the format type of the field. The format of a field can be changed at any time.

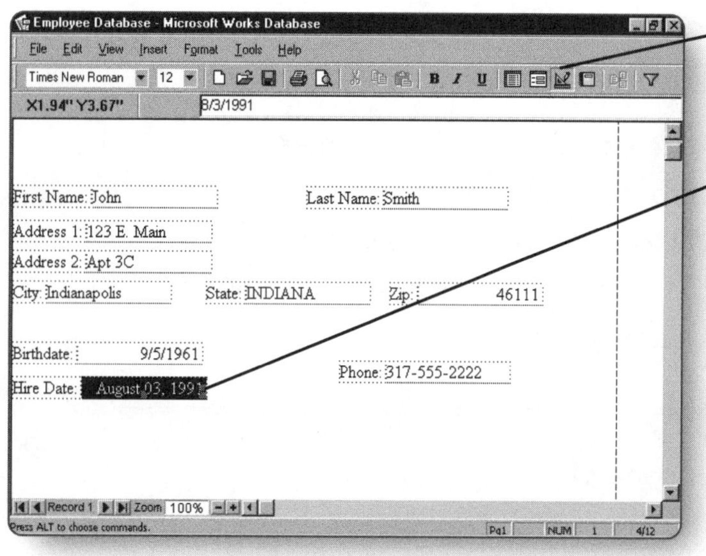

1. Click on the **Form Design View button**. The database will appear in Form Design view.

2. Click on the **field** to be modified. The field will be highlighted.

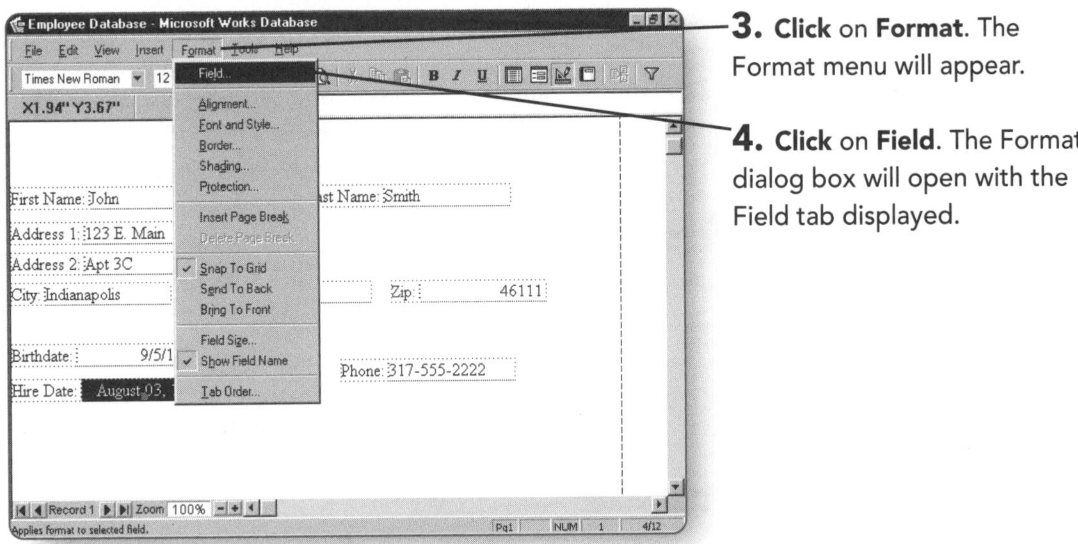

3. Click on **Format**. The Format menu will appear.

4. Click on **Field**. The Format dialog box will open with the Field tab displayed.

5. Click on a **format**. The option will be selected, and any appearance options will be displayed.

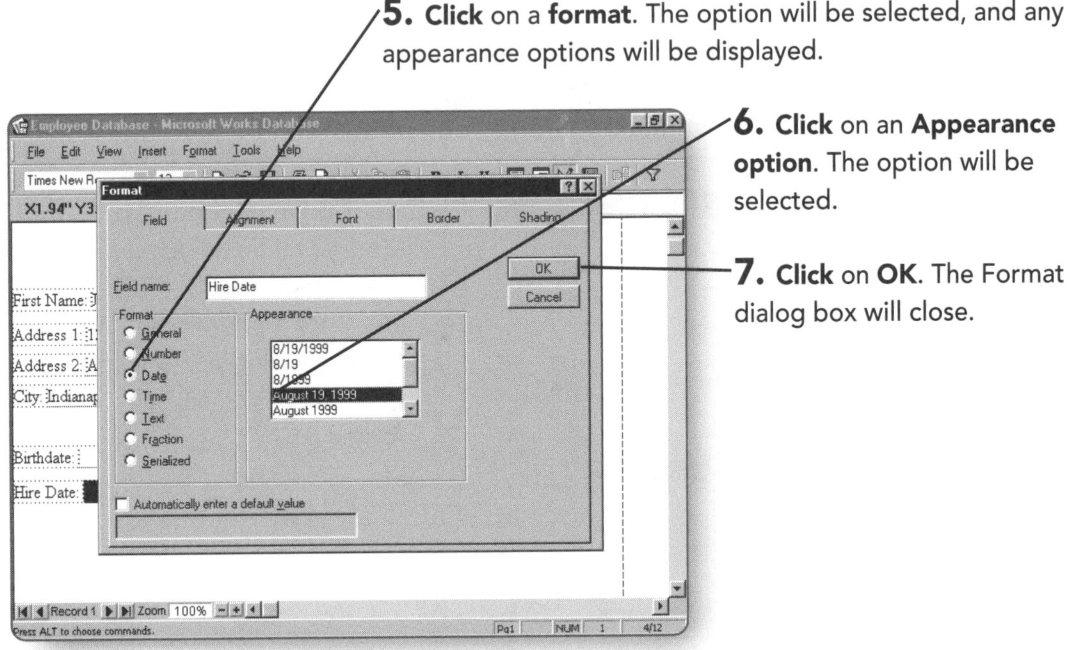

6. Click on an **Appearance option**. The option will be selected.

7. Click on **OK**. The Format dialog box will close.

Changing the Alignment of a Field

The default alignment of field contents is General. Text items are aligned to the left, whereas dates and numerically formatted fields are aligned to the right. You can override the default alignment and set any field to line up on the right, left, or center of the field.

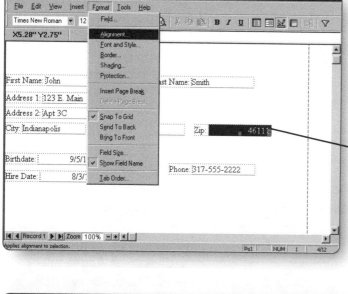

1. If necessary, **click** on the **Form Design button**. The database will be in Form Design view.

2. **Click** on the **field** to be modified. The field will be highlighted.

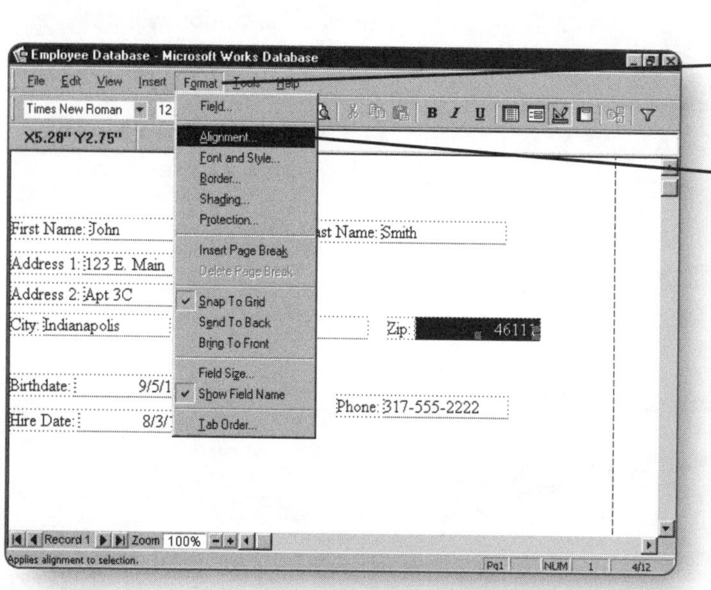

3. **Click** on **Format**. The Format menu will appear.

4. **Click** on **Alignment**. The Format dialog box will open with the Alignment tab displayed.

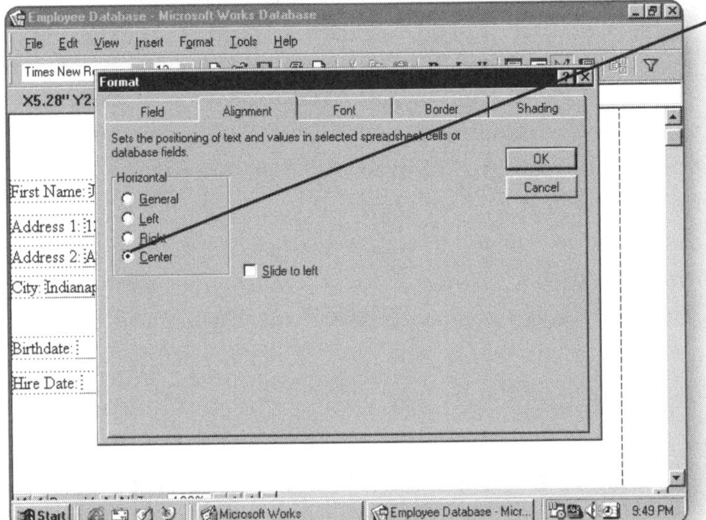

5. Click on a **Horizontal alignment option**. The option will be selected.

> **NOTE**
>
> The alignment choices pertain to the overall width of the field contents, not the page. The next section discusses field width.

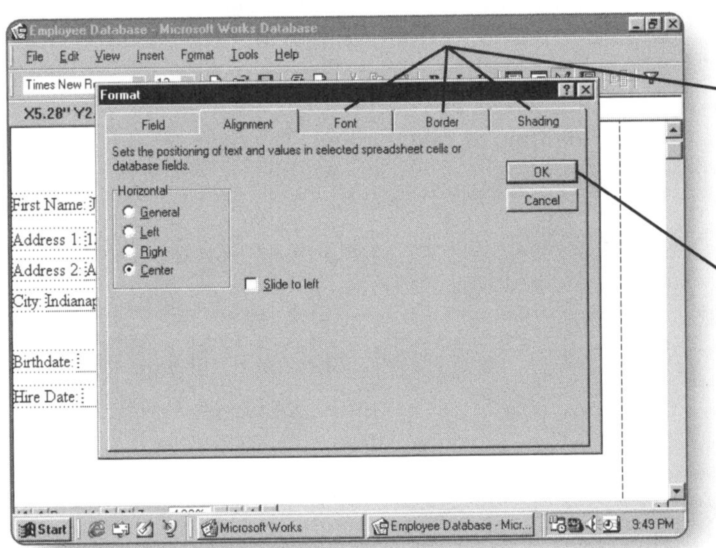

> **TIP**
>
> Click on the Font, Border, or Shading tabs to select these options.

6. Click on **OK**. The Format dialog box will close. The field alignment will be modified to your specifications.

Changing the Size of a Field

When the fields are first created, Works makes each field the same size—20 characters for each field. Perhaps that is too much—or not enough. For example, only two characters may be needed for a State field, whereas you might need 40 for an Address field. If you've included a field to store miscellaneous information, such as a Note field, you might even want to have the data take up several lines of text. When a field height is set to more than one line, Works wraps the text to the next line when the text is longer than the field width.

Changing Field Size Using the Menu

Fields can be a maximum of 325 characters wide and 325 lines long.

1. If necessary, **click** on the **Form Design button**. The database will be in Form Design view.

2. **Click** on the **field** to be modified. The field will be highlighted.

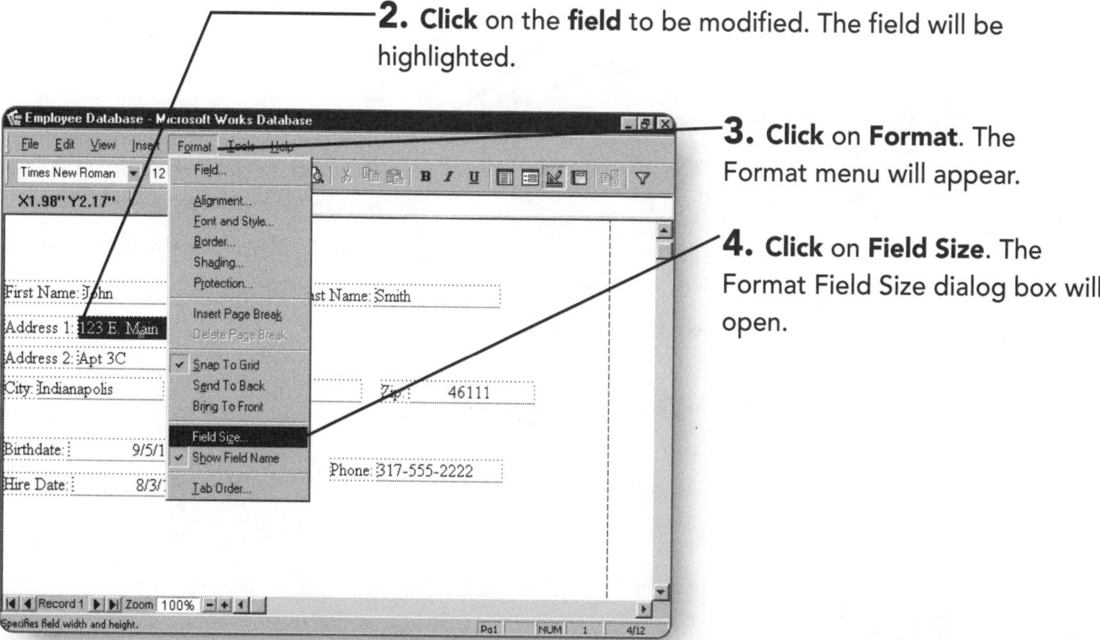

3. **Click** on **Format**. The Format menu will appear.

4. **Click** on **Field Size**. The Format Field Size dialog box will open.

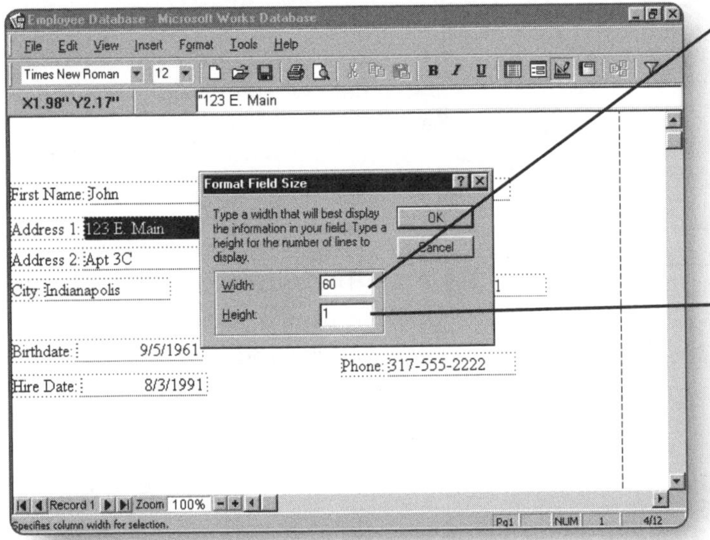

5. **Type** a **size** in the Width: text box. The new value will appear.

6. **Press** the **Tab** key. The Height: text box will be highlighted.

7. **Type** a **size** for the field height. The new value will appear.

8. **Click** on **OK**. The Format Field Size dialog box will close, and the field will change to the specified width and height.

Changing Field Size by Dragging

Visually resize the field by using the mouse.

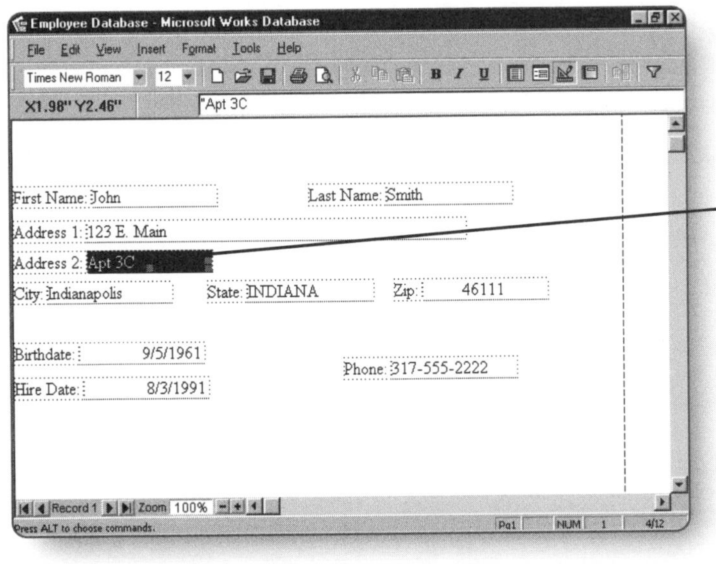

1. If necessary, **click** on the **Form Design button**. The database will be in Form Design view.

2. **Click** on the **field** to be modified. The field will be highlighted.

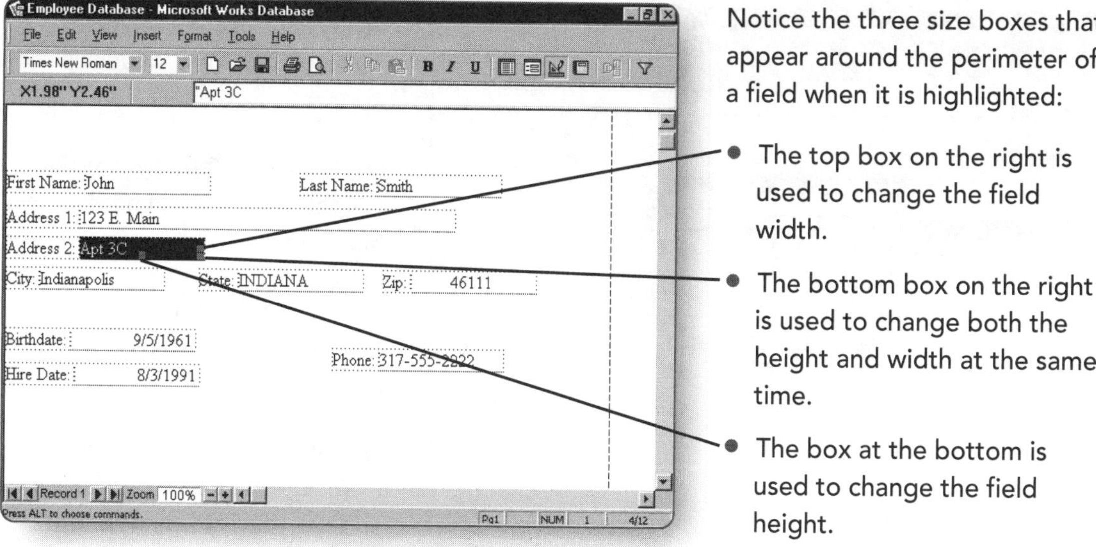

Notice the three size boxes that appear around the perimeter of a field when it is highlighted:

- The top box on the right is used to change the field width.
- The bottom box on the right is used to change both the height and width at the same time.
- The box at the bottom is used to change the field height.

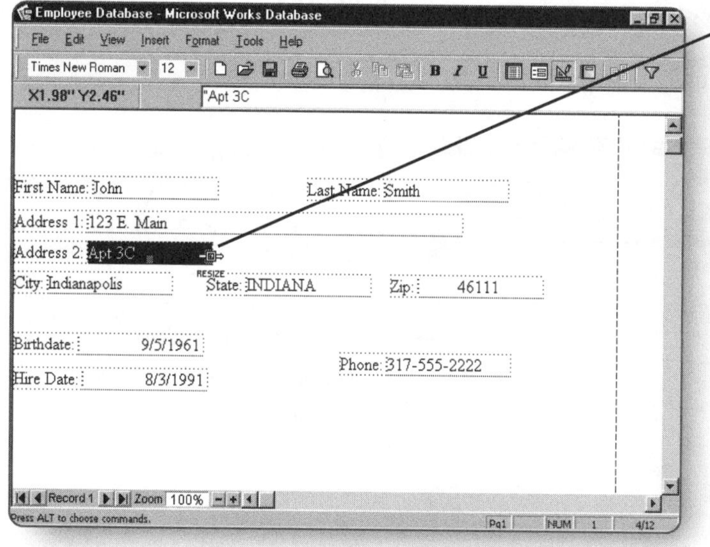

3. Position the **mouse pointer** on one of the size boxes. The mouse pointer will change to an arrow with the word "RESIZE" displayed.

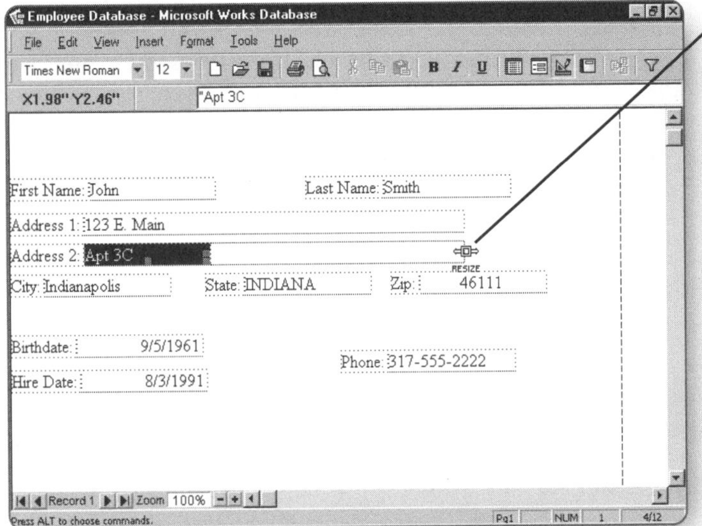

4. Drag the **size box** to the desired size. A dotted box will indicate the new size.

5. Release the **mouse button**. The field will be resized.

> **NOTE**
>
> Field text that previously did not display because the field size was too small may now appear.

Renaming a Field

The name originally assigned to a field can be changed. Field names can be up to 15 characters including spaces and punctuation.

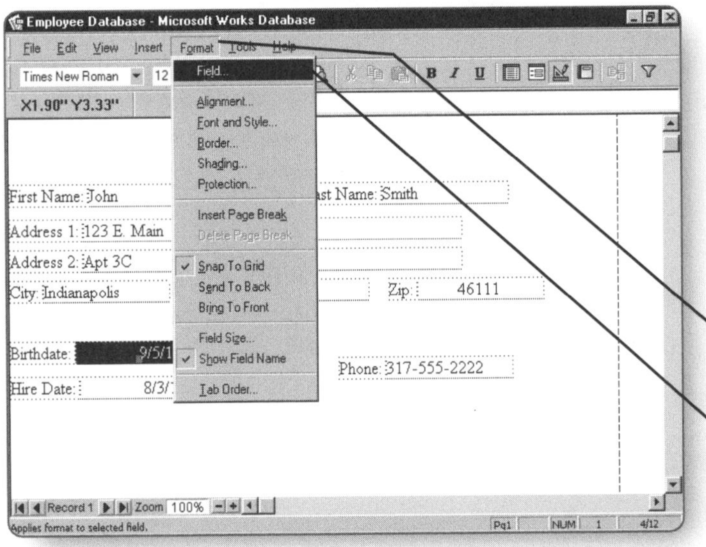

1. If necessary, **click** on the **Form Design button**. The database will be in Form Design view.

2. Click on the **field** to be modified. The field will be highlighted.

3. Click on **Format**. The Format menu will appear.

4. Click on **Field**. The Format dialog box will open with the Field tab displayed.

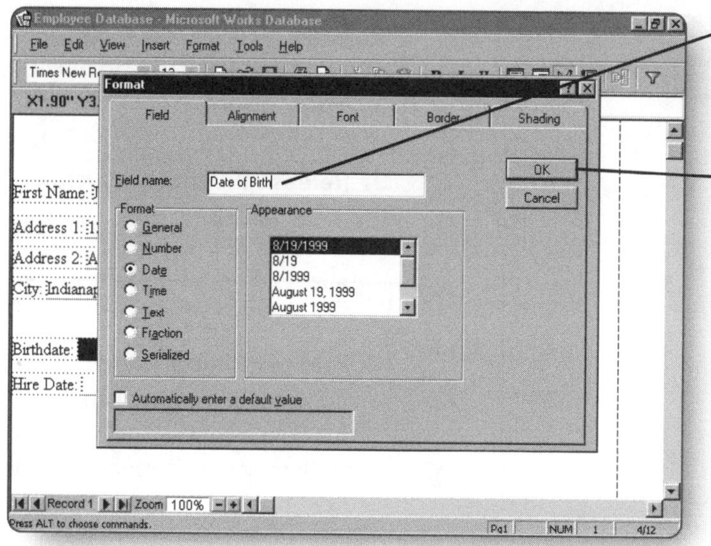

5. Type a new field **name**. The text will be displayed in the Field name: text box.

6. Click on **OK**. The field name will be changed.

> **NOTE**
>
> No data is changed when renaming a field.

Adding Non-Field Text

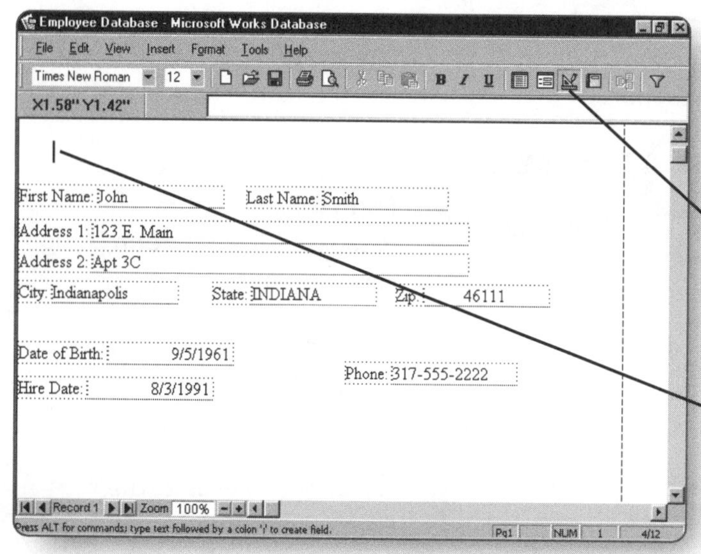

Text that is not related to a field can be added. Add items such as your company name or a description of the information you're storing in the database.

1. If necessary, **click** on the **Form Design button**. The database will be in Form Design view.

2. Click the **mouse** where you want the text to be located. A blinking insertion point will appear.

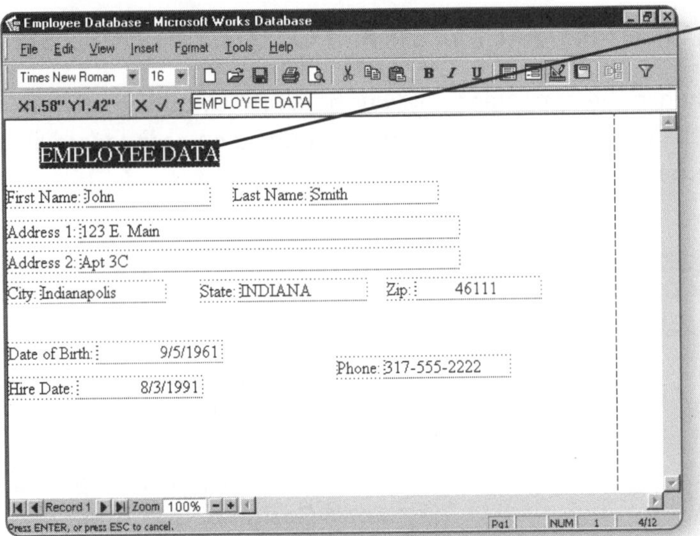

3. Type text. The text will be displayed and highlighted.

4. Click anywhere in the database. The text will be deselected.

NOTE

Do not type any colons (:) in the text. Works treats an item with a colon as a new field.

TIP

Click on the non-field text object and format or move in the same manner as field text.

Adding Artwork to a Database

Enhance the appearance of your database by adding artwork to the design. Any artwork added appears on each record in the database.

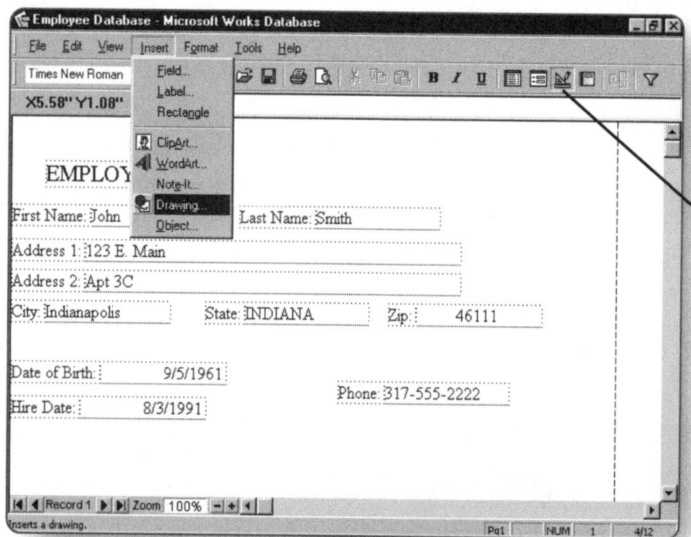

Adding a Logo

You can add your company logo or other graphic to be displayed on each record of the database.

1. If necessary, **click** on the **Form Design button**. The database will be in Form Design view.

2. Click the **mouse** where you want the logo to be located. A blinking insertion point will appear.

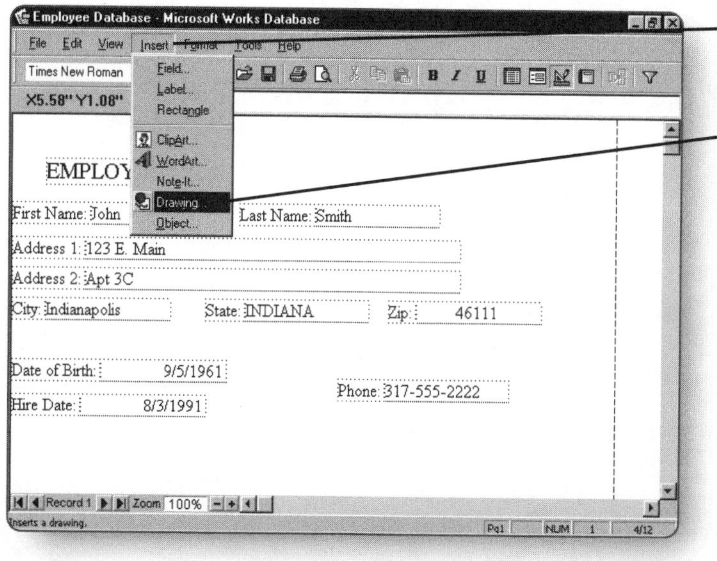

3. Click on **Insert**. The Insert menu will appear.

4. Click on **Drawing**. A Microsoft Drawing window will appear.

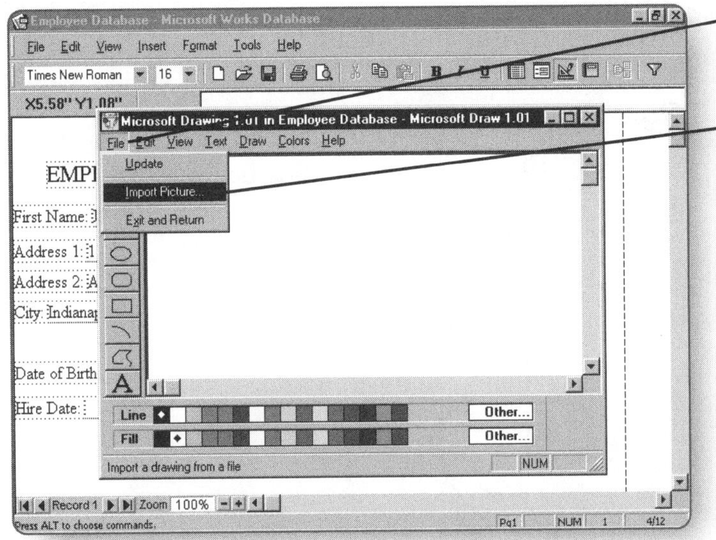

5. Click on **File**. The File menu will appear.

6. Click on **Import Picture**. The Open dialog box will open.

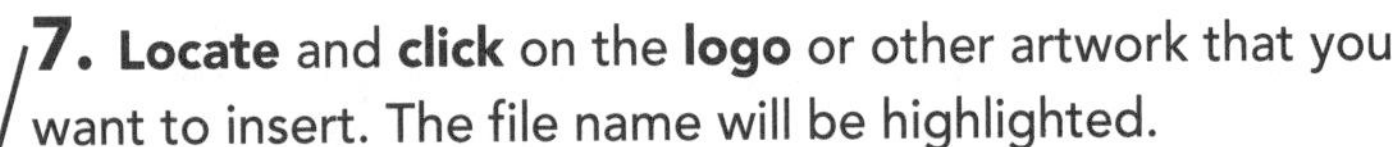

7. Locate and **click** on the **logo** or other artwork that you want to insert. The file name will be highlighted.

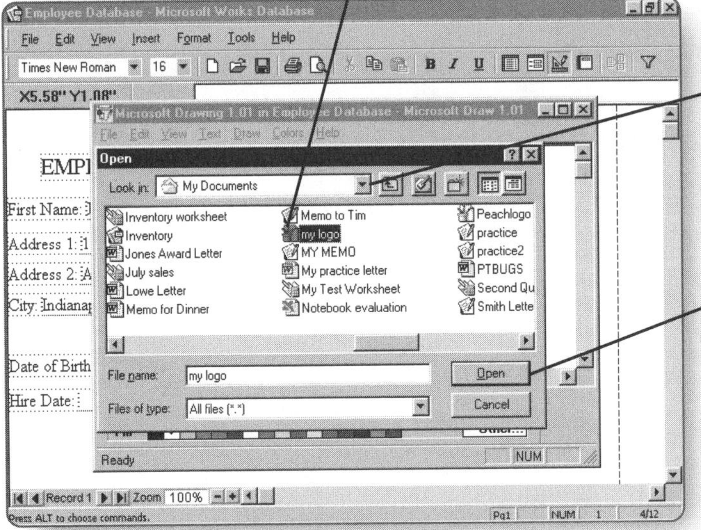

TIP

Click on the down arrow (▼) of the Look in: list box to navigate to the folder containing your artwork.

8. Click on **Open**. The drawing will be inserted into the Microsoft Drawing window.

The next step is to insert the drawing into the database window.

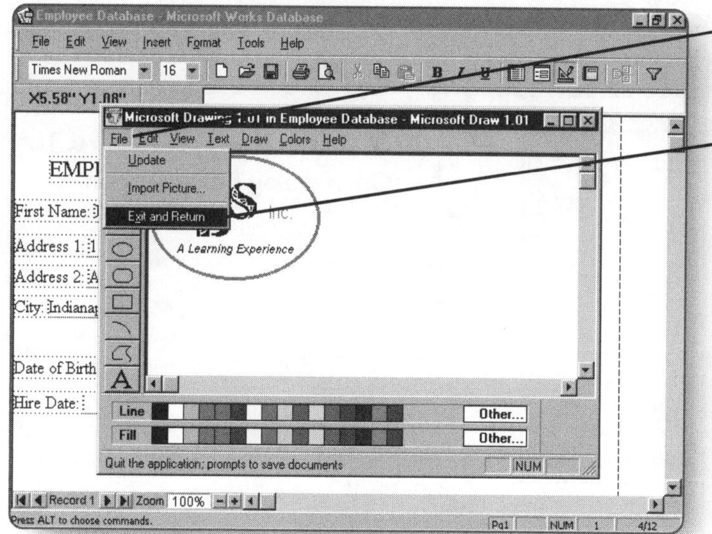

9. Click on **File**. The File menu will appear.

10. Click on **Exit and Return**. A message box will open.

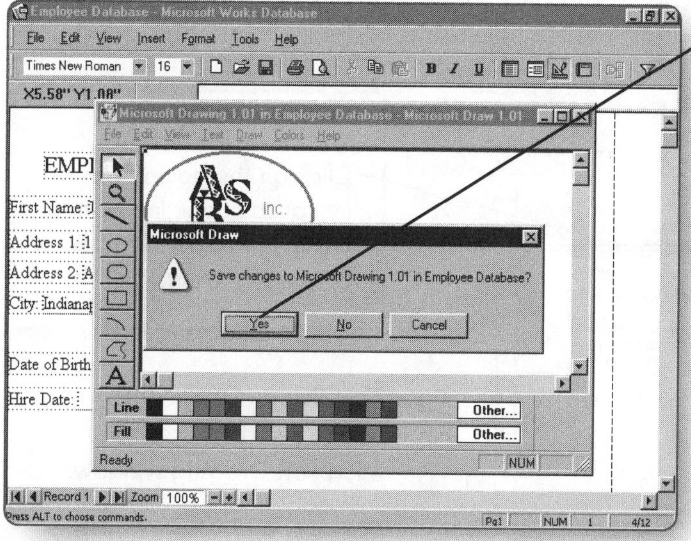

11. Click on **Yes**. The image will be inserted into the database form.

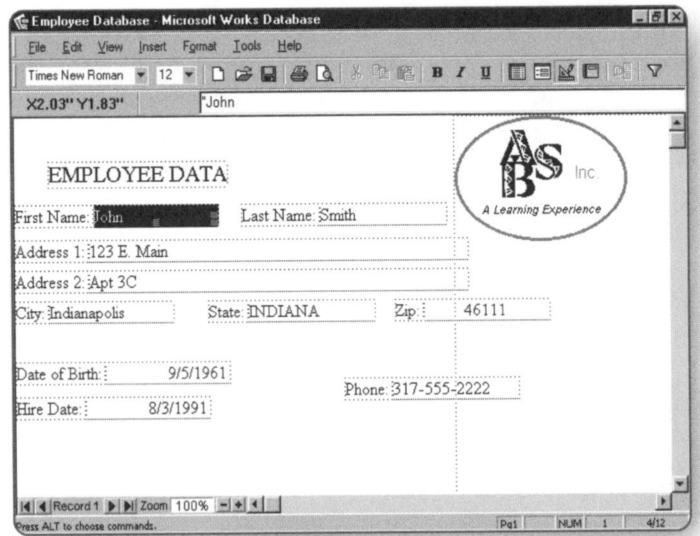

TIP

Resize artwork by clicking and dragging on one of the eight handles surrounding the image.

Adding Clip Art

Don't want to insert a logo? You can still enhance your database by adding one of the many pieces of clip art or photographs supplied with Microsoft Works.

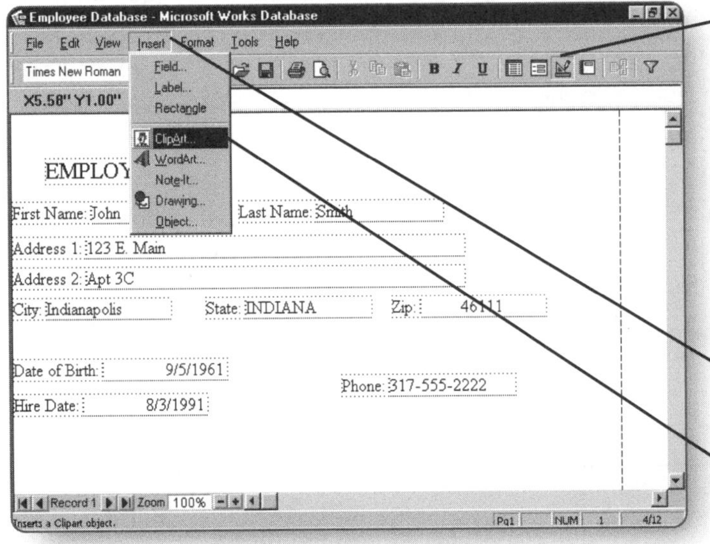

1. If necessary, **click** on the **Form Design button**. The database will be in Form Design view.

2. **Click** the **mouse** where you want the artwork to be located. A blinking insertion point will appear.

3. **Click** on **Insert**. The Insert menu will appear.

4. **Click** on **ClipArt**. The Microsoft Clip Gallery dialog box will open.

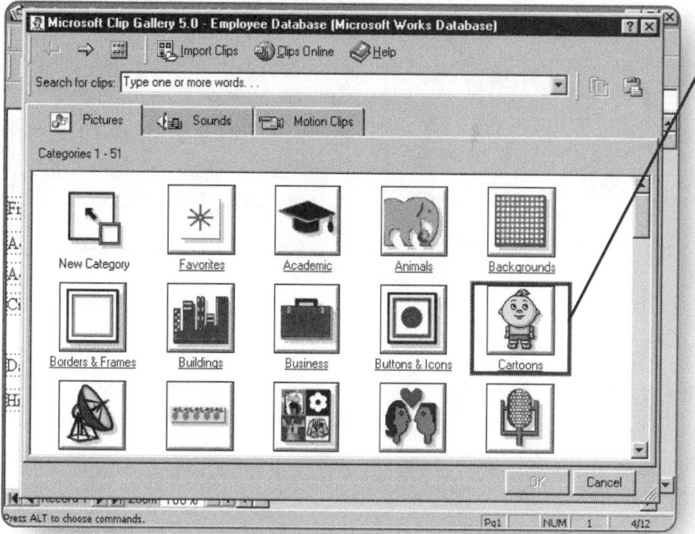

5. Click on the category of **image** that you want to use. The selection of available artwork will appear.

TIP

Click on the Back button to return to the category selections.

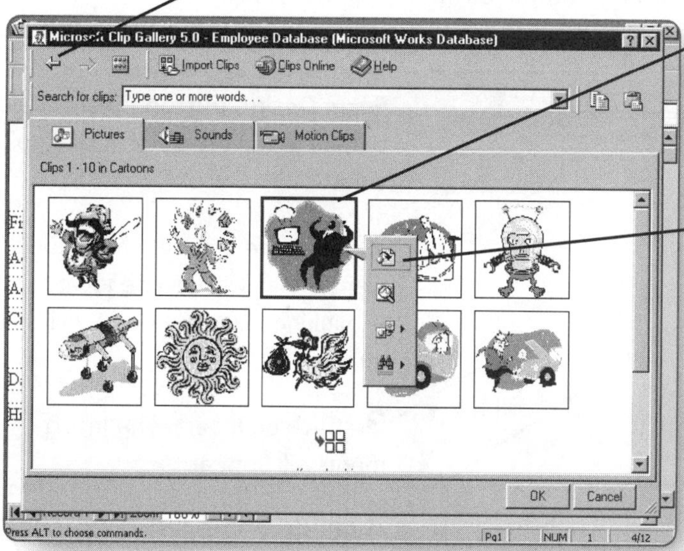

6. Click on the **image** you want to insert. The selection will be surrounded by a black box. The drawing toolbar will also display.

7. Click on **Insert**. The clip art image or picture will be inserted into your database.

TIP

Move the artwork by placing the mouse pointer in the middle of the artwork and dragging it to the desired location.

19

Working with Filters

Filtering information allows you to select which records you want to work with. Based on conditions you specify, you can tell Works to be very specific in which records to display. In this chapter, you'll learn how to:

- Create filters
- Apply a filter
- Rename or delete filters

Filtering Records

Filtering records is the process of letting Works know which records to select from the database. For example, you could create a filter named "Chicago Smiths" that includes only the people named Smith who live in Chicago. You could create another filter named "Youth" that includes only the people under 21 years of age.

Creating a Filter the First Time

The first time you create a filter in the database, a Filter Name box appears. This box does not appear on subsequent filters.

1. **Click** on **Tools**. The Tools menu will appear.

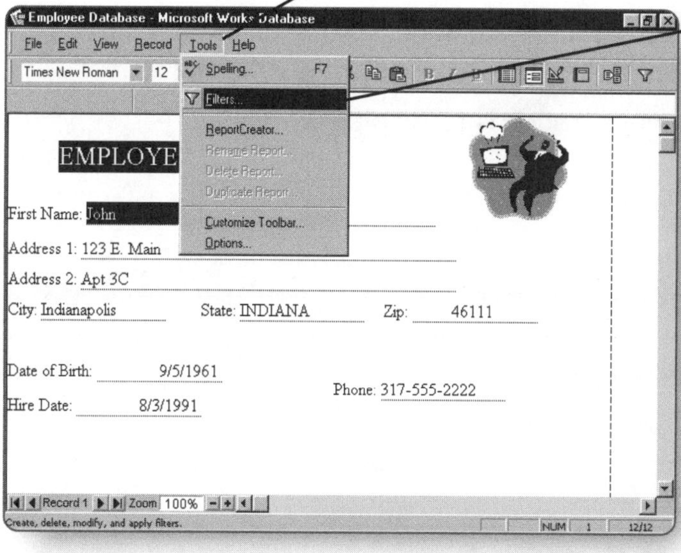

2. **Click** on **Filters**. The Filter Name dialog box will open.

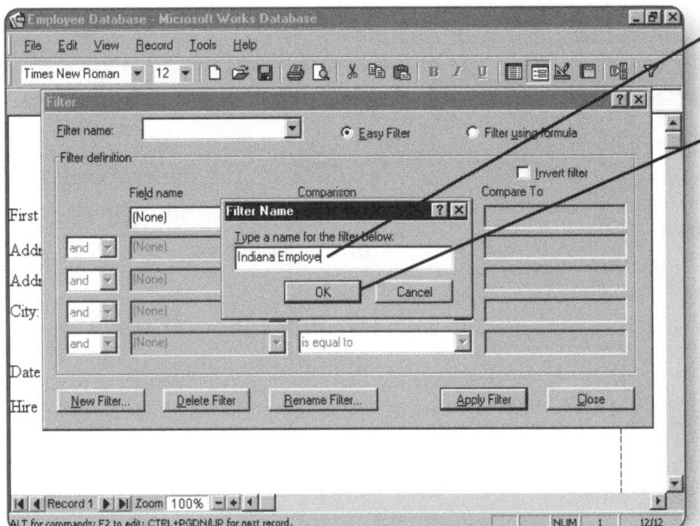

3. Enter a **name** for the filter. The default name is Filter1.

4. Click on **OK**. The Filter dialog box will open.

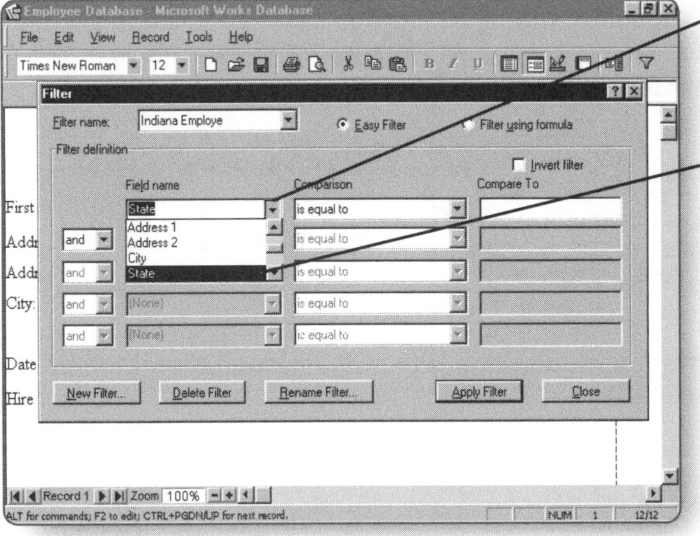

5. Click on the **Field name down arrow (▼)**. A list of field names will appear.

6. Click on the first **Field name** that you want to filter. The name will appear in the Field name text box.

7. Press the **Tab key**. The highlight will jump to the Comparison box.

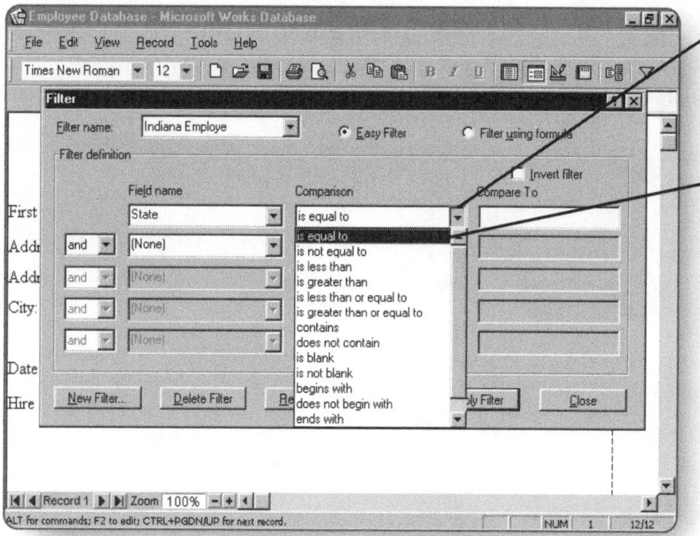

8. **Click** on the **Comparison down arrow** (▼). A list of comparison types will appear.

9. **Click** on the desired **option**. The option will appear in the Comparison box.

10. **Press** the **Tab key**. The highlight will jump to the Compare To box.

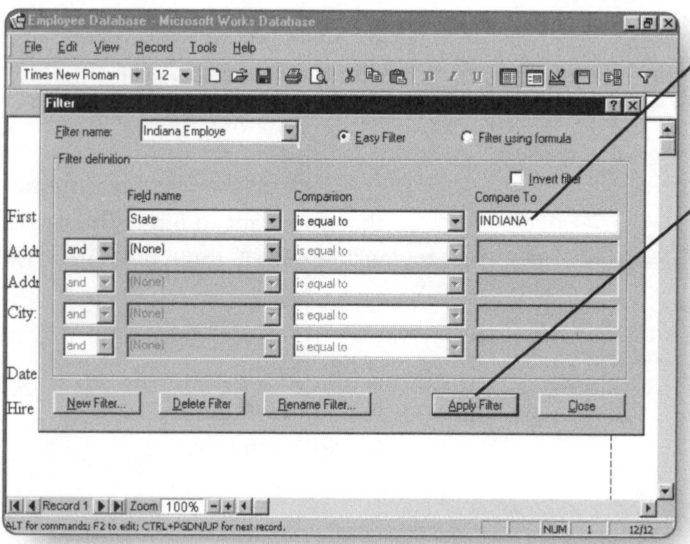

11. **Type** the **value or criterion** to be compared. You can type text or numbers.

12. **Click** on **Apply Filter**. The Filter dialog box will close, and only records that match the filter will be displayed.

Creating Additional Filters

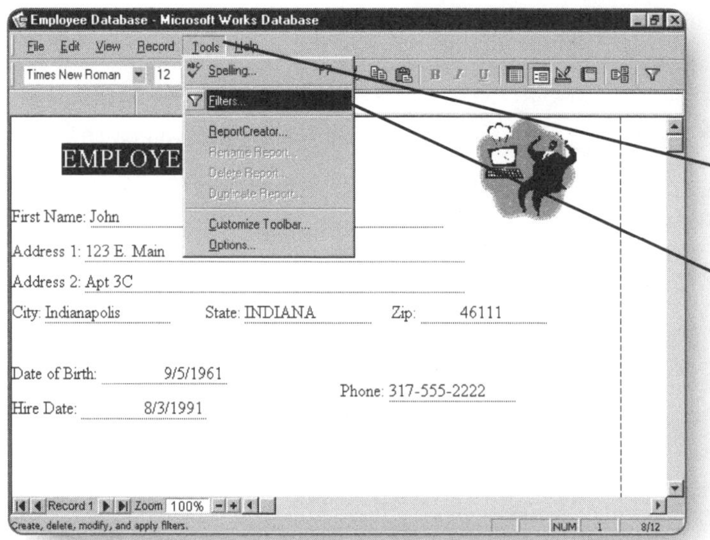

A database can have up to eight filters. Filters can be created in List View or Form View.

1. **Click** on **Tools**. The Tools menu will appear.
2. **Click** on **Filters**. The Filter dialog box will open with the last filter you created.

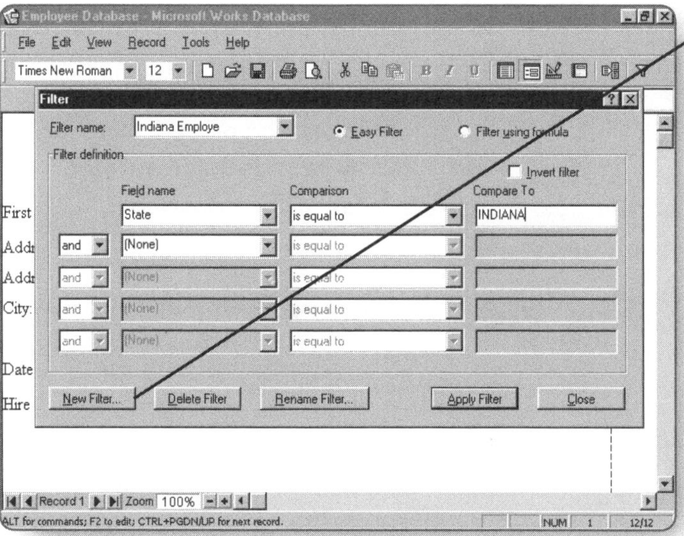

3. **Click** on **New Filter**. The Filter Name dialog box will open.

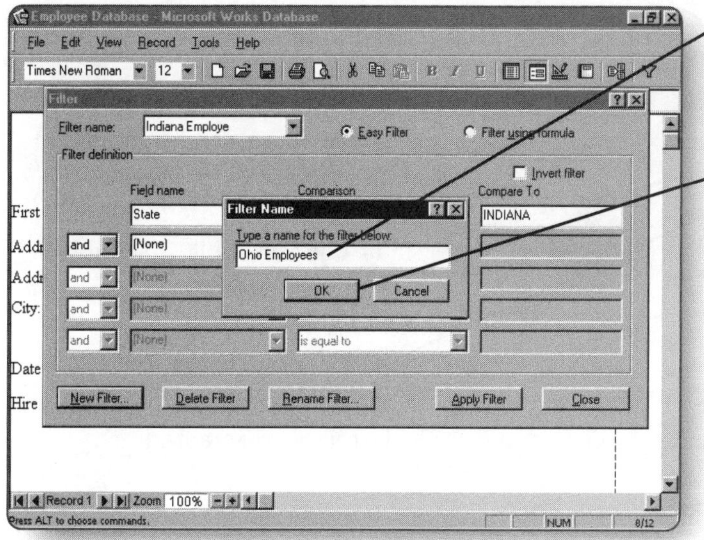

4. Enter a **name** for the new filter. The name will appear in the dialog box.

5. Click on **OK**. The Filter Name dialog box will close.

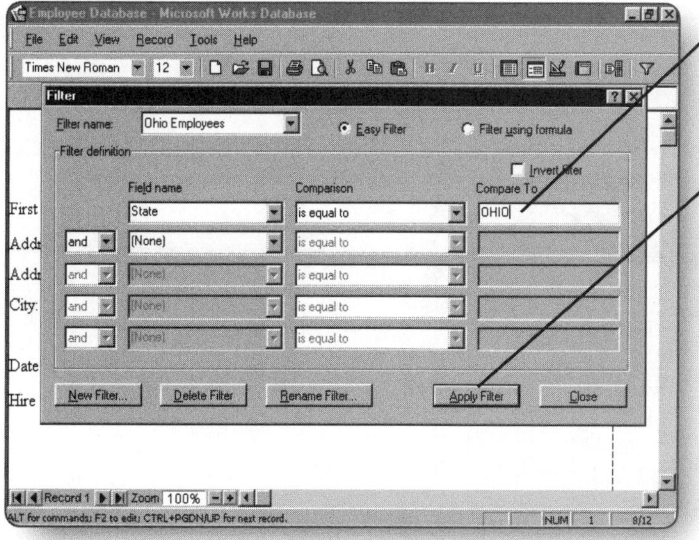

6. Apply the **filter information** as you learned in the previous section.

7. Click on **Apply Filter**. The Filter dialog box will close, and only records that match the filter will be displayed.

Selecting Multiple Filter Criteria

You can define up to five criteria for Works to match. Each additional criterion will use the logical operators AND or OR. For example, you could choose the last name Smith AND he must live in Chicago. This would exclude a person named Smith who lives in Indianapolis. If you use OR in the preceding example, the criteria would include anyone named Smith (regardless of where they lived), and it would include anyone who lives in Chicago, regardless of whether their last name was Smith, Jones, Koers, or whatever.

1. **Click** on **Tools**. The Tools menu will appear.

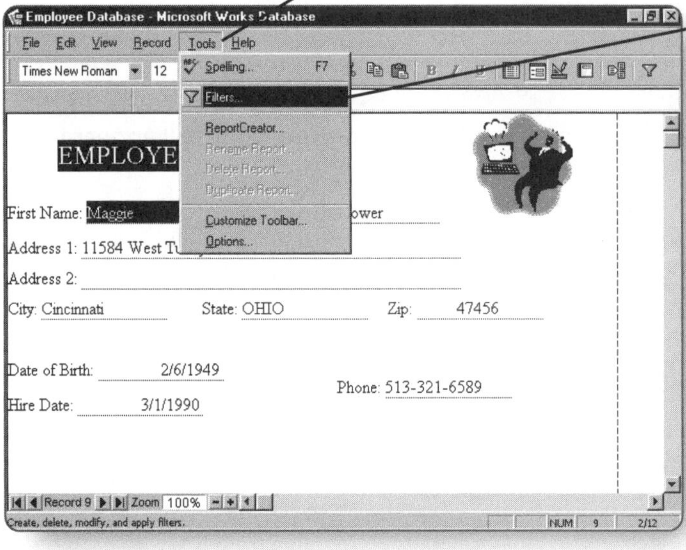

2. **Click** on **Filters**. The Filter dialog box will open with the last filter you created.

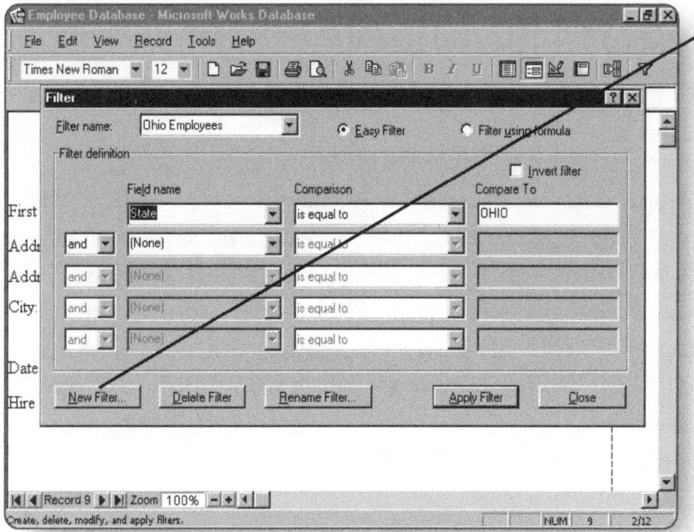

3. Click on **New Filter**. The Filter Name dialog box will open.

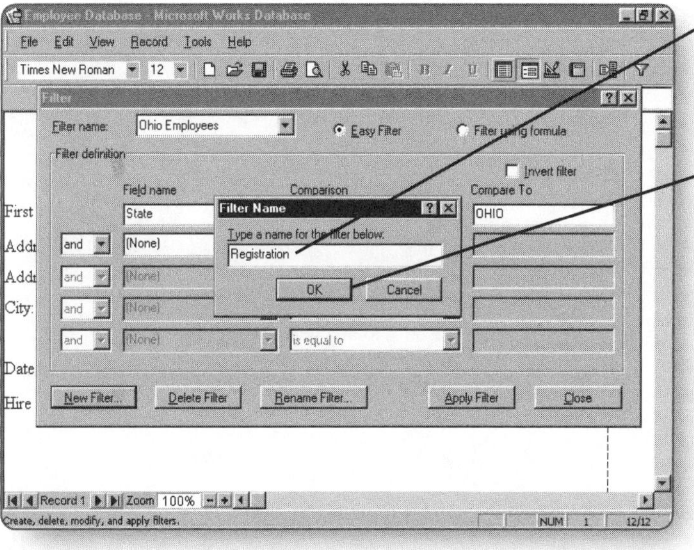

4. Enter a **name** for the new filter. The name will appear in the dialog box.

5. Click on **OK**. The Filter Name dialog box will close.

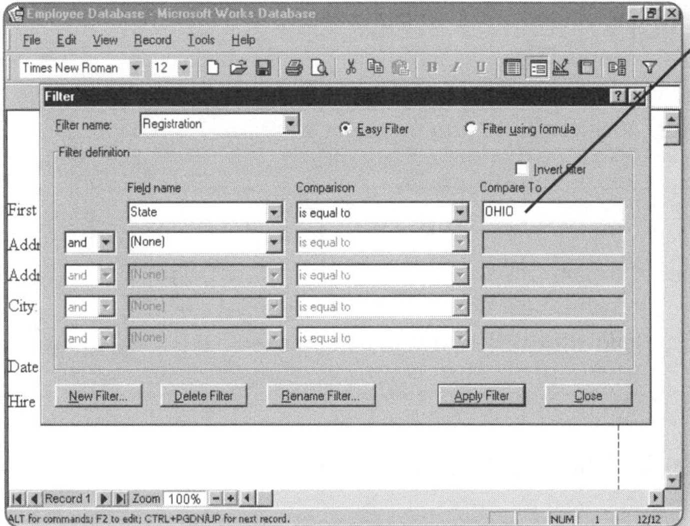

6. Set the **Field name, Comparison, and Compare To information** for the first criteria. The options will display.

7. Press the **Tab key**. The highlight will move to the second criterion line.

8. Click on the comparative **down arrow (▼)**. A selection of choices will appear.

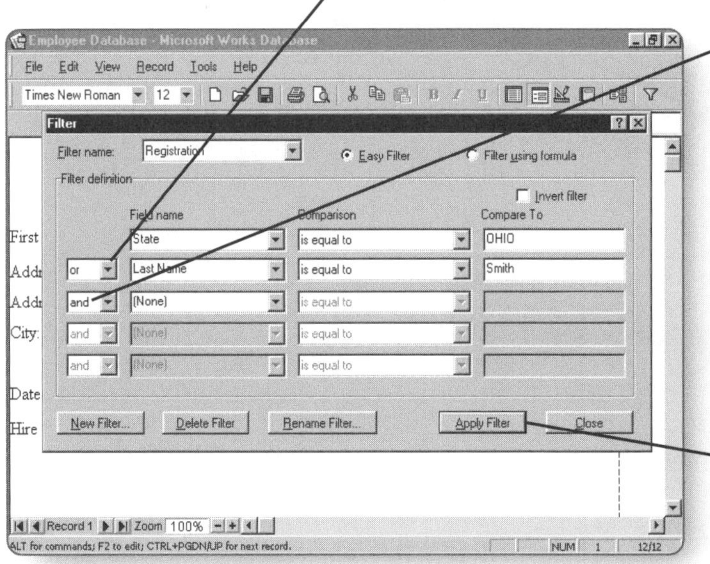

9. Click on **AND** or **OR**. The option will appear.

10. Press the **Tab key**. The highlight will move to the second Field name box.

11. Repeat steps 6 through **8** for each criterion that you want to specify.

12. Click on **Apply Filter**. The Filter dialog box will close, and only records that match the filter will be displayed.

Applying a Filter

If you want to select records from a filter that you previously created, Works allows you to select the filter from a list.

> **NOTE**
>
> The figures in this section show the filters from the List view; however, you can apply filters from either List view or Form view.

1. Click on **Record**. The Record menu will appear.

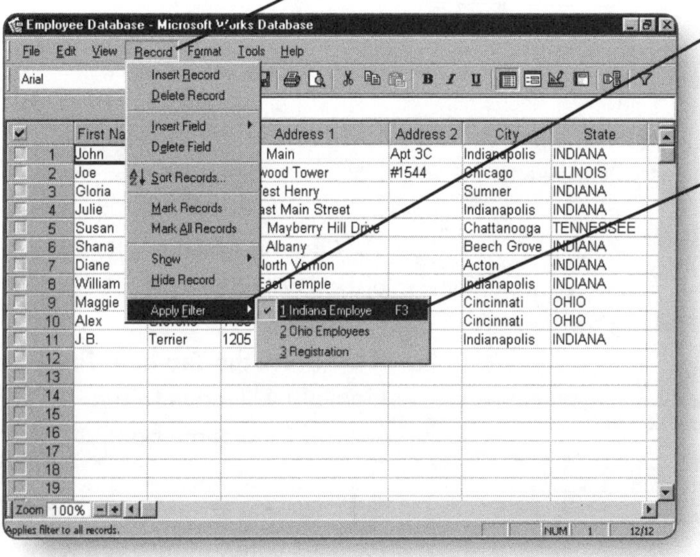

2. Click on **Apply Filter**. The Apply Filter submenu will appear.

3. Click on the **Filter name** to be used. The filter will be applied.

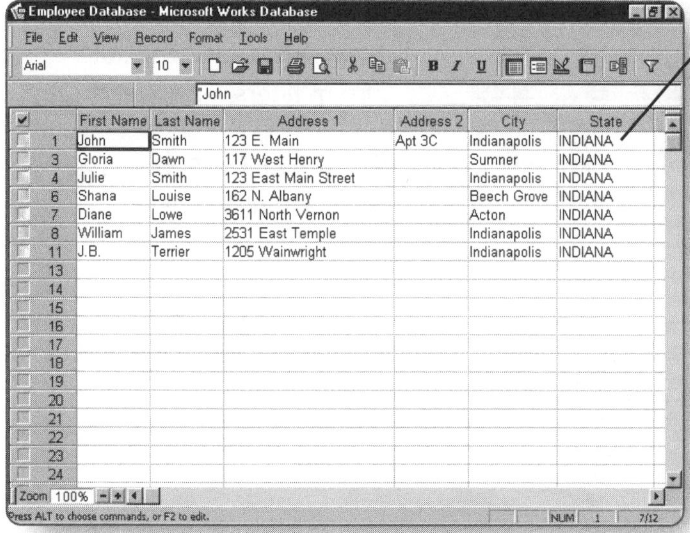

	First Name	Last Name	Address 1	Address 2	City	State
1	John	Smith	123 E. Main	Apt 3C	Indianapolis	INDIANA
3	Gloria	Dawn	117 West Henry		Sumner	INDIANA
4	Julie	Smith	123 East Main Street		Indianapolis	INDIANA
6	Shana	Louise	162 N. Albany		Beech Grove	INDIANA
7	Diane	Lowe	3611 North Vernon		Acton	INDIANA
8	William	James	2531 East Temple		Indianapolis	INDIANA
11	J.B.	Terrier	1205 Wainwright		Indianapolis	INDIANA

The records that match the filtered criteria will display.

Renaming a Filter

If the name you originally selected for your filter doesn't seem appropriate, rename it. Filters can be renamed at any time.

1. **Click** on **Tools**. The Tools menu will appear.

2. **Click** on **Filters**. The Filter dialog box will open.

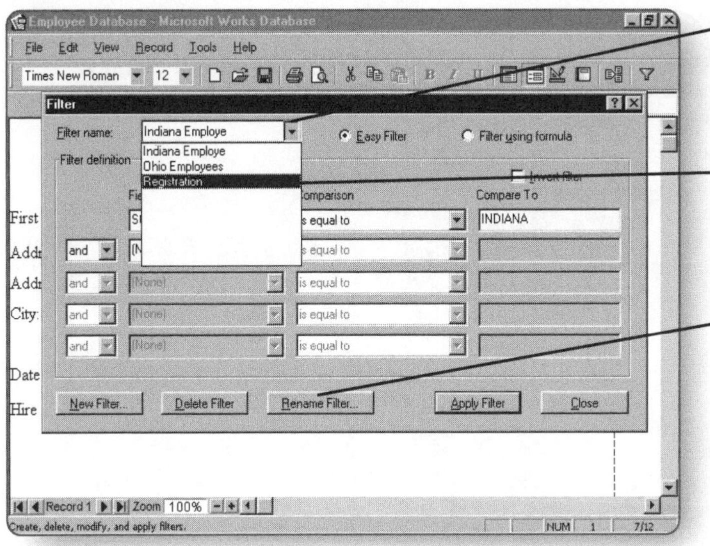

3. **Click** on the **Filter name: down arrow (▼)**. A list of current filters will appear.

4. **Click** on the **Filter name** to be renamed. The filter information will appear.

5. **Click** on **Rename Filter**. The Filter Name dialog box will open.

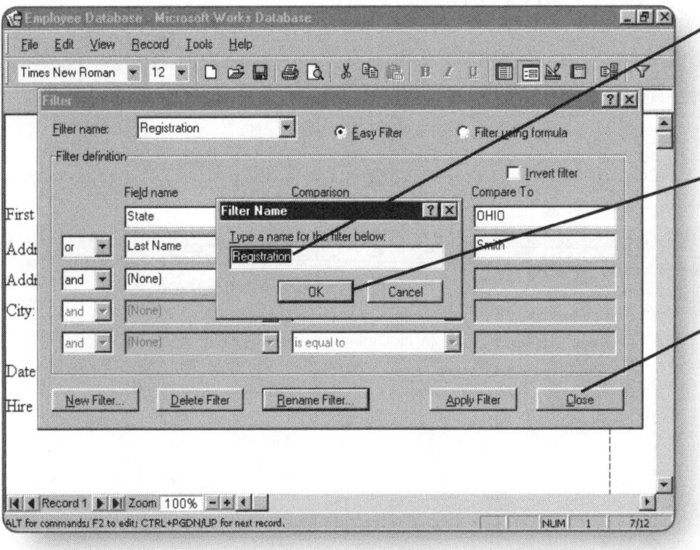

6. **Type** a **new name** for the filter. The text will appear in the text box.

7. **Click** on **OK**. The Filter Name dialog box will close, and the filter will be renamed.

8. **Click** on **Close**. The Filter dialog box will close.

Deleting a Filter

You can easily delete filters. When you delete a filter, you are not deleting any records or fields, only the instructions to filter it.

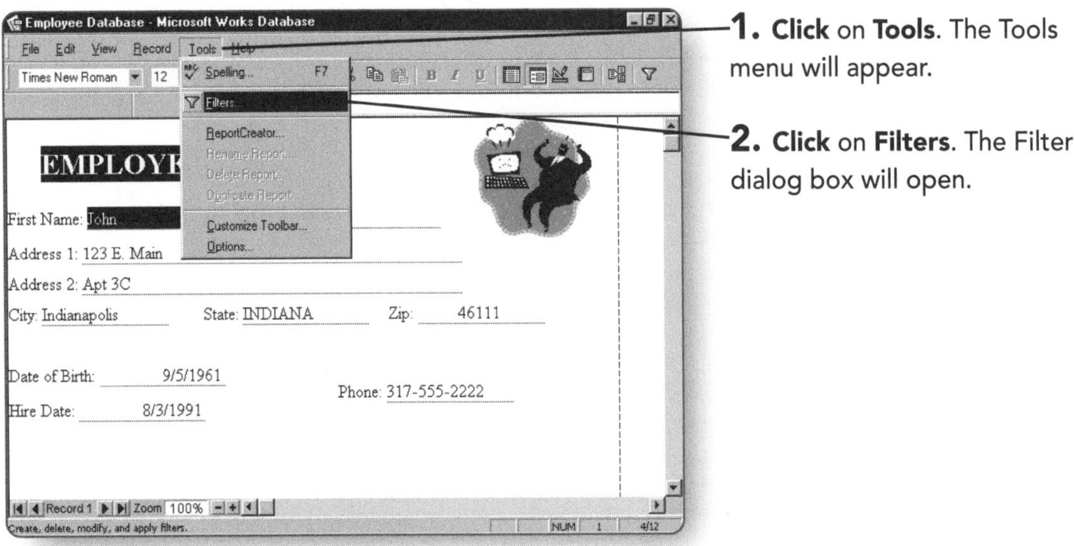

1. **Click** on **Tools**. The Tools menu will appear.

2. **Click** on **Filters**. The Filter dialog box will open.

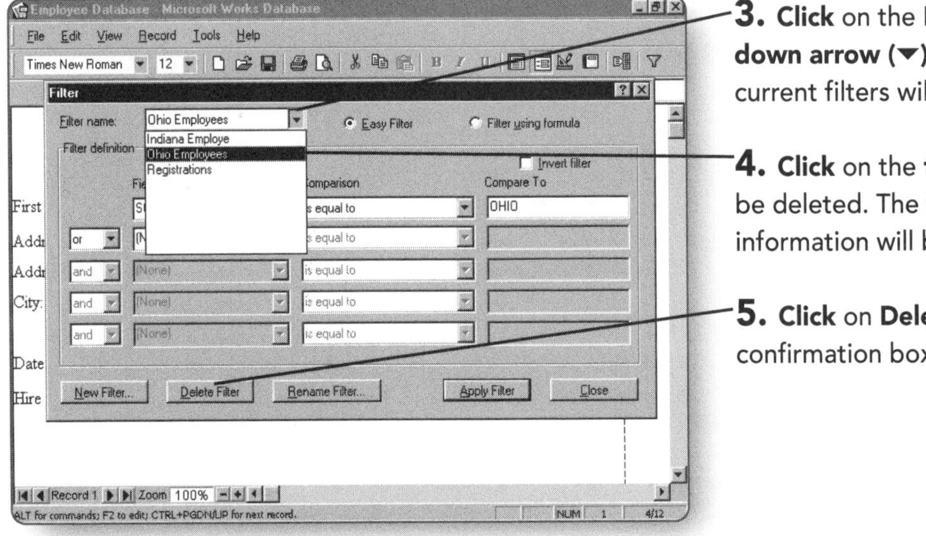

3. **Click** on the **Filter name: down arrow (▼)**. A list of current filters will appear.

4. **Click** on the **filter name** to be deleted. The filter information will be displayed.

5. **Click** on **Delete Filter**. A confirmation box will open.

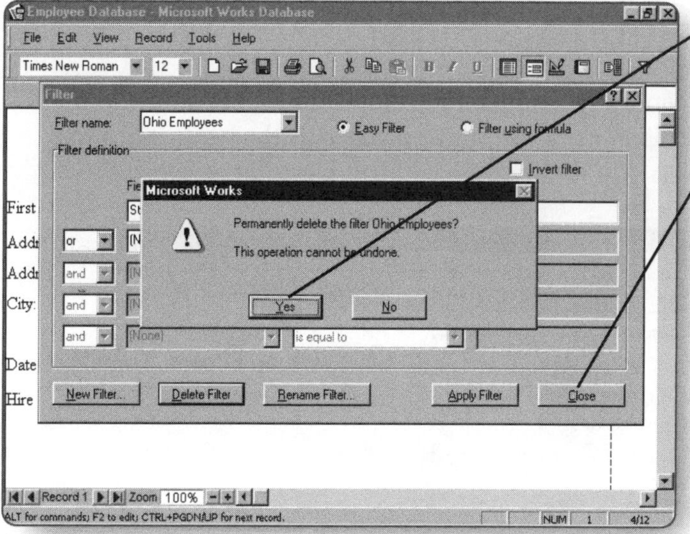

6. **Click** on **Yes**. The filter will be removed from the filter list.

7. **Click** on **Close**. The Filter dialog box will close.

20

Using Reports

Works allows you to decide how your printed data should look by letting you create reports. Using reports, you can control the format of the report, which fields and records are included in the report, and whether you want totals. In this chapter, you'll learn how to:

- Use the ReportCreator
- Modify reports
- Delete reports
- Print reports

Creating a Report

Reports organize and summarize the database information. When you create a report, you can specify which fields to print and where on the page to print them. You can also sort and group information as well as include calculations such as totals or averages. Each database can include up to eight reports.

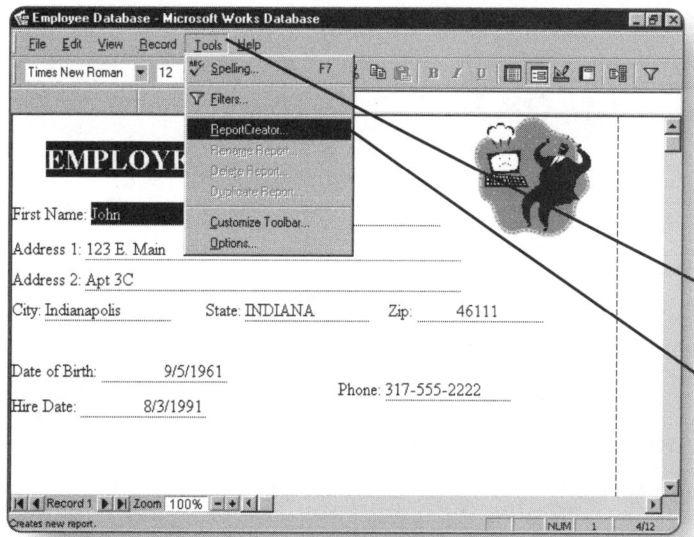

Using the ReportCreator

Use the ReportCreator to create a database report that has been sorted and formatted.

1. **Click** on **Tools**. The Tools menu will appear.
2. **Click** on **ReportCreator**. The Report Name dialog box will open.

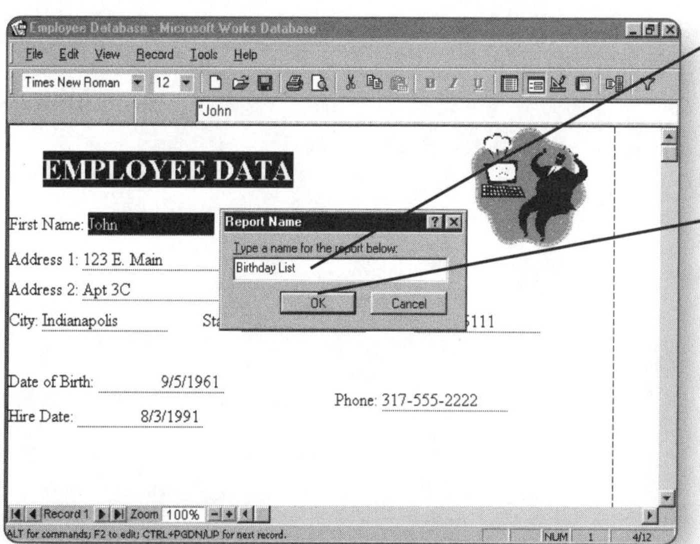

3. **Enter** a **name** for the report. Report names can be up to 15 characters in length including spaces.
4. **Click** on **OK**. The ReportCreator Wizard will open.

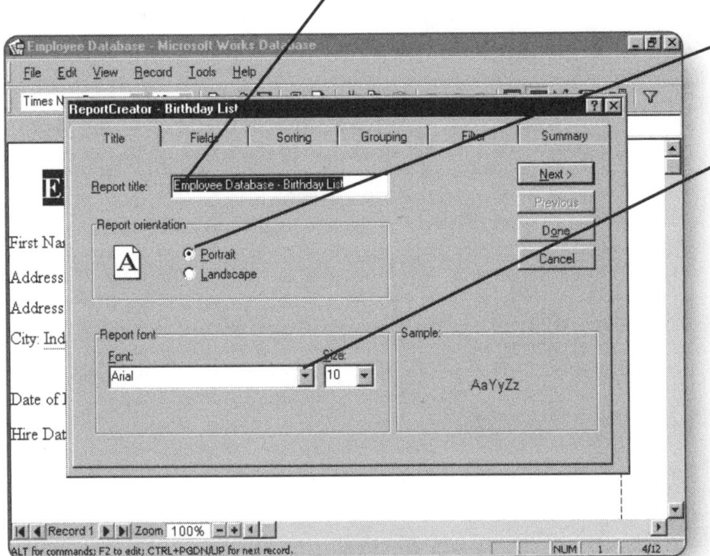

5. **Type** a **title** for your report. The title will print on the report and can be up to 255 characters including spaces.

6. **Click** on an **orientation**. The option will be selected.

7. **Click** on the **Font: down arrow (▼)**. A list of available fonts will appear.

8. **Click** on a **font**. The font name will be displayed.

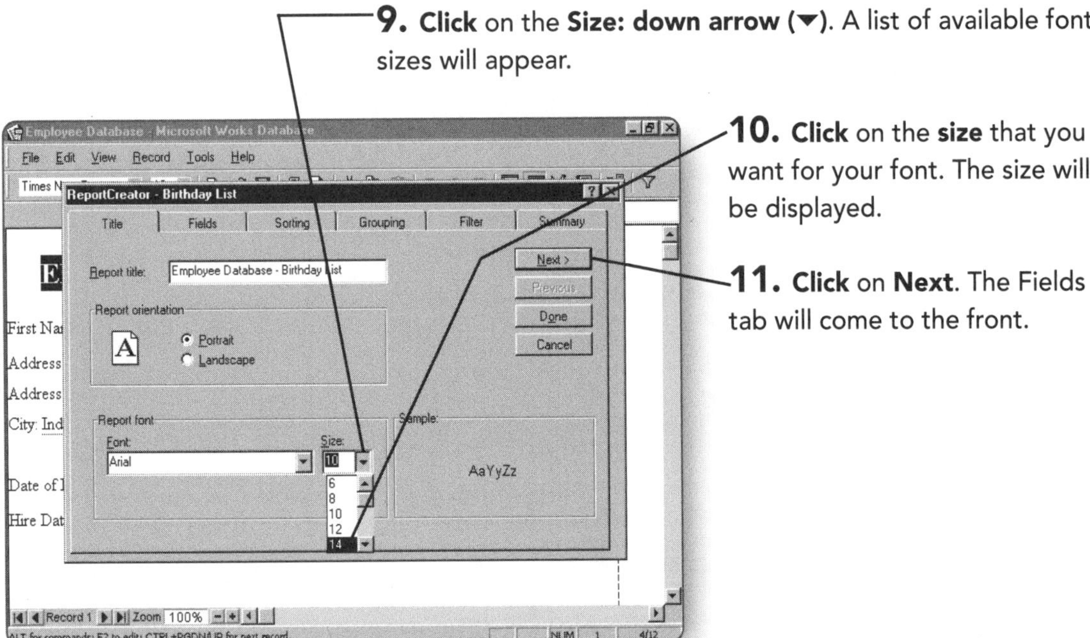

9. **Click** on the **Size: down arrow (▼)**. A list of available font sizes will appear.

10. **Click** on the **size** that you want for your font. The size will be displayed.

11. **Click** on **Next**. The Fields tab will come to the front.

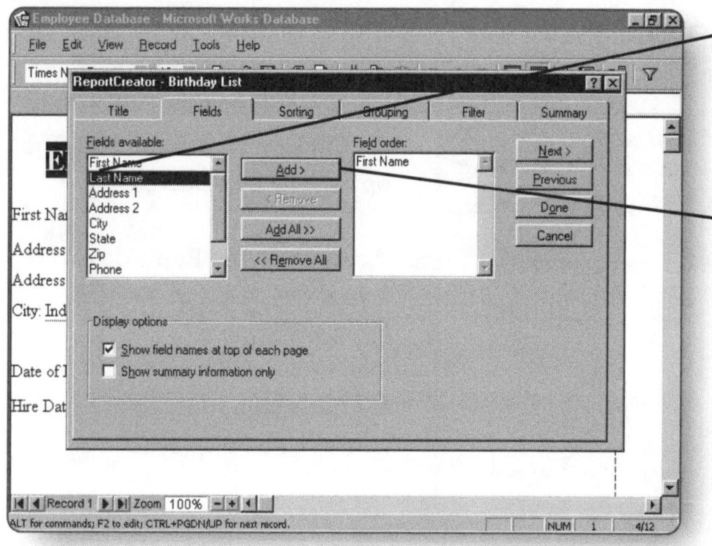

12. Click on the **first field name** that you want to display in the report. The field name will be highlighted.

13. Click on **Add**. The field name will be added to the Field order list.

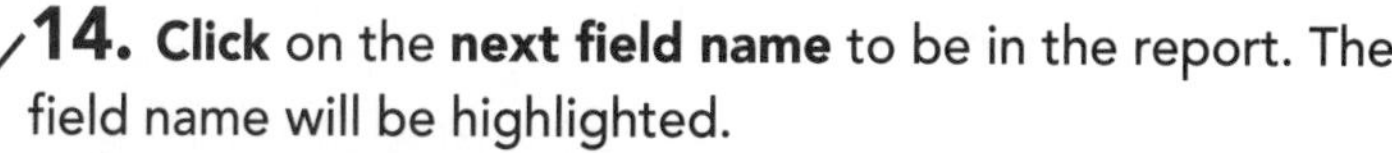

14. Click on the **next field name** to be in the report. The field name will be highlighted.

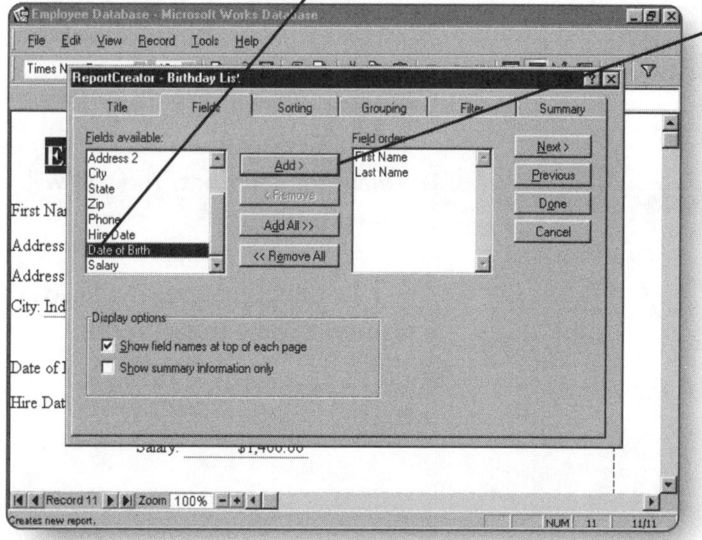

15. Click on **Add**. The field name will be added to the Field order list.

16. Repeat steps 14 and **15** for each field to be included in the report.

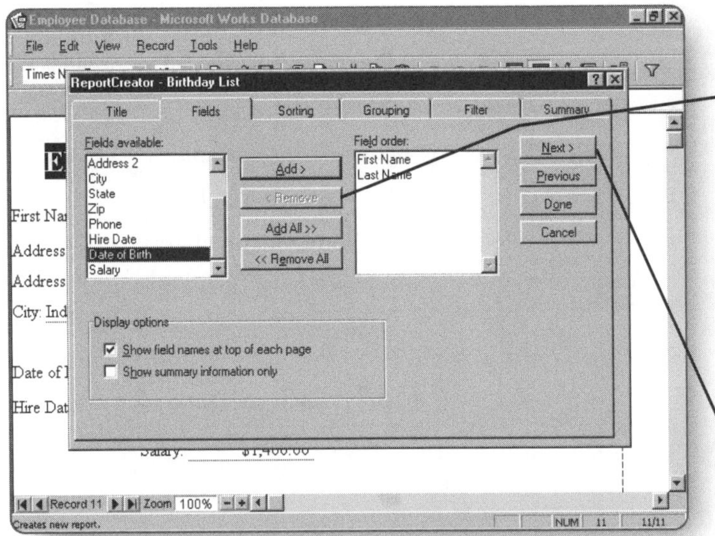

TIP

To remove a field from the report, click on the field name in the Field order list, and then click on Remove. The field is only removed from the report, not from the database.

17. Click on **Next**. The Sorting tab will come to the front.

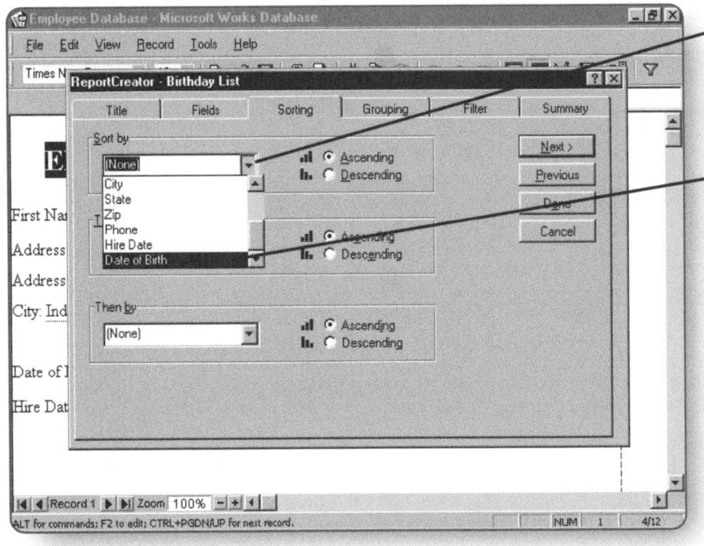

18. Click on **Sort by down arrow (▼)**. A list of field names will appear.

19. Click on the **field** to sort by. The field name will appear.

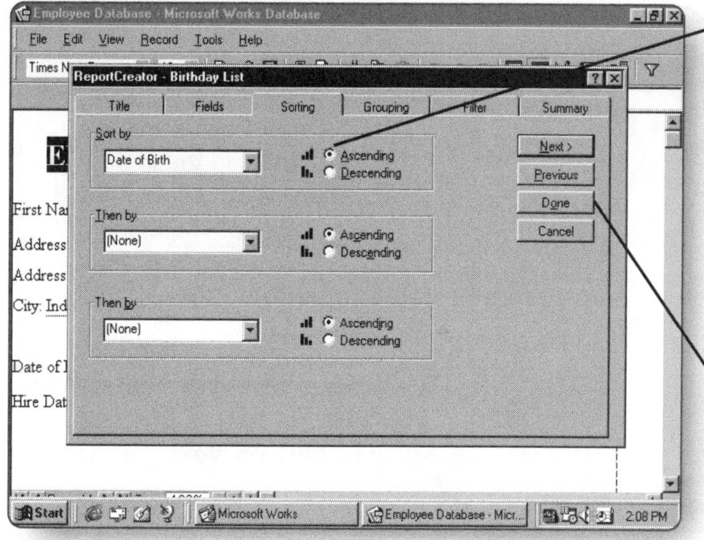

20. Click on **Ascending** or **Descending**. The option will be selected.

> **NOTE**
>
> You can specify up to three sort requests.

21. Click on **Done**. A message box will appear.

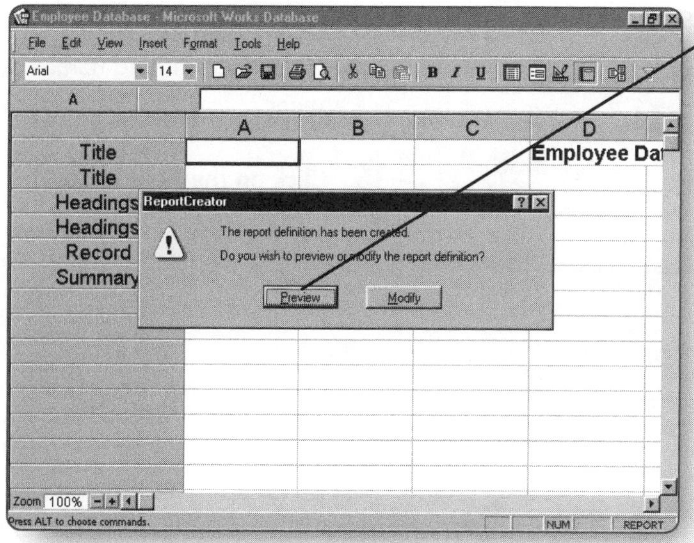

22. Click on **Preview**. The report will display with the data as specified.

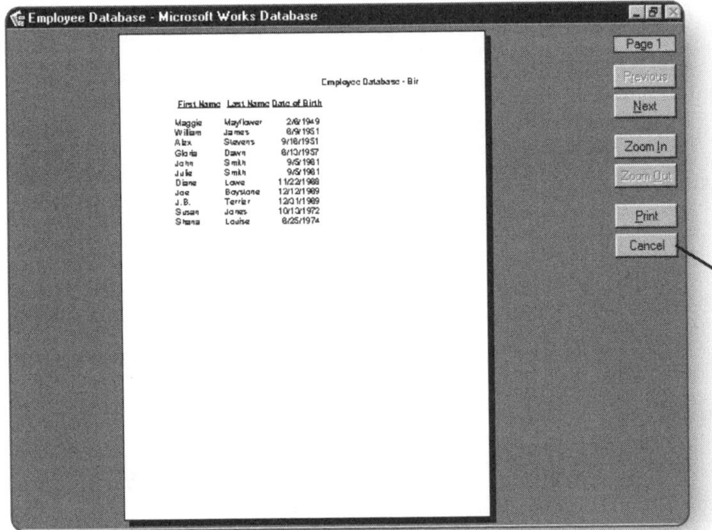

> **TIP**
>
> Click the mouse on the report to zoom in and take a closer look.

23. Click on **Cancel**. The database report layout will appear.

Creating Summary Reports

Let a Works report summarize your data with totals, averages, or other statistical information.

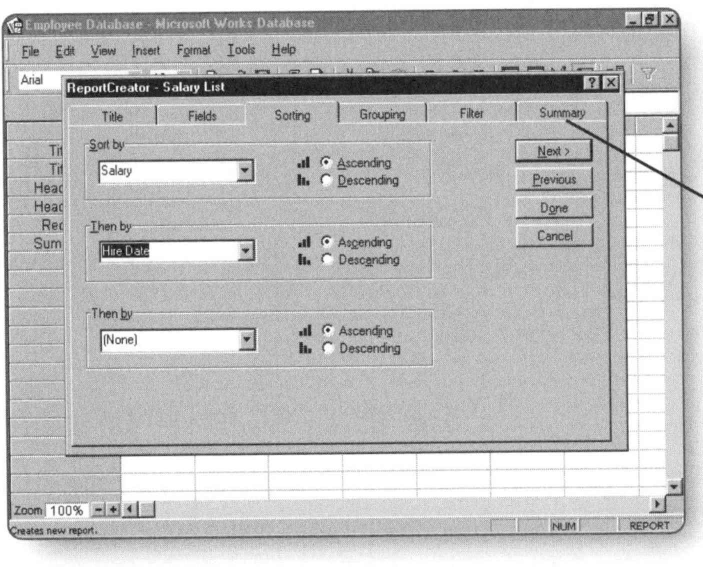

1. Create a **report** following steps 1 through 20 of the previous section "Using the ReportCreator."

2. Click on the **Summary tab**. The tab will come to the front.

3. Click on the **field name** to summarize by. The field name will be highlighted.

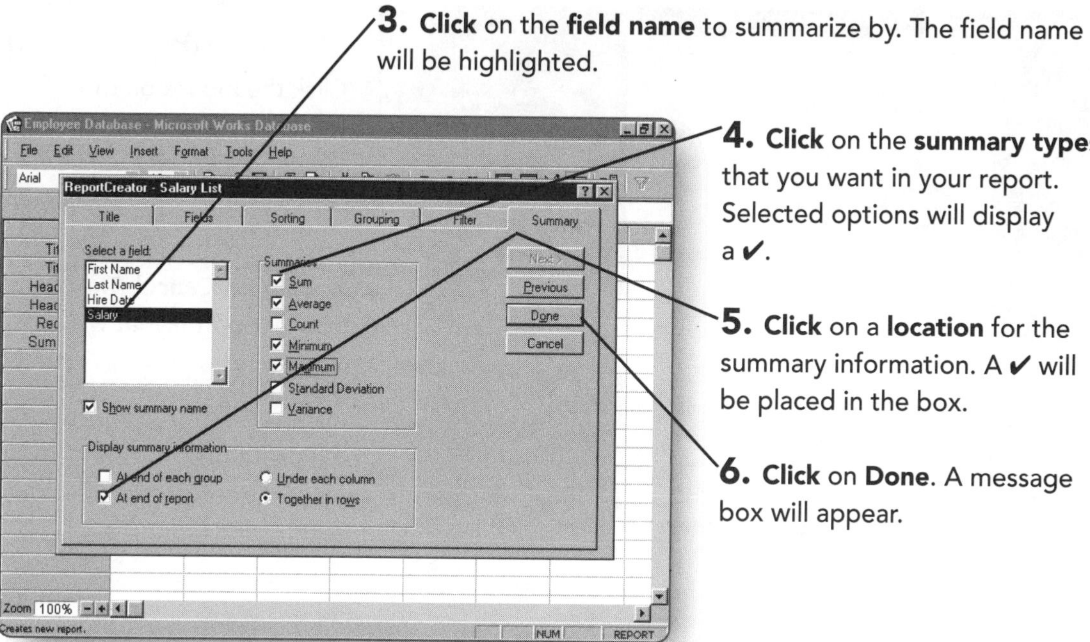

4. Click on the **summary types** that you want in your report. Selected options will display a ✔.

5. Click on a **location** for the summary information. A ✔ will be placed in the box.

6. Click on **Done**. A message box will appear.

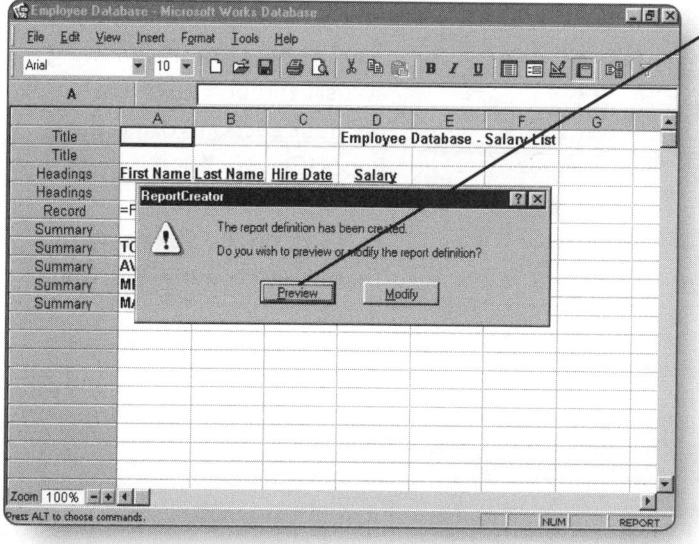

7. Click on **Preview**. The report will appear with the specified data.

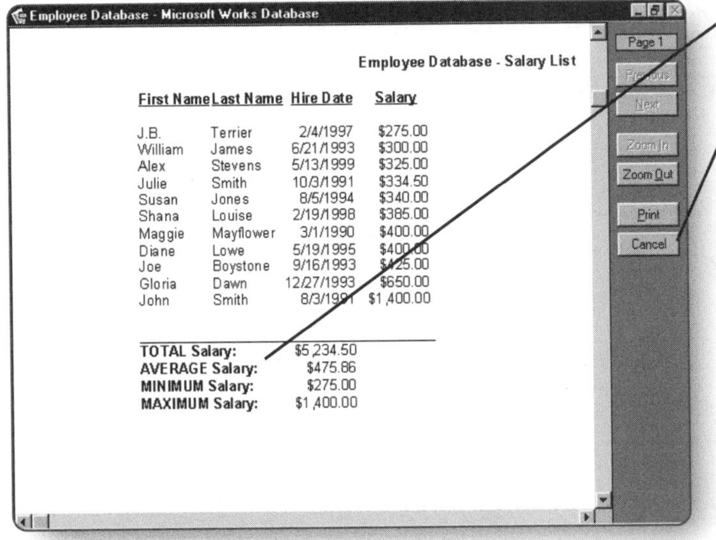

The summarized fields are displayed.

8. Click on **Cancel**. The database report layout will appear.

Modifying a Report

You may want to modify the appearance of the report data. Working in the report editor is similar to working with a Works spreadsheet except that instead of row numbers, the rows are named with the type of data to be displayed.

Editing Report Column Headings

By default, each column in a report is displayed with the field name, which you can easily edit.

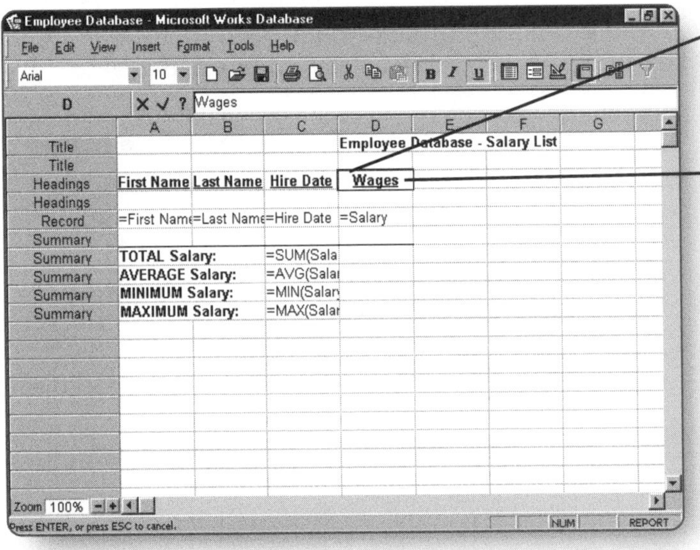

1. Click on the **heading** that you want to modify. The cell will be selected.

2. Type a **new heading**. The new text will appear.

3. Press Enter. The new heading will replace the old heading. The field heading will remain the same; only the heading for the report will be changed.

Changing Column Width

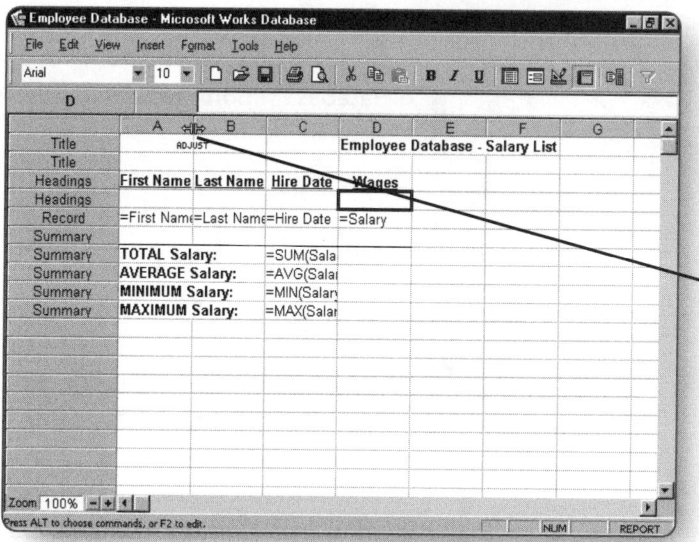

Use your mouse to widen a column. A line located at the right edge of each column heading divides the columns. Use this line to change the column width.

1. Position the **mouse pointer** on the right column line for the field that you want to change. The mouse pointer will become a double-headed white arrow with the word "ADJUST" displayed under it.

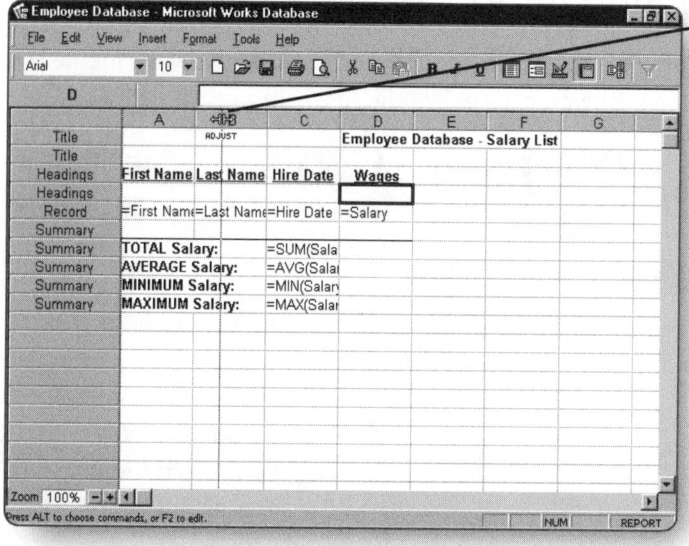

2. Press and **hold** the **mouse button** and **drag** the column line. If you drag it to the right, the column width will increase; if you drag it to the left, the column width will decrease.

3. Release the **mouse button**. The column width will be changed.

Increasing Row Height

Add more room between each record in your report by increasing row height.

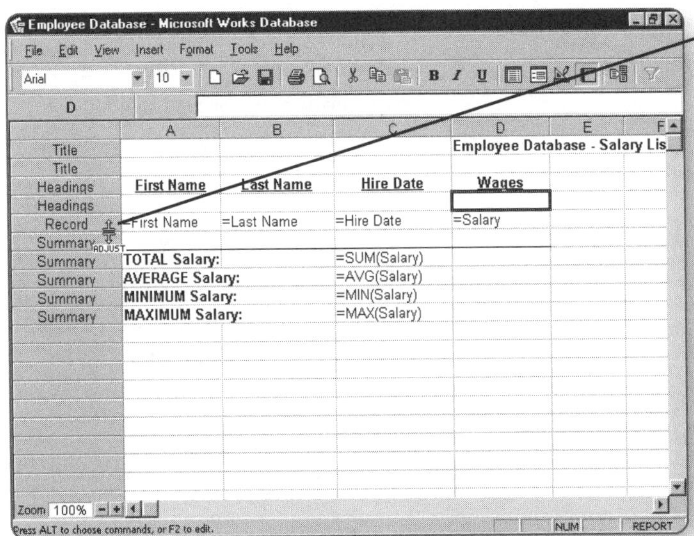

1. **Position** the **mouse pointer** on the lower row line for the row that you want to change. The mouse pointer will become a double-headed white arrow with the word "ADJUST" displayed under it.

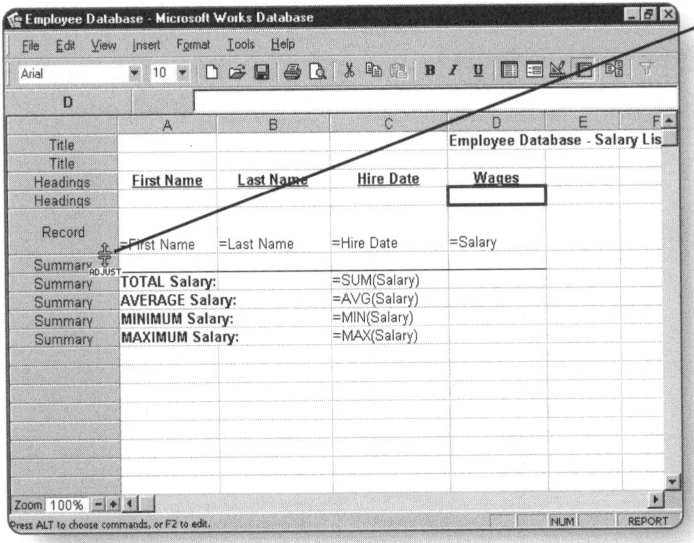

2. **Press** and **hold** the **mouse button** and **drag** the column line. If you drag it down, the row height will increase; if you drag it up, the row height will decrease.

3. **Release** the **mouse button**. The column width will be changed.

Modifying Alignment

Change the alignment of any field column, row, or individual field data.

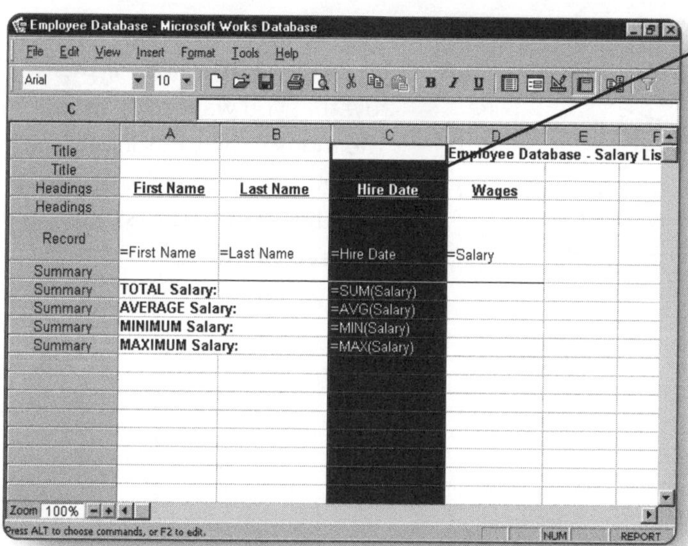

1. Click on a **field column, row, or cell** to modify. The column, row, or cell will be highlighted.

> **NOTE**
>
> To select an entire row, click on the row description; to select an entire column, click on the column letter.

2. Click on **Format**. The Format menu will appear.

3. Click on **Alignment**. The Format dialog box will open with the Alignment tab in front.

4. Click on an **Alignment** option. The option will be selected.

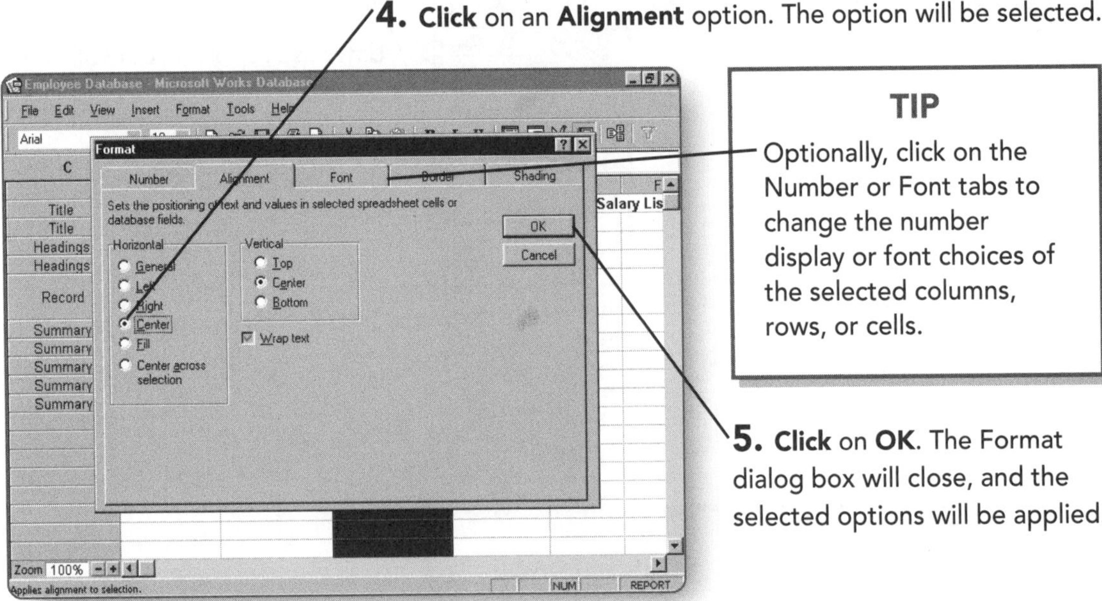

TIP

Optionally, click on the Number or Font tabs to change the number display or font choices of the selected columns, rows, or cells.

5. Click on **OK**. The Format dialog box will close, and the selected options will be applied.

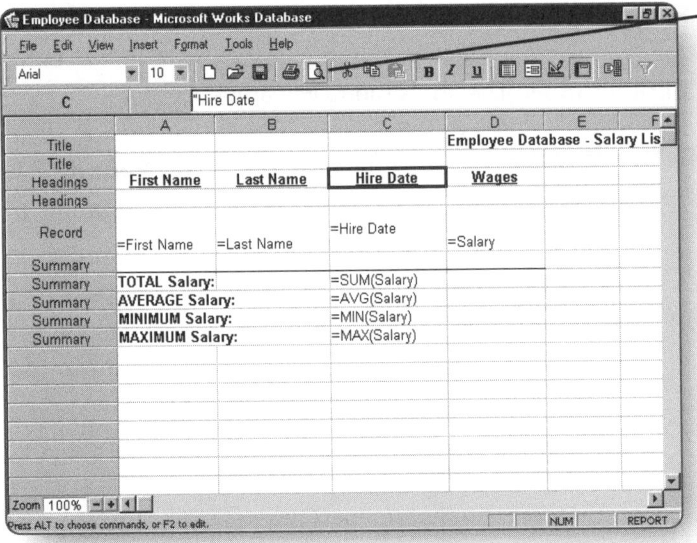

6. Click on the **Print Preview button**. The complete report will appear.

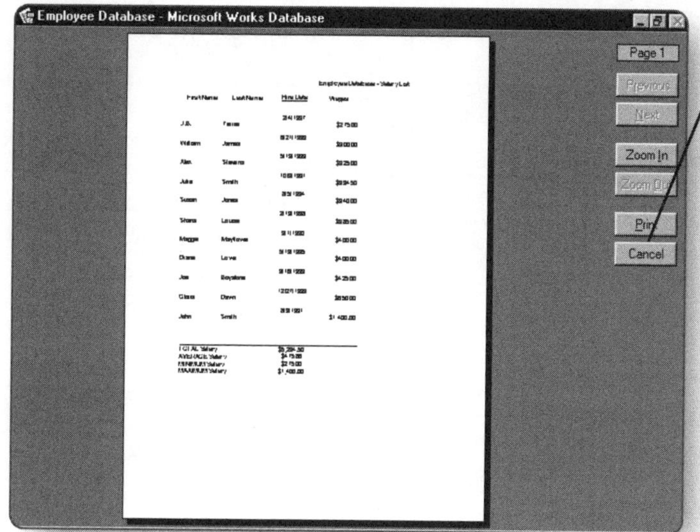

7. Click on **Cancel**. The database report layout will appear.

Deleting a Report

Works has a limit of eight reports per database. You may need to delete unwanted or old reports.

1. Click on **Tools**. The Tools menu will appear.

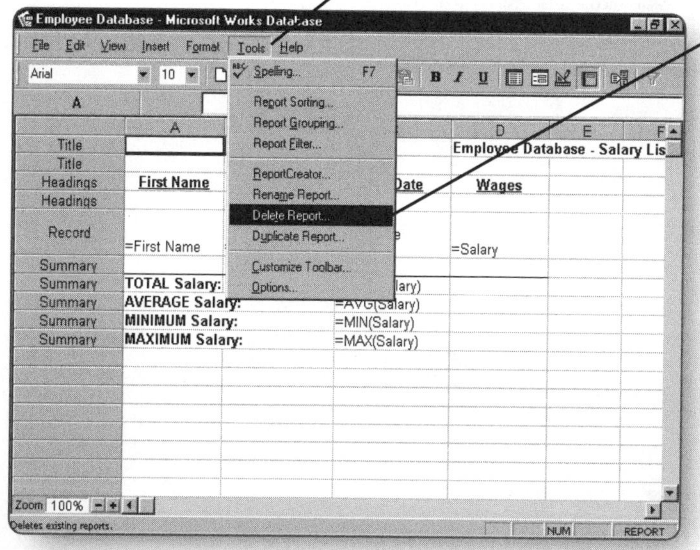

2. Click on **Delete Report**. The Delete Report dialog box will open.

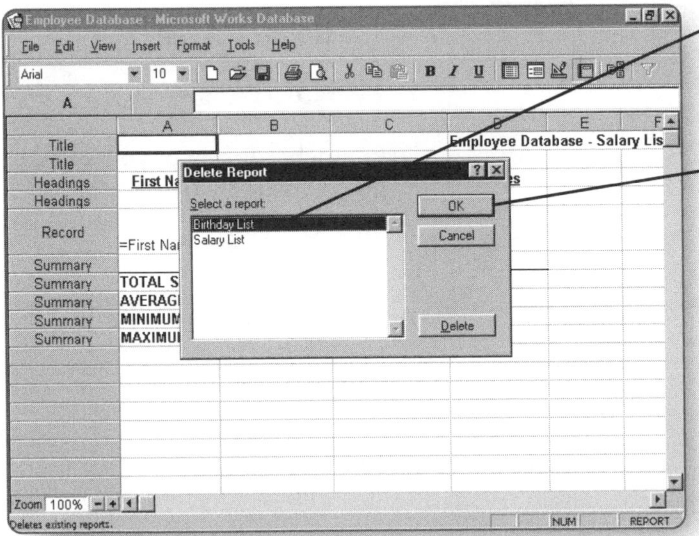

3. Click on the **Report name** to be deleted. The report name will be highlighted.

4. Click on **OK**. A confirmation message will appear.

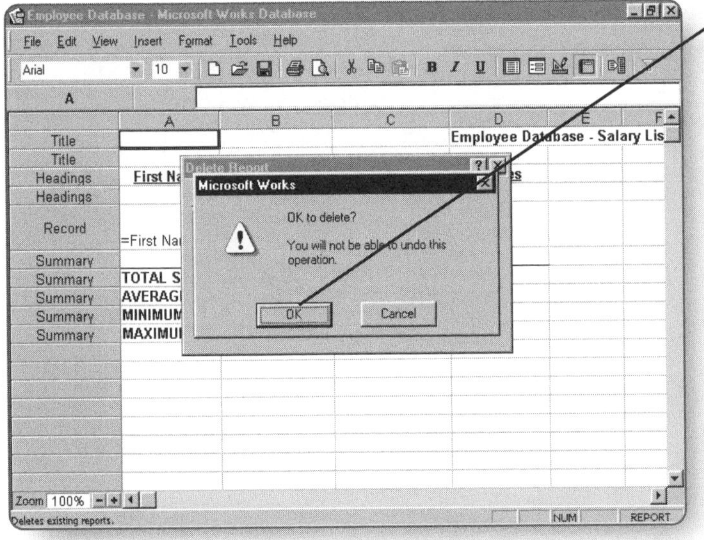

5. Click on **OK**. The report will be deleted.

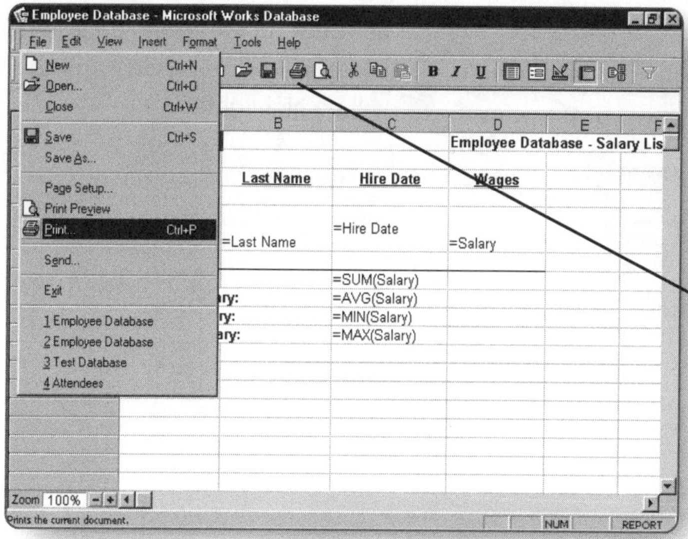

Printing a Report

Print a hard copy of your report for your files or to distribute to others.

1a. Click on the **Print button**. The report will print with standard options.

OR

1b. Click on **File**. The File menu will appear.

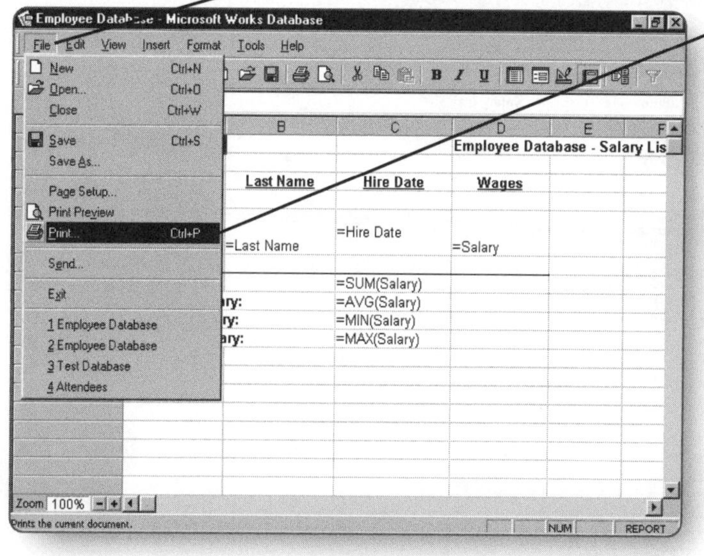

2. Click on **Print**. The Print dialog box will open.

Many options are available from the Print dialog box.

3. Click on any desired **option.** The option will be activated.

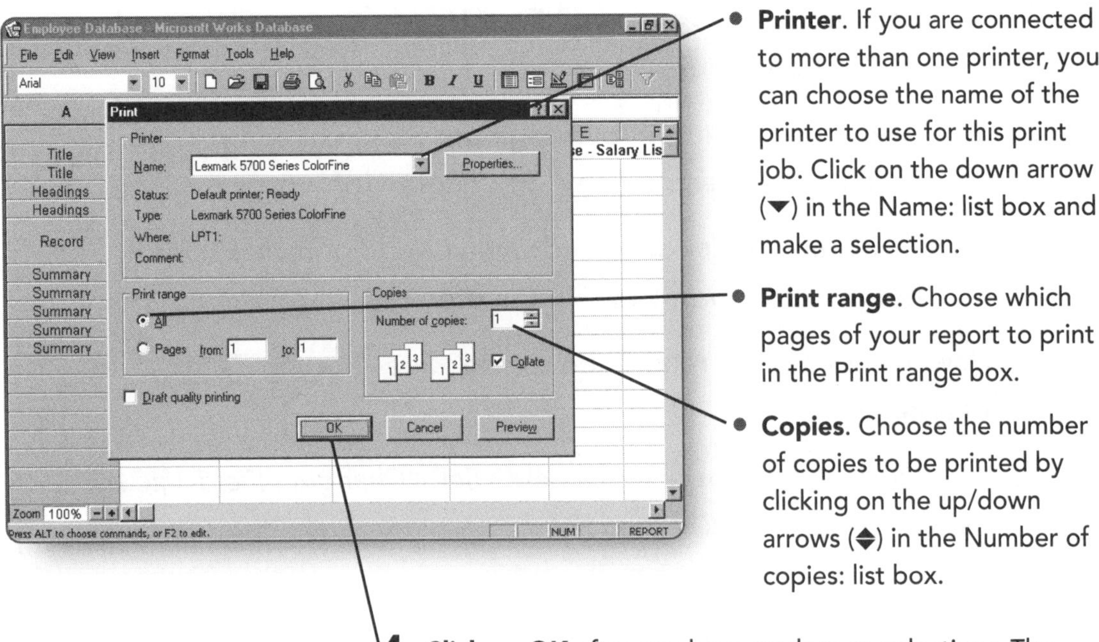

- **Printer**. If you are connected to more than one printer, you can choose the name of the printer to use for this print job. Click on the down arrow (▼) in the Name: list box and make a selection.
- **Print range**. Choose which pages of your report to print in the Print range box.
- **Copies**. Choose the number of copies to be printed by clicking on the up/down arrows (⬍) in the Number of copies: list box.

4. Click on **OK** after you have made your selections. The report will be sent to the printer.

Part IV Review Questions

1. In a database, what is a record? *See "Understanding Fields and Records" in Chapter 16*
2. What view must be active to change the design of a form? *See "Looking at the Different Views" in Chapter 16*
3. How many records are displayed when using Form view? *See "Entering Data in Form View" in Chapter 17*
4. How many ways can records be sorted? *See "Sorting Records" in Chapter 17*
5. What is the maximum size of a field? *See "Changing Field Size by Using the Menu" in Chapter 18*
6. When adding graphics to a database, on what records will the graphic display? *See "Adding Artwork to a Database" in Chapter 18*
7. How many filters can a database have? *See "Creating Additional Filters" in Chapter 19*
8. What do reports do to database information? *See "Creating a Report" in Chapter 20*
9. What feature does Works provide to assist you in creating a report? *See "Using the ReportCreator" in Chapter 20*
10. How can a report summarize your data? *See "Creating Summary Reports" in Chapter 20*

PART V

Discovering Works Tools

21

Saving Information in the Address Book

Works contains an address book that you can use to maintain a variety of information about business and personal contacts. You can use the address book to print a phone or address list, telephone a contact, or send e-mail to a contact. In this chapter, you'll learn how to:

- Add an Address Book entry
- Delete a contact
- Print a contact list

Opening the Address Book

The Works Address Book can be accessed through the Works Task Manager.

1. Click on **Programs**. A listing of the Works components will appear.

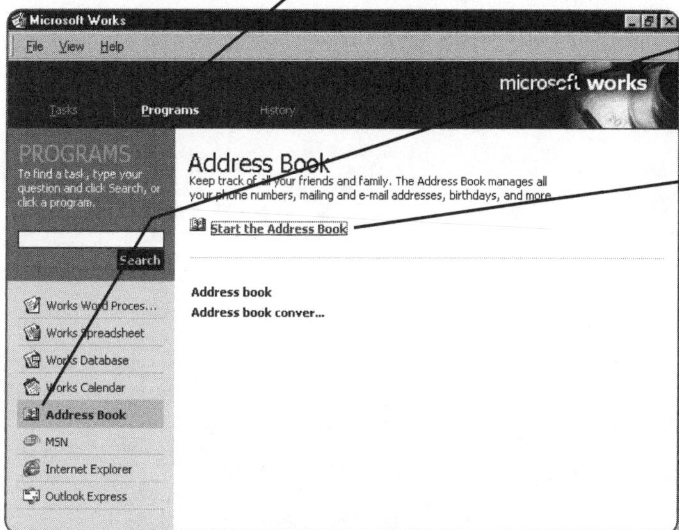

2. Click on **Address Book**. A list of Address Book tasks will appear.

3. Click on **Start the Address Book**. The Address Book will open.

Adding an Address

It is easy to add entries to the address book in Works. As you add contacts, they will be listed in alphabetical order by last name.

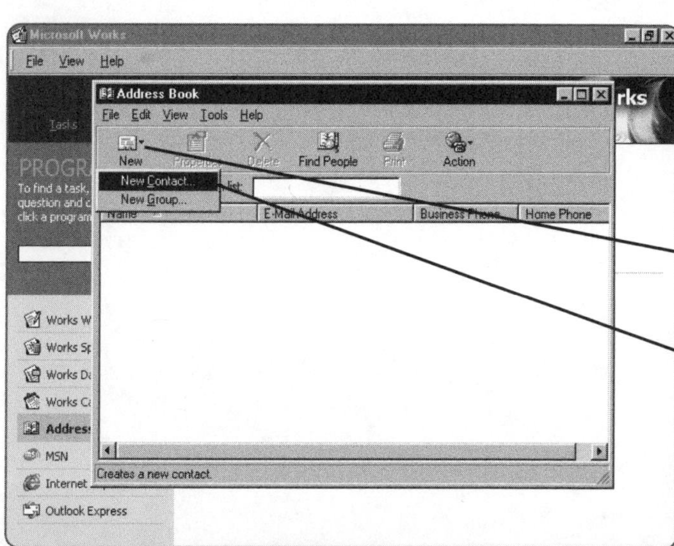

1. Click on the **New button**. A drop-down list will appear.

2. Click on **New Contact**. The Properties dialog box will open.

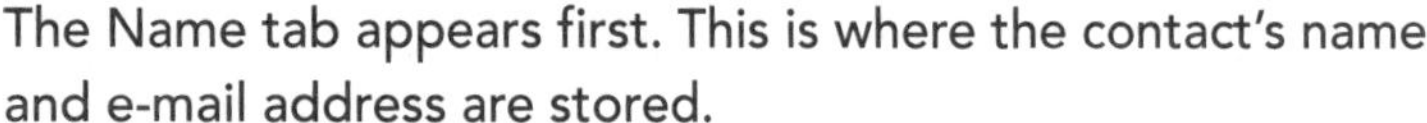

The Name tab appears first. This is where the contact's name and e-mail address are stored.

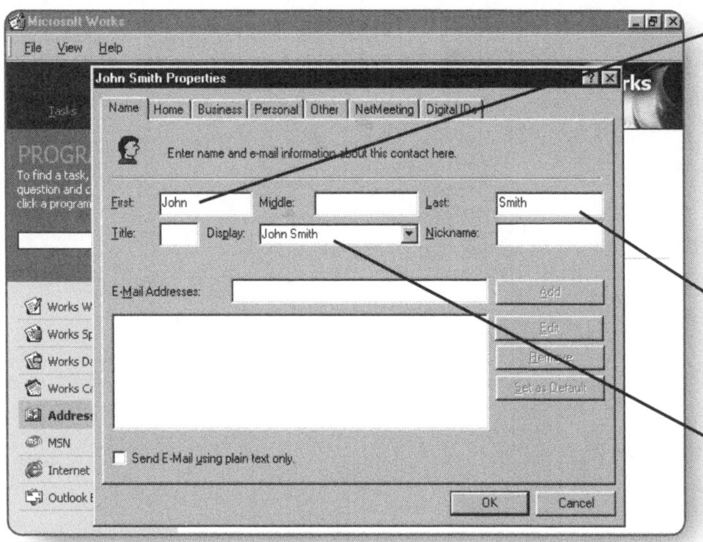

3. Type the contact's **first name**. The name will appear in the First: text box.

4. Press the **Tab key twice**. The insertion point will move to the Last: text box.

5. Type the contact's **last name**. The name will appear in the Last: text box.

As you enter the name, Works automatically fills in the Display: text box.

6. Press the **Tab key** four times. The blinking insertion point will be in the E-Mail Addresses: text box.

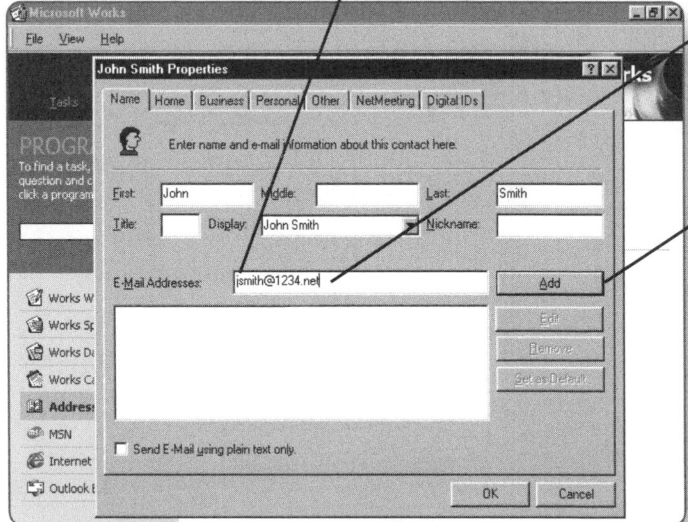

7. Type the contact's **e-mail address**. The e-mail address will appear in the E-Mail Addresses: text box.

8. Click on **Add**. The e-mail address will be added.

> **TIP**
>
> Repeat steps 7 and 8 to add as many e-mail addresses as you want for this contact.

9. **Click** on the **Home tab**. The tab will come to the front.

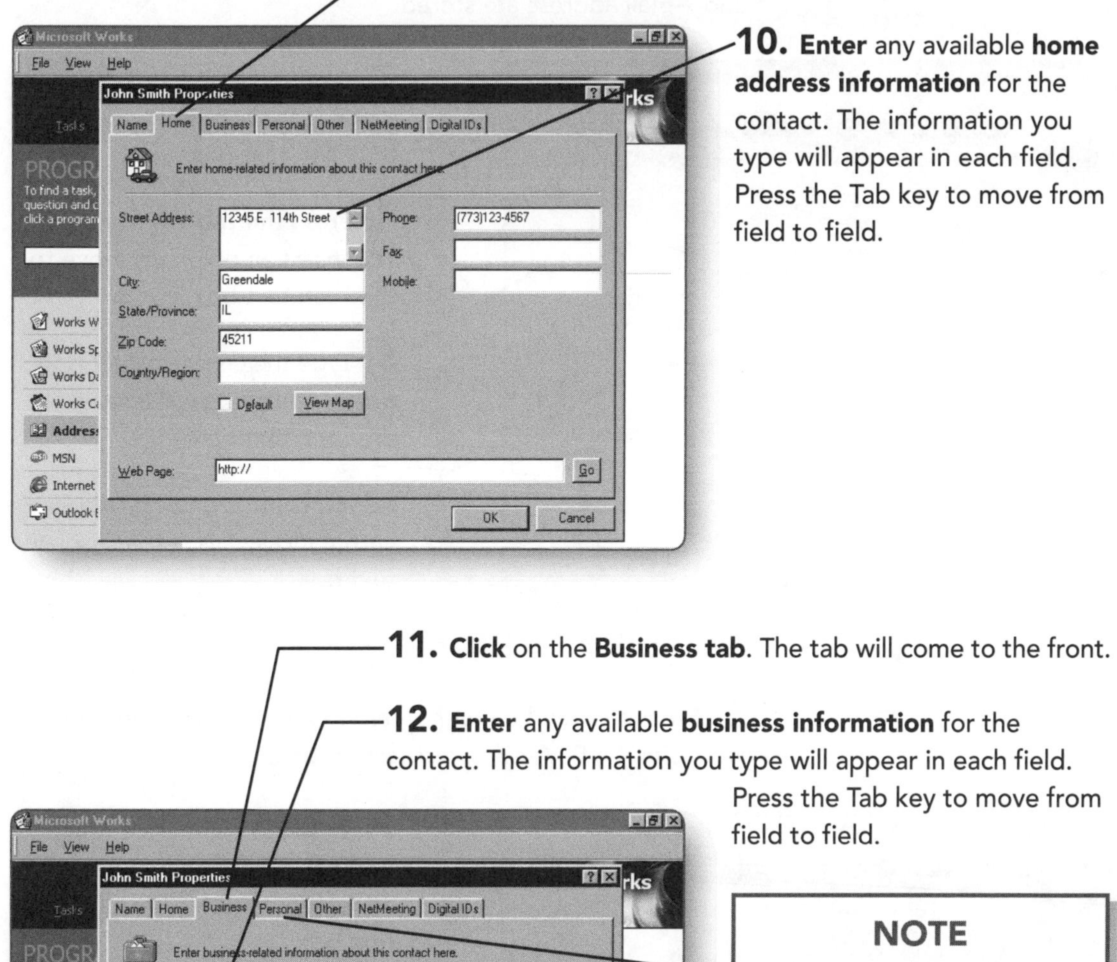

10. **Enter** any available **home address information** for the contact. The information you type will appear in each field. Press the Tab key to move from field to field.

11. **Click** on the **Business tab**. The tab will come to the front.

12. **Enter** any available **business information** for the contact. The information you type will appear in each field. Press the Tab key to move from field to field.

NOTE

Click on the Personal tab to store personal information, such as spouse and children names, birthday or anniversary dates.

13. **Click** on **OK**. The Properties dialog box will close.

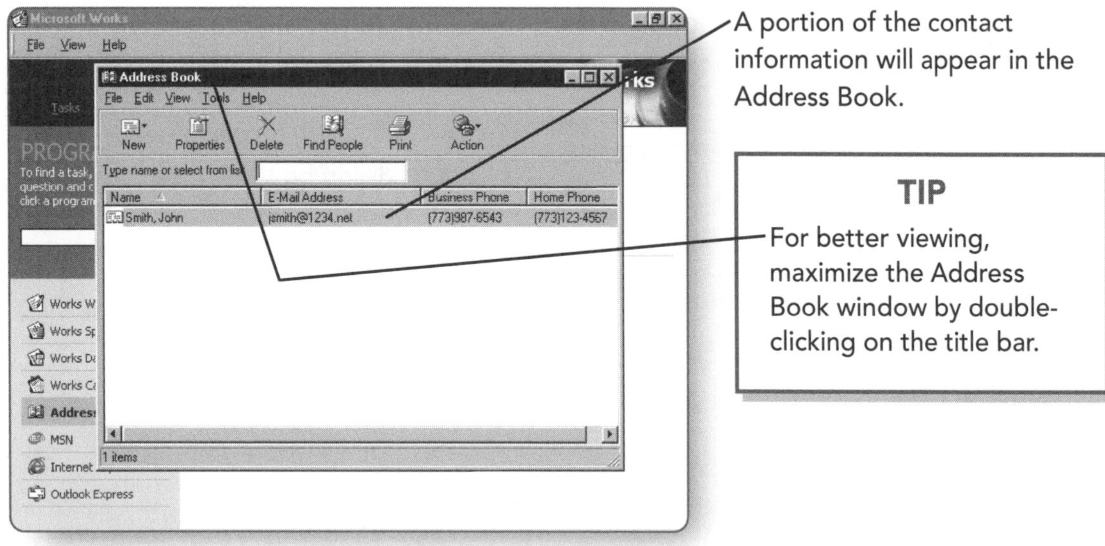

A portion of the contact information will appear in the Address Book.

TIP

For better viewing, maximize the Address Book window by double-clicking on the title bar.

Displaying Contact Information

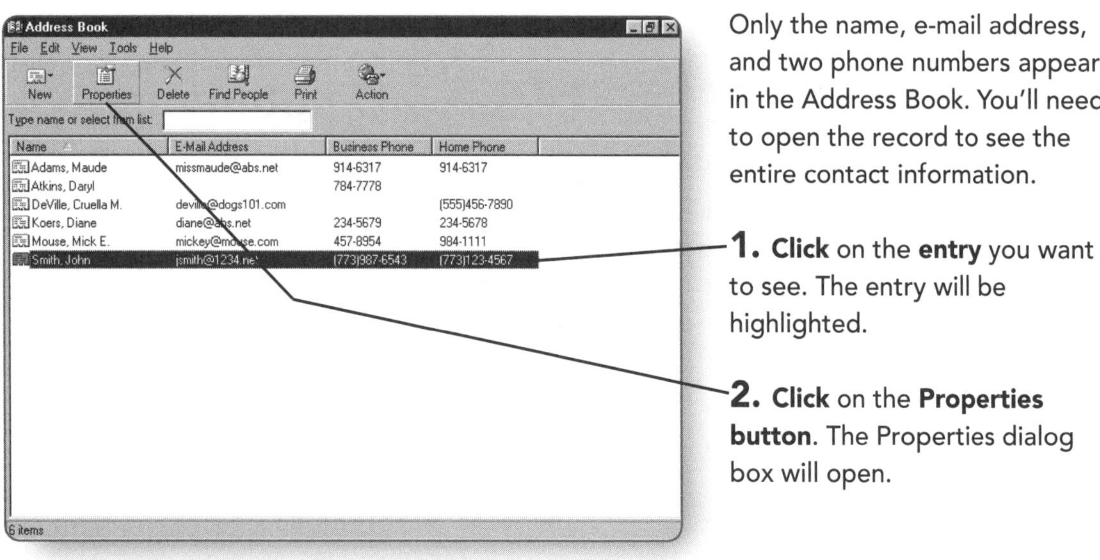

Only the name, e-mail address, and two phone numbers appear in the Address Book. You'll need to open the record to see the entire contact information.

1. **Click** on the **entry** you want to see. The entry will be highlighted.
2. **Click** on the **Properties button**. The Properties dialog box will open.

3. Click on the **information tab** you want to see. The information on the selected contact will appear.

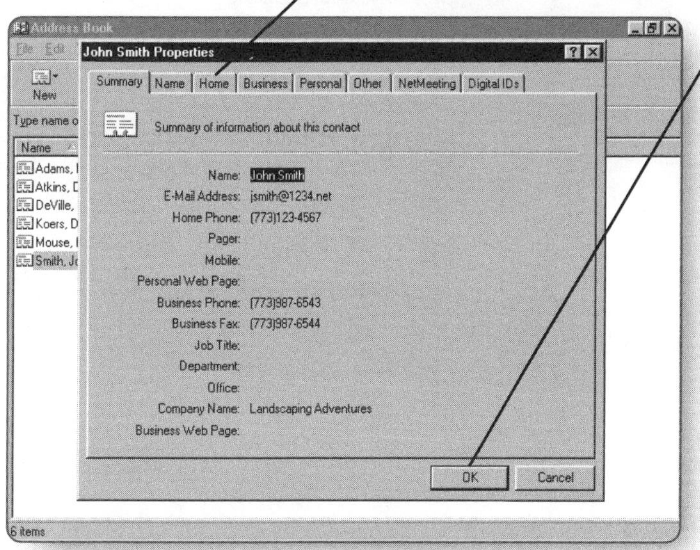

4. Click on **OK**. The Properties dialog box will close.

Deleting an Address

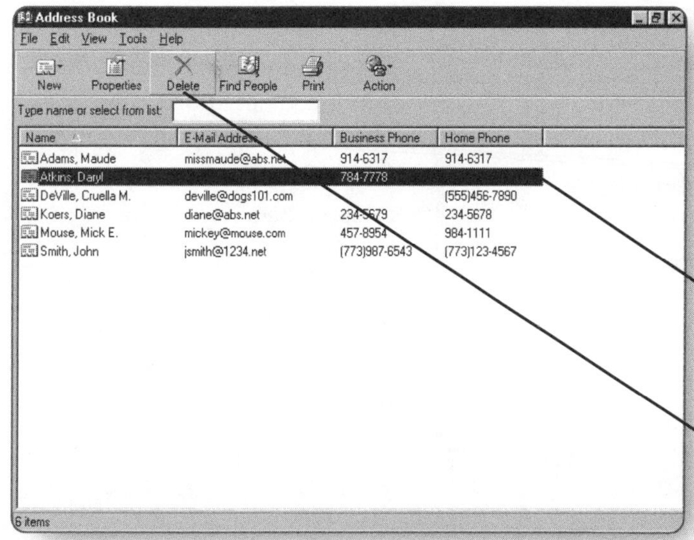

If you no longer want a contact listed in your Address Book, you can easily delete it.

1. Click on the **contact name** to be deleted. The name will be selected.

2. Click on the **Delete button**. A confirmation box will appear.

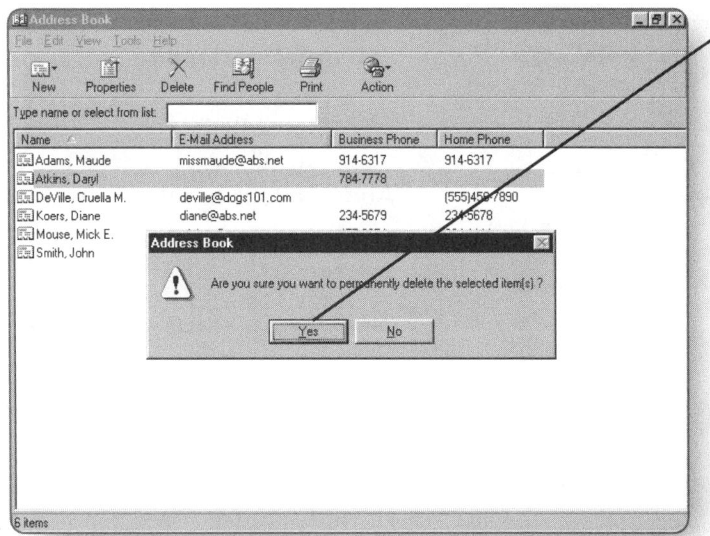

3. Click on **Yes**. The contact and all its information will be deleted.

> **NOTE**
>
> You cannot undo the delete action.

Using an Address Entry

Provided that you have e-mail on your system, you can send e-mail to your Address Book contacts.

1. Click on the **contact** you want to e-mail. The contact will be highlighted.

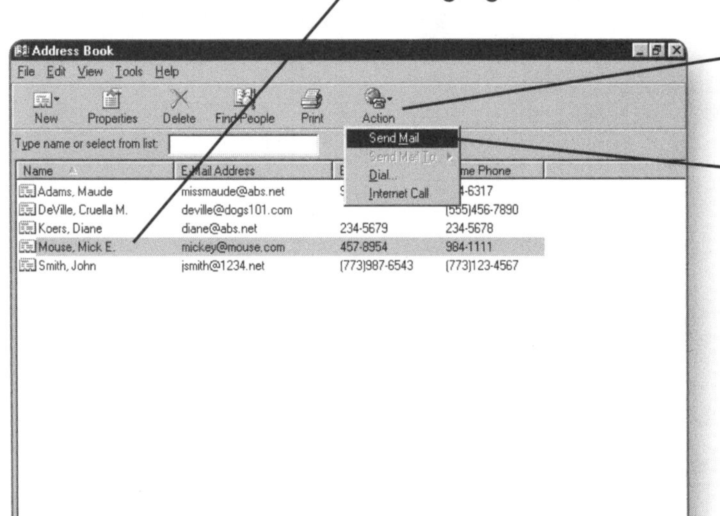

2. Click on the **Action button**. A list of tasks will appear.

3. Click on **Send Mail**. The New Message dialog box will open.

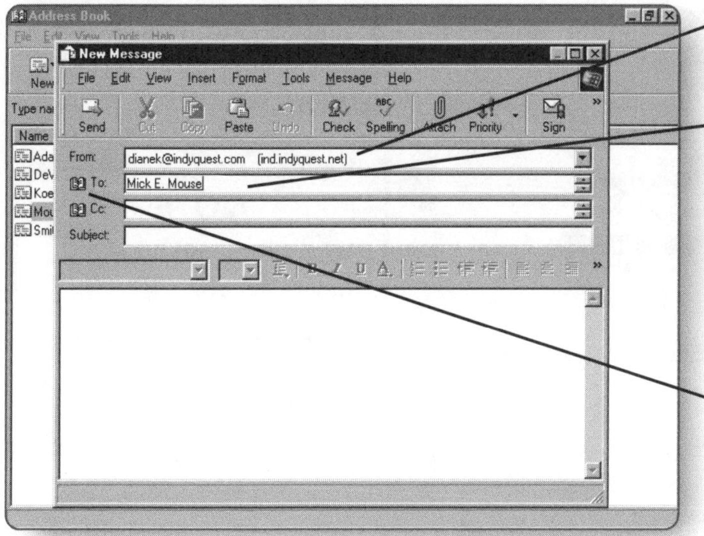

Your return e-mail address will automatically display.

The contact name will automatically display. Works Address Book has the contact e-mail address associated with this contact.

> **TIP**
>
> Optionally, click on the To: icon to locate and add message recipients from your Address Book.

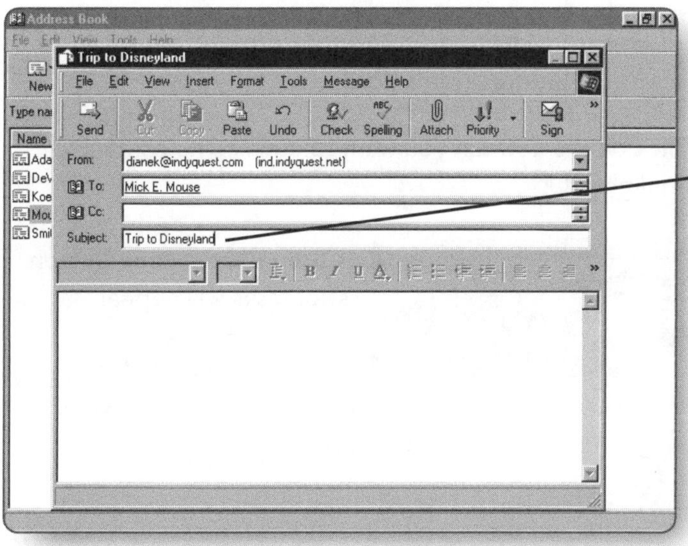

4. Press the **Tab key twice**. The insertion point will move to the Subject: text box.

5. Type a **subject** for the message. The text will appear in the Subject: text box.

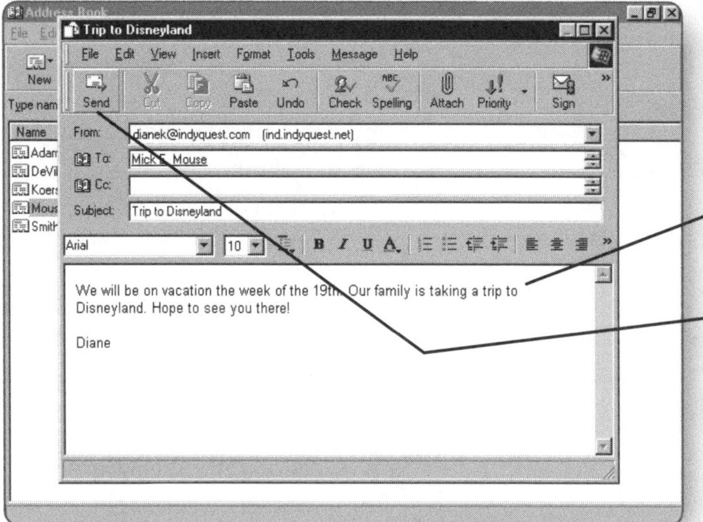

6. Press the **Tab key**. The insertion point will move to the body of the e-mail message box.

7. Type the e-mail **message**. The text will appear in the box.

8. Click on **Send**. The e-mail message will be sent.

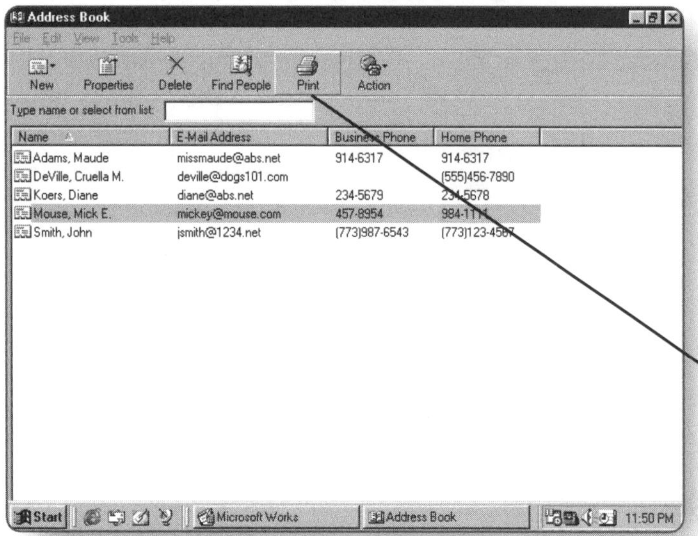

Printing a Phone List

You can print the information you store about your contacts in a variety of formats: Memo Style, Business Card Style, and Phone List Style.

1. Click on the **Print button**. The Print dialog box will open.

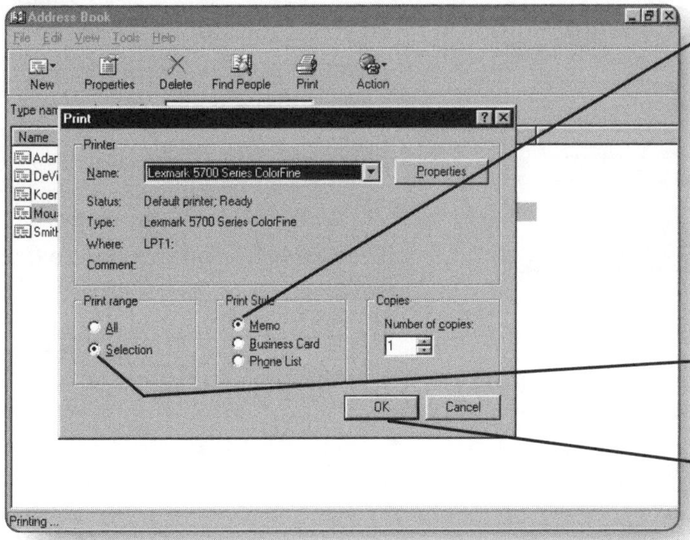

2. Click on a **print style**. The style will be highlighted.

You can print your entire contact list, or only the currently selected record—the one highlighted before you clicked on the Print button.

3. Click on a **print range**. The option will be selected.

4. Click on **OK**. The Address Book contacts will print.

Exiting the Address Book

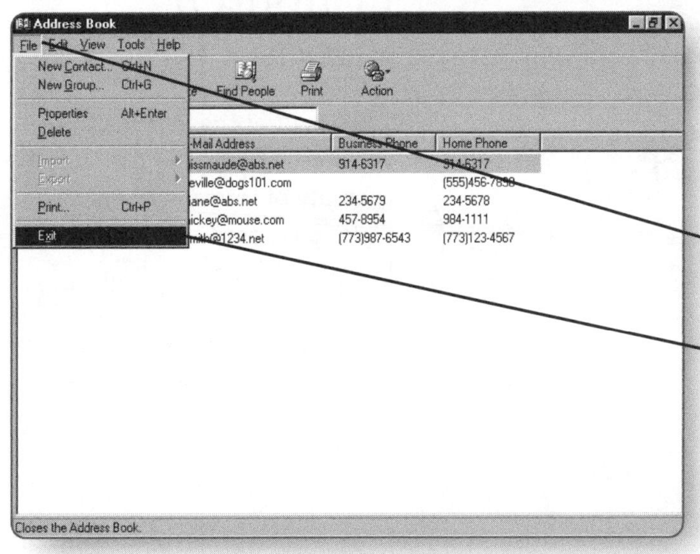

Works automatically saves the information in the Address Book. When you are finished with the Address Book, close it like any other Works application.

1. Click on **File**. The File menu will appear.

2. Click on **Exit**. The Address Book will close, and the Works Task Launcher will appear.

22

Working with Graphics

Microsoft Works provides several ways to add graphics to your document. One method is to use the Microsoft Draw program to create your own simple graphics. Another interesting tool is the WordArt program. In this chapter, you'll learn how to:

- Create a WordArt object
- Enhance a WordArt object
- Draw objects with Microsoft Draw
- Edit drawn objects

Using WordArt

Works includes a tool to reshape, rotate, and add special effects to text. Make your text come alive with the shapes that you create with WordArt! Start with a word processing document.

1. **Click** on **Insert**. The Insert menu will appear.

2. **Click** on **Picture**. The Picture submenu will appear.

3. **Click** on **WordArt**. A WordArt window will appear.

Menu selections have changed.

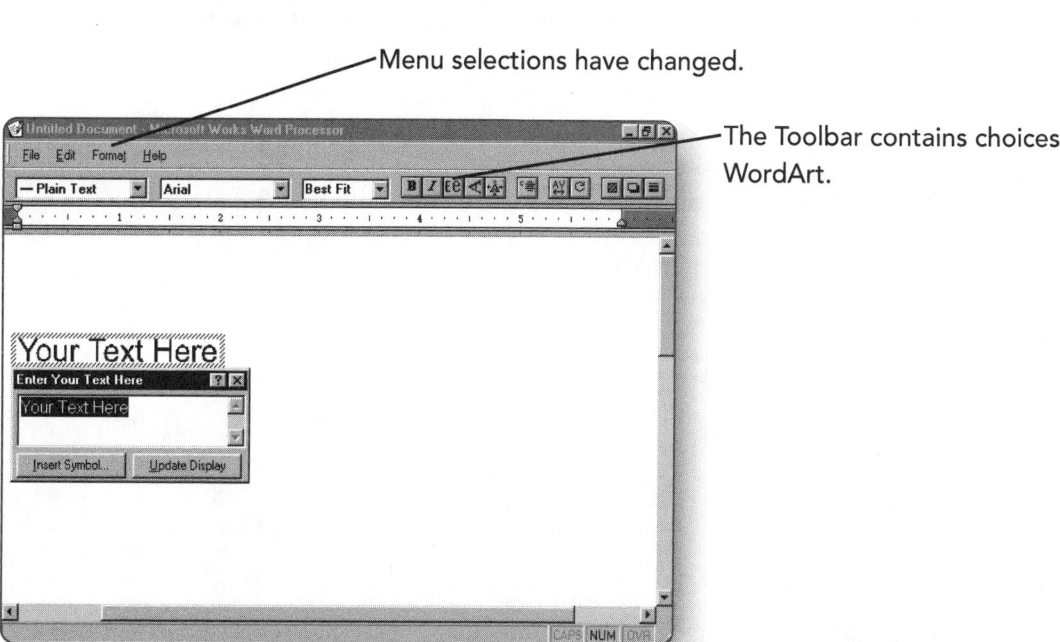

The Toolbar contains choices for WordArt.

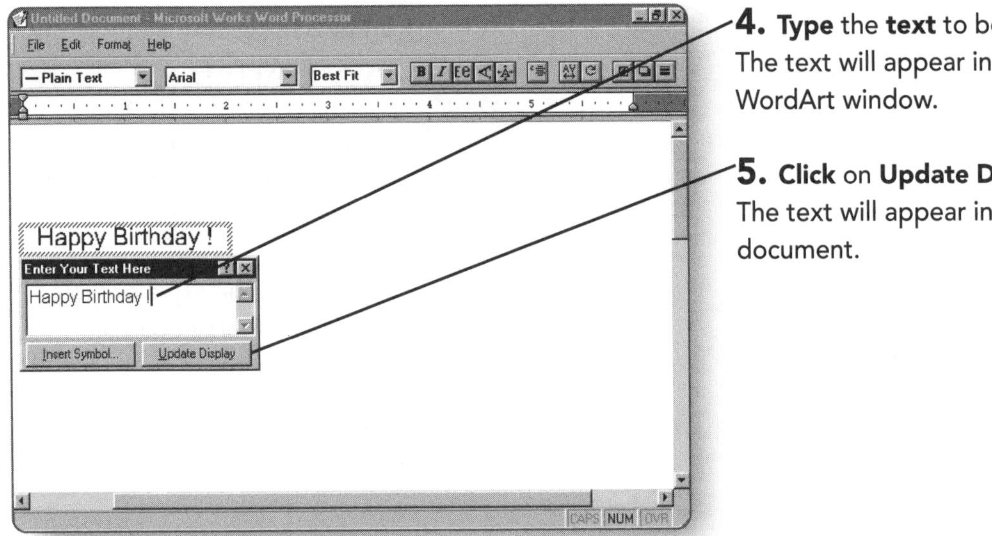

4. Type the **text** to be used. The text will appear in the WordArt window.

5. Click on **Update Display**. The text will appear in the document.

6. Click on **Format**. The Format menu will appear.

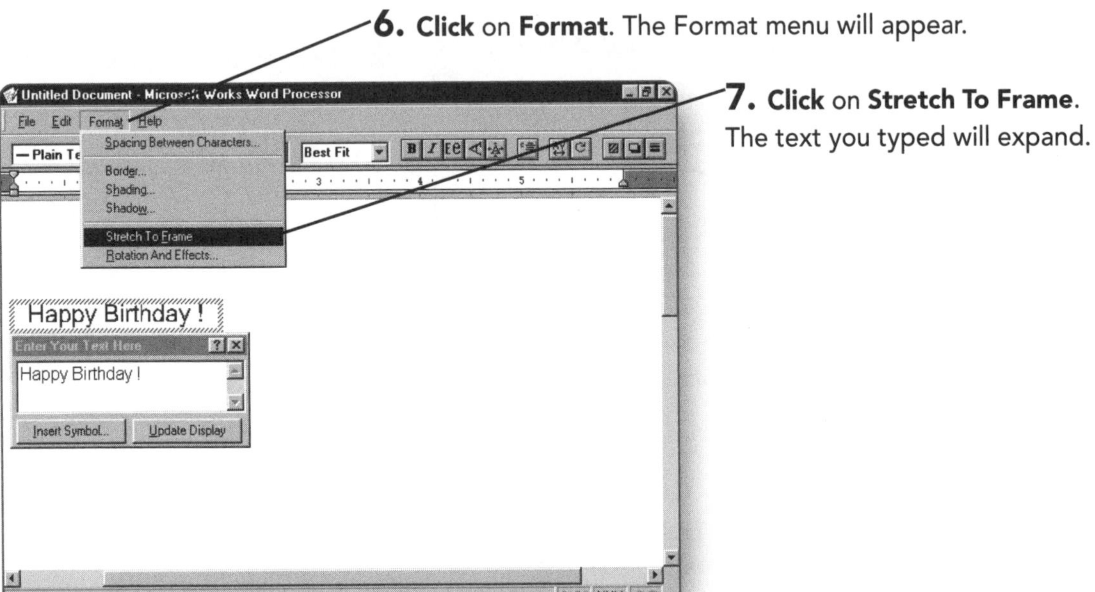

7. Click on **Stretch To Frame**. The text you typed will expand.

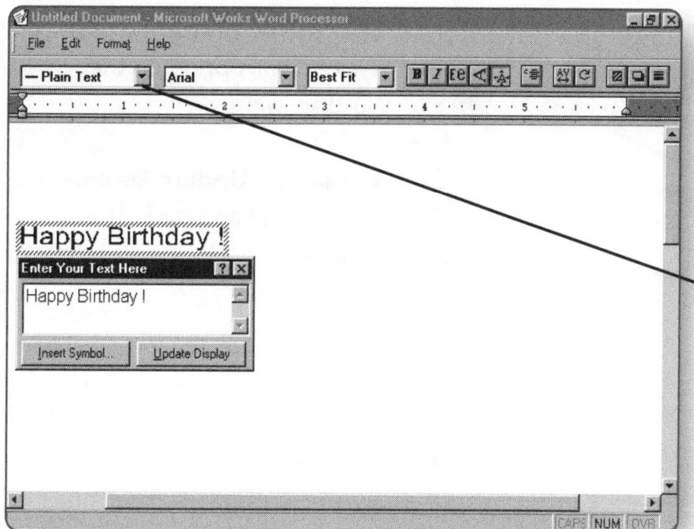

Shaping WordArt Text

Change the shape of the typed text to circular, triangular, or any other different shape.

1. **Click** on the **Style down arrow (▼)**. A collection of shapes will appear.

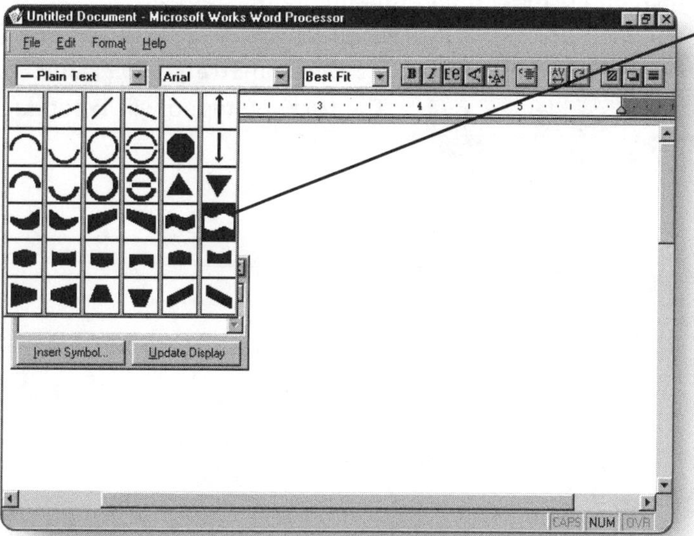

2. **Click** on the **shape** you want your text to take. The text will be reshaped.

Changing the Font of WordArt

WordArt text can be displayed in any font available on your computer.

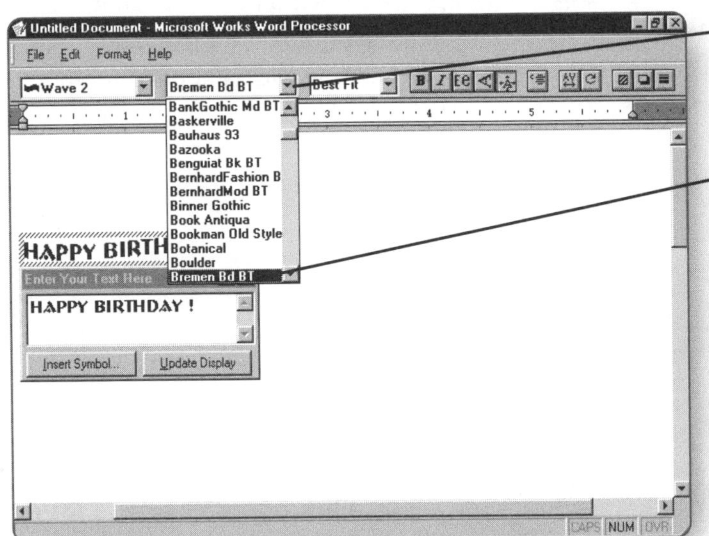

1. **Click** on the **Font down arrow (▼)**. A list of available fonts will appear.

2. **Click** on the desired **font**. The text will be modified to the selected font.

> **NOTE**
>
> Your list of fonts may vary from the ones shown.

Adding a Text Shadow

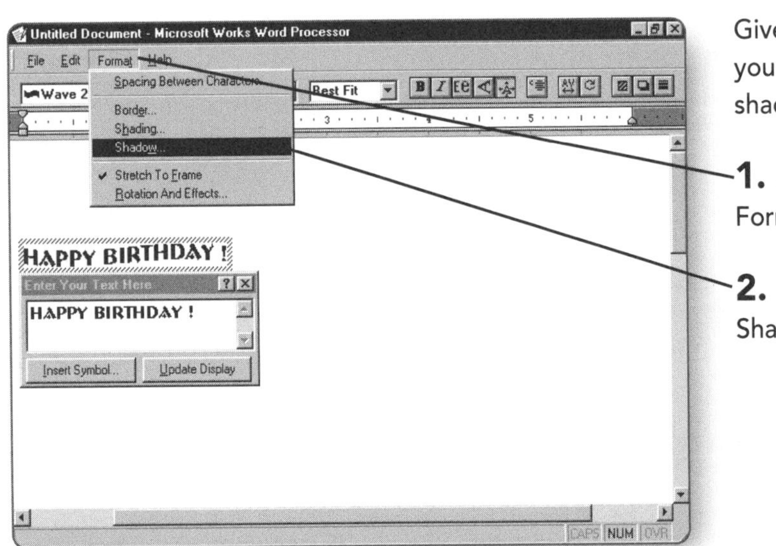

Give depth and a 3-D effect to your WordArt by adding a shadow.

1. **Click** on **Format**. The Format menu will appear.

2. **Click** on **Shadow**. The Shadow dialog box will open.

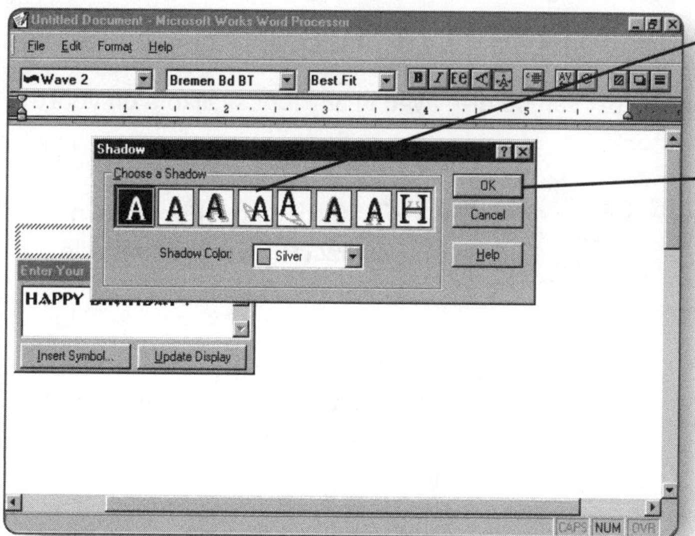

3. Click on a **shadow effect**. The selected effect will be highlighted.

4. Click on **OK**. The Shadow dialog box will close, and the shadow will be applied to your WordArt.

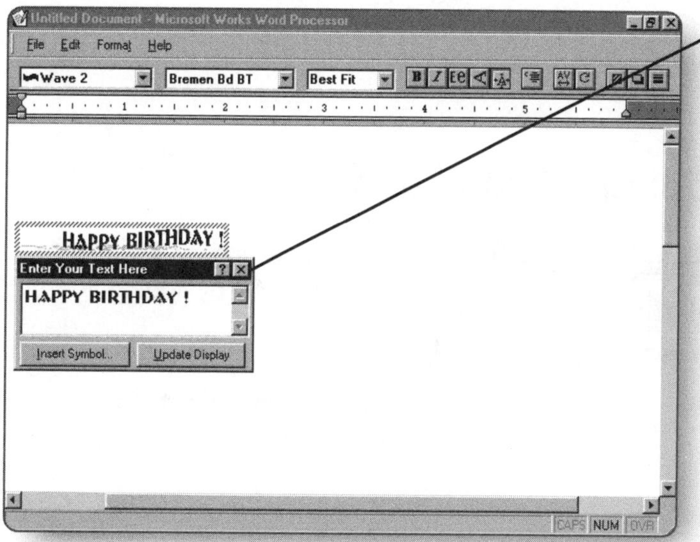

5. Click on the WordArt **Close button** (X). The WordArt box will close.

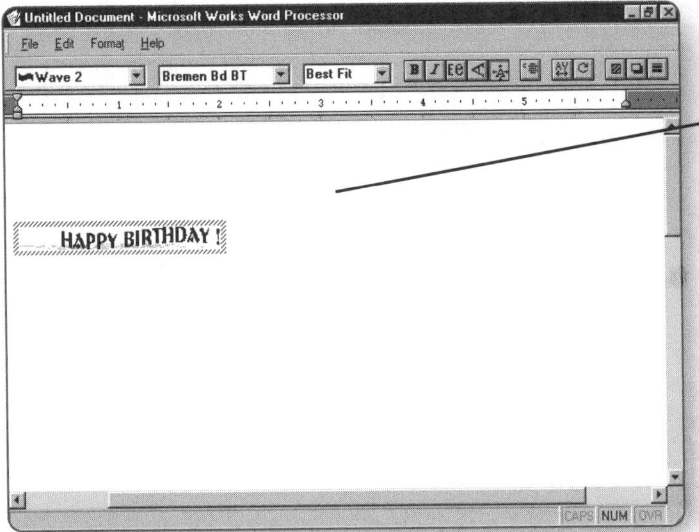

The WordArt object will appear in your document.

6. **Click** anywhere in the **document body**. The object will still be deselected.

Resizing a WordArt Object

A selected WordArt object has eight handles for resizing the object. The handles on the top or bottom resize the height of the object, whereas the handles on the left or right side change the width of the object. The four corner handles resize both the width and height at the same time.

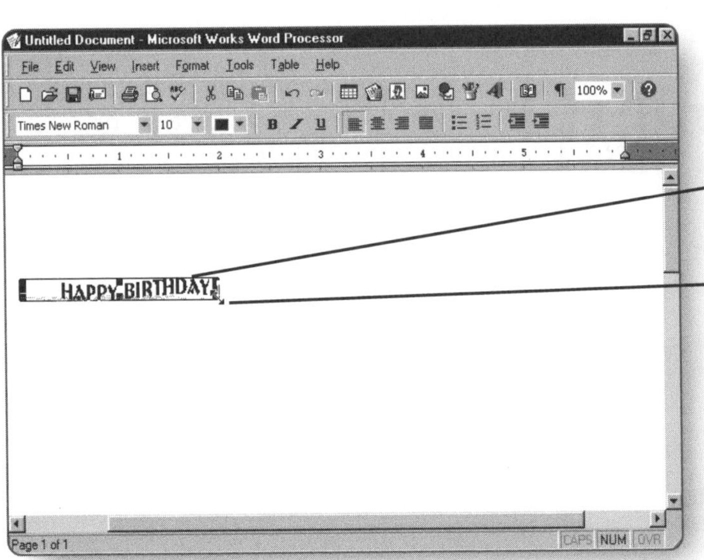

1. **Click** on a **WordArt object.** The object will be selected.

2. **Position** the **mouse** over one of the handles. The mouse will change to a double-headed arrow.

Depending on the object size, font, and other attributes, these handles may be difficult to see.

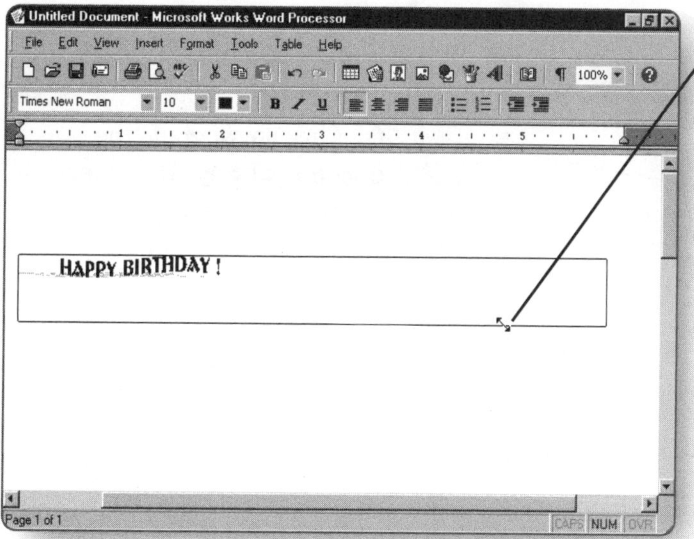

3. Click and **drag** the **handle** until the object is the desired size. A dotted line will indicate the new object size.

4. Release the **mouse button**. The object will be resized.

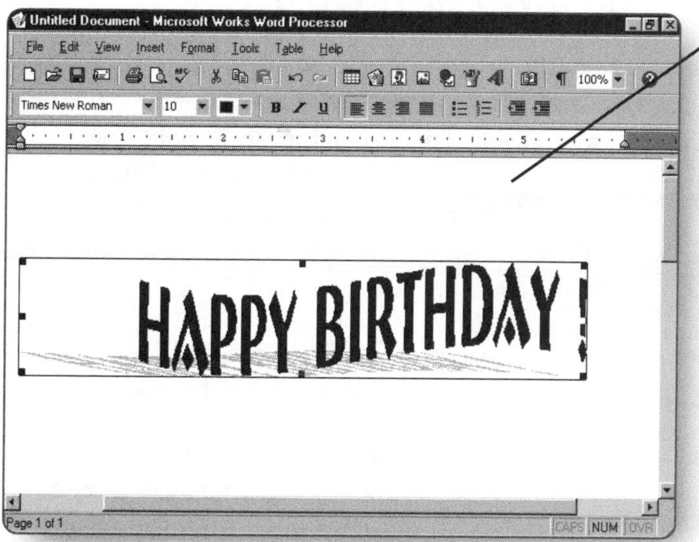

5. Click anywhere outside the WordArt object. The object will be deselected.

TIP

Double-click on the object to edit the text, shape, shadow, color, or fill of the object.

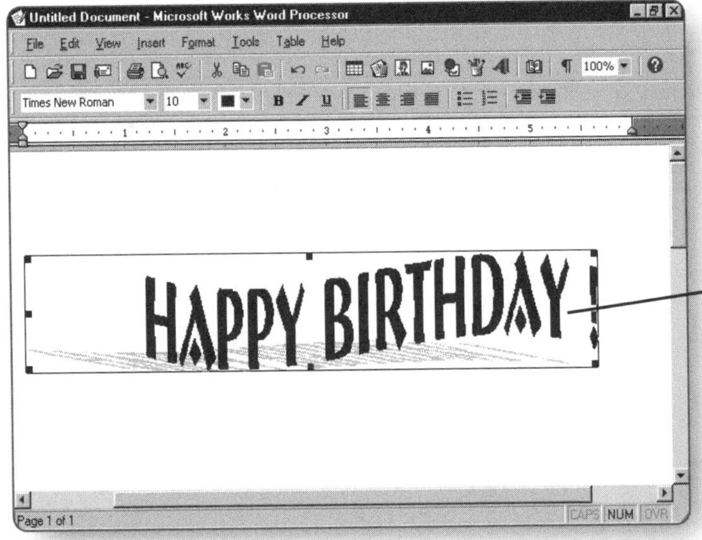

Deleting a WordArt Object

If an object is no longer needed, you can delete it with just the push of a key.

1. Click on a **WordArt object**. The object will be selected.

2. Press the **Delete key**. The object will be deleted.

Using Microsoft Draw

Even if you think that you can't draw a straight line, you can with Microsoft Draw. Use Microsoft Draw to create maps and other drawings to be included in a Works document.

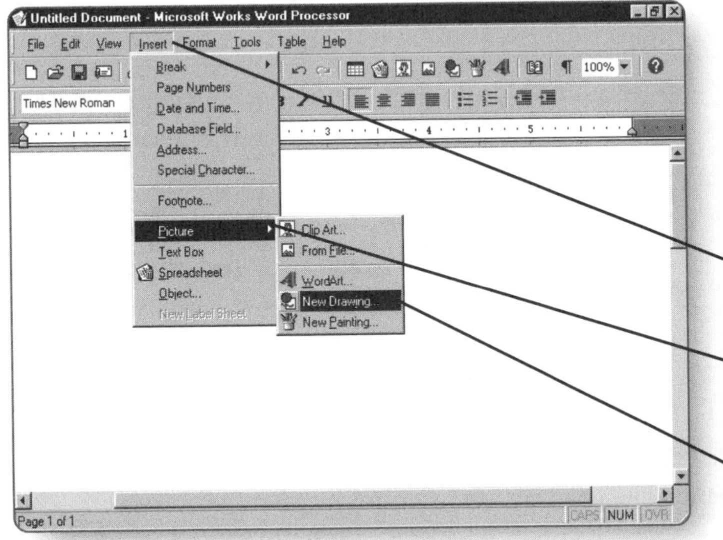

Starting Microsoft Draw

Microsoft Draw creates an embedded drawing right in your Microsoft Works document.

1. Click on **Insert**. The Insert menu will appear.

2. Click on **Picture**. The Picture submenu will appear.

3. Click on **New Drawing**. The Microsoft Drawing window will appear.

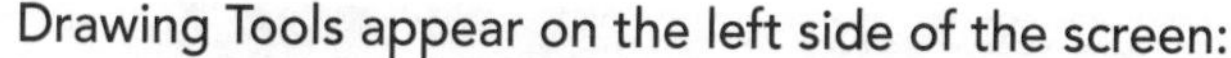

Drawing Tools appear on the left side of the screen:

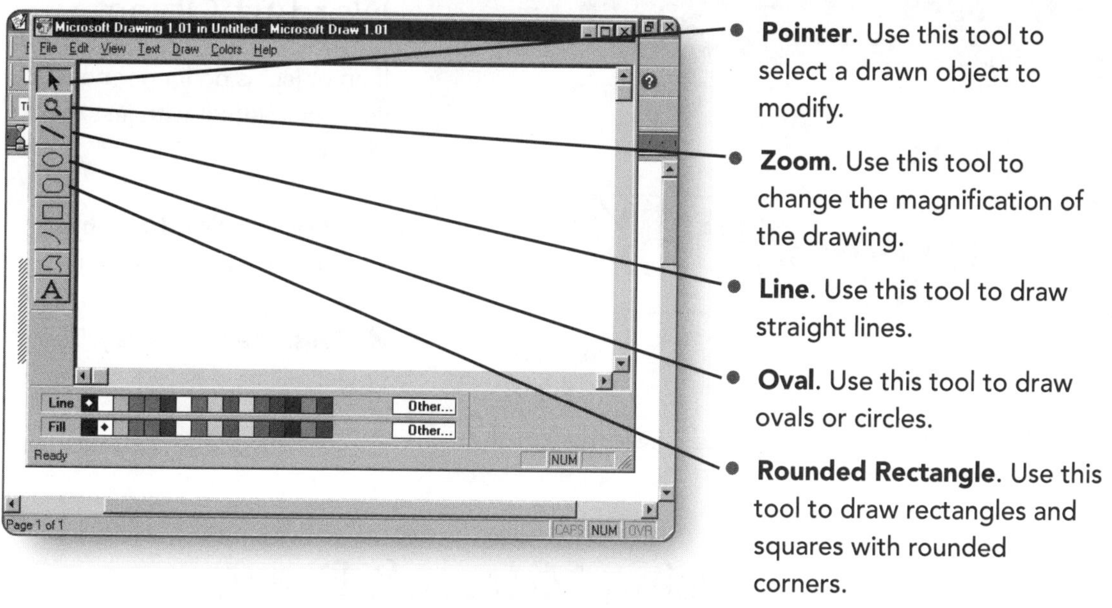

- **Pointer**. Use this tool to select a drawn object to modify.
- **Zoom**. Use this tool to change the magnification of the drawing.
- **Line**. Use this tool to draw straight lines.
- **Oval**. Use this tool to draw ovals or circles.
- **Rounded Rectangle**. Use this tool to draw rectangles and squares with rounded corners.

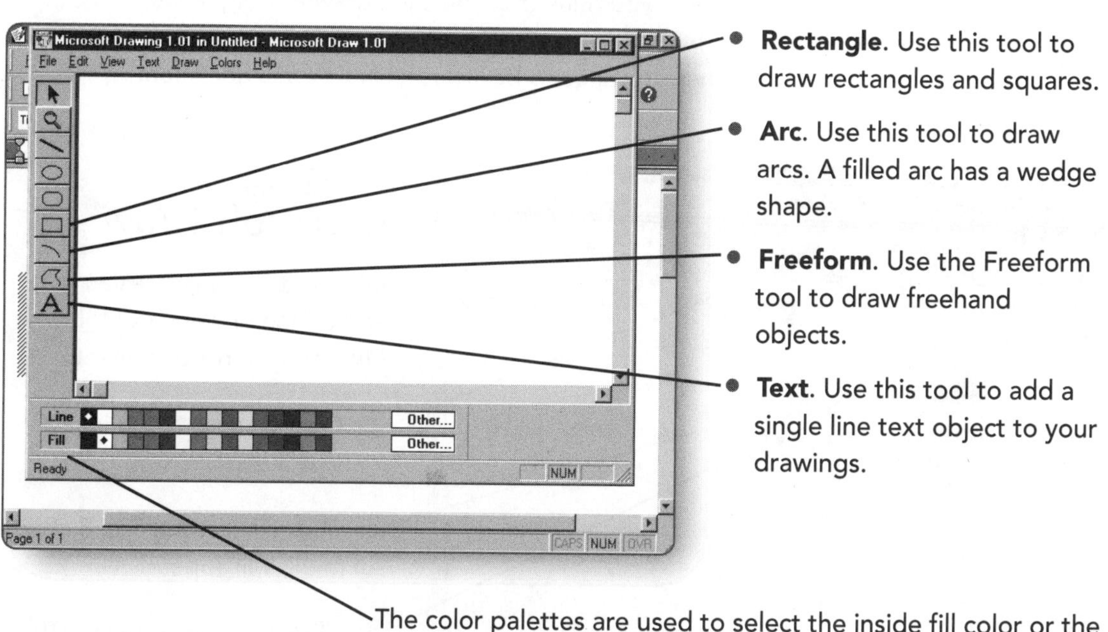

- **Rectangle**. Use this tool to draw rectangles and squares.
- **Arc**. Use this tool to draw arcs. A filled arc has a wedge shape.
- **Freeform**. Use the Freeform tool to draw freehand objects.
- **Text**. Use this tool to add a single line text object to your drawings.

The color palettes are used to select the inside fill color or the outside line color of a drawn object.

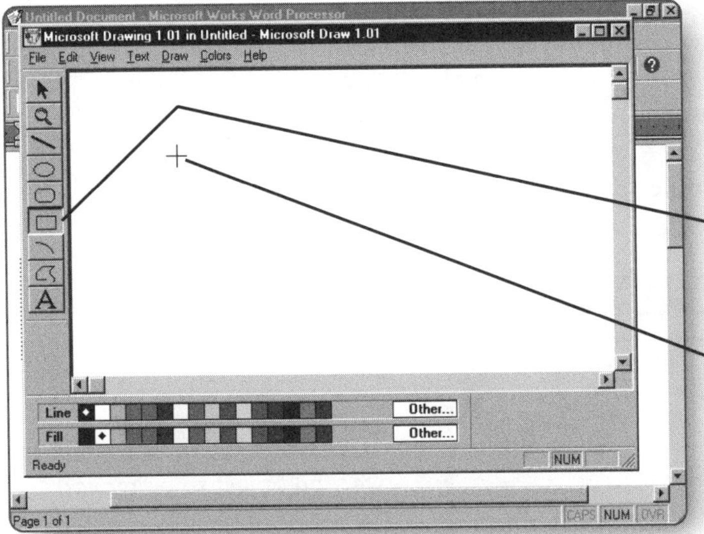

Drawing Shapes

Draw circles and ellipses or rounded or square cornered rectangles.

1. **Click** on a **shape tool** such as the Rectangle tool. The tool will be selected.

2. **Position** the **pointer** at one corner of the shape that you want to draw. The mouse pointer will change to a black cross.

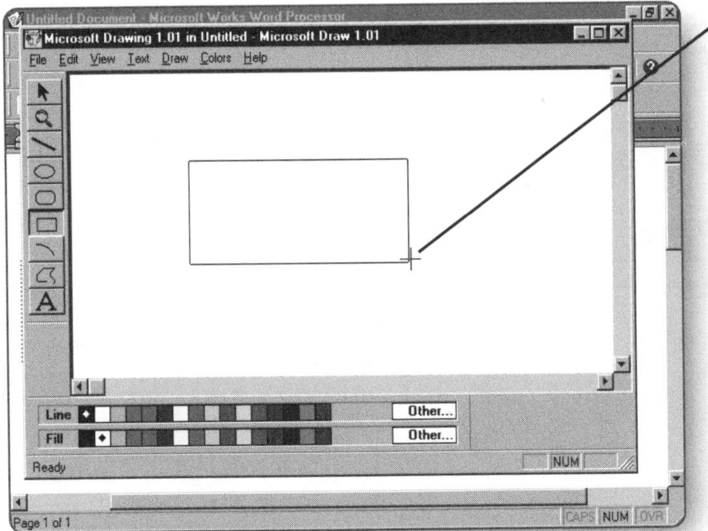

3. **Click** and **drag** the mouse. An outline of the shape will appear.

4. **Release** the **mouse button**. The shape will appear.

> **TIP**
>
> To draw a perfect circle, or perfect square, press the Shift key and hold it down as you drag.

A shape object can be resized using the same methods you learned earlier in this chapter. See the previous section, "Resizing a WordArt Object."

Moving Objects

You can move a drawn object to a different position on the page.

1. **Click** on the **Pointer tool**. The Pointer tool will be selected.

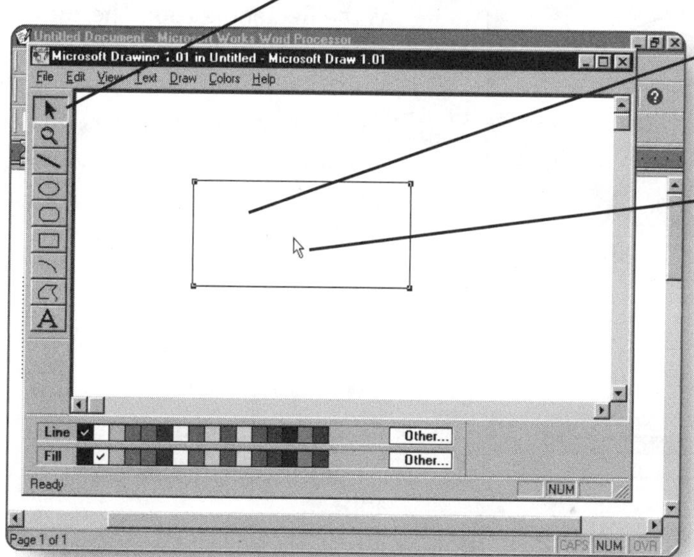

2. **Click** on the **object** to be moved. The object will be selected.

3. **Position** the **mouse pointer** over the object to be moved. Do *not* position it over one of the sizing handles.

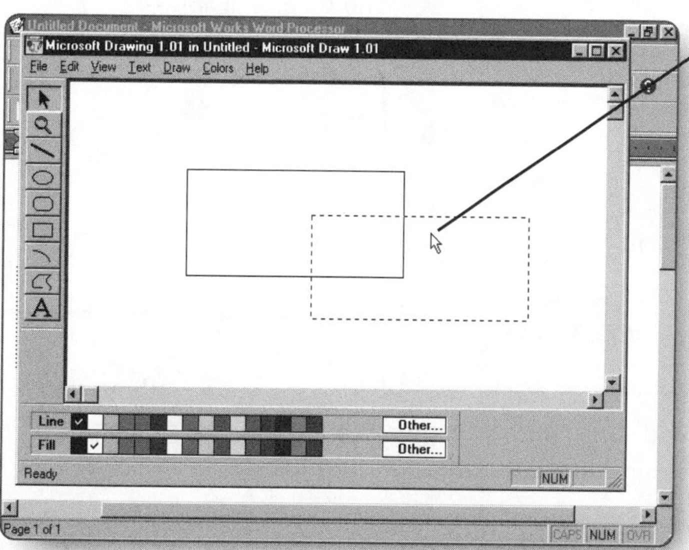

4. **Press** the **mouse button** and **drag** the **object** to the new location. A dotted line will indicate the new object position.

5. **Release** the **mouse button**. The object will be moved.

Changing Object Fill Color

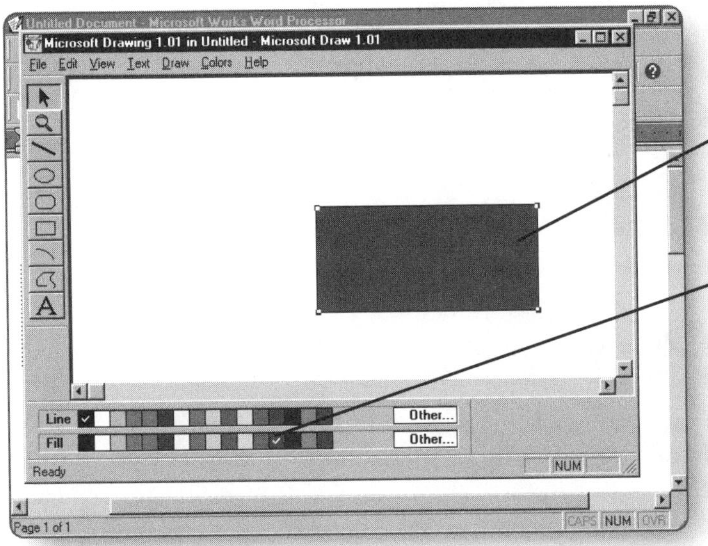

Change any object to any color displayed on the color palette.

1. Click on the **object** to be modified. The object will be selected.

2. Click on the **desired color** from the Fill color palette. The fill color of the object will be changed.

Adding the Drawing to a Document

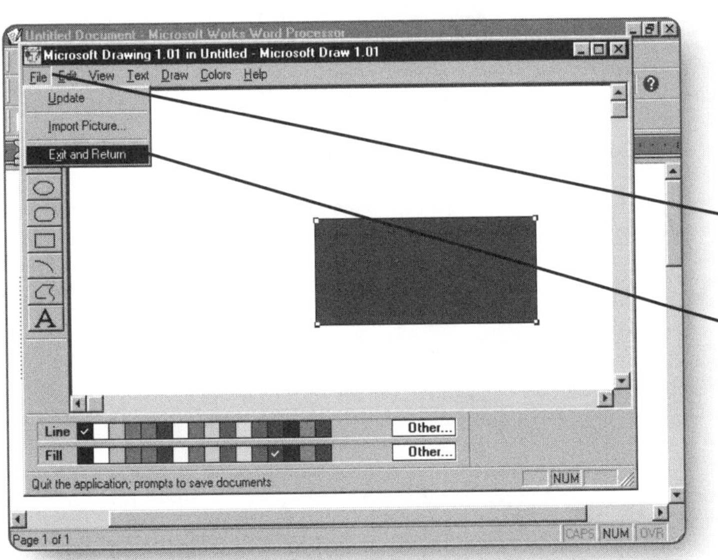

When your drawing is complete, you can return to your Microsoft Works document with the drawing included.

1. Click on **File**. The File menu will appear.

2. Click on **Exit and Return**. A message dialog box will appear.

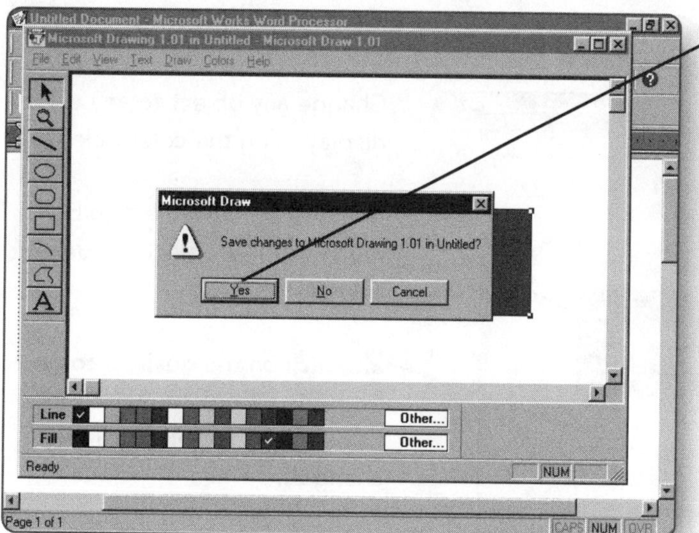

3. Click on **Yes**. The Microsoft Draw program will close, and your Works document will appear.

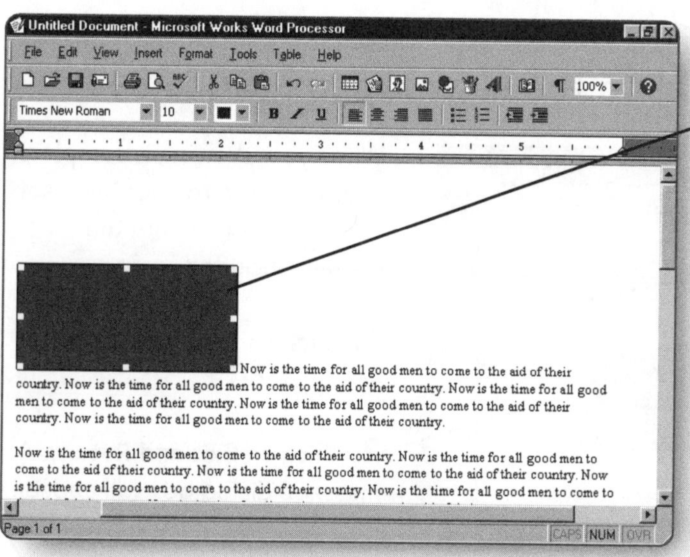

TIP

Double-click on the drawing object to return to the Microsoft Draw program for further editing of the selected object.

23

Creating Form Letters Using Mail Merge

Form letters are multiple printed copies of the same document, with different information such as names and addresses printed on each copy automatically.

We've all received such letters—like the ones telling us, "You may already be a winner." If creating a form letter seems intimidating, you can relax. In Part II, "Using the Word Processor," you learned how to create a document using the word processing feature of Works, and in Part IV, "Using a Database," you learned how to create and work with a database. By merging a document and a database, you can create form letters for mass mailings. In this chapter, you'll learn how to:

- Use the Form Letter Wizard
- Preview and print form letters

Preparing to Merge

When preparing a document for merging, leave the space blank where the variable information, such as name and address, will appear.

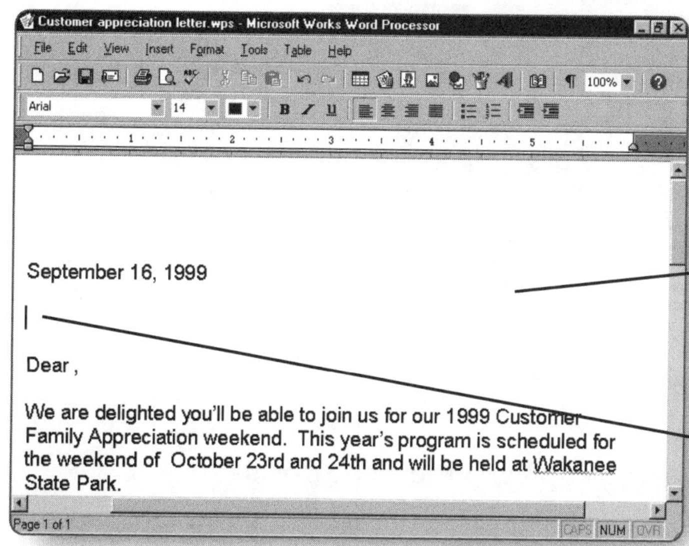

Using the Form Letter Wizard

The Form Letter Wizard assists you in preparing a form letter.

1. Open or **create** the **letter** with the common information. The document will be active in the Works window.

2. Click the **mouse** where the first field is to appear. The blinking insertion point will appear.

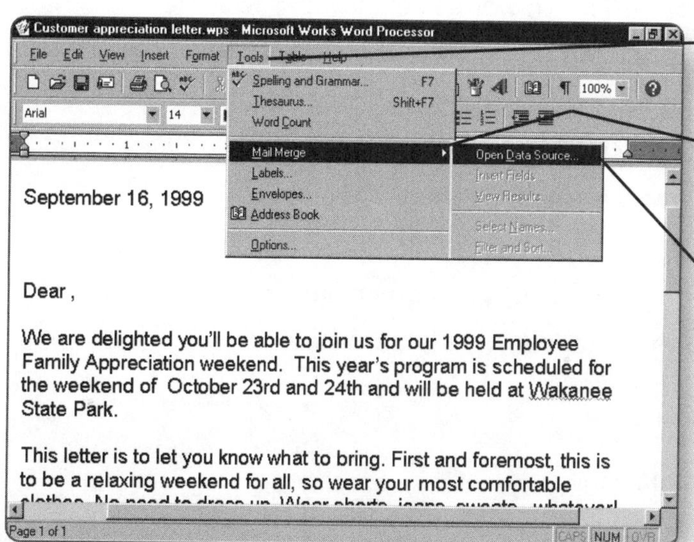

3. Click on **Tools**. The Tools menu will appear.

4. Click on **Mail Merge**. The Mail Merge submenu will appear.

5. Click on **Open Data Source**. The Open Data Source dialog box will open.

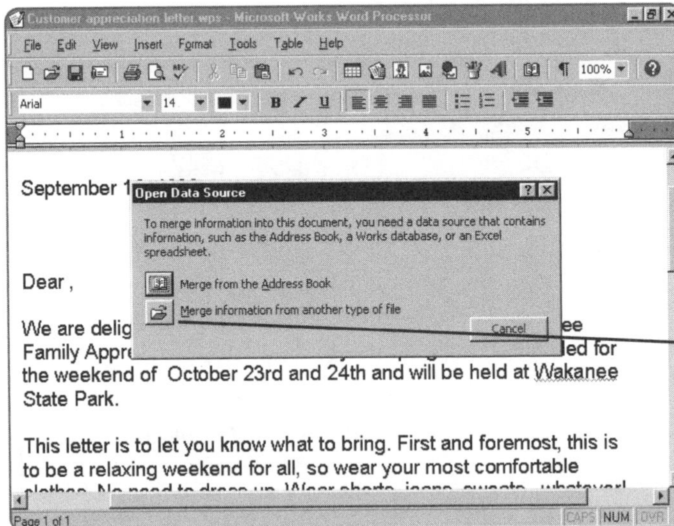

You'll need to specify whether the data will come from the Works address book or from another source such as a Works database or Excel spreadsheet. For this chapter, we'll merge with the database created earlier in this book.

6. **Click** on **Merge information from another type of file**. The Open Data Source dialog box will open.

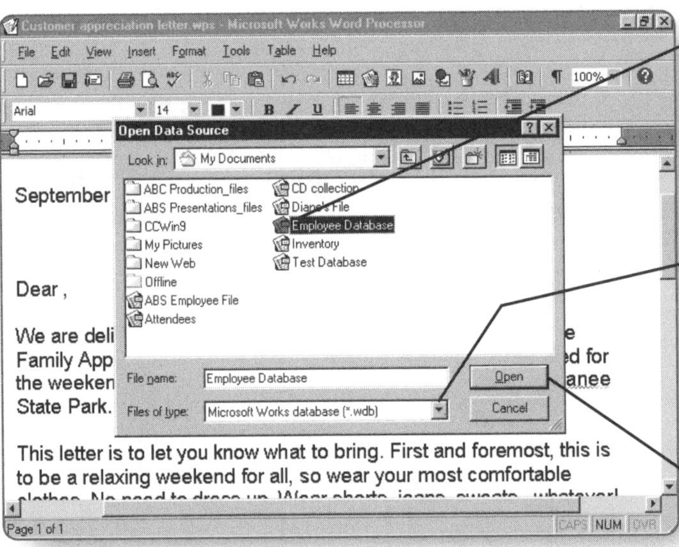

7. **Click** on the **data file** you want to merge. The file name will be highlighted.

TIP

If the data file is not a Works database, click on the Files of type: down arrow (▼) to choose a different file type.

8. **Click** on **Open**. The Insert Fields dialog box will open.

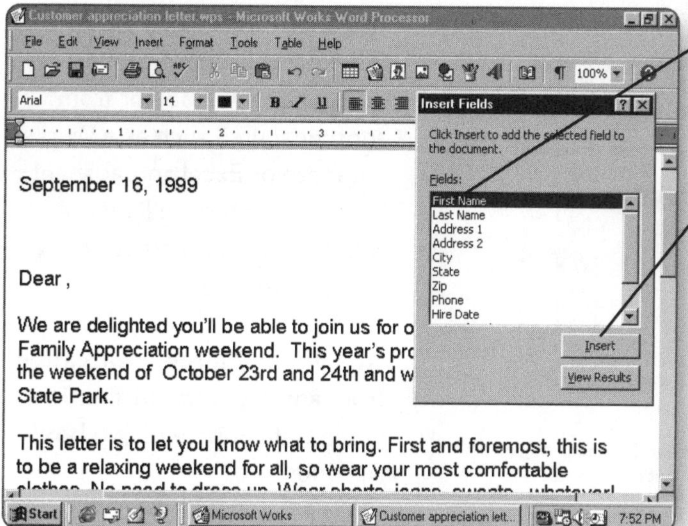

9. **Click** on the **first field** to be added in the form letter. The field will be highlighted.

10. **Click** on **Insert**. A field name placeholder will be added to the Works document.

> **NOTE**
>
> Field name placeholders appear as <<field name>> in a form letter.

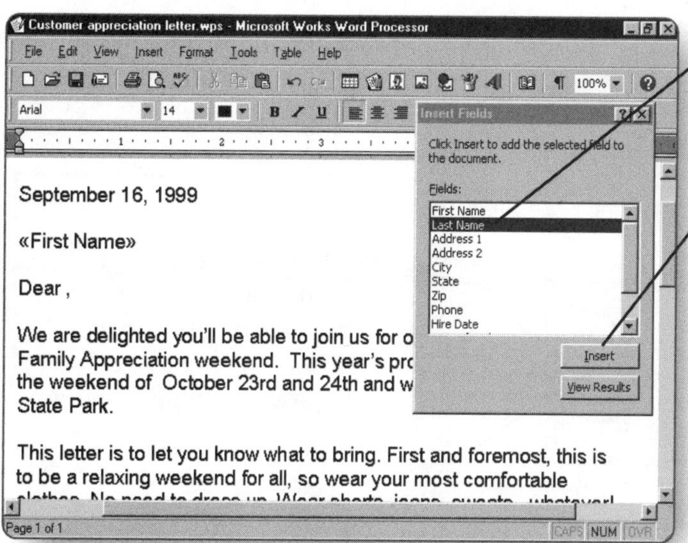

11. **Click** on the **next field** to be added to the form letter. The field name will be highlighted.

12. **Click** on **Insert**. The field name will be inserted into the Works document.

> **NOTE**
>
> Not all fields have to be used in the document, and any field can be used more than once.

13. Repeat steps 11 and **12** until all fields have been added. The fields will appear in the document.

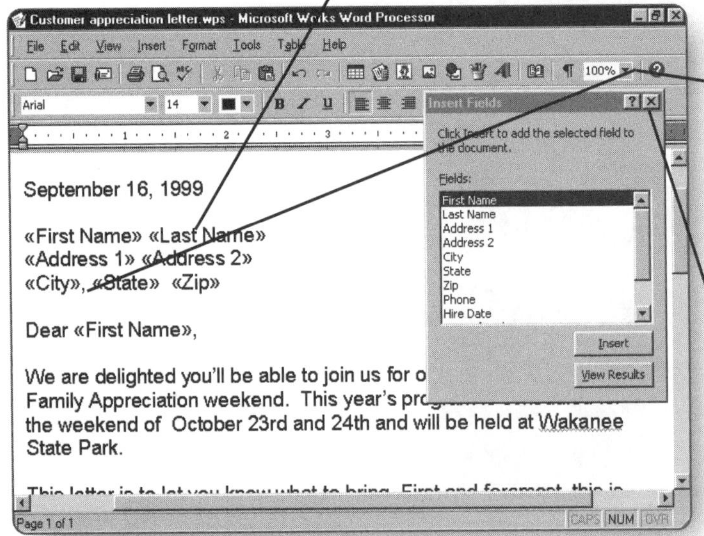

TIP

Place any necessary spaces or punctuation between the fields. The spaces or punctuation marks should not be between the << and >> field markers.

14. Click on the Insert Fields **Close button** (☒). The dialog box will close.

Previewing a Merge

To check for errors before printing, use the Works Print Preview feature.

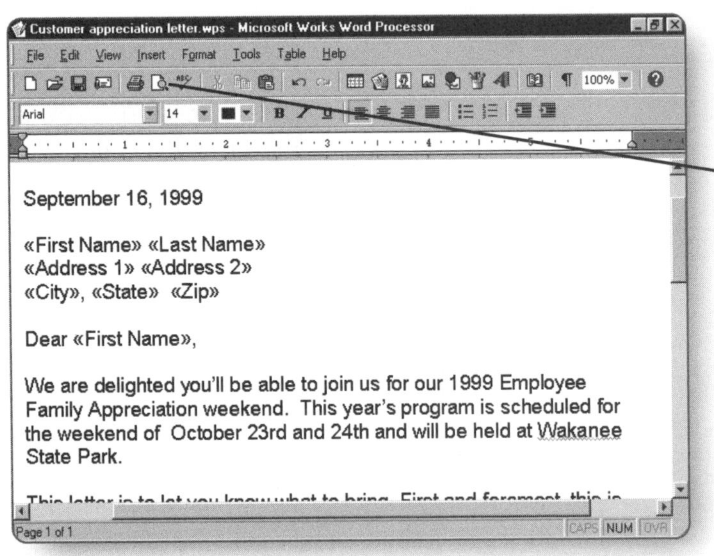

1. Click on the **Print Preview button**. The merged data will appear.

2. Click on the **Magnifier**. The mouse pointer will turn into a magnifying glass with a plus.

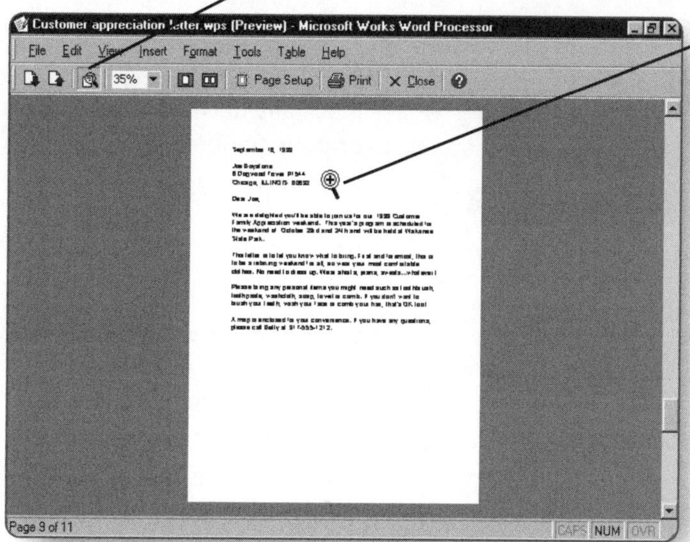

3. Click on the **document**. The first merged record will be enlarged.

4a. Click on **Next** to view the next merged record. The next record will appear.

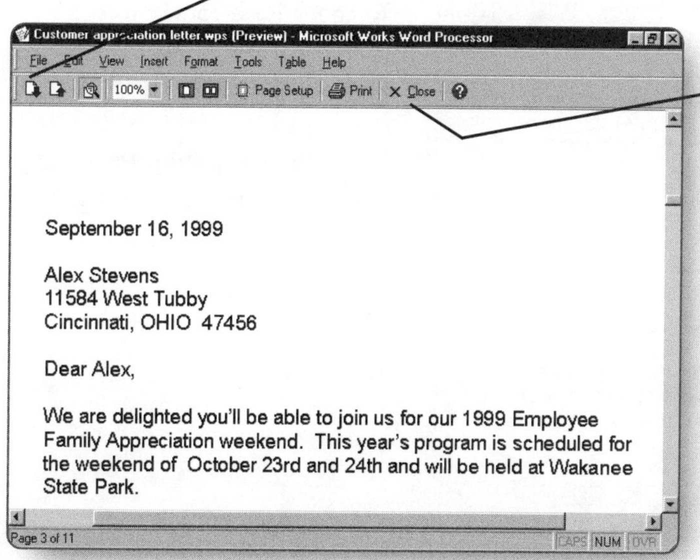

OR

4b. Click on **Close.** The view will return to the document.

Printing Merged Records

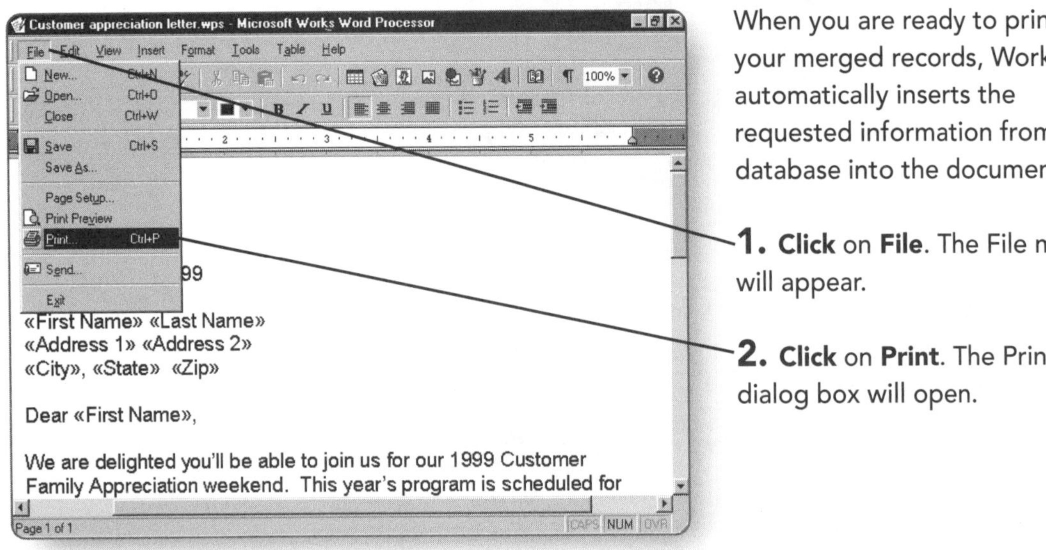

When you are ready to print your merged records, Works automatically inserts the requested information from the database into the document.

1. Click on **File**. The File menu will appear.

2. Click on **Print**. The Print dialog box will open.

3. Change any desired printing **options**. The options will be selected.

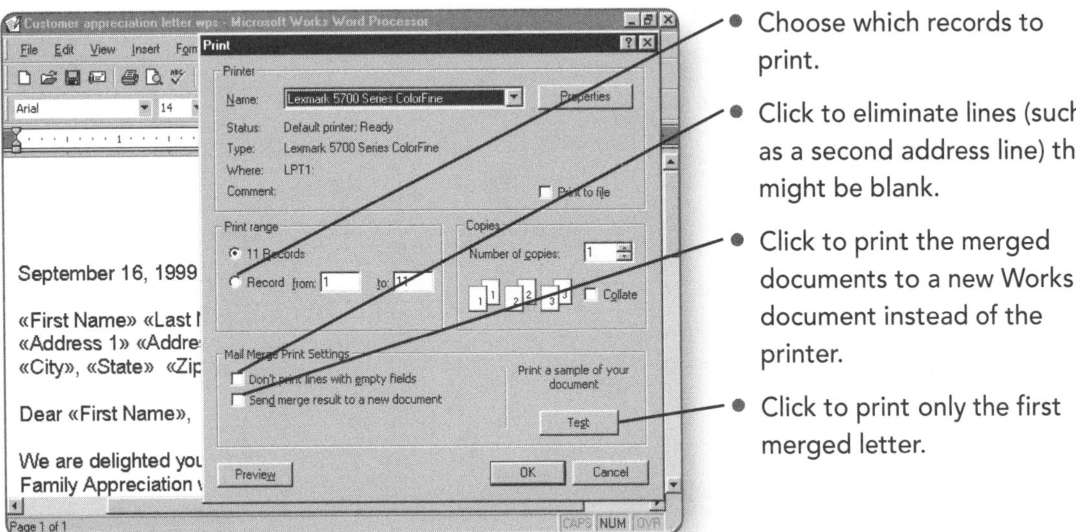

- Choose which records to print.
- Click to eliminate lines (such as a second address line) that might be blank.
- Click to print the merged documents to a new Works document instead of the printer.
- Click to print only the first merged letter.

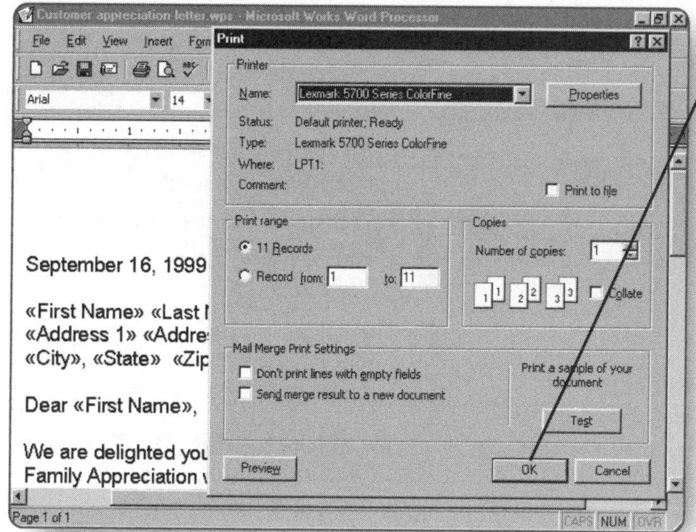

4. Click on **OK**. The merged letters will print to your specifications.

24

Scheduling Using the Calendar

Do you need to track when and where your child has practice? Do you lose track of time or forget appointments? An *appointment* is anything that requires your time during a specific period. Items such as meetings, calls to clients, or interviews are considered appointments. Works has a brand-new calendar program. In this chapter, you'll learn how to:

- View the Calendar
- Add and delete appointments
- Assign reminders to appointments
- Find appointments
- Print a calendar

Starting the Works Calendar

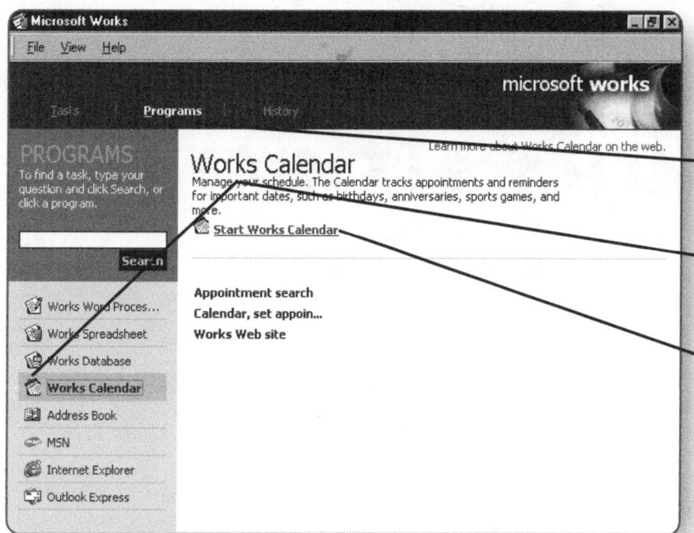

Like other Works components, the calendar is opened from the Task Launcher.

1. **Click** on **Programs**. The Programs menu will appear.
2. **Click** on **Works Calendar**. A list of calendar tasks will appear.
3. **Click** on **Start Works Calendar**. A message box will appear.

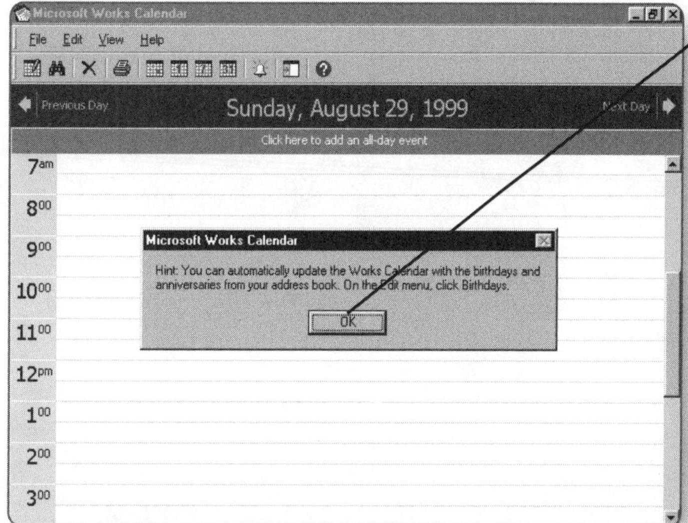

4. **Click** on **OK**. The calendar will open in Day view.

> **NOTE**
>
> The first time the Calendar is opened, a message may display, asking if you would like to make Works your default calendar. Click on Yes. The message box will close.

Viewing the Calendar

Although the calendar opens in Day view—allowing you to see the appointments for the current day—you can also view it in Month or Week view.

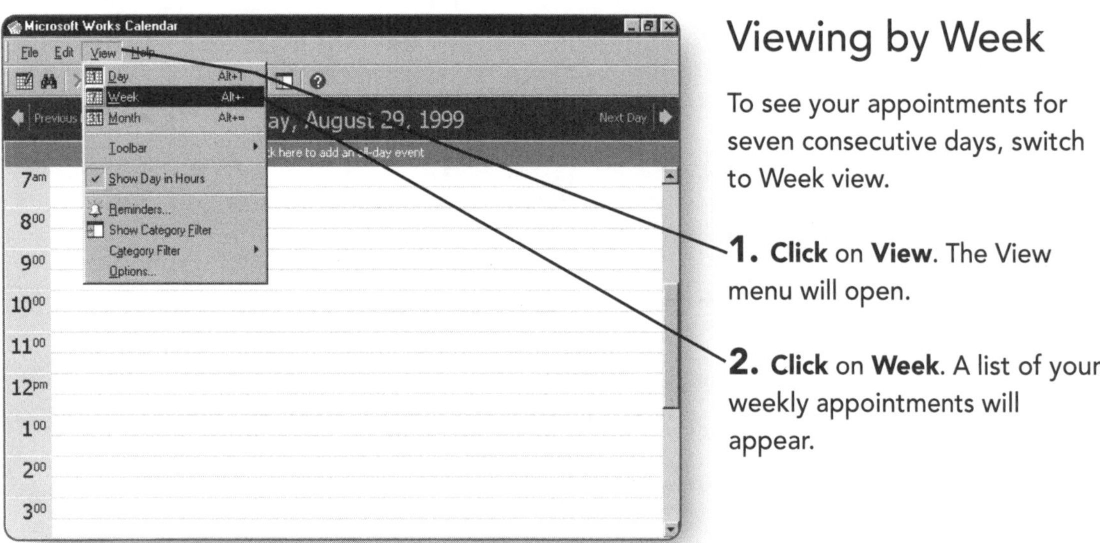

Viewing by Week

To see your appointments for seven consecutive days, switch to Week view.

1. **Click** on **View**. The View menu will open.

2. **Click** on **Week**. A list of your weekly appointments will appear.

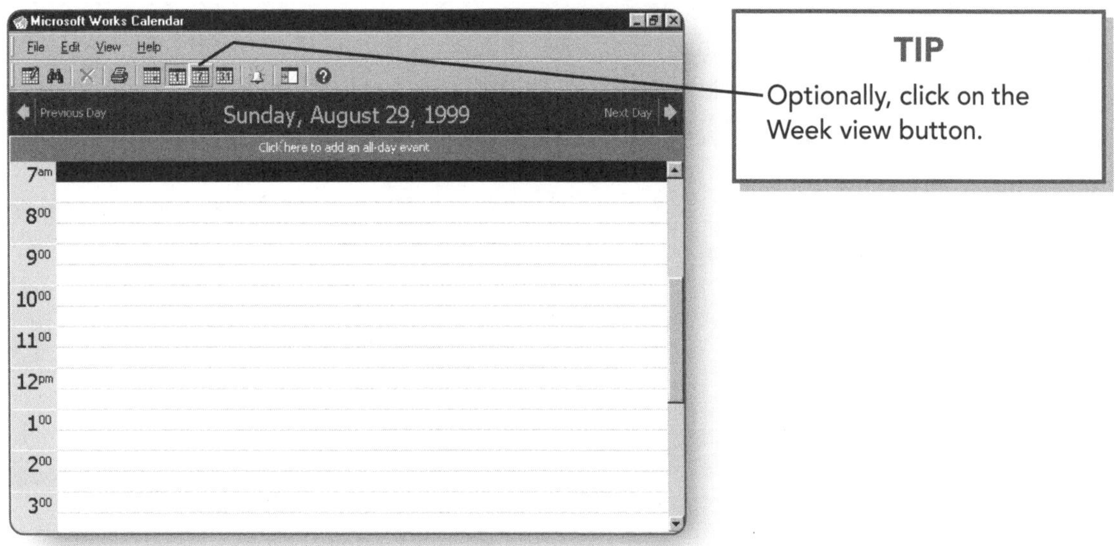

TIP

Optionally, click on the Week view button.

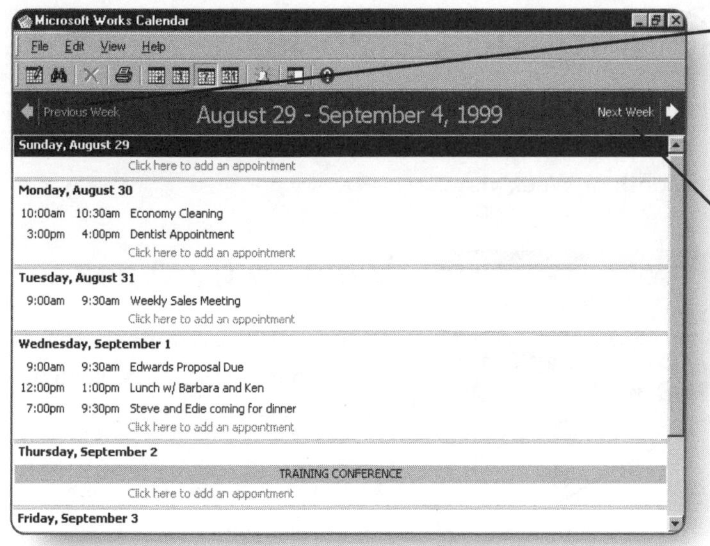

3a. Click on **Previous Week**. The prior week's appointments will appear.

OR

3b. Click on **Next Week**. The next week's appointments will appear.

Viewing by Month

View your appointments for an entire month.

1. Click on the **View Month button**. Appointments for the month will appear.

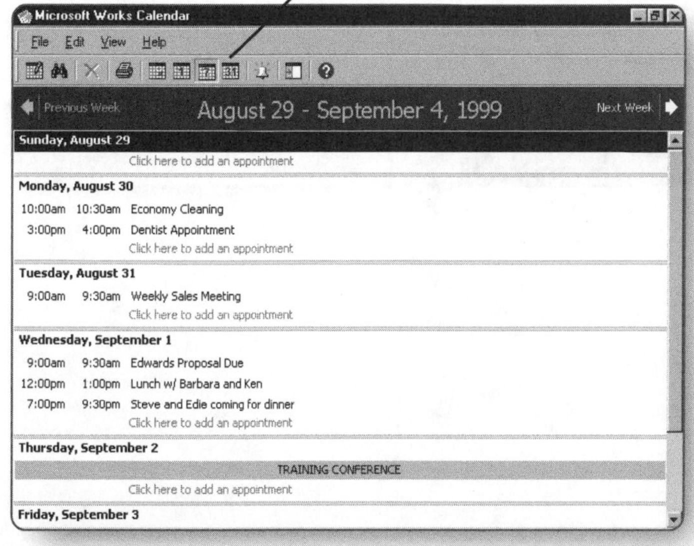

TIP

Optionally, click on the View menu and choose Month.

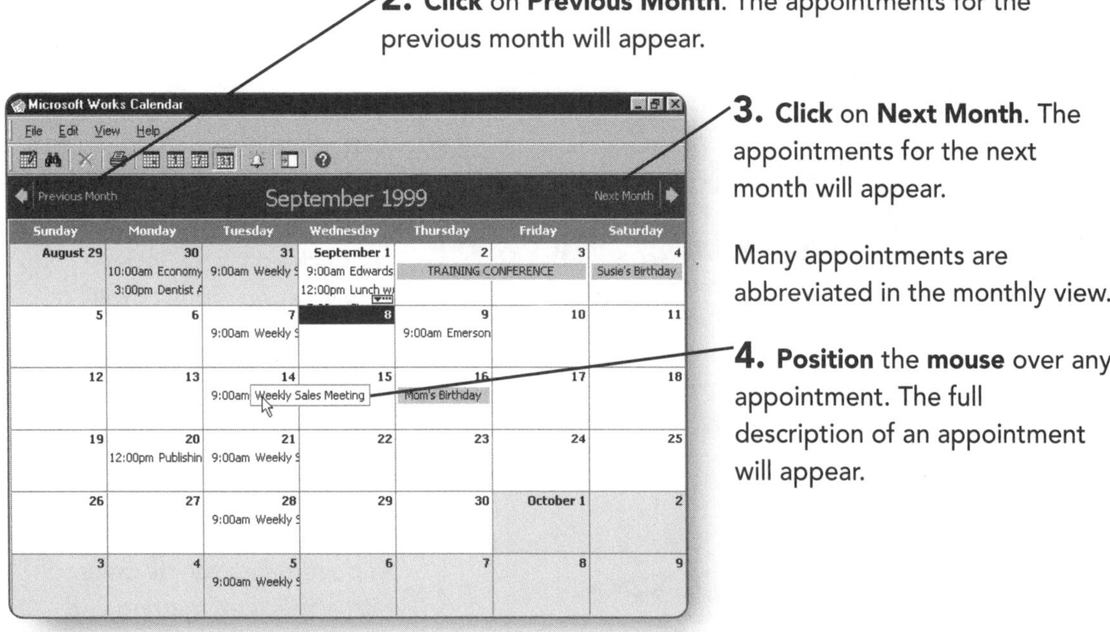

2. **Click** on **Previous Month**. The appointments for the previous month will appear.

3. **Click** on **Next Month**. The appointments for the next month will appear.

Many appointments are abbreviated in the monthly view.

4. **Position** the **mouse** over any appointment. The full description of an appointment will appear.

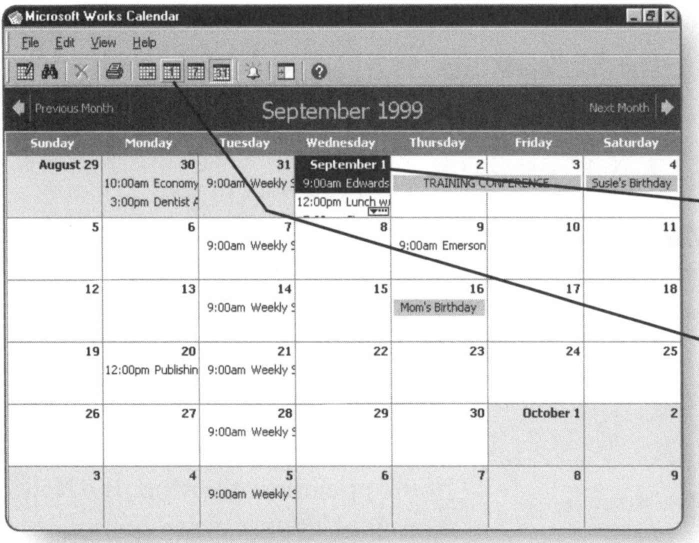

Viewing by Day

Returning to Day view is only a mouse click away.

1. **Click** on the **day** to be viewed. The date will be highlighted.

2. **Click** on the **View Day button**. Appointments will appear for the selected day.

3. Click on **Previous Day**. The previous day's appointments will appear.

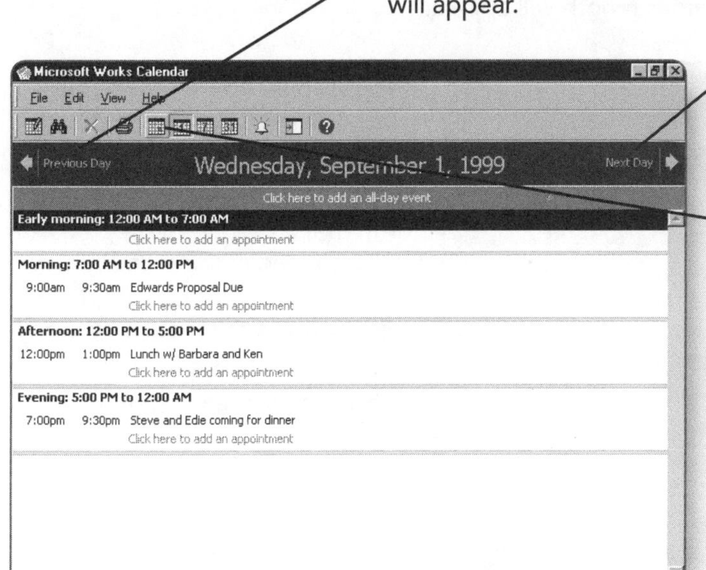

4. Click on **Next Day**. The next day's appointments will appear.

5. Click on **Go To Today**. Today's appointments will appear.

Creating a New Appointment

Appointments can be created with a specified starting and ending time, as an all-day event, or as a recurring event, such as a birthday or weekly meeting.

Adding an All-Day Event

Do you want to take an extra day off to enjoy the sunshine? You can add that as an all-day event in your calendar. Appointments can be added from any view: daily, weekly, or monthly.

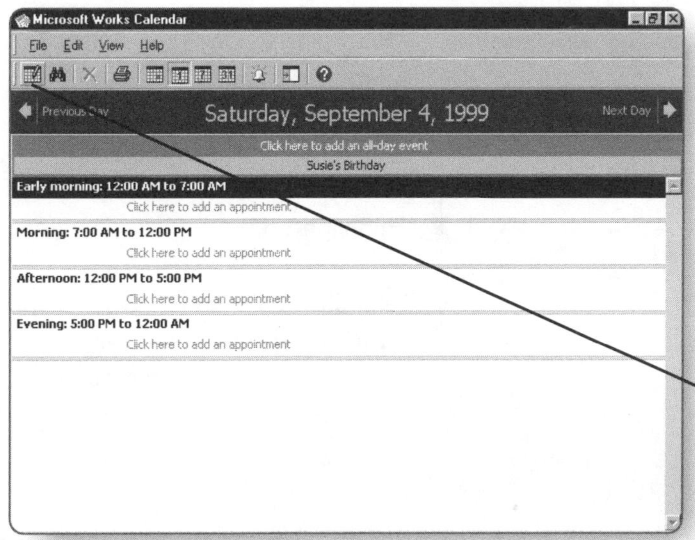

1. Click on the **New Appointment button**. The New Appointment dialog box will open.

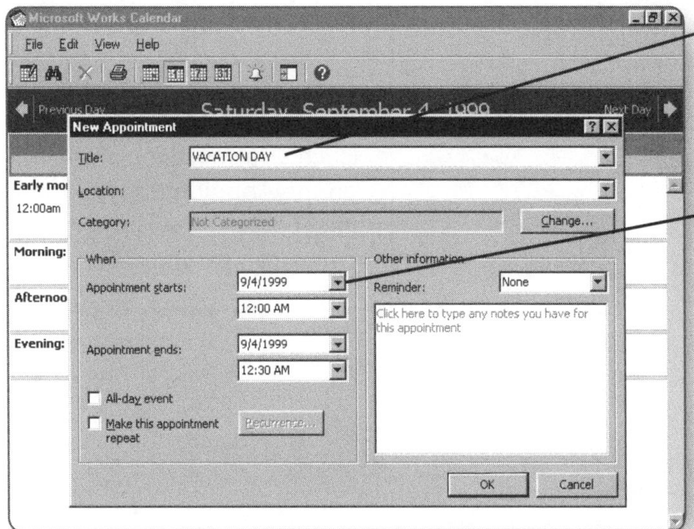

2. Type a **description** of the appointment in the Title: text box. The description will appear in the Title: text box.

3. Click on the **Appointment starts: down arrow (▼)**. A monthly calendar will appear.

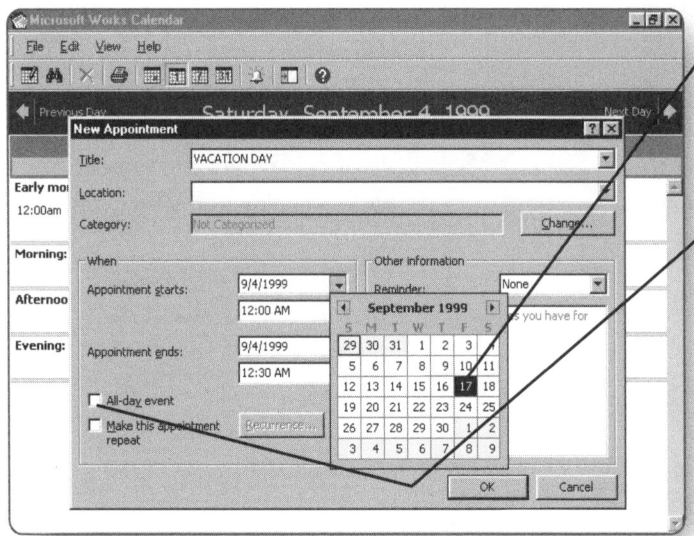

4. Click on the **starting date** for the appointment. The date will appear in the Appointment starts: text box.

5. Click in the **All-day event check box**. A ✔ will be placed in the box.

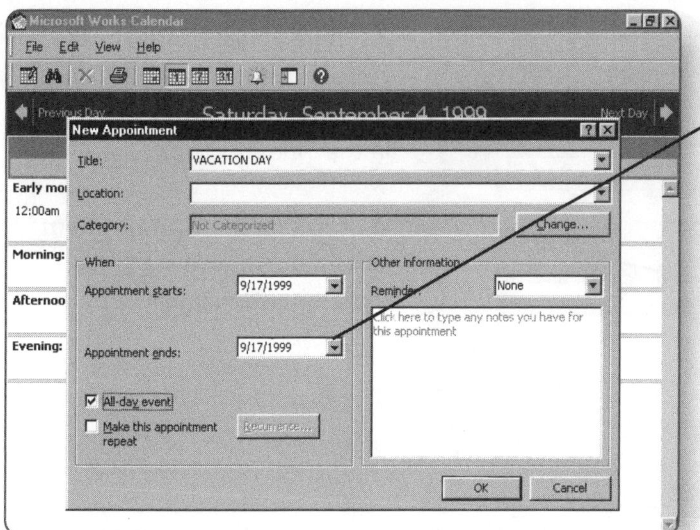

TIP

To create an appointment that spans multiple days, (such as a vacation), click on the Appointment ends: down arrow (▼) and choose an ending date.

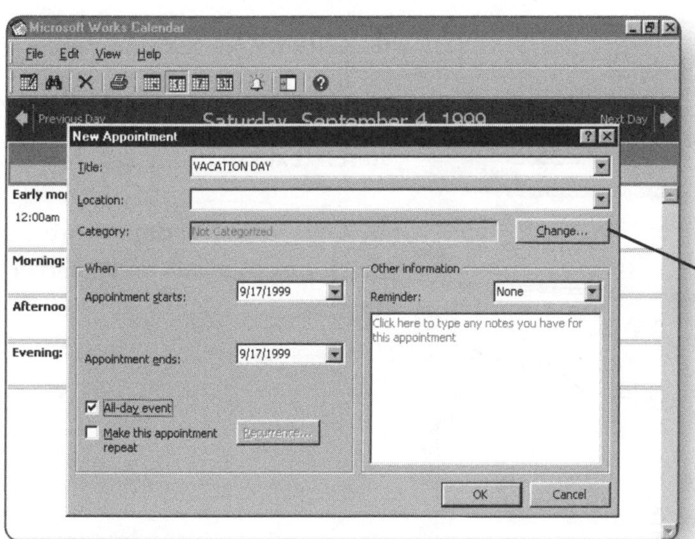

The Works Calendar includes 11 predefined categories for you to optionally assign your appointments. Applying a category allows you to search for or display items by category.

6. Click on the **Change: button**. The Choose Categories dialog box will open.

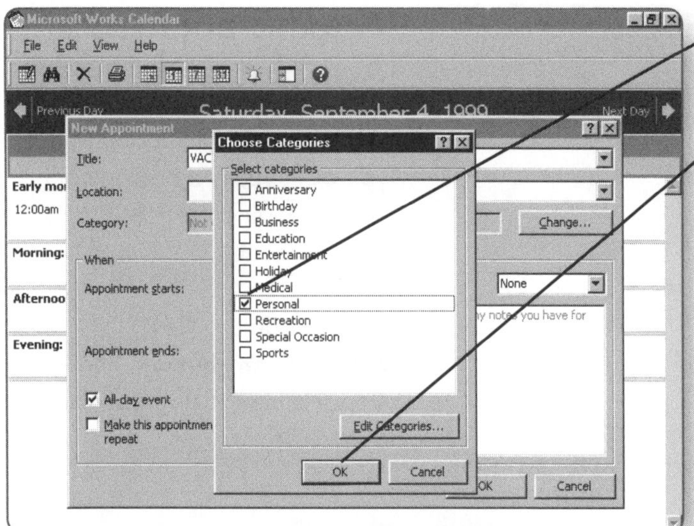

7. Click on a **category**. The option will be selected.

8. Click on **OK**. The Choose Categories dialog box will close.

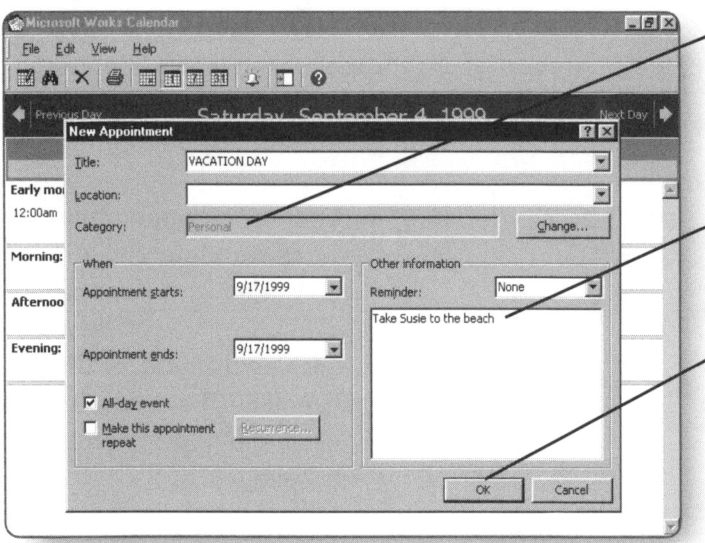

The selected category name will appear in the Category: box.

TIP

Optionally, type any notes about the appointment.

9. Click on **OK**. The appointment will be added.

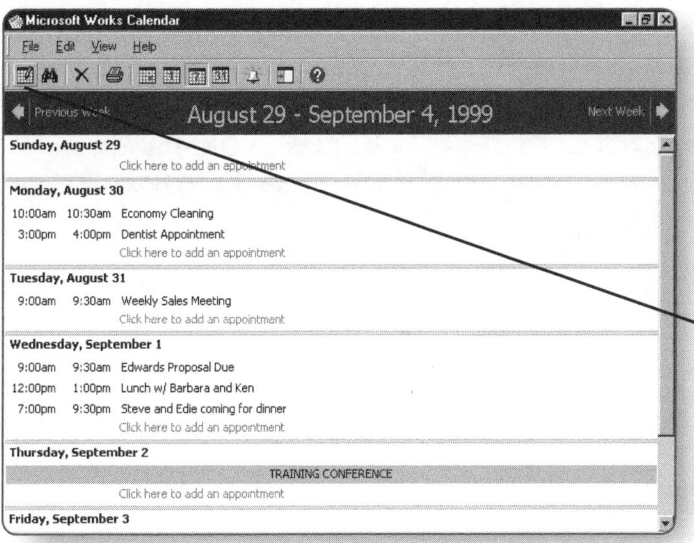

Adding a Timed Appointment

When creating an appointment, you can specify a beginning and/or ending time for the appointment.

1. Click on the **New Appointment button**. The New Appointment dialog box will open.

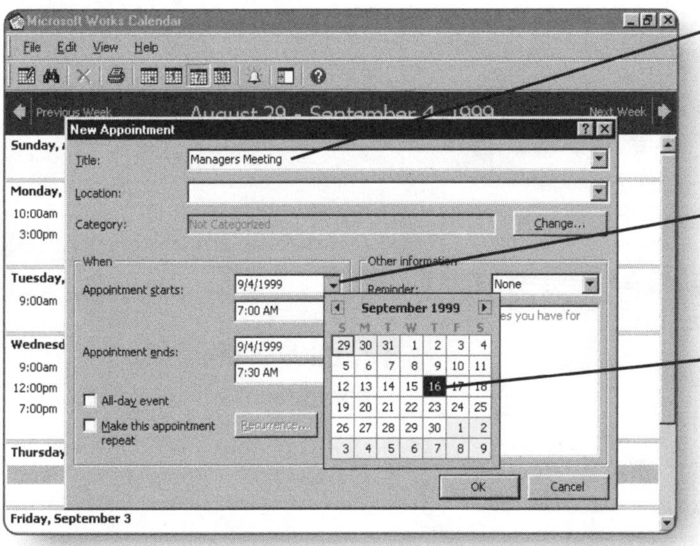

2. Type a **description** of the appointment in the Title: text box. The description will appear in the Title: text box.

3. Click on the **Appointment starts: down arrow (▼)**. A monthly calendar will appear.

4. Click on the **date** for the appointment. The date will appear in the Appointment starts: text box.

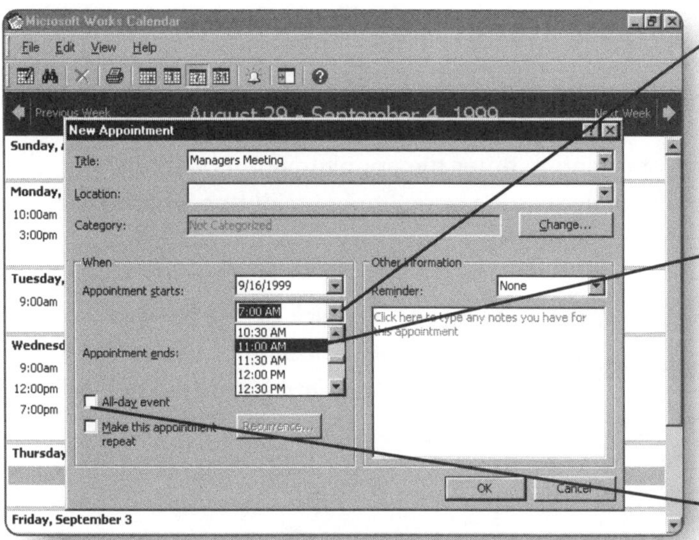

5. Click on the **Appointment starts: down arrow (▼)** in the box below the Appointment starts: text box. A list of times will appear.

6. Click on the **starting time** for the appointment. The time will appear in the starting time text box.

> **NOTE**
>
> Make sure that the All-day event box is not checked. If the All-day event box is checked, no starting and ending times will be displayed.

Works assumes that the appointment will end 1/2 hour after it begins. You can set an appointment ending time.

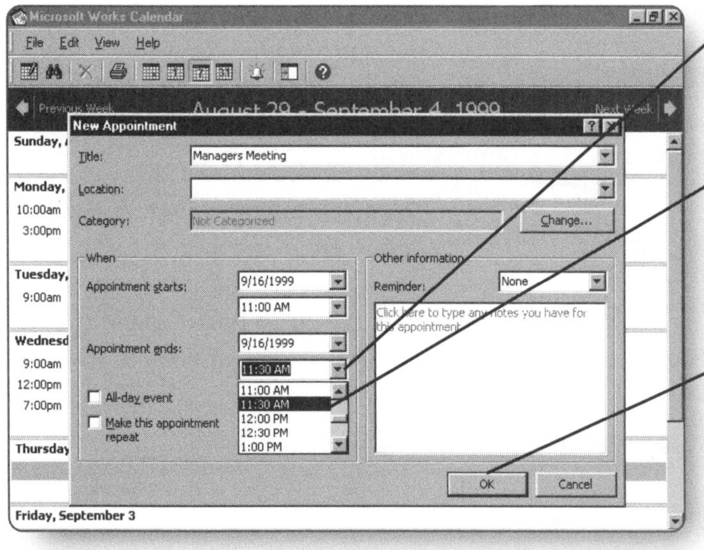

7. Click on the **Appointment ends: down arrow (▼)**. A list of times will appear.

8. Click on the **ending time** for the appointment. The time will appear in the ending time text box.

9. Click on **OK**. The appointment will be added.

Adding a Recurring Appointment

A *recurring appointment* is one that you schedule at the same time every day, week, month, and so on. This saves you the effort of having to enter the appointment repeatedly. An example of a recurring appointment might be a birthday or weekly sales meeting.

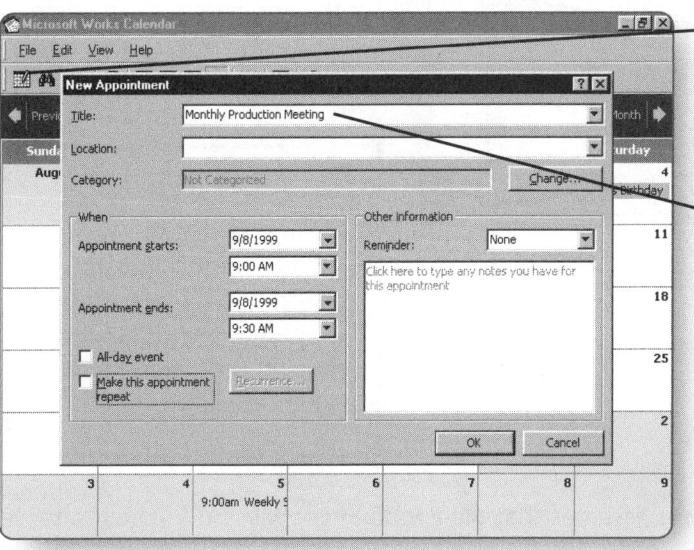

1. Click on the **New Appointment button**. The New Appointment dialog box will open.

2. Type a **description** of the appointment in the Title: text box. The description will appear in the Title: text box.

> **TIP**
>
> Decide on the starting and ending dates and times and, if necessary, mark the event as an all-day event before proceeding to step 3.

3. Click on **Make this appointment repeat**. A ✔ will be placed in the box.

4. Click on **Recurrence**. The Recurrence Options dialog box will open.

5. **Click** on a recurrence **frequency.** The options displayed will vary with the frequency selected.

6. **Choose** the appropriate **option**. The option will be selected.

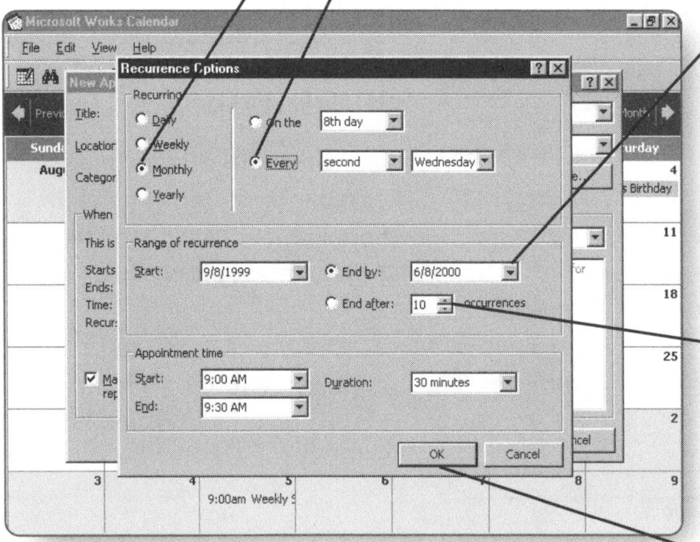

7a. **Choose** an **ending date** using the drop-down arrow (▼) in the End by: text box under the Range of recurrence options. The date will be displayed.

OR

7b. **Click** on the **up/down arrows** (⬍) to select the maximum number of occurrences in the End after: text box.

8. **Click** on **OK**. The Recurrence Options dialog box will close.

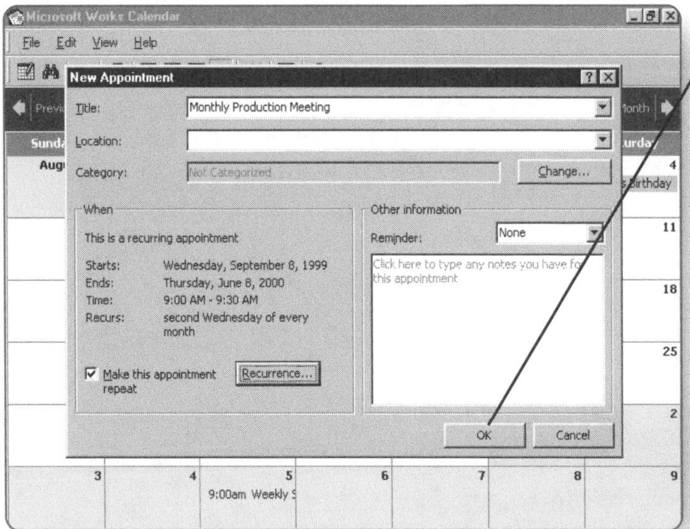

9. **Click** on **OK**. The New Appointment dialog box will close, and the appointment will be repeated at the specified intervals.

Editing Appointments

It's a fact of life—plans change. It's simple to update an event in your Works Calendar.

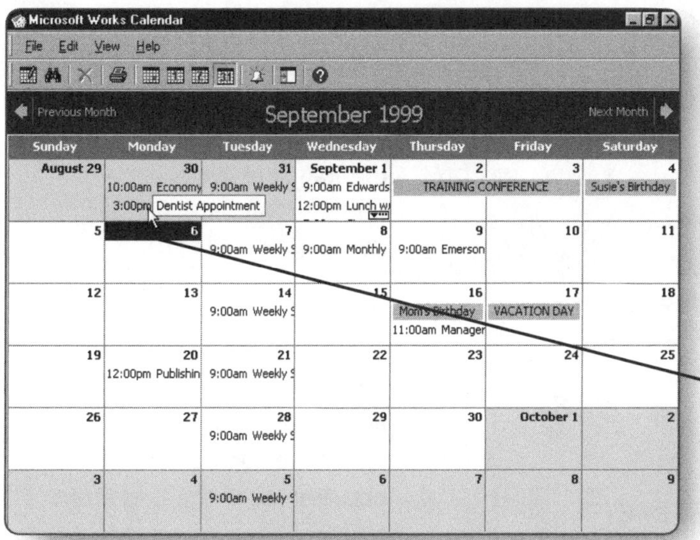

Editing Appointment Information

If you need to change the text or reminder information of an appointment, you'll use the Edit Appointment dialog box.

1. **Double-click** on the **appointment** to be edited. The Edit Appointment dialog box will open.

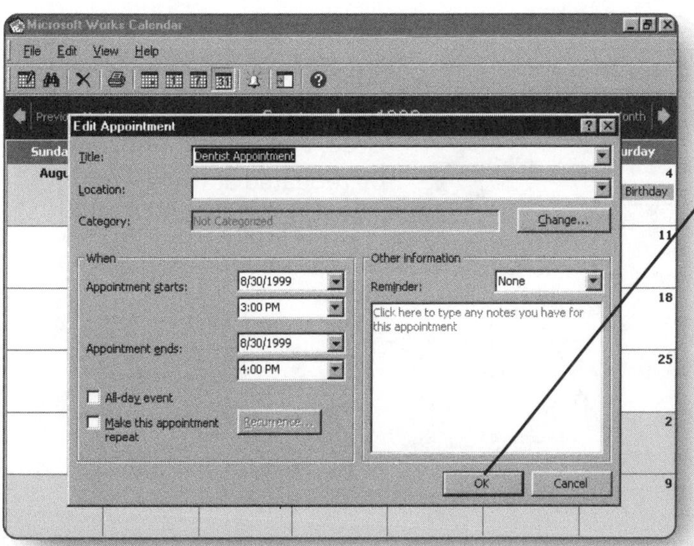

2. **Make** any **changes** to the appointment. The changes will appear in the dialog box.

3. **Click** on **OK**. The Edit Appointment dialog box will close.

Rescheduling Events

If your company picnic has been postponed to the next weekend, move it by using the Month view.

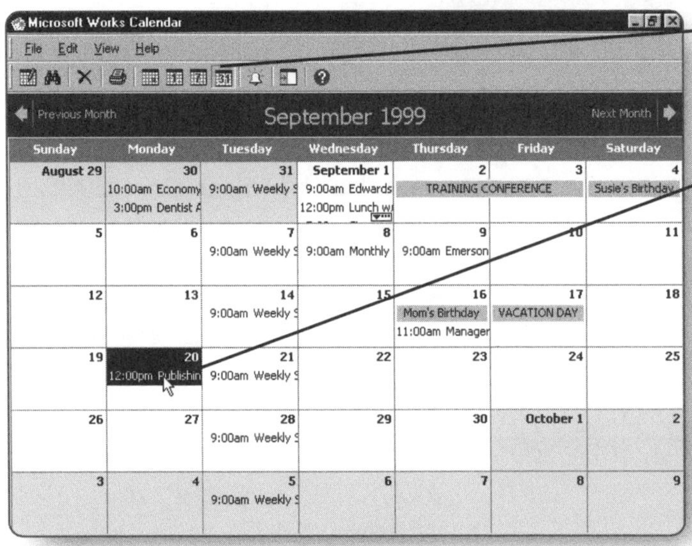

1. **Click** on the **Month View button**. The calendar will be displayed by the month.
2. **Press** and **hold** the **mouse** over the **event** to be moved. The event will be highlighted.

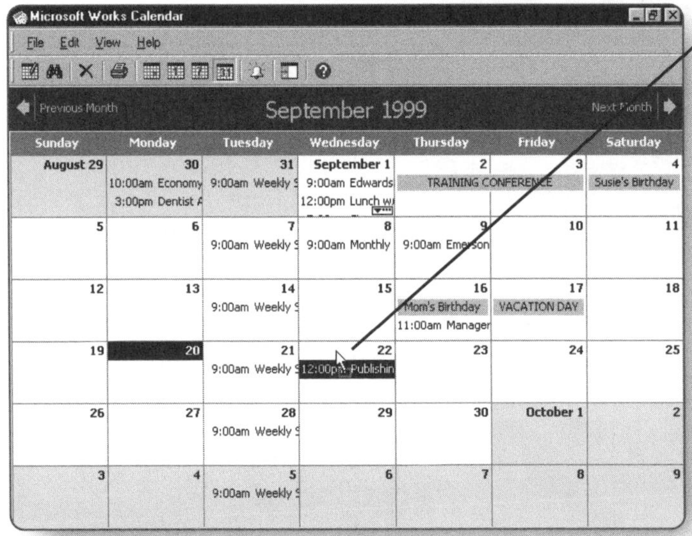

3. **Drag** the **event** to the new date. Both the new and old dates will be highlighted.
4. **Release** the **mouse button**. The event will be rescheduled.

> **TIP**
>
> If you're moving your appointment to a different time on the same day, move it in the Day view.

Deleting Appointments

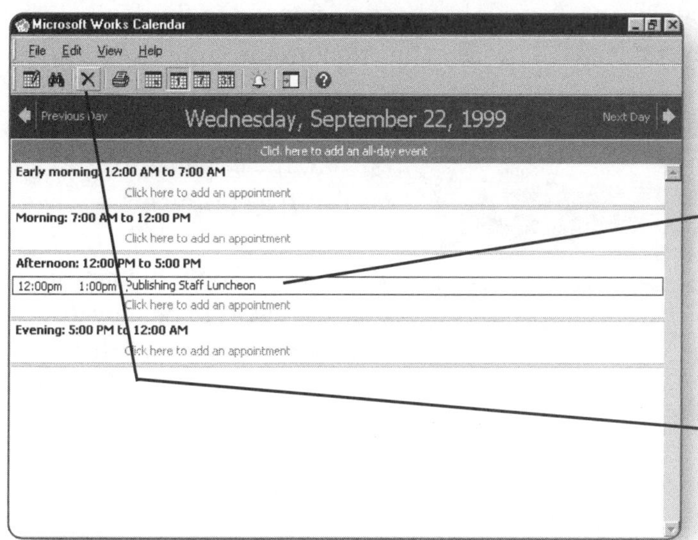

If an appointment has been canceled, delete it from your calendar. It doesn't matter which view you are using.

1. **Click** on the **appointment** to be deleted. The appointment will be highlighted, or a blinking insertion point will appear on the appointment.

2. **Click** on the **Delete button**. A confirmation box will appear.

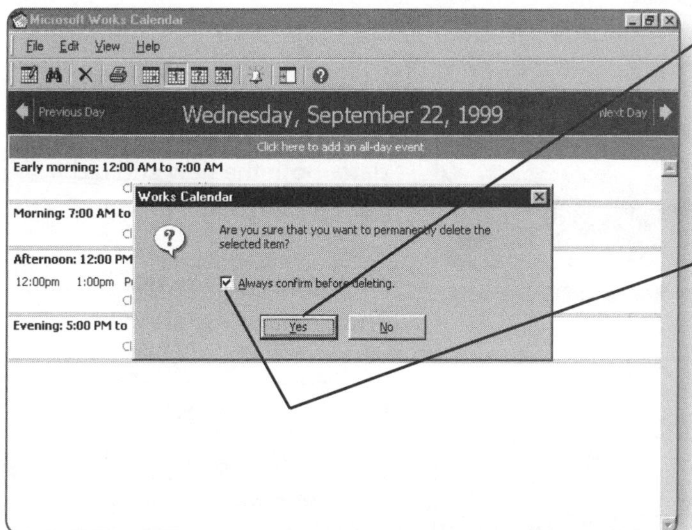

3. **Click** on **Yes**. The appointment will be permanently deleted.

TIP

To avoid the confirmation box in the future, remove the ✔ from the Always confirm before deleting box.

NOTE

The Windows Undo command does not work with deleted appointments.

Finding Appointments

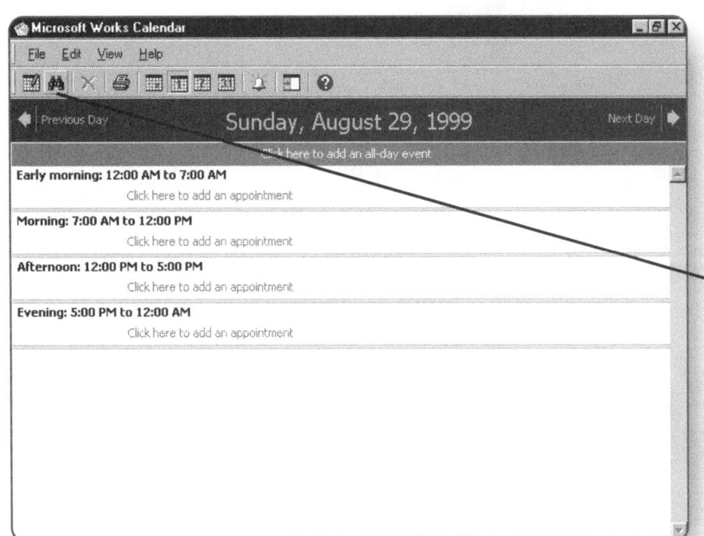

Can't remember when a particular appointment is scheduled? Let Calendar locate the appointment for you. The Find command locates appointments from any view.

1. **Click** on the **Find button**. The Find dialog box will open.

2. **Type** the **search text** under the Keyword tab. The text will appear in the Find appointments that contain the following words: text box.

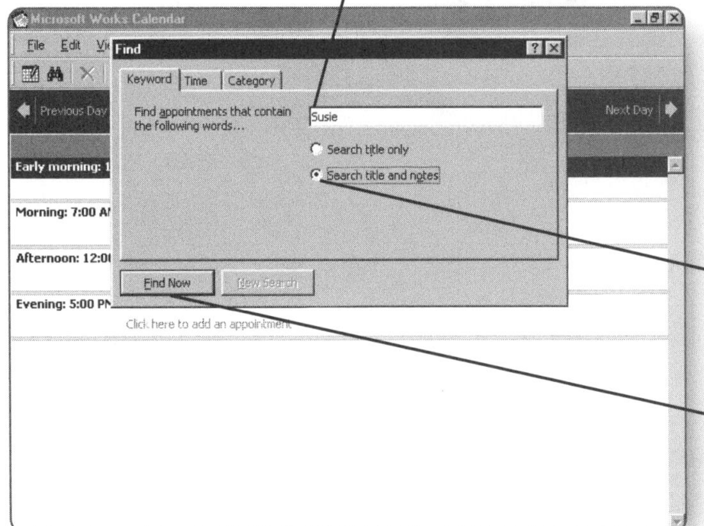

> **NOTE**
>
> You can also choose to search for appointments by time or category.

3. **Click** on a search location **option**. The option will be selected.

4. **Click** on **Find Now**. A list of all appointments that match the criteria will appear.

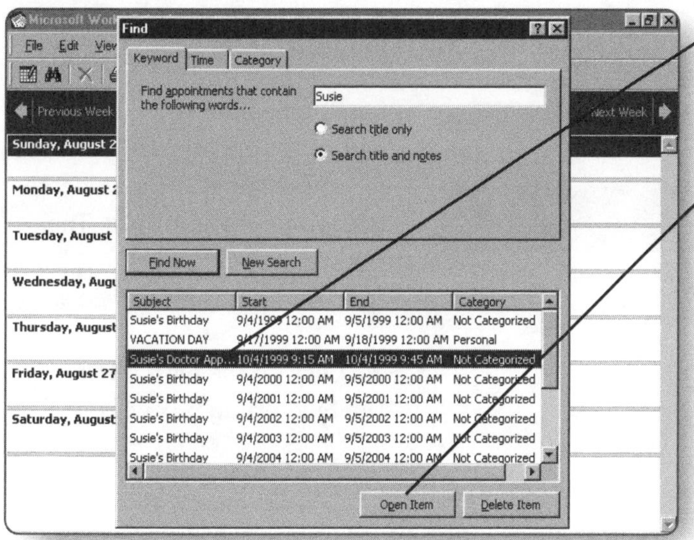

5. Click on the **item to be viewed**. The appointment will be highlighted.

6. Click on **Open Item**. The Edit appointment dialog box will open.

You can then review or edit the appointment.

7. Click on **OK**. The Edit appointment dialog box will close.

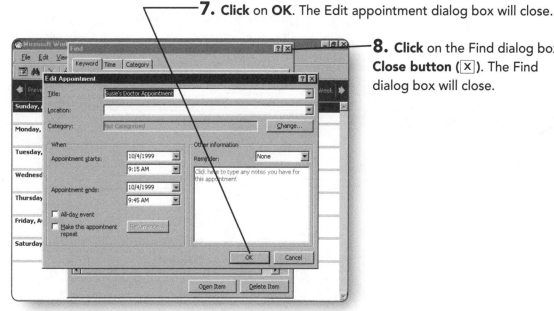

8. Click on the Find dialog box **Close button (X)**. The Find dialog box will close.

Printing a Calendar

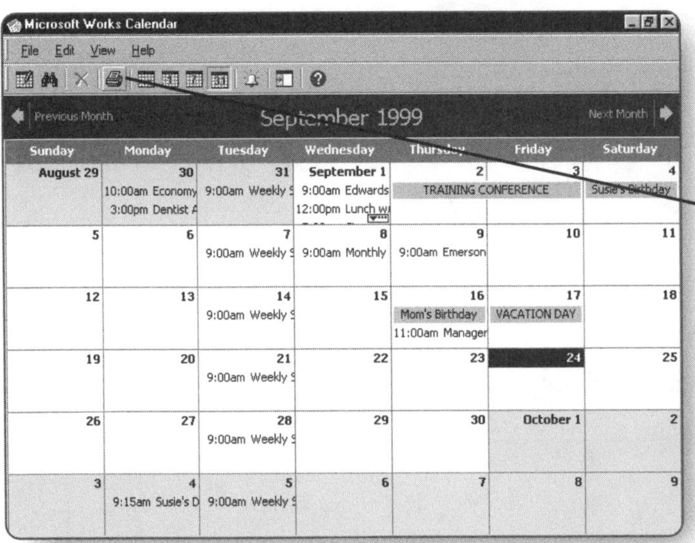

If you need a paper copy of your calendar, you can print it by the day, week, month, or even hour of the appointments.

1. Click on the **Print button**. The Print dialog box will open.

> **TIP**
>
> Optionally, click on the File menu and choose Print.

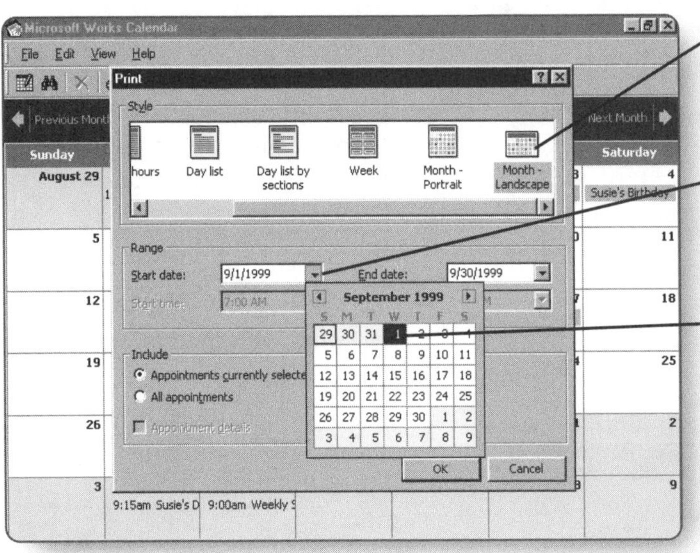

2. Click on the calendar **Style** to be printed. The style will be highlighted.

3. Click on the **Start date: down arrow** (▼). A monthly calendar will appear.

4. Click on the **starting date** that you want to print. The date will appear in the Start date: text box.

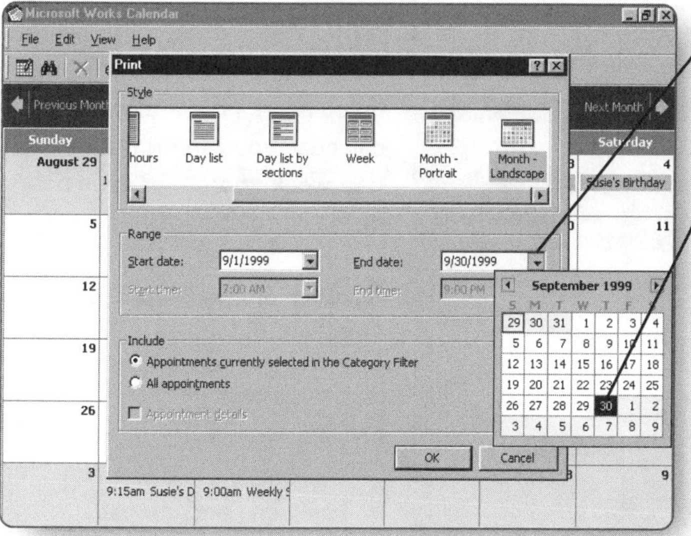

5. **Click** on the **End date: down arrow (▼)**. A monthly calendar will appear.

6. **Click** on the **ending date** that you want to print. The date will appear in the End date: text box.

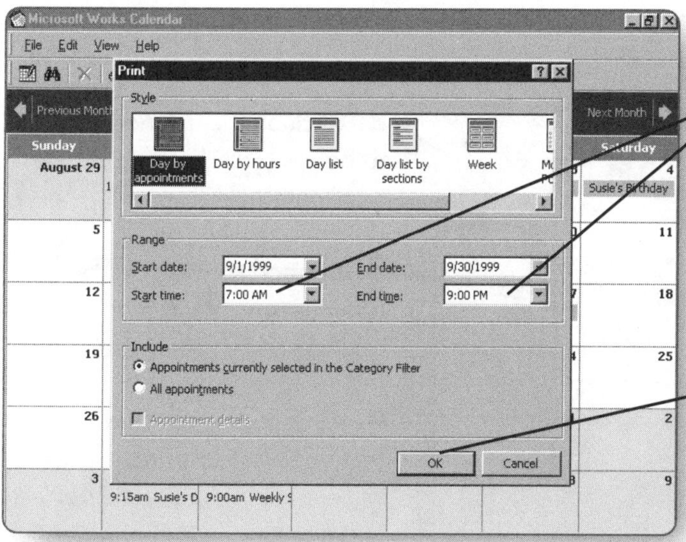

NOTE

If you select Day by appointments or Day by hours for the style to be printed, you'll also need to select the starting and ending time to be printed.

7. **Click** on **OK**. The calendar will print with the options that you specified.

Exiting the Works Calendar

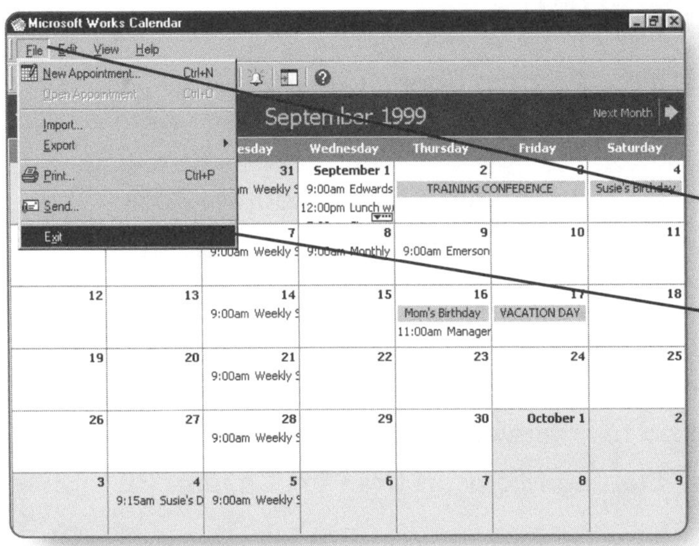

There is no Save command necessary for the Works Calendar. It is automatically saved each time you exit.

1. Click on **File**. The File menu will appear.

2. Click on **Exit**. The Works Calendar will close, and the Task Launcher will appear.

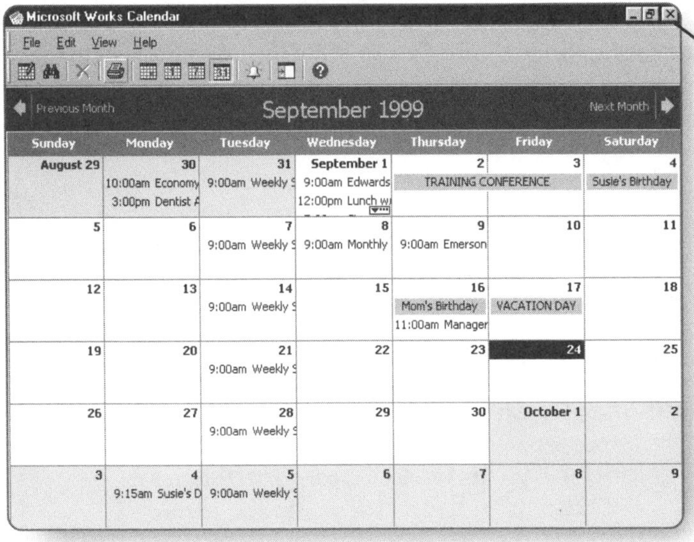

TIP

Optionally, click on the Calendar Close button (X).

Part V Review Questions

1. As contacts are added to the Address Book, how are they displayed? *See "Adding an Address" in Chapter 21*
2. What button do you click on to send e-mail to an Address Book contact? *See "Using an Address Entry" in Chapter 21*
3. What does WordArt do to text? *See "Using WordArt" in Chapter 22*
4. What is the program used to create embedded drawings in a Works document? *See "Starting Microsoft Draw" in Chapter 22*
5. What key can be pressed to draw a perfect circle? *See "Drawing Shapes" in Chapter 22*
6. What two types of documents are combined to do a mail merge? *See "Creating Form Letters Using Mail Merge" in Chapter 23*
7. What is a recurring appointment? *See "Adding a Recurring Appointment" in Chapter 24*
8. What feature does Calendar provide to help you locate a scheduled appointment? *See "Finding Appointments" in Chapter 24*
9. Does the Save command need to be used with Calendar? *See "Exiting the Works Calendar" in Chapter 24*
10. How do you print your calendar by the week? *See "Printing a Calendar" in Chapter 24*

PART VI

Appendixes

Installing Works

Installing Microsoft Works 2000 is a painless process. In this appendix, you'll learn how to:

- Determine hardware requirements
- Install Microsoft Works 2000
- Uninstall Microsoft Works 2000

Discovering System Requirements

Works 2000 has minimum requirements to run properly. The following table lists these specifications:

Component	Requirement
Processor	Multimedia PC P90 or higher
Operating System	Win 95, 98, or NT
Memory	16MB RAM
Disk Space	145MB disk
CD	2X or higher CD-ROM drive
Monitor	Super VGA 256 color
Mouse	Microsoft mouse or compatible

Installing Works 2000

Microsoft Works 2000 comes on a single CD. The Works installation disk includes the Works program and Internet Explorer version 5.

NOTE

See Prima Tech's *Internet Explorer 5.0 Fast & Easy* for assistance with Internet Explorer.

TIP

Before installing Microsoft Works 2000, be sure to temporarily disable any anti-virus programs running on your system and close any open applications.

1. Place the **Installation CD** in your CD-ROM drive. If your computer has the autoplay feature, the setup program will automatically begin.

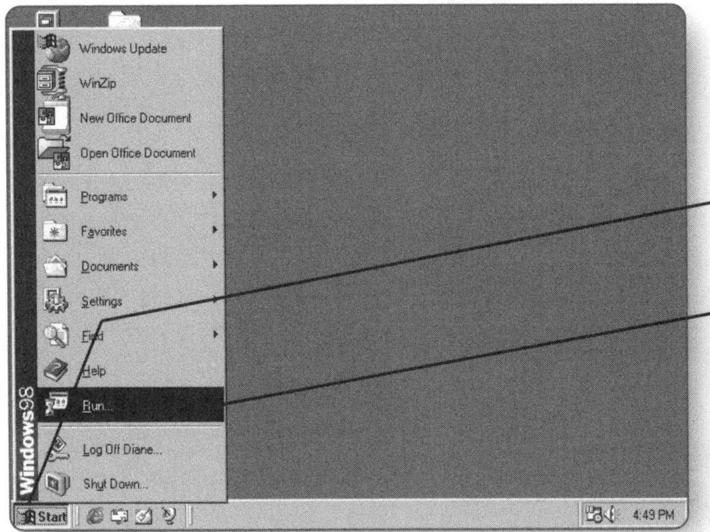

If the setup program appears, skip to step 6. If the setup program does not begin, you'll have to start it manually.

2. Click on **Start**. The Start menu will appear.

3. Click on **Run**. The Run dialog box will open.

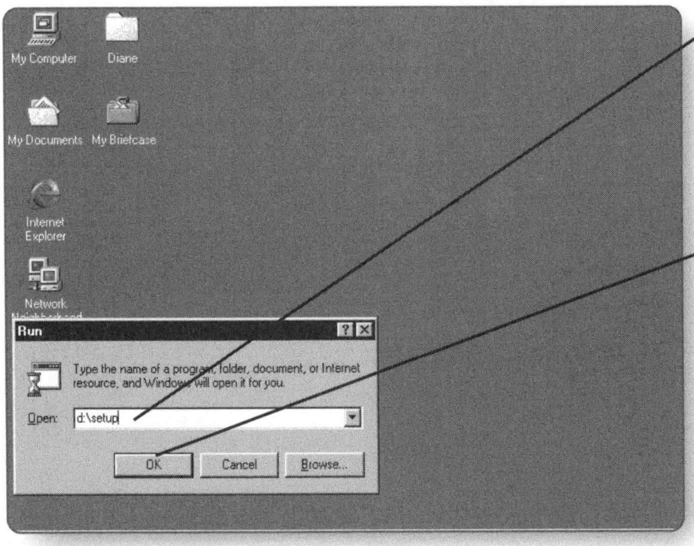

4. Type D:\setup.exe in the Open: text box substituting for D the drive letter for your CD-ROM drive. The text will display in the Open text box.

5. Click on **OK**. The Microsoft Works 2000 Setup welcome screen will appear.

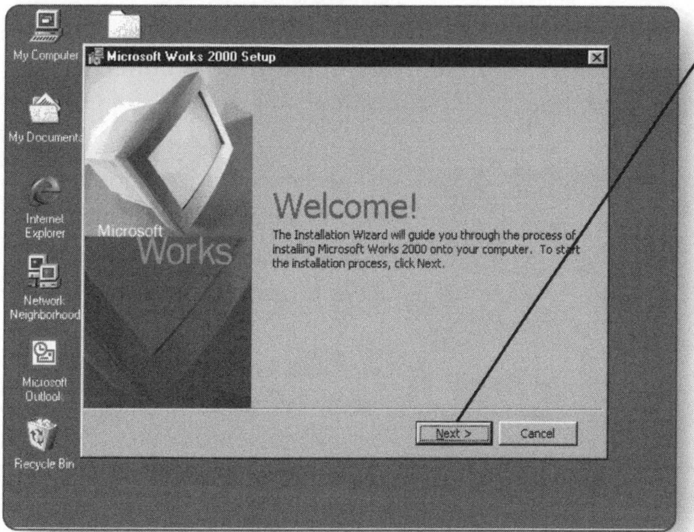

6. Click on **Next**. The installation folder screen will appear.

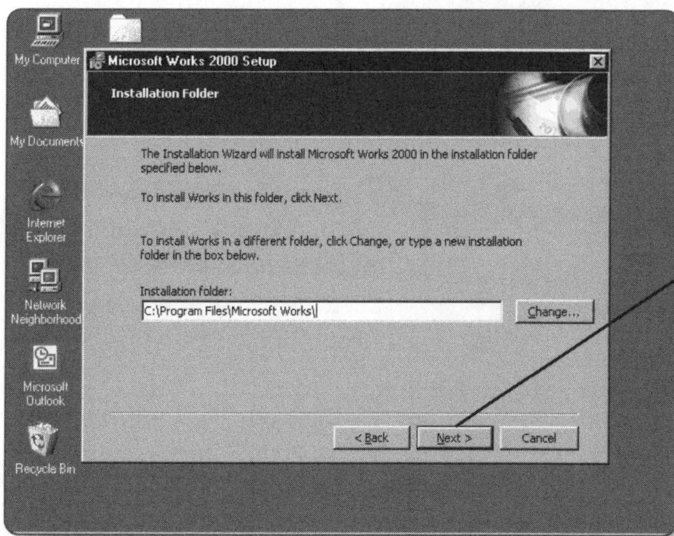

This option prompts you for a folder in which to install Microsoft Works. The easiest method is to accept the choice provided by Microsoft.

7. Click on **Next**. The installation option screen will appear.

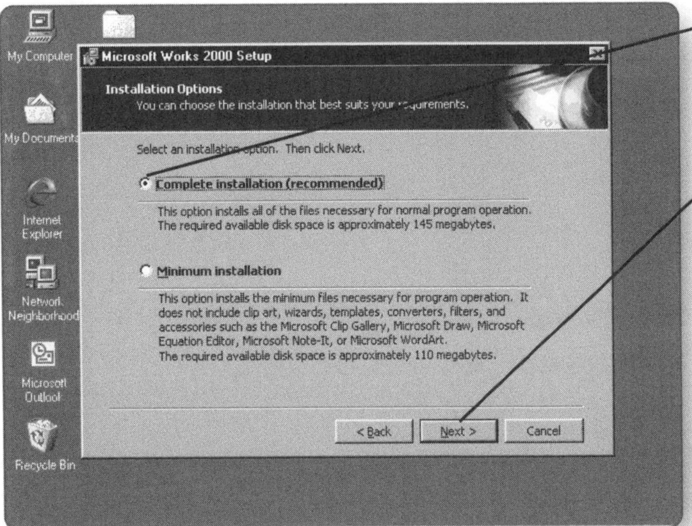

8. Click on **Complete installation**. The option will be selected.

9. Click on **Next**. The next installation screen will appear.

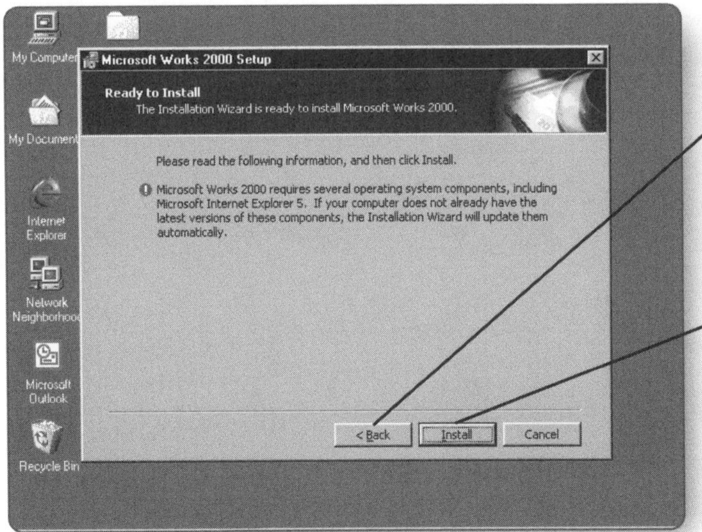

TIP

Click on the Back button to change any of the options you previously selected.

10. Click on **Install**. The installation process will begin.

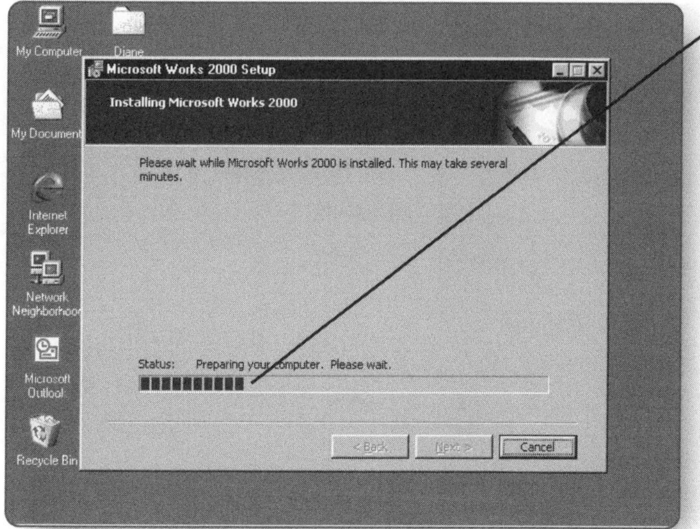

A progress indicator will appear.

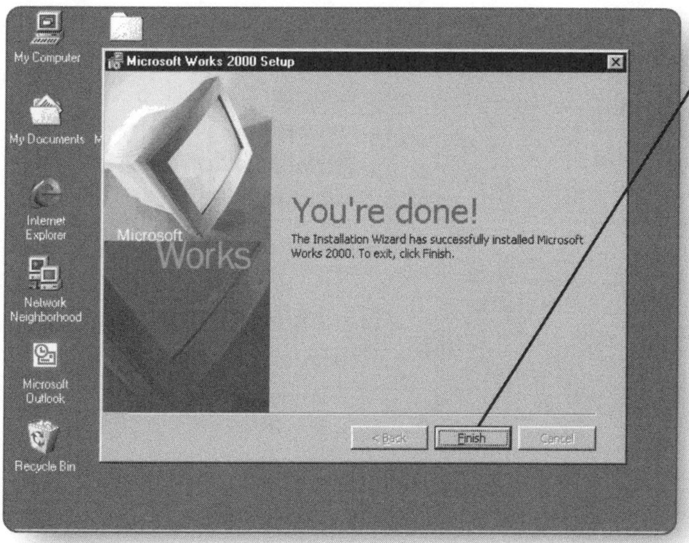

11. Click on **Finish**. The setup program will close, and you will be prompted to restart your computer.

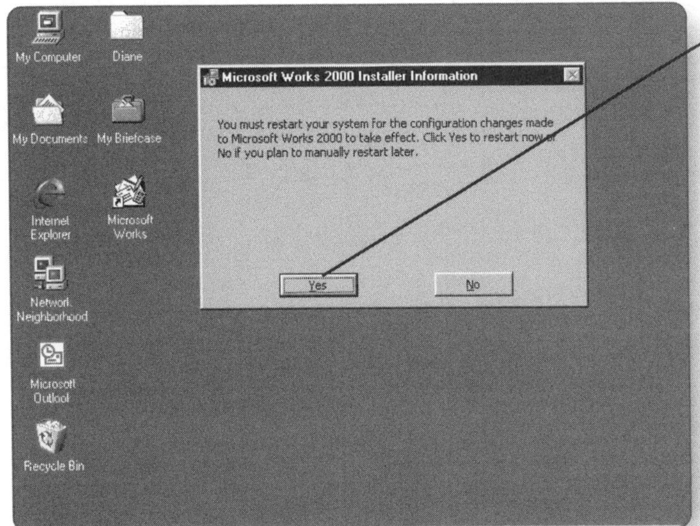

12. Click on **Yes**. Your computer will restart, and you'll be ready to run Microsoft Works.

Uninstalling Works 2000

If you no longer want Microsoft Works on your system, you can easily uninstall it.

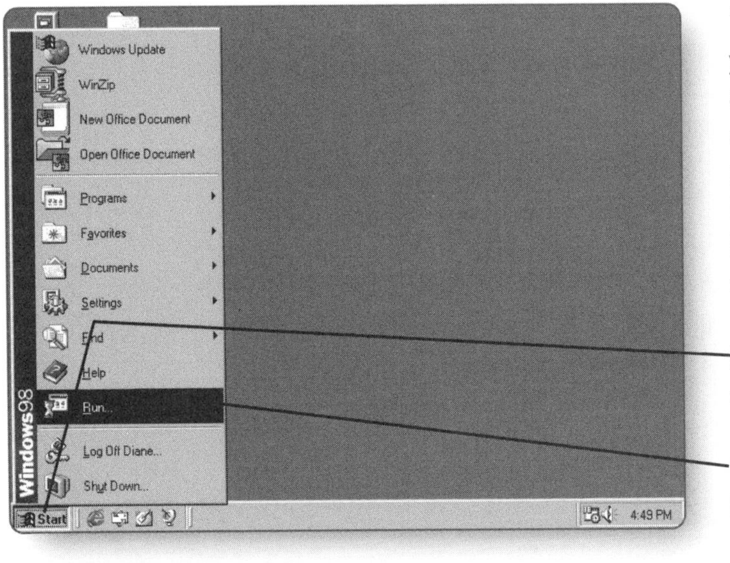

1. **Place** the **Installation CD** in your CD-ROM drive. If you have autoplay, the setup program will automatically begin. If the setup program appears, skip to step 6. If the setup program does not begin, you'll have to start it manually.
2. **Click** on **Start**. The Start menu will appear.
3. **Click** on **Run**. The Run dialog box will open.

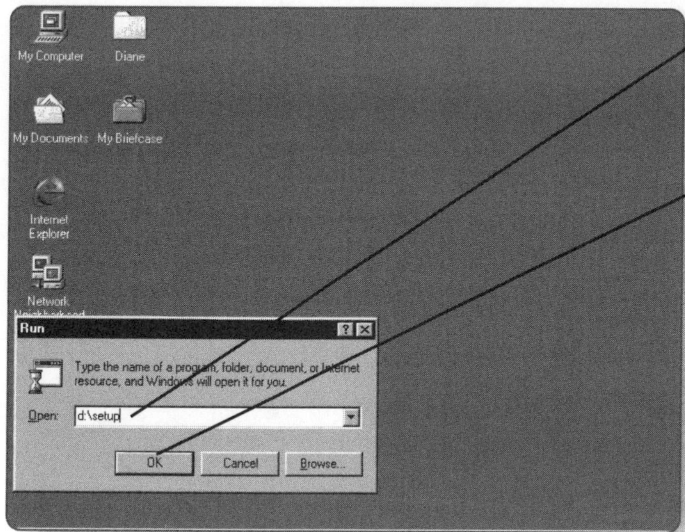

4. Type D:\setup.exe. Substitute for D the drive letter to your CD-ROM drive.

5. Click on **OK**. The Microsoft Setup Wizard will begin with a Welcome Back message.

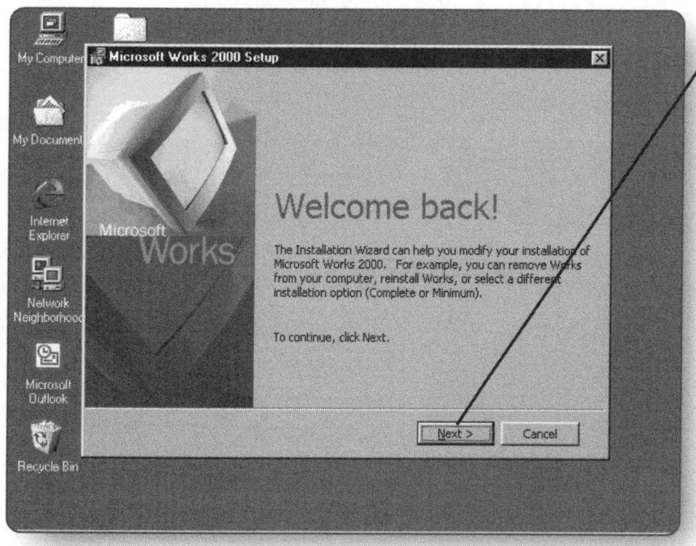

6. Click on **Next**. The options screen will appear.

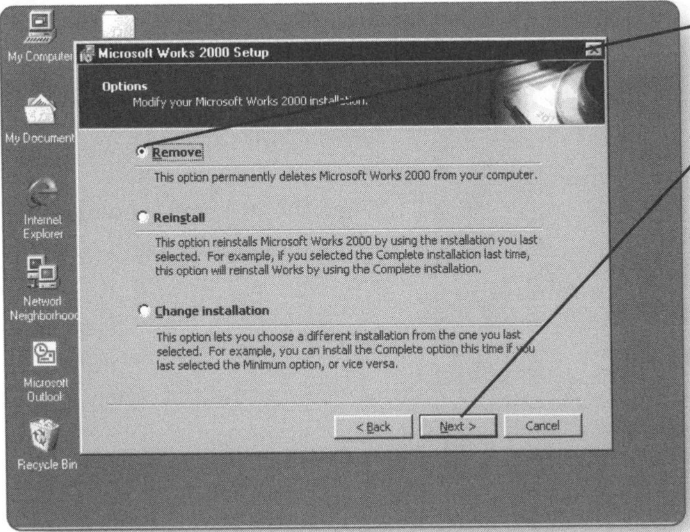

7. Click on **Remove**. The option will be selected.

8. Click on **Next**. An option to save your calendar information will appear.

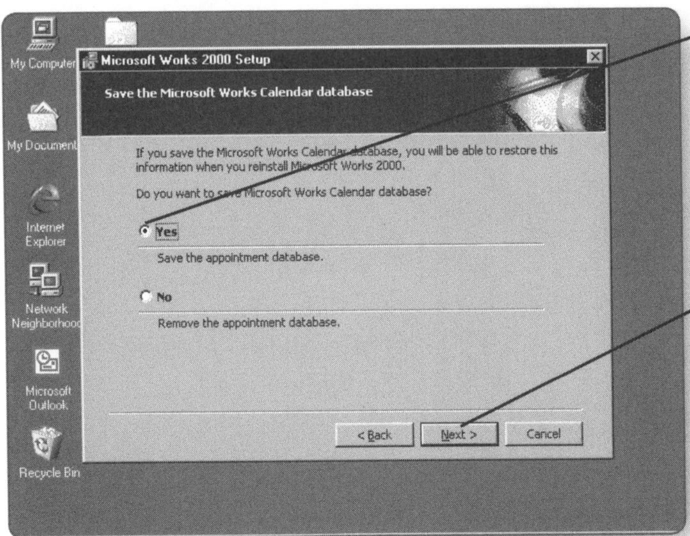

9. Click on an **option**. If you click on Yes, the option will be selected, and your calendar information will be saved in the event you reinstall Microsoft Works 2000.

10. Click on **Next**. A confirmation message will appear.

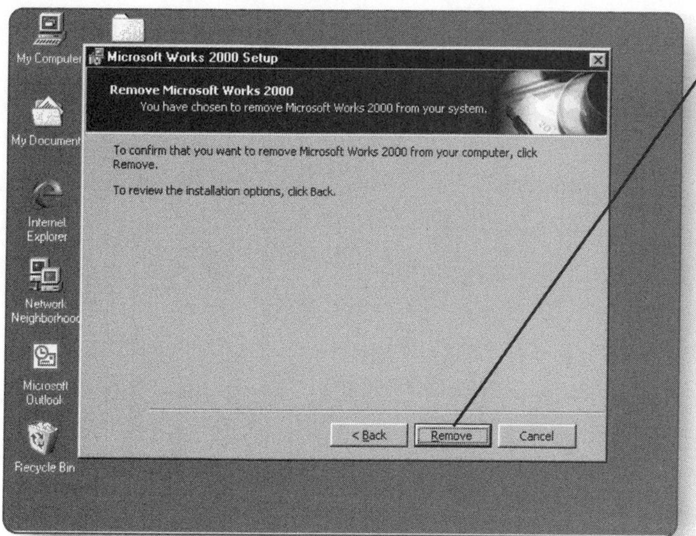

11. Click on **Remove**. The program will be removed. A status bar will appear to indicate the uninstall progress.

When the uninstall is complete, a final message will appear.

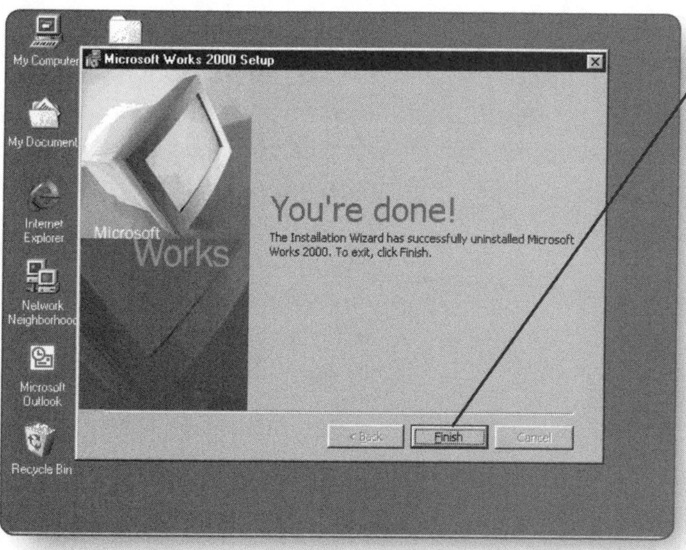

12. Click on **Finish**. You'll be prompted to restart your computer.

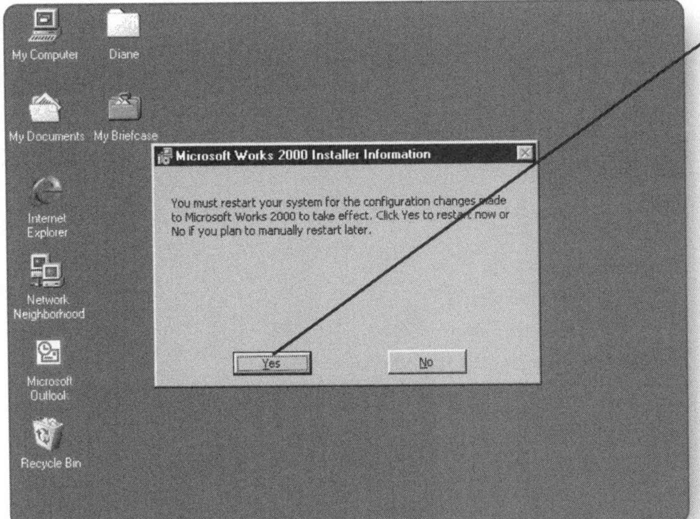

13. Click on **Yes**. Your computer will restart.

B

Using Task Wizards

Numerous task wizards are included with the Microsoft Works program that can be used for home, business, employment, education, volunteer, and civic activities. A task wizard is a shortcut for creating a document. You make a few choices, and the task wizard sets up a document for you. You can then edit the document as usual. In this appendix, you'll learn how to:

- Create a loan analysis spreadsheet using a task wizard
- Create a garage sale flyer using a ask wizard

Starting a Task Wizard

Task wizards are predesigned documents that you can use. All you do is replace the sample data with your information. Some task wizards use the word processing module of Works, whereas others use the spreadsheet or database module.

Creating a Loan Analysis Spreadsheet

Discover how much the payments would be on that new house or car you've been thinking about!

1. **Click** on **Tasks**. A list of task categories will appear.

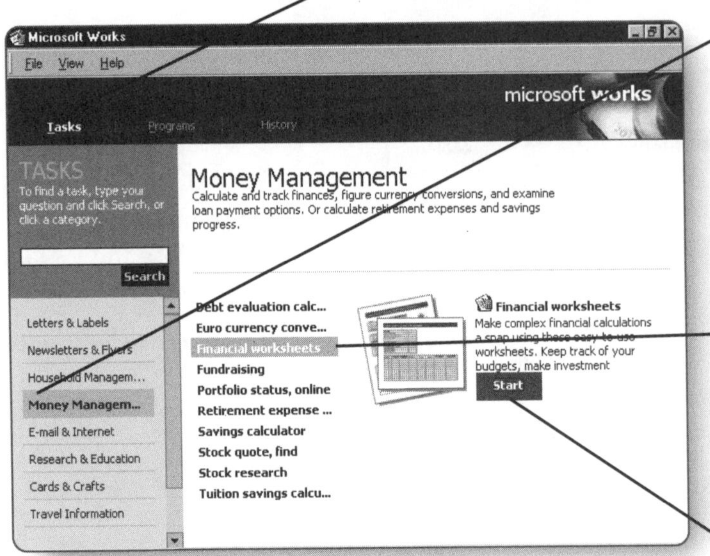

2. **Choose** the **category** of your project. For our example of a loan worksheet, choose **Money Management**. A selection of projects will appear. A description of each wizard will appear as you click on it.

3. **Click** on a **project**. For the loan worksheet, choose **Financial worksheets**. Instructions will appear on the right side of the screen.

4. **Click** on **Start**. The Works Financial Worksheets Wizard will display a variety of financial worksheets.

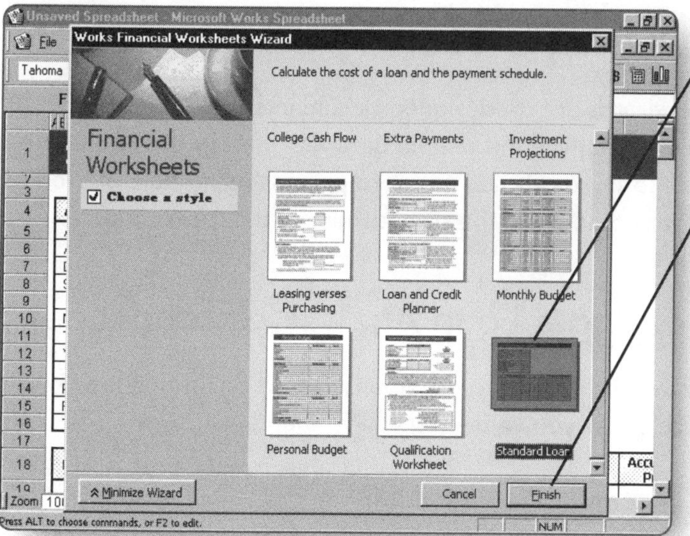

5. Click on **Standard Loan**. A green box will appear around the selection.

6. Click on **Finish.** A loan schedule using a Works spreadsheet will be created for you.

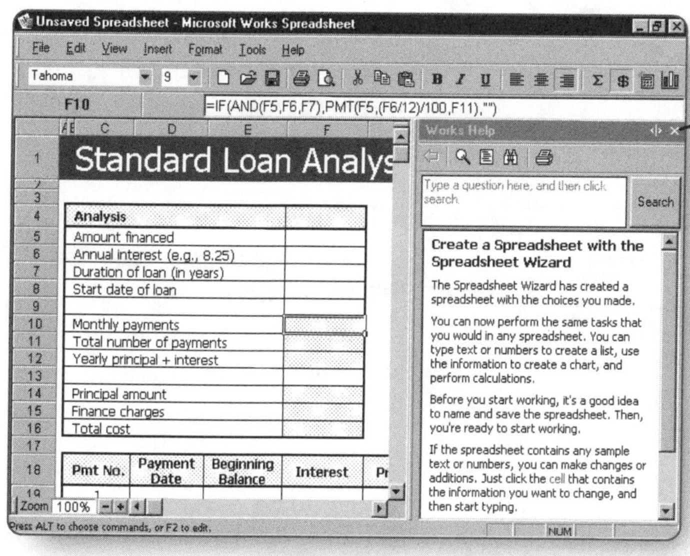

TIP

To see more of the spreadsheet, close the Works Help window.

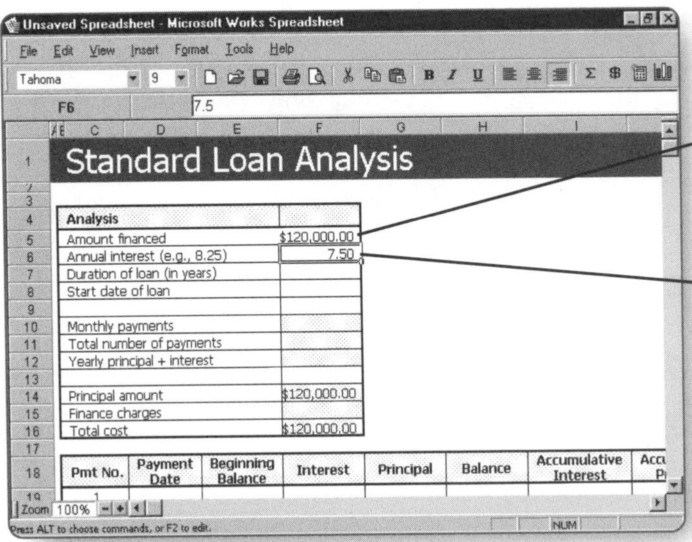

7. **Click** cell **F5**. The cell will be selected.

8. **Enter** the **amount of loan** to be financed. The value will be displayed.

9. **Enter** the annual **interest rate in cell F6**. The value will be displayed.

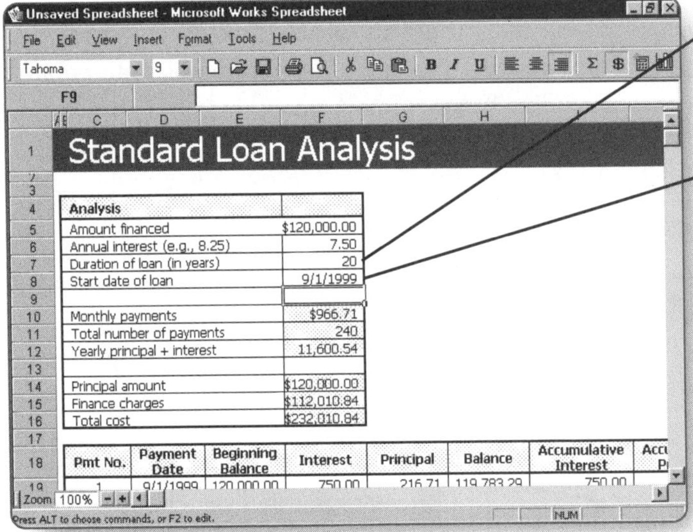

10. In cell F7, **enter** the **duration** of the loan (in years). The value will be displayed.

11. **Enter** the **starting date** of the loan in cell F8. The value will be displayed.

12. **Press Enter**. The loan amounts and an amortization table will be calculated.

> **NOTE**
>
> Do not enter data in any cells other than F5 through F8. Doing so can alter the structure of the spreadsheet.

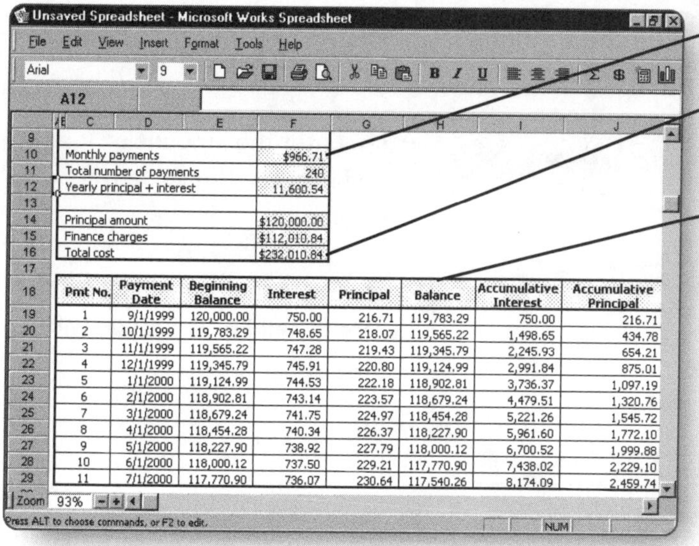

Your monthly payment amount.

Your total cost of the purchase—including interest.

Amortization of the payments.

Creating a Garage Sale Flyer

Having a garage sale? There's a lot to do, so save yourself some time by using the Works predefined template to create a flyer you can distribute.

1. **Click** on **Tasks**. A list of task categories will appear.

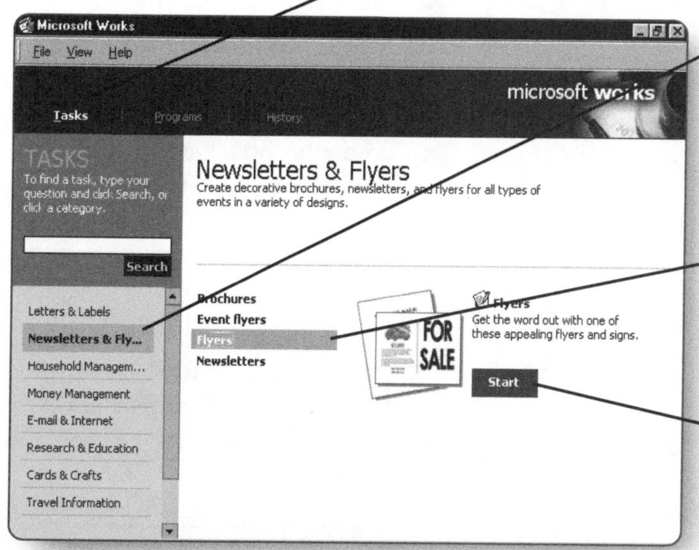

2. **Choose** the **category** of your project. For our example of a garage sale flyer, choose **Newsletters & Flyers**. A selection of projects will appear.

3. **Click** on a **project**. For the garage sale flyer, choose **Flyers**. Instructions will appear on the right side of the screen.

4. **Click** on **Start**. The Works Flyer Wizard will display a variety of flyers.

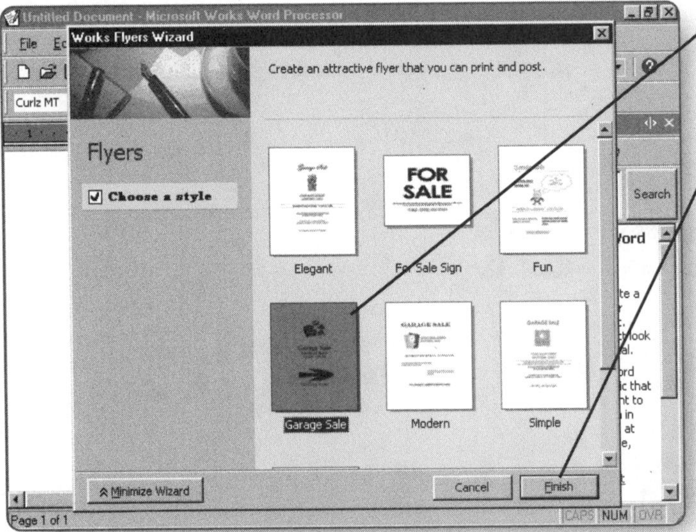

5. Click on **Garage Sale**. The item will be selected.

6. Click on **Finish**. A new Works word processing document will be created with sample information supplied.

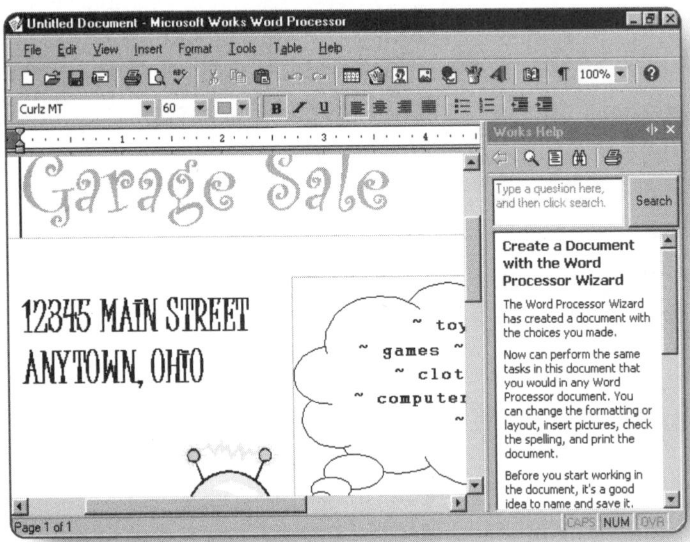

Edit the flyer to display your information. You can change the formatting, graphics, or layout as you would in any Works word processing document.

Looking at Additional Works Applications

In this book you've seen the basic applications of the Microsoft Works programs: word processing, spreadsheets, databases, and the calendar. You've also seen how to integrate those applications.

You should know that several additional applications are now included with Microsoft Works that are beyond the scope of this book. These applications include Internet Explorer, Outlook Express, and the Microsoft Network (MSN).

Internet Explorer

Internet Explorer is a popular Web browser used when accessing the Internet. With Internet Explorer you can visit Web sites, mark them as Favorites so you can easily return to them, or track your Web usage with the History button.

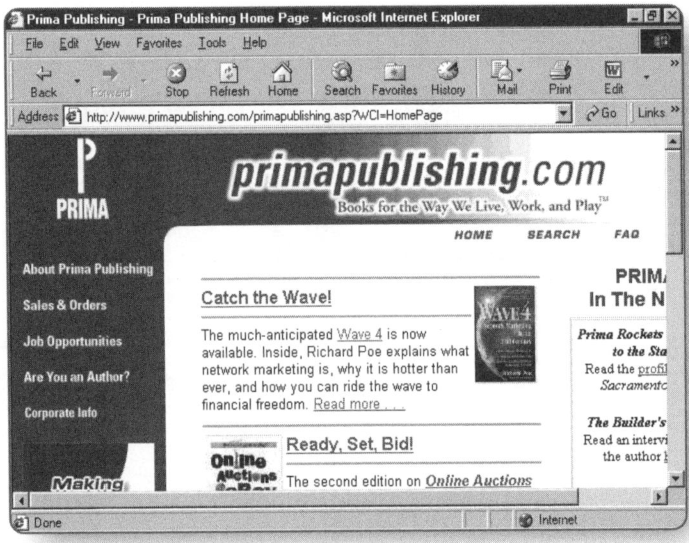

For more information on using Internet Explorer, you might want to take a look at a book published by Prima Tech entitled *Internet Explorer 5 Fast & Easy* by Coletta Witherspoon, ISBN 0-76151742-1.

Outlook Express

Outlook Express is an easy-to-use e-mail client program. With Outlook Express you can send and receive e-mail or transfer files to others.

For more information on using Outlook Express, you might want to take a look at a book published by Prima Tech entitled *Internet Explorer 5 Fast & Easy* by Coletta Witherspoon, ISBN 0-76151742-1. This book includes a section on using Outlook Express. Outlook Express is also covered in *Windows 98 Fast & Easy* by Diane Koers (Yes, that's me), ISBN 0-7615-1006-0.

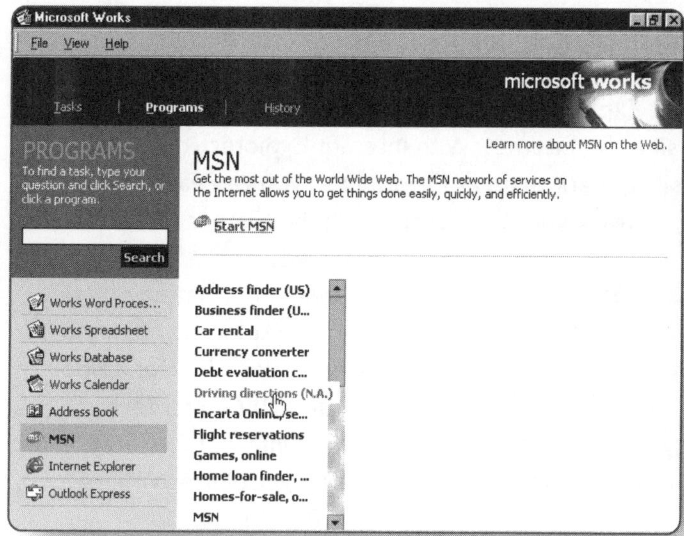

MSN

As you probably already know, you must have some type of Internet Service Provider (ISP) to connect to the Internet. MSN, also known as Microsoft Network, is one of the many services you can subscribe to for a network of Internet services.

Glossary

=AVG. A Works function that calculates the average of a list of values. SYNTAX: =AVG(*list*)

=COUNT. A Works function that counts the nonblank cells in a list of ranges. SYNTAX: =COUNT(*list*)

=**MAX**. A Works function that finds the largest value in a a list. SYNTAX: =MAX(*list*)

=**MIN**. A Works function that finds the smallest value in a list. SYNTAX: =MIN(*list*)

=**SUM**. A Works function that adds a range of cells. See also *AutoSum*. SYNTAX: =SUM(*list*)

Absolute reference. In a formula, a reference to a cell that does not change when you copy the formula. An absolute reference always refers to the same cell or range. It is designated in a formula by the dollar sign ($).

Active cell. The selected cell in a worksheet. Designated with a border surrounding the cell.

Address Book. Stores names, addresses, and phone numbers in one handy location.

Alignment. The position of data in a document, cell, range, or text block; for example, centered, right-aligned, or left-aligned. Also called *justification*.

Attributes. Items that determine the appearance of text such as bolding, underlining, italics, or point size.

AutoSum. A function that adds a row or column of figures when you click on the AutoSum button on the toolbar. Same as *=SUM*.

Axes. Lines that form a frame of reference for the chart data. Most charts have an x axis and a y axis.

Bar chart. A type of chart that uses bars to represent values. Normally used to compare items.

Bold. A font attribute that makes text thicker and brighter.

Border. A line surrounding paragraphs, pages, table cells, or objects.

Browser. A software program especially designed for viewing Web pages on the Internet.

Bullet. A small black circle or other character that precedes each item in a list.

Cell. The area where a row and column intersect in a worksheet or table.

Chart. A graphic representation of data. Also called *graph*.

Choose. To use the mouse or keyboard to pick a menu item or option in a dialog box.

Circular reference. A cell that has a formula that contains a reference to itself.

Click on. To use the mouse or keyboard to pick a menu item or option in a dialog box.

Clip art. Drawings that can be inserted into a Works application.

Clipboard. An area of computer memory where text or graphics can be stored temporarily.

Close. To shut down or exit a dialog box, window, or application.

Close button. Used to shut down or exit a dialog box, window, or application.

Column. A set of cells that appear vertically on a worksheet. A single Works worksheet has 256 columns.

Command. An instruction given to a computer to carry out a particular action.

Command button. A button in a dialog box, such as Open, Close, Exit, OK, or Cancel, that carries out a command. The selected command button is indicated by a different appearance, such as a dotted rectangle or another color.

Compound formula. A formula, usually in a spreadsheet, that has multiple operators. An example might be A2*C2+F4.

Copy. To take a selection from the document and duplicate it on the Clipboard.

Cut. To take a selection from the document and move it to the Clipboard.

Data. The information to be entered into a spreadsheet or database.

Database. A file composed of records, each containing fields together with a set of operations for searching or sorting.

Default. A setting or action predetermined by the program unless changed by the user.

Deselect. To remove the ✔ from a check box or to remove highlighting from a menu item or selected text in a document.

Desktop. The screen background and main area of Windows where you can open and manage files and programs.

Dialog box. A box that appears and lets you select options or displays warnings and messages.

Document. A letter, memo, proposal, or other file created in the Works program.

Drag and drop. To move text or an object by positioning the mouse pointer on the item you want to move, pressing and holding down the mouse button, moving the mouse, and then releasing the mouse button to drop the material into its new location.

E-mail. The exchange of text messages or computer files over a local area network or the Internet.

Export. The capability to copy data from one program to another.

Field. A piece of information used in a database.

File. Information stored on a disk under a single name.

File format. The arrangement and organization of information in a file. File format is determined by the application that created the file.

Fill. The changing of interior colors and patterns or the completion of data in a series of spreadsheet cells.

Fill Data. A function that allows Works to automatically complete a series of numbers or words based on an established pattern.

Folder. An organizational tool used to store files.

Font. A group of letters, numbers, and symbols with a common typeface.

Footer. Text repeated at the bottom of each page of a document or spreadsheet.

Footnote. Reference information that prints at the bottom of the page.

Form. A type of database document with spaces reserved for fields to enter data.

Format. To change the appearance of text or objects with features such as the font, style, color, borders, and size.

Form Design view. The view in a Works database that allows the structure of the database to be modified.

Formula. An entry in a worksheet that performs a calculation on numbers, text, or other formulas.

Formula bar. The location where all data and formulas are entered for a selected cell.

Form view. A view in a Works database where one record is displayed at a time.

Freezing. The prevention of sections of a worksheet from scrolling offscreen when you move down the page.

Function. A series of predefined formulas used in Works spreadsheets. Functions perform specialized calculations automatically.

Go To. A feature that enables you to jump to a specific cell or worksheet location quickly.

Graph. See *Chart*.

Greater than. A mathematical operator that limits the results of a formula to be higher than a named number or cell.

Gridlines. The lines dividing rows and columns in a table or worksheet.

Handles. Small black squares that appear when you select an object, which enable you to resize the object.

Header. Text entered in an area of the document that will be displayed at the top of each page of the document.

Help. A feature that gives you instructions and additional information on using a program.

Help topic. An explanation of a specific feature, dialog box, or task. Help topics usually contain instructions on how to use a feature, pop-up terms with glossary definitions, and related topics. You can access Help topics by choosing any command from the Help menu.

Hypertext link. Used to provide a connection from the current document to another document or to a document on the World Wide Web.

Icon. A small graphic image that represents an application, command, or tool. An action is performed when an icon is clicked or double-clicked.

Import. The capability to receive data from another program.

Indent. To move a complete paragraph one tab stop to the right.

Internet Explorer. A browser made by Microsoft and used to view documents on the World Wide Web.

Justification. See *Alignment*.

Label. Any cell entry you begin with a letter or label-prefix character.

Landscape. Orientation of a page in which the long edge of the paper runs horizontally.

Legend. A box containing symbols and text, explaining what each data series represents. Each symbol is a color pattern or marker that corresponds to one data series in the chart.

Less than. A mathematical operator that limits the results of a formula to be lower than a named number or cell.

Line spacing. The amount of space between lines of text.

List view. A view in a Works database that allows the records to be viewed in a vertical format similar to a spreadsheet.

Mailbox. An area of memory or disk assigned to store any e-mail messages sent by other users.

Mail Merge. A feature that combines a data file with a word processing document to produce personalized letters.

Margin. The width of blank space from the edge of the page to the edge of the text. All four sides of a page have margins.

Modem. A device used to connect a personal computer with a telephone line so that the computer can be used for accessing online information or communicating with other computers.

Mouse pointer. A symbol that indicates a position onscreen as you move the mouse around on your desktop.

Netiquette. Short for *network etiquette*. Internet rules of courtesy for sending e-mail and participating in newsgroups.

Object. A picture, map, or other graphic element that you can place in a Works application.

Open. To start an application, to insert a document into a new document window, or to access a dialog box.

Operator. The element of a formula that suggests an action to be performed, such as addition (+), subtraction ([ms]), division (/), multiplication (*), greater than (>), or less than (<).

Orientation. A setting that designates whether a document will print with text running along the long or short side of a piece of paper.

Page Break. A command that tells the application where to begin a new page.

Page Setup. A command that tells the application what paper size, orientation, margins, and other items that are applicable to the entire document.

Password. A secret code word that restricts access to a file. Without the password, the file cannot be opened.

Paste. The process of retrieving the information stored on the Clipboard and inserting a copy of it into a document.

Patterns. Predefined shading and line arrangements used to format cells in a worksheet.

Pie chart. A round chart type in which each pie wedge represents values.

Point. To move the mouse until the tip of the mouse pointer rests on an item.

Point size. A unit of measurement used to indicate font size. One point is 1/72-inch in height.

Portrait. The orientation of the page in which the long edge of the page runs vertically.

Print area. The portion of a worksheet you designate to print.

Print Preview. Shows you how your printed document will look onscreen before you print it.

Properties. The characteristics of text, objects, or devices. Text properties might include font, size, or color.

Queue. A waiting or holding location, usually for printing documents or sending e-mail messages.

Range. A collection of cells, ranging from the first named cell to the last.

Range name. An "English" name that identifies a range and that can be used in commands and formulas instead of the range address.

Record. The collection of field information about one particular element. For example, Joe Smith's record might include field information such as name, address, and phone number.

Redo. To reverse the last Undo action.

Reference. In a formula, a name or range that refers the formula to a cell or set of cells.

Relative. In a formula, a reference to a cell or a range that changes when you copy the formula. A relative reference refers to the location of the data in relation to the formula. A relative reference can be an address or range name.

Right align. To line up text with the right side of a cell, tab setting, or document margin, as with a row of numbers in a column.

Row. Cells running from left to right across a worksheet.

Ruler. A feature that lets you easily change page format elements such as tabs and margins.

Save. To take a document residing in the memory of the computer and create a file to be stored on a disk.

Save As. To save a previously saved document with a new name or properties.

Scroll bars. The bars on the right side and bottom of a window that let you move vertically and horizontally through a document.

Shape. Item such as a circle, rectangle, line, polygon, or polylines in your document.

Shortcut. An icon that represents a quick way to start a program or open a file or folder.

Simple formula. A formula, usually in a spreadsheet, that has only one operator. An example might be B4+B5.

Sizing handle. The small solid squares that appear on the borders of a graphics box or a graphics line that has been selected. You can drag these handles to size the box and its contents.

Sort. To arrange data in alphabetical or numeric order.

Spell Check. A feature that checks the spelling of words in your document against a dictionary and flags possible errors for correction.

Spreadsheet. The component in Works that handles calculations and data needing to be placed in a columnar or linear format. Data is stored in small locations called cells.

Status bar. The line at the bottom of a window that shows information, such as the current page in a document.

Style. A way to format similar types of text such as headings and lists.

Submenu. An additional list of menu items opening from a single menu item. Also called a *cascading menu*.

Symbols. Characters that are not on your keyboard, such as iconic symbols, phonetic characters, and characters in other alphabets.

Syntax. The exact structure of functions and formulas.

Table. A set of rows and columns of cells that you fill in with text, numbers, or graphics.

Tabs. Settings in your document to determine where the insertion point moves when you press the tab key or use the indent feature.

Taskbar. The bar (usually at the bottom of the screen) that lists all open folders and active programs.

Task Wizards. An interactive Help feature that prompts the user for key pieces of information and then, using that information, completes a project.

Template. A predesigned file with customized formatting, content, and features.

Thesaurus. A feature used to find synonyms (words that are alike) and antonyms (words that are opposite).

Tile. A display format for open windows. Tiled windows are displayed side by side, with no window overlapping any other window.

Titles. Descriptive pieces of text. Used in charts and spreadsheets.

Toolbar. Appears at the top of the application window and is used to access many commonly used features of the Works applications.

Undo. To reverse the last editing action.

Uppercase. A capital letter.

Value. An entry that is a number, formula, or function.

Views. Ways of displaying documents to see different perspectives of the information in that document.

WordArt. A feature that allows blocks of text to be manipulated into varying shapes and formats.

Word processing. The ability to type, edit, and save a document.

Word Processor. The component in Microsoft Works that allows the user to do word processing.

Word Wrap. To let text in a paragraph automatically flow to the next line when it reaches the right margin.

World Wide Web. A series of specially designed documents—all linked together—to be viewed over the Internet.

Wrapping. A function that causes text to automatically wrap to the next line when it reaches the right edge of a cell or page margin.

X-axis. In a chart, a reference line marked in regular intervals to display the categories with descriptive labels.

Y-axis. In a chart, a reference line marked in regular intervals to display the values of a chart.

Zoom. To enlarge or reduce the way text is displayed on the screen. It does not affect how the document will print.

Index

T

U

V

W

Z